Contemporar
in Act

CW01510469

MERCER
UNIVERSITY PRESS

Endowed by
TOM WATSON BROWN
and
THE WATSON-BROWN FOUNDATION, INC.

Contemporary Studies in Acts

edited by
THOMAS E. PHILLIPS

Mercer University Press
May 2009

MUP / P386

Library of Congress Cataloging-in-Publication Data

Contemporary studies in Acts / edited by Thomas E. Phillips.
p.   cm.
Includes bibliographical references and index.
ISBN-13: 978-0-88146-145-9 (pbk. : alk. paper)
ISBN-10: 0-88146-145-8 (pbk. : alk. paper)
1. Bible. N.T. Acts–Criticism, interpretation, etc.
I. Phillips, Thomas E.
BS2625.52.C65 2009
226.6'06--dc22

2009011289

Contents

Abbreviations

AB	Anchor Bible
ABD	*Anchor Bible Dictionary*
ACNT	Augsburg Commentary on the New Testament
ACW	Ancient Christian Writers
AGJU	Arbeiten zur Geschichte des antiken Judentums und des Urchristentums
AnBib	Analecta biblica
ANF	*The Ante-Nicene Fathers*
ANRW	Aufstieg und Niedergang der römishen Welt
ANTC	Abingdon New Testament Commentaries
APATS	American Philological Association Textbook Series
AUS	American University Studies
BAFCS	Book of Acts in Its First Century Setting
BBR	*Bulletin for Biblical Research*
BDAG	Bauer-Danker-Arndt-Gingrich, *Greek-English Lexicon of the New Testament and Other Early Christian Literature*, 3rd ed.
BECNT	Baker Exegetical Commentary on the New Testament
BETL	Bibliotheca ephemeridum theologicarum lovaniensium
BGBE	Beiträge zur Geschichte der biblischen Exegese
BGU	*Aegyptische Urkunden aus den Königlichen Staatlichen Museen zu Berlin, Griechische Urkunden*
BHT	Beiträge zur historischen Theologie
Bib	*Biblica*
BINS	Biblical Interpretation Series
BSac	*Bibliotheca Sacra*
BJRL	*Bulletin of John Rylands Library*
BJS	Brown Judaic Studies
BNTC	Black's New Testament Commentaries
BW	*Biblical World*
BZ	*Biblische Zeitschrift*
BZAW	Beihefte zur Zeitschrift für die alttestamentliche Wissenschaft
BZNW	Beihefte zur Zeitschrift für die neutestamentliche Wissenschaft
CBQ	*Catholic Biblical Quarterly*
CBQMS	CBQ Monograph Series
CBR	*Currents in Biblical Research*
CCCM	Corpus Christianorum, Continuatio Mediaevalis
CCS	Cambridge Classical Studies
CCSA	Corpus Christianorum, Series Apocryphorum
CCSL	Corpus Christianorum, Series Latina
CP	*Classical Philology*
CQ	*Classical Quarterly*

CSEL	Corpus scriptorium ecclesiasticorum latinorum
CTM	*Concordia Theological Monthly*
CurTM	*Currents in Theology and Mission*
DACL	*Dictionnaire d'archéologie chrétienne et de liturgie*
EKKNT	Evangelisch-katholisher Kommentar zum Neuen Testament
ETL	*Ephemerides theologicae lovanienses*
EvT	*Evangelische Theologie*
ExpTim	*Expository Times*
FRLANT	Forschungen zur Religion und Literatur des Alten und Neuen Testaments
GIF	*Giornale Italiano di Filologia*
HDR	Harvard Dissertations in Religion
HTKNT	Herders theologischer Kommentar zum Neuen Testament
HTR	*Harvard Theological Review*
HTS	Harvard Theological Studies
IBS	*Irish Biblical Studies*
ICC	International Critical Commentary
Int	*Interpretation*
JAC	*Jahrbuch für Antike und Christenum*
JBL	*Journal of Biblical Literature*
JEH	*Journal of Ecclesiastical History*
JETS	*Journal of the Evangelical Theological Society*
JHB	*Jahrbuch der theologischen Hochschule Bethel*
JHC	*Journal of Higher Criticism*
JR	*Journal of Religion*
JSNT	*Journal for the Study of the New Testament*
JSNTSup	JSNT Supplement Series
JTS	*Journal of Theological Studies*
KEK	Kritisch-exegetischer Kommentar über das Neue Testament
LCBI	Literary Currents in Biblical Interpretation
LCL	Loeb Classical Library
LD	Lectio divina
LNTS	Library of New Testament Studies
LSJ	Lidell-Scott-Jones, *A Greek-English Lexicon*, 9th ed.
MBCBS	Mnemosyne Bibliotheca Classica Batava Supplmentum
MNTC	Moffatt New Testament Commentary
NCBC	New Century Bible Commentary
NHS	Nag Hammadi Studies
NIB	*The New Interpreter's Bible*
NICNT	New International Commentary on the New Testament
NIGTC	New International Greek Testament Commentary

NovT	*Novum Testamentum*
NovTSup	Novum Testamentum Supplement Series
NTAbh	Neutestamentliche Abhandlungen
NTD	Das Neue Testament Deutsch
NTG	New Testament Guides
NTS	New Testament Studies
NTTS	New Testament Tools and Studies
PEGLBS	*Proceedings of the Eastern Great Lakes Biblical Society*
PEGLMBS	*Proceedings of the Eastern Great Lakes and Midwest Biblical Societies*
PG	Patrologia graeca
PL	Patrologia latina
PRS	*Perspectives in Religious Studies*
QD	*Quaestiones disputatae*
RB	*Revue Biblique*
RECHSR	*Recherches de Science Religieuse*
RMP	*Rheinisches Museum für Philologie*
RTP	*Revue de théologie et de philosophie*
SBLDS	Society of Biblical Literature Dissertation Series
SBLMS	SBL Monograph Series
SBLRBS	SBL Resources for Biblical Studies
SBLSP	SBL Seminar Papers
SBLSPS	SBL Sources for Biblical Studies
SBLSymS	SBL Symposium Series
SBLTT	SBL Texts and Translations
SBT	Studies in Biblical Theology
SC	Sources chrétiennes. Paris: Cerf, 1943- .
SEÅ	*Svensk exegetisk årsok*
SecCen	*Second Century*
SNTS	Society for New Testament Studies
SNTSMS	SNTS Monograph Series
SP	Sacra Pagina
ST	*Studia theologica*
SUSIA	Skrifter Utgivna av Svenska Institutet i Athen
TDNT	*Theological Dictionary of the New Testament*, 10 vols.
Them	*Themelios*
Theo	*Theology*
ThSt	Theologische Studiën
TNTC	Tyndale New Testament Commentaries
TRev	*Theologische Revue*
TRu	*Theologische Rundschau*

TSR	*Trinity Seminary Review*
TU	Texte und Untersuchungen
TWAS	*Twayne's World Author Series*
TynBul	*Tyndale Bulletin*
TZ	*Theologische Zeitschrift*
VC	*Vigiliae Christianae*
VE	*Vox Evangelica.*
WBC	Word Biblical Commentary
WUNT	Wissenschaftliche Untersuchungen zum Neuen Testament
ZNW	Zeitschrift für die neutestamentliche Wissenschaft und die Kunde der älteren Kirche
ZTK	Zeitschrift für Theologie und Kirche

*In fond appreciation for
three gifted friends
and former colleagues,*

David A. Williams,

Janet Rumfelt,

and Frank Ritchel Ames

Preface

In many ways the book of Acts is unique in the New Testament. The gospels offer the teachings of Jesus, teachings which were preserved in order to inspire believers toward the lofty vision and nobler existence to which the gospel writers believed Christ had called them. The letters in the New Testament, particularly those of Paul, reveal churches in their unavoidable this-worldliness and admid their struggles to define themselves on the run. Acts does neither. It neither preserves the lofty and inspiring words of Jesus nor reveals the church in the midst of its present struggles to live up to those teachings. Acts does something different. Acts portrays the early church neither as it was (the letters) nor as it wished to be (the gospels), but as later generations remembered it—not quite as messy as in the epistles, but neither as lofty as the gospels would call it to be. It is, I think, this "otherness" that has made Acts the foster child of New Testament studies, not depised, sometimes even well cared for, but always an awkward member of the family.

This volume is a part of an ongoing endeavor among a number of gifted scholars to wipe some of the tarnish off the nameplate "Acts scholar." The twin themes of this volume are that Acts is not only an intriguing book today (theme one), but that it also has an intriguing history of interpretation behind it (theme two). In the first half of the volume, a group of largely senior scholars offer their seasoned reflections on the origin and use of Acts in the second century and beyond. In the second half of the book, a group of largely younger scholars offer new insights into the meaning of the book. Each chapter in this book had its origin in the Society of Biblical Literature's section on Acts and has benefited from the conversation accompanying the oral presentations in 2005 and 2006. The papers are offered in this format in order to draw increased attention to the very stimulating work being done on the Book of Acts in that section of the SBL.

As cochair of the SBL section on Acts, I have been fortunate to work with my cochair, F. Scott Spencer, and four other exceptional scholars, Pamela Hedrick, Loveday Alexander, Mikeal Parsons, and Steve Walton. I take this opportunity to publicly thank them for their work. I would also like to thank my colleague, Mark G. Bilby, for his considerable assistance in helping me to standard the pastristic references in this book and my former student, Dale C. Frederickson, for his extensive work in creating large portions of the bibliography and indexes for this volume. Finally, I would like to thank the administration at Point Loma Nazarene University for their support in the production of this volume, particularly for their financial support in the form of an institutional research grant.

Advent 2007   *Thomas E. Phillips*

Wrestling with and for Paul: Efforts to Obtain Pauline Support by Marcion and the Author of Acts[1]

Joseph B. Tyson

The author of 2 Peter, writing probably in the mid-second century, observed that Paul's letters were hard to understand and that "the ignorant and unstable twist [them] to their own destruction, as they do the other scriptures" (2 Pet 3:16). This author, who writes in the name of Peter, reveals that the writings of Paul had become problematic for second-century Christians, but the writer's irritation is probably only the tip of the iceberg. Paul himself was clearly the subject of a good deal of controversy during his lifetime, and his death did little to resolve it. It has long been observed that the deuteropauline letters serve to show that controversy about Paul continued for many decades.[2]

The legacy of Paul was a matter of great concern for some time. Struggles for Pauline support must have begun shortly after his death and continued for over a century afterward. I want to call your attention to Marcion and the author of Acts, who, in my judgment, were among those contending for Pauline support. I think we can best understand the role of

---

[1]Some parts of this article have been adapted from my book, *Marcion and Luke-Acts: A Defining Struggle* (Columbia: University of South Carolina Press, 2006) and are used with permission.

[2]See, e.g., Francis Watson who observed that the author of Colossians invoked the name of Paul to support a form of Christian belief that saw the gospel as autonomous and did away with Torah. Watson added that this form of belief did not need the Hebrew Scriptures either as law or prophets and deemed the revelation of the Father of Jesus Christ as something new. Noting that this form of thought sounds a lot like some second-century heresies, Watson wrote, "Admittedly, it is anachronistic to ascribe to the author of Colossians the view of scripture that later readers such as Valentinus and Marcion may have found here. The issue would not yet have posed itself in such sharply polarized form. Yet, arguably, the Paul of Colossians is moving away from the scriptural matrix of the earlier Pauline tradition, in the direction of later assertions of the self-sufficiency of the gospel." Watson, " 'In Whom are Hid All the Treasures of Wisdom and Knowledge': Colossians and the Autonomy of the Gospel," paper presented at the annual meeting of the SNTS, Halle, Germany, 5 August 2005, 3.

the author of Acts in the history of early Christianity if we view him as, among other things, a contender, against Marcion, for Pauline support.

I begin with an expression of agreement with Richard I. Pervo on the revised date for the composition of Acts. In my judgment he has presented a substantial argument for dating it in the period between 100–130 CE.[3] Although the consensus dating of Acts in ca. 85 CE has long held, few scholars have been willing to lay out convincing arguments either for this date or for a meaningful context for its composition. Pervo, by contrast, marshals impressive arguments to show that the author of Acts made use of Josephus's *Antiquities of the Jews*, as well as a collection of Pauline letters, and he thus establishes a firm *terminus a quo* for the composition of Acts at 100 CE. Since Pervo's arguments are presented elsewhere in this volume, I need not go into the details of his argument. I only want to commend his work to readers.

Assuming that Pervo is right about the composition of Acts in the first quarter of the second century, there is still the question of the context for it. In my own book I have attempted to answer this question by reconsidering some propositions of John Knox, in his 1942 study, *Marcion and the New Testament*, a book that, in my judgment, has received insufficient attention among critical scholars.[4] Knox there argued that the book of Acts was written as a reaction against Marcion. In my recent book, I reflect on Knox's argument and attempt to flesh it out.[5]

Marcion's views are sufficiently well known that they need little rehearsing here. I would, however, want to stress that his views were shaped largely by reading Paul's letters, which formed a major part of his canon. Limited as we are by the lack of unbiased sources dealing with Marcion, we can only cite the ways in which his theology and practices were perceived by his opponents. Having said this, it is yet significant that we are able to form a remarkably coherent impression of Marcion's theology. It is probably safe to say that Marcion found irresolvable contrasts between the Hebrew Scriptures and the letters of Paul. For him there was an

---

[3]See Richard I. Pervo, *Dating Acts: Between the Evangelists and the Apologists* (Santa Rosa CA: Polebridge Press, 2006). Also see Pervo's essay in the next chapter of this volume.

[4]See John Knox, *Marcion and the New Testament: An Essay in the Early History of the Canon* (Chicago: University of Chicago Press, 1942).

[5]See Joseph B. Tyson, *Marcion and Luke-Acts*.

irreconcilable contrast between a God who enacted laws and judged humans in accordance with their obedience or disobedience of them and a God who justified sinners. He was also struck with the contrast between what he understood to be the teachings of Jesus and those of the Hebrew Scriptures, and he could not be convinced that Jesus and Paul meant to signify a deity who was known through the Hebrew Scriptures. These convictions evidently led Marcion to conclude that the God who was revealed by Jesus was totally unknown before his time. What Jesus revealed and Paul taught was fundamentally new and unanticipated.

Marcion also evidently concluded that Paul was the only true apostle of Jesus and that Peter and the others were false apostles, who attempted to retain a relation between Jewish religion and belief in Jesus. Marcionite Christianity is, therefore, an impressive example of the attempt to gain support from the Pauline legacy.[6]

I. The Characterization of Paul in Acts

I intend to focus attention on some aspects of Acts that may be illuminated by reference to the Marcionite controversy. These features in Acts do not prove the theory of its Marcionite context, but acquaintance with the probable context should have a bearing on the interpretation. Further, if it should turn out that a second-century post-Marcionite setting for Acts allows us to address some difficult issues in new and convincing ways, our confidence in this proposed *Sitz im Leben* would be increased. Such is the case with a number of classic problems of Acts interpretation, but here I

---

[6]Marcion is usually thought of as active in the middle of the second century, and comments by his opponents confirm this tendency. But close study of the sources shows that Marcion's teachings were known in the East during the first quarter of the second century. The argument is complex, but by way of summary, we should note that from Justin we learn that Marcion had had an extensive ministry in the East prior to 150 CE and that from Polycarp we can conclude that his teachings were known by 130 CE (see Justin, *First Apology* 26, 58; Polycarp, *Phil* 7:1). Indications from the Pastorals (e.g. 1 Tim 6:20) suggest even earlier dates. We probably will not be far off if we conclude that Marcion's views were known, at least in part and in some locations, as early as 115–120 CE. For further details, see R. Joseph Hoffman, *Marcion: On the Restitution of Christianity: An Essay on the Development of Radical Paulinist Theology in the Second Century*, AAR Academy Series 46 (Chico: Scholars Press, 1984).

wish to concentrate on a particularly difficult set of problems, connected with the characterization of Paul.

An intriguing aspect of the characterization of Paul in Acts is the parallelism with Peter. Both characters deliver speeches, perform healings and resurrections, defeat workers of magic, correct inadequate teaching, are miraculously released from prison, and witness the giving of the Spirit and the phenomenon of glossolalia among converts. This parallelization has long been noted.[7] The work of Matthias Schneckenberger (1841)[8] inspired F. C. Baur to characterize Acts as an attempt to harmonize Jewish and Gentile Christianity by falsely harmonizing its leaders.[9] Thus, for Baur, Acts gives us a characterization of Paul that is at odds with what may be drawn from his letters.

Adolf von Harnack faced the objections of Baur and his colleagues in an effort to defend the characterization of Paul in Acts. Believing that Acts was written by a companion of Paul, he cautioned against exaggerating its differences with the letters and explained them by reference to the supposed differences in religious temperament between Paul and Luke. Harnack further called attention to references in the letters that suggest that Paul's attitude was more complex than it had been represented to be.[10]

---

[7]See, e.g., Charles H. Talbert who treats parallelism as fundamental to the entire structure of Luke-Acts. *Literary Patterns, Theological Themes and the Genre of Luke-Acts*, SBLMS 20 (Missoula MT: Scholars Press, 1974). More recently, Andrew Clark has subjected the parallels in Acts to exhaustive treatment. *Parallel Lives: The Relation of Paul to the Apostles in the Lucan Perspective* (Carlisle UK: Paternoster Press, 2001).

[8]See Matthias Schneckenberger, *Über den Zweck der Apostelgeschichte* (Bern: Fischer, 1841).

[9]See esp. Ferdinand Christian Baur, *Paul, the Apostle of Jesus Christ, His Life and Work, His Epistles and His Doctrine. A Contribution to the Critical History of Primitive Christianity*, 2nd ed., 2 vols., ed. Eduard Zeller, trans. Allan Menzies (London: Williams & Norgate, 1876).

[10]In Gal 5:11, Paul is accused of still preaching circumcision, and, says Harnack, there must be some ground for the accusation. In 1 Cor 7:18-20, Paul implies "that the converted Jew should remain faithful to the customs and ordinances of the fathers." Harnack, *The Date of Acts and of the Synoptic Gospels*, trans. J. R. Wilkinson, New Testament Studies 4 (London: Williams & Norgate; New York: G. P. Putnam's Sons, 1911) 43. The discourse in Romans 9–11 constitutes a serious qualification to Paul's judgments in Galatians, since here he holds out a future hope

The issue of the characterization of Paul in Acts was most sharply treated by Philip Vielhauer, writing in 1950.[11] His work has been influential on a generation of Acts scholarship. Vielhauer maintained that the theology attributed to Paul in Acts was generally unrelated to that found in the letters but that the most dramatic contrasts are to be found on the issue of Torah observance and connection with Judaism. In Acts Paul is a faithful Pharisaic Jew, believing everything in the Scriptures and devoutly adhering to the customs and requirements of this faith. Vielhauer catalogued the practices in Acts that demonstrate Paul's adherence to Jewish customs, including his submission to the Jerusalem apostles, his circumcision of Timothy (Acts 16:3), his spreading of the apostolic decree (Acts 16:4), and his repeated assertions that he is a Pharisee.[12] All of these activities stress Paul's observance of Torah and his connection with Judaism and the Jewish people. And, to cap it off, Paul never in Acts hints at any critical attitude toward Torah. Only two verses in Acts may be cited as suggestions of Paul's views, and one of them was expressed by Peter rather than Paul (Acts 13:38-39; 15:11).

Writing only a few years after Vielhauer, Ernst Haenchen comes to essentially the same conclusions. He stresses that Paul and Luke are in basic agreement on the legitimacy of the Gentile mission without the law. Luke, says Haenchen, takes it for granted but is *"unaware of Paul's solution"*[13] and unable to justify it "from within," as Paul was.[14] "He must therefore seize on a justification 'from without'—God willed the mission, and that

---

for historical Israel. Strict logic would have required Paul to abandon this hope, but "the Jew in him was still too strong and his reverence for the content of the Old Testament still too devoted!" Harnack, *Date of Acts*, 49. Also in 1 Cor 9:20, Paul says, "To the Jews I became as a Jew, in order to win Jews."

[11]See Philip Vielhauer, "Zum 'Paulinismus' der Apostelgeschichte," *EvT* 10 (1950–1951): 1-15. ET: "On the 'Paulinism' of Acts," in *Studies in Luke-Acts. Essays Presented in Honor of Paul Schubert*, ed. Leander E. Keck and J. Louis Martyn, trans. William C. Robinson, Jr. and Victor P. Furnish (Nashville: Abingdon Press, 1966) 33-50. References below are to the English translation.

[12]Vielhauer, "Paulinism," 38.

[13]Ernst Haenchen, *The Acts of the Apostles: A Commentary*, ed. and trans. Bernard Noble, Gerald Shinn, Hugh Anderson, and R. McL. Wilson (Oxford UK: Blackwell; Philadelphia: Westminster, 1971) 112; emphasis in original.

[14]Haenchen, *Acts*, 113.

was sufficient."[15] Furthermore, in Haenchen's view, Luke's portrait of Paul differs from the Paul of the letters in significant ways: in Acts Paul is a miracle worker and a great orator, but not an apostle. Further, Acts misses the real point of Paul's theology: "From beginning to end, according to Acts, the Jewish hostility to the Christians was kindled by the latter's preaching of the Resurrection (Acts 4:2, 28:23)."[16] But, in fact, says Haenchen, the real bone of contention was Torah. This point surfaces from time to time in Acts, but only as a charge against Paul, a charge of which Paul is said to be not guilty.

The challenges of Vielhauer and Haenchen have not gone unanswered. Jacob Jervell reminds us that the letters of Paul were occasional letters, which do not require full biographical information. He writes, "As such they [the Pauline letters] obviously conceal parts of Paul's preaching and activity, since it was not necessary to treat such in a letter."[17] Jervell maintains that "The Lukan Paul, the picture of Paul in Acts, is a completion, a filling up of the Pauline one, so that in order to get at the historical Paul, we cannot do without Acts and Luke."[18] He emphasizes the Lukan treatment of Paul as a practicing Pharisee and calls attention to those places in the Pauline letters where Paul claims to have lived as a Jew (Rom 9:7; 11:2; Gal 2:15; 2 Cor 11:22; and especially 1 Cor 9:20). In general these references certify the context in which Paul saw himself. And it is as a Pharisee faithful to Torah that Paul is represented in Acts. Jervell concedes that Luke built his portrait of Paul "on material to be found in the marginal notes in Paul's letters."[19] But the Acts picture can be harmonized theologically with an important section of one of Paul's letters, namely Romans 9-11. Here Paul emphasizes the irrevocable covenant of God with Israel and projects the expectation of the eventual inclusion of all Israel in the believing community.[20]

---

[15]Haenchen, *Acts*, 113.

[16]Haenchen, *Acts*, 115.

[17]Jacob Jervell, *The Unknown Paul: Essays on Luke-Acts and Early Christian History* (Minneapolis: Augsburg Publishing House, 1984) 90.

[18]Jervell, *Unknown Paul*, 70.

[19]Jervell, *Unknown Paul*, 67.

[20]But Marianne Bonz has recently challenged this apparent harmony between Acts and Romans 9–11. See Marianne Palmer Bonz, "Luke's Revision of Paul's Reflections in Romans 9–11," in *Early Christian Voices in Texts, Traditions, and*

Stanley E. Porter faced the challenges from Vielhauer and Haenchen directly in a book originally published in 1999.[21] He noted Haenchen's claim that the Acts portrait of Paul stresses him as miracle worker and orator but not apostle and contended that there is no necessary contradiction with Paul's letters on the first two points. On the matter of apostleship, Porter called attention to Acts 14:4,14, where Barnabas and Paul are called apostles. Haenchen said that these verses were unimportant, but Porter notes that of the 28 uses of the word "apostle" in Acts, two apply to Paul, and he maintains that this cannot be overlooked as unimportant. Porter also questions Haenchen's claim that Luke was unaware of Paul's solution to the issue of the Gentile mission without the law.[22] Porter concludes that whatever differences may be found between the letters and Acts are not as significant as Vielhauer and Haenchen maintained and that they simply occur when different writers use different genres for writing.

Daniel Marguerat and a few recent scholars have framed the question somewhat differently and have proposed interesting solutions to our problem.[23] Marguerat acknowledges that, in some respects, the portrayals of

---

Symbols. Essays in Honor of François Bovon, ed. Ann Graham Brock, David W. Pao, and David H. Warren (Boston: Brill Academic Publishers, 2003) 143-51.

[21]Stanley E. Porter, *The Paul of Acts*, WUNT 115 (Tübingen: Mohr Siebeck, 1999).

[22]Porter, *Paul of Acts*, 199. Porter calls attention to a number of places in Acts where Paul is accused of disobeying the law and instructing others to do so. In Acts, however, these are regarded as false charges.

[23]See Daniel Marguerat, "L'Image de Paul dans les Actes des Apôtres," in *Les Actes des Apôtres: Histoire, récit, théologie*, ed. Michel Berder, Association catholique française pour l'étude de la Bible (Paris: Les editions du Cerf, 2005) 121-54. See also Marguerat, *The First Christian Historian: Writing the "Acts of the Apostles,"* SNTSMS 121 (Cambridge UK and New York: Cambridge University Press, 2002); Jürgen Roloff, "Die Paulus-Darstellung des Lukas: Ihre geschichtlichen Voraussetzungen und ihr theologisches Ziel," *EvT* 39 (1979): 510-31; Karl Löning, "Paulinismus in der Apostelgeschichte," in *Paulus in den Neutestamentlichen Spätschriften: Zur Paulusrezeption im Neuen Testament*, ed. Karl Kertelge, QD 89 (Freiburg, Basel, Wien: Herder, 1981) 202-32; Josef Pichler, "Das theologische Anliegen der Paulusrezeption im lukanischen Werk," in *The Unity of Luke-Acts*, ed. J. Verheyden, BETL 142 (Leuven: Leuven University Press, 1999) 731-43. See also Mark D. Nanos, *The Irony of Galatians: Paul's Letter in First-Century Context* (Minneapolis: Fortress Press, 2002).

Paul in Acts and in the Pauline letters are very close together and that in others there is a great distance. He calls this a "paradox," and the result is that "the image of Paul displayed in Acts and the image which results from the Pauline correspondence cannot be superimposed on one another. There is a tension between the undeniable biographical proximity and the gaping theological distance."[24] Marguerat emphasizes the complex phenomenon of the reception of Paul. Luke, he writes, lives in a community that both reveres and adapts Paul, and Luke's work does not depend on a reading of Paul's letters, but on the memory of his activity in founding communities.

In my estimation, Marguerat's refusal to attempt to reconcile the two views of Paul is correct. However he might appear in the letters, the Paul of Acts is a faithful Jew who observes Torah and the customs of his people, believes the Hebrew Scriptures, and intends to convince one and all that Jesus is the fulfillment of Jewish expectations. He is a Pharisee, who, like other Pharisees, believes in resurrection. He works hand-in-hand with the Jerusalem apostles and is even subservient to them on occasion. How can one reconcile the views expressed in the Pauline letters with a Paul who in Acts 16 would circumcise Timothy? How might one reconcile Paul's rejection of his past in Phil 3:1-11 with his maintenance of it in Acts 23:6?[25] How can one reconcile Paul's vehement definition of himself as an apostle in Gal 1:1 and his repeated claims to the designation in Rom 1:1; 11:13; 1 Cor 1:1; 9:1, 2; 15:9; 2 Cor 1:1; 12:12 with the almost total denial of the title to him in Acts?

Marguerat has helpfully pointed the way forward, and I think it is in line with his suggestions to add something further about the contextualization of Acts. The author of Acts surely represents a community that lives with the heritage of Paul, and this means a community that both reveres and adapts him. It is at this point that the late dating and contextualizing of Acts present us with an intriguing solution to our problem. If Acts was written in the early second century, as Pervo has convincingly shown, its characterization of Paul and Pauline theology may be understood as an

---

[24]Marguerat, "L'Image de Paul," 124.

[25]In Phil 3:1-11, Paul refers to his life as a Pharisee in highly derogatory terms, but Acts 23:6 conveys only a sense of pride. In the former it is clear that Paul looks upon his Pharisaic identification as past, a stage of his life not to be continued, but in Acts 23:6 he announces his Pharisaic identification as a matter of the present: "I am a Pharisee, a son of Pharisees."

extraordinarily appropriate attempt not only to revere Paul, but to adapt him. In my judgment, the author of Acts is not dealing directly with the real Paul, whom he did not know, but with the Paul of Marcion. In this respect, the issue is not the accuracy of his characterization of Paul, but the adequacy of his response to Marcion. In the effort to rescue Paul from the Marcionites, the author of Acts portrayed him as a faithful Pharisaic Jew who worked in tandem with the other apostles.

If Acts was written, at least in part, as a reaction against the Marcionite interpretation of the Pauline letters, it is not difficult to understand the characterization of Paul that meets us in this book. To explore this point, it will be useful to focus on specific features of the characterization of Paul and to suggest how they may have been intended to counter Marcionite claims. In what follows, I will comment on two of the major items in the characterization of Paul: the relationship between Paul and the Jerusalem apostles; and the representation of Paul as a faithful Pharisaic Jew.

II. Paul and the Jerusalem Apostles

Two interrelated issues are involved here: the question of Paul as apostle; and his relationship to the Jerusalem leaders. The author of Acts employed a number of literary techniques to dispute Marcionite claims, including the characterization of Peter as the leader of the early community and chief of the apostles. Further, the parallelization of Peter and Paul negates any concept of Pauline autonomy. But the parallelism between Peter and Paul is not complete, since the title "apostle" is almost totally confined to Peter and the Jerusalem leaders and used apparently to designate Paul (and Barnabas) only in two verses (Acts 14:4, 14). Is this not a direct reversal of the Marcionite claim that Paul is *the* apostle, who stands opposed to Peter and the others? For the author of Acts, there is complete harmony between Peter and Paul; the Jerusalem leaders are undoubtedly apostles, but Paul's official position is ambiguous.

The question of the apostleship of Paul in Acts is a particularly thorny one that has elicited a great deal of debate. A discussion of it should begin with the observation that the requirements set forth by Peter in his first speech in Acts 1:21-22 define apostleship in such a way that Paul could not have been accorded the title.[26] The narrative in Acts 1 makes it clear that the

---

[26]These verses link with the pericope in Luke 6:12-16, where Jesus himself chooses twelve of his disciples and grants them the title "apostle." As if to remove

apostles must be twelve in number, since the original twelfth apostle must be replaced. Moreover, the author of Acts is careful not only to number the apostles but also to include a list that does not have Paul in it. Given these stipulations, there is no way for Paul to be called an apostle in Acts. He was not appointed by Jesus; he was not with the others from the time of Jesus' baptism to the time of the ascension; his name is absent from what we may call Luke's official list; and his inclusion as apostle would expand a group whose number must remain constant.

As is well known, however, the title is apparently applied to Paul and Barnabas in Acts 14:4, 14. There is not sufficient space here to give these verses the consideration they deserve. At this point I concede that they present us with an inconsistency on the author's part but I also insist that they do not seriously compromise the understanding that the title "apostle" is denied to Paul.[27]

The Peter-Paul parallelism and the stress on the apostolicity of the Jerusalem leaders have yet another consequence. The community's inclusion of Gentiles, a major theme in Acts, is exhibited in an exemplary way in the work of Peter, not Paul (Acts 10:1-11:18). This section of Acts is particularly important, as its size and complexity make clear. The story of Cornelius and Peter, in my judgment, depicts the conversion of the first godfearing Gentile. But this conversion is unlike that of Jews as described in the previous chapters of Acts.[28] Something more is necessary, something

---

any doubt, the names of the apostles are given in Luke 6:14-16 as well as in Acts 1:13. The lists are identical except for slight changes in the order and for the omission of Judas Iscariot in the Acts list. One might object that even those listed in Luke 6 and Acts 1 did not meet the requirements set out in Acts 1:21-22, since none of them were present at Jesus' baptism, which was reported in Luke 3:21-22. But in the face of the lists of named apostles in Luke and Acts, the objection seems trivial.

[27]Pace Porter. On Acts 14:4, 14, see further, Tyson, *Marcion and Luke-Acts*, 70-72. Also see Thomas E. Phillips, "Narrative Characterizations of Peter and Paul in Early Christianity," *ARC: Journal of the Faculty of Religious Studies at McGill University* 30 (2002): 139-57. Phillips argues that Paul is portrayed as "post-apostolic" in Acts.

[28]C. K. Barrett's comment at this point is germane: "The drift of the section as a whole, especially when it is viewed in the setting provided for it by Luke, is that the event marks a notable step in the extension of the Gospel to the world outside Judaism. . . . Yet within the narrative, Luke goes out of his way to show how close

that will permit both Jews and Gentiles to be members of the community without disturbing its unity. The necessary permission comes through Peter's vision, in which the distinction of clean and unclean foods is abolished, and in Peter's interpretation of the vision that no persons are profane or unclean (see Acts 10:28; cf. 11:18; 15:9).[29] In his speech at the home of Cornelius, Peter stresses his role as witness to all that Jesus had done, from the baptism (Acts 10:37) to the resurrection (Acts 10:40), and he recalls the choice of the witnesses and the commission given to them (Acts 10:41-42). The reader would be reminded of the requirements for apostleship from Acts 1:21-22.[30] But for the author of Acts there must be an authoritative confirmation of the validity of the new move of Peter, and that is given in Acts 11:1-18. Here Peter is called to give account of his actions in regard to this godfearing Gentile, and after he does so, the Jerusalem apostles agree that repentance has also been granted to Gentiles (Acts 11:18). It is important to observe that, for the author of Acts, the story is not over until all the apostles have agreed that Gentiles may be members of the community and that their admission will not create disharmony.

Cornelius was to Judaism." Barrett, *A Critical and Exegetical Commentary on the Acts of the Apostles*, 2 vols. ICC (Edinburgh: T.&T. Clark, 1994, 1998) 1:493.

[29]The contrast between the vision and its interpretation presents critics with a number of thorny issues. Martin Dibelius concluded that the author of Acts had access to a traditional conversion story similar to that of the Ethiopian and that he altered it so that it would serve as a precedent to be invoked in Acts 15. Dibelius, *Studies in the Acts of the Apostles*, ed. Heinrich Greeven, trans. Mary Ling (New York: Charles Scribner's Sons, 1956) 109-22. Similar explanations are provided by Gerd Lüdemann, *The Acts of the Apostles: What Really Happened in the Earliest Days of the Church* (Amherst NY: Prometheus Books, 2005) 138-49; Jacob Jervell, *Die Apostelgeschichte*, 17th ed., KEK 3 (Göttingen: Vandenhoeck & Ruprecht, 1998) 299-320; and François Bovon, "Tradition et redaction en Actes 10,1-11,18," *TZ* 36 (1970): 22-45. Bovon concludes that "tradition gives a literal sense to the vision, redaction a figurative sense" (p. 34). Haenchen, however, rejects Dibelius's views on the grounds that such stories were inappropriate for Christians under the influence of their eschatological convictions. See Haenchen, *Acts*, 343-63. For a compelling critique of Dibelius, see Klaus Haacker, "Dibelius und Cornelius: Ein Beispiel formgeschichtlicher Überlieferungskritik," *BZ* 24 (1980): 234-51.

[30]Note, however, that the terminal point in Acts 1 is the ascension, whereas in Acts 10 it is the resurrection appearances.

Interpreters of Acts have long regarded it as curious that the one who in his letters claimed to be an apostle to Gentiles played no role in that momentous model conversion. But, in fact, the narrative in Acts 10:1-11:18 is fully controlled by a theme that plays out in the book as a whole. For the author of Acts, the importance of order in the community requires that the conversion of the first Gentile be the work of an apostle and that it be authorized by the entire group of Jerusalem apostles. Such an important event as the inclusion of the first Gentile cannot be seen as an unauthorized departure or a disruption of order and harmony in the community. How distant this is from the Marcionite claim that Paul was the only apostle![31]

The relation of Paul to the leaders in Jerusalem is most vividly treated in Luke's narrative of the apostolic conference in Acts 15. Recent studies of Acts 15 have shown that Luke used Paul's letter to the Galatians as a source for his narrative and that he intentionally subverted it.[32] Why would he do so? It would be difficult to explain the reasons for this treatment of Galatians if Acts had been written by a companion or follower of the historical Paul. The treatment is born of an effort to read Galatians in a way that would not call attention to rifts between Paul and the other apostles and would not lead readers to think that Paul and his followers were unfaithful to Jewish traditions and practices. It is not unreasonable to think that it resulted from an effort to reconcile followers of Paul with followers of Peter, as the Tübingen School maintained. One of the most notable aspects of the chapter is the short speech in Acts 15:7-11, which puts Pauline words into Peter's mouth.[33] It seems more reasonable, however, to think that there

---

[31]Note also that, in Acts 15:7, Peter claims to be the apostle to Gentiles.

[32]See, e.g., William O. Walker, "Acts and the Pauline Corpus Revisited: Peter's Speech at the Jerusalem Conference," in *Literary Studies in Luke-Acts. Essays in Honor of Joseph B. Tyson*, ed. Richard P. Thompson and Thomas E. Phillips (Macon GA: Mercer University Press, 1998) 77-86; see also Pervo, *Dating Acts*, 79-96.

[33]Dibelius regarded Acts 15 as literary theology, not history (*Studies in Acts*, 93-101). He noted that the reference to Cornelius in Acts 15 would have meaning only for readers of Acts and would not have stood independently of the story in Acts 10–11. Dibelius did, however, believe that the decree was not part of Luke's invention; Luke drew on a source for the four requirements, but it was a source that did not go back to the time of Paul and Peter. Philip F. Esler recognizes the contribution of Luke: "The particular method employed by Luke to legitimate Jewish-

was a serious and specific challenge that the author of Acts intended to meet, a challenge that stressed the distance between Jewish and Christian practices and the opposition of Paul to the imposition on Gentile Christians not only of circumcision but of any requirements coming from Torah.

Such a challenge came from Marcionite Christians, who stressed Paul's claim not to yield to the opponents of Gentile freedom for a moment (Gal 2:5). How better to counter these Marcionite assertions than by publishing a narrative of this very meeting that Paul described in Galatians, and by showing that there was no genuine disagreement between Paul and the other apostles and that the meeting ended in full accord with an agreement that some requirements from Torah were imposed on Gentile believers. The fact that the requirements as listed in Acts are said to be minimal is not the issue. Rather, the imposition of any such requirements on Gentile believers would signal to Luke's readers that Marcionite Christians were in error. Their total separation of Jewish and Christian practices is not to be countenanced; Peter cannot be regarded as a false apostle; and the distance between Jewish and Christian practices is not as great as Marcion had said. Paul's spreading of the apostolic decree (Acts 16:4) underscores his own agreement with it and leads the reader to understand Paul as quite different from the way the Marcionites portrayed him. Again, it is difficult to see why the author of Acts would have so altered the material from Galatians except under the threat of a serious challenge such as that of Marcion.

III. Paul as a Faithful Jew and a Pharisee

For Vielhauer and other scholars, the assertion that Paul continued to think of himself as a Pharisee even toward the evident end of his life rings false to the assertions Paul makes about himself in the letters. I agree, but I also think that the characterization of Paul in Acts is fundamentally a literary answer to Marcion. In addition, the content of Paul's preaching in Acts seems intended to counter the claims of Marcionite Christianity. While

---

Gentile table-fellowship against the background of persistent opposition from the Jerusalem church in the period before the events of 67–70 CE is both simple and yet thoroughly audacious—he rewrites the history of early Christianity relating to this subject and assigns to Peter, James, and the church in Jerusalem exactly the opposite roles to those which they played in fact." Esler, *Community and Gospel in Luke-Acts: The Social and Political Motivations of Lucan Theology*, SNTSMS 57 (Cambridge UK and New York: Cambridge University Press, 1987) 107.

Marcion would totally divorce the Hebrew Scriptures, the prophets, and Jewish messianic expectation from Jesus, Paul in Acts asserts that Jesus is the fulfillment of these very expectations.

A major objective of the scenes in Acts where Paul is on trial appears to be to portray him as a Torah-abiding Jew. In his appearances before the Sanhedrin, Felix, Festus, and Agrippa and Bernice, Paul is consistent in his claims to "worship the God of our ancestors" and to believe "everything laid down according to the law or written in the prophets" (Acts 24:14).[34] When in Acts 26:22, Paul asserts that he proclaims "nothing but what the prophets and Moses said would take place," we know that the Paul who speaks here has nothing whatsoever to do with the Marcionite Paul. In fact, however, the attentive reader of Acts would not be surprised by this claim, because the author has prepared for it by portraying a number of incidents in which Paul is shown to be just what he claims to be in his trials, one of the most important of which is Acts 21:18-28.

When viewed as a response to the Marcionite challenge, the narrative of Acts 21:18-28 is very interesting. It tells of Paul's arrival in Jerusalem and of the news that greeted him there. We learn categorically that there are myriads of believers among the citizens of Jerusalem and that "they are all zealous for the law" (Acts 21:20). For Marcion, who saw the role of Jesus

---

[34]Dibelius regards Paul's claims at his trials as part of the author's political apologetic (*Studies in Acts*, 213). "These themes are intended to emphasise the fact that Christians have not rebelled against the emperor, nor against the temple, nor against the law, but that the essential matter of dispute between them and the Jews is the question of the resurrection." John A. Darr recommends that we should not take Paul's claims at these points seriously: "Given Paul's desperate situation, the reader will take these words about his membership in the Pharisaic party with a grain of salt. In any event, the emphasis of Paul's claim seems to fall on his affiliation through heritage ('a son of Pharisees'), not on the status of his present membership." Darr, *On Character Building: The Reader and the Rhetoric of Characterization in Luke-Acts*, LCBI (Louisville: Westminster/John Knox, 1992) 123. Robert Tannehill argues that Luke intends to present Paul "as a resourceful witness from whom other missionaries can learn." As such, later Christians can learn how to address Jews. Tannehill adds: "This view does imply that there is a continuing concern in Acts with a mission to Jews, even though relations have been poisoned by controversy." Tannehill, *The Acts of the Apostles*, vol. 2 of *The Narrative Unity of Luke-Acts: A Literary Interpretation* (Minneapolis: Fortress, 1990) 290.

and Paul as freeing believers from the domination of Torah, the existence of such a group would probably have been attributed to the work of "false apostles." Then we learn that Paul had been accused of teaching diaspora Jews to forsake Moses, to forego circumcision for their sons, and not to observe the customs (Acts 21:21). These are clearly regarded as false charges against Paul, and he is to demonstrate their falsity by participating in a ritual of purification and paying the expenses of four other men under a vow.

There should be no doubt that the purpose of this series of actions is to show that Paul did not teach the abolition of Torah. James's statement in Acts 21:25 makes the point explicitly.[35] But why such a strong defense unless Paul had actually been charged with anti-Torah teaching? It is as if the author of Acts is saying to the reader: "You may have heard Marcionite Christians say falsely that Paul did not observe Torah, but here is what he really said and did." Paul willingly engaged in the practices recommended by James but the charges against him persisted. He was seized by Asian Jews, who shouted: "This is the man who is teaching everyone everywhere against our people, our law, and this place" (Acts 21:28). The author of Acts knows this to be a vicious falsehood, and he here attributes it to Jews from Asia. But we know it also as a claim made by Marcion. The message to the reader is that Paul was not as Marcion said he was, but he was arrested because people believed this falsehood.

Conclusion

The characterization of Paul in Acts is internally consistent. He is a loyal Jew, obedient to Torah and faithful to Jewish practices. His message is that Jesus fulfills the words of the Hebrew prophets: he is the Messiah of Israel. Paul does not act unilaterally but only in harmony with Peter and the Jerusalem apostles. It is they who establish the authentic Christian tradition, and Paul neither adds to it nor subtracts from it. The author of Acts has made use of the characterization of Paul to produce an engaging narrative that responds, almost point by point, to the Marcionite challenge. Readers of Acts learn that the God of Jesus is the God of the Jews, that Jesus is the ful-

---

[35]On the appropriateness of James's advice to Paul, see Jacob Neusner, "Vow-Taking, the Nazirites, and the Law: Does James' Advice to Paul Accord with Halakhah?" in *James the Just and Christian Origins*, ed. Bruce Chilton and Craig Evans (Leiden: Brill, 1999) 59-82.

fillment of Jewish expectation as announced by the Hebrew prophets, and that the early Christian leaders continued to observe Torah and Jewish practices.

I have attempted here to provide a few examples of features and incidents in Acts that, in my judgment, make sense when seen as reactions against Marcion. Neither these few examples nor the entire characterization of Paul in Acts proves that the author of Acts wrote with Marcion in mind. But together with the evidence that Richard Pervo brings forward to support his contention that Acts was written in the first quarter of the second century, this reading of Acts as a reaction against emerging Marcionite Christianity helps in determining its probable historical context. It makes good sense of Acts and provides a way to understand some major themes. In particular, it opens the way for us to appreciate this text as a major chapter in the controversy over the legacy of Paul.

Acts in the Suburbs of the Apologists

Richard I. Pervo

I. Preface

My recent reflections on the date of Acts began in particular as a response to a contribution by Joe Tyson to the Acts Seminar of the Westar Institute[1] and in general as a parergon to a commentary being prepared for the Hermeneia series.[2] For a good three decades I had assumed that ca. 100 CE was a reasonable date for the composition of Acts.[3] The consensus date of ca. 80–85 CE has never seemed particularly viable to me. The perspective of (Luke and) Acts is that of the third generation. Participation in a group at the International SBL at Leuven in 1994 reinforced the understanding that the phrase "legitimating narrative" comprehended the majority of views about the genre/genres, theology and purposes of (Luke and) Acts.[4] This established the *termini* of a trajectory with evangelists like Mark at one pole and such apologists as Justin at the other.[5] The relation between Acts and apologetic was scarcely a new idea. Scholarship agrees upon the presence of apologetic elements, however delineated and understood.[6] This trajectory is not necessarily chronological, but it does have implications for chronology that require evaluation.[7]

---

[1]Tyson's paper was published as Joseph B. Tyson, "The Date of Acts: A Reconsideration," *Forum* n.s. 5 (2002): 33-51.

[2]Richard I. Pervo, *Acts: A Commentary*, Hermeneia (Minneapolis: Fortress Press, 2008).

[3]Hans Conzelmann, "Luke's Place in the Development of Early Christianity," in *Studies in Luke-Acts*, ed. Leander E. Keck and J. Louis Martyn (Nashville: Abingdon, 1966) 298-316, exercised a strong influence in this direction.

[4]For a concise statement indicating what "legitimating narrative" means, see Richard I. Pervo, "Israel's Heritage and Claims upon the Genre(s) of Luke and Acts: The Problems of a History," in *Jesus and the Heritage of Israel: Luke's Narrative Claim upon Israel's Legacy*, ed. David P. Moessner (Harrisburg PA: Trinity Press International, 1999) 127-43, 136.

[5]A useful introduction to the world and thought of the apologists is Robert M. Grant, *Greek Apologists of the Second Century* (Philadelphia: Westminster, 1988).

[6]For a recent survey, see Loveday C. A. Alexander, *Acts in Its Ancient Literary Context: A Classicist Looks at the Acts of the Apostles*, LNTS 298 (London: T.&T. Clark, 2005) 183-206.

[7]Gospels continued to be written throughout the second century and beyond. Although many apologetic features can be found in the New Testament (Arthur J. Droge, "Apologetics, New Testament," *ABD on CD-ROM*, ver. 2.0, ©1995, 1996),

By the mid-90s I had begun to question the assumption that Luke did not draw from the letters of Paul. The thesis that Luke must have known that Paul wrote letters but refused to look at them became increasingly difficult to swallow. Acts 9:23-25 (the escape from Damascus) seemed to reflect 2 Corinthians, and the Miletus speech rippled with possible allusions.[8] Steve Mason's handbook to Josephus showed the strengths of the hypothesis that Luke knew at least the later books of the *Antiquities*.[9] An attendant perception is that the some of the conclusions reached in the patient and excellent labor expended to refute F. C. Baur deserved reexamination.[10] These discarded old hypotheses reemerged as potential solutions to a number of knotty problems.[11] With these possibilities in mind, I turned, in 2002, to study of the date of Acts, producing a paper for the Acts Seminar that I subsequently hoped could be turned, without undue padding, into a 120 page book.[12] The manuscript was drafted by October 2002 and appeared in November 2006 as *Dating Acts: Between the Evangelists and the Apologists* at 528 pages in length.

Initial investigation revealed that very little detailed and penetrating research had been devoted to the question of the date of Acts in recent decades. The consensus of ca. 80–85 CE was more of a political compromise

---

the first formal apologists (Quadratus, Aristides) appear in the 120s.

[8]Even a superficial examination of Lars Aejmelaeus, *Die Rezeption der Paulusbriefe in der Miletrede* (Helsinki: Suomalienen Tiedeakatemia, 1987) raised doubts about a hermetic seal protecting Luke from Paul's letters.

[9]Steve Mason, *Josephus and the New Testament* (Peabody MA: Hendrickson, 1992). This led one back to Max Krenkel, *Josephus und Lukas: Der schriftstellerische Einfluß des jüdischen Geschichtschreibers auf der christlichen nachgewiesen* (Leipzig: H. Hässel, 1894), a work that, despite its well-advertised flaws, has many useful proposals.

[10]Not all of Baur's opponents rejected the possibility that Luke knew Paul's letters. William Ramsay, for example, took this for granted. Richard I. Pervo, *Dating Acts: Between the Evangelists and the Apologists* (Santa Rosa CA: Polebridge, 2006) 51. F. C. Burkitt agreed that Luke knew Josephus (*Dating Acts*, 149).

[11]Very few of the proposals about literary dependence presented in *Dating Acts* are original to me. The chapters devoted to that subject (pp. 29-199) are largely syntheses and summaries of the findings of others.

[12]Richard I. Pervo, "Dating Acts," Acts Seminar, Santa Rosa CA, 19 October 2002—a paper written in the spring of that year, and published under that title in *Forum* n.s. 5/1 (Spring 2002): 53-72.

than the result of scientific analysis, a compromise allowing conversation between both those who believed that the author was a one-time companion of Paul and those who held that the book looked back to Paul's activity from a subsequent generation. Such compromises have their value, but are likely to endure only as long as the subject is deemed relatively unimportant. This particular compromise was unraveling, for creative scholarship on the leading edge was leaning toward ca. 90 CE or later as a *terminus a quo*.[13] Argument against a *communis opinio* often requires detail. This helps to explain, if not justify, the length of the book.[14]

The general principle is that a work must be dated by reference to the latest datable material in the text's final, integral, form.[15] This may seem too obvious to require iteration, but the influential work of Adolph von Harnack,[16] whose arguments were basically restated by J. A. T. Robinson and Colin Hemer, attempted the opposite,[17] essentially by identifying views

---

[13]See Pervo, *Dating Acts*, appendix III, 359-63.

[14]An additional justification was a firm commitment to make this scholarly argument intelligible to nonexperts, a goal of the Westar Institute.

[15]"Final" applies to the hand of the author. Two difficulties arise. Scholars are sometimes tempted to ask whether Acts was properly and finally revised by the author. Over the course of more than a century a few authorities have argued that the D-text (i.e., "The Western Text") represents such an authorial revision. Since the text of Acts is unstable and arguably corrupt in a number of places, the adjective "final" must be qualified. Such qualifications do not seriously impugn the hypotheses here advanced. "Integral" refers to alleged supplements, appendixes, etc. I do not regard John 21, e.g., as part of the integral text of the Fourth Gospel, but as a contribution to the history of its reception. (The same judgment applies to the bulk of the D-text tradition.)

[16]Adolf von Harnack, *The Acts of the Apostles*, trans. J. R. Wilkinson (New York: G. P. Putnam's Sons, 1909) 290-97. See also Harnack, *The Date of Acts and of the Synoptic Gospels*, trans. J. R. Wilkinson (New York: G. P. Putnam's Sons, 1911). For a review of Harnack's views of the date of Acts (which moved from relatively late to early) see Joseph B. Tyson, *Marcion and Luke-Acts: A Defining Struggle* (Columbia: University of South Carolina Press, 2006) 6-9.

[17]J. A. T. Robinson, *Redating the New Testament* (Philadelphia: Westminster, 1976) 88-92; Colin J. Hemer, *The Book of Acts in the Setting of Hellenistic History*, ed. Conrad Gempf (Winona Lake IN: Eisenbrauns, 1990) 365-410. A recent reiteration of these arguments is Andreas Mittelstädt, *Lukas als Historiker: Zur Datierung des Lukanischen Doppelwerkes*, Texte und Arbeiten zum neuestesta-

and data deemed early. Another, possibly debatable, principle deploys Ock-ham's razor, which privileges simplicity in the construction of hypotheses. Known sources are preferred to unknown. Rather than posit another, albeit lost, historian of Jewish affairs who wrote somewhat earlier than Josephus,[18] one prefers the known historian. When Luke reflects some of the biases and viewpoints of Josephus, the probability that he used Josephus rises precipitously.[19] In place of the liturgical and creedal traditions alleged to account for many similarities with the epistles, traditions that are often vague and frequently unverifiable, one ought to prefer the known data of the epistles. This hypothesis that Luke knew both Josephus and a collection of Paul's letters gains strength from the application of recent theories about intertextuality and such tools as the TLG, which can show that an allegedly traditional phrase is attested only in Galatians or Romans and Acts, for example.[20] We do not know how Paul spoke; what is known is how he *wrote*. Luke and Acts exhibit features of that written style. To this it might be added that much of New Testament source theory falls under the influence of the analysis of relations among the Synoptic Gospels or between Colossians and Ephesians. Close verbal contact is not the only manifestation of intertextuality. Ancient authors were expected to rewrite their sources in their own style.[21]

Another useful approach to hypotheses is to ask whether a particular proposal solves more problems than it creates. All theories generate some problems and raise new questions. That does not invalidate them, *per se*. An

---

mentlichen Zeitalter 43 (Tübingen: Francke, 2006).

[18]Justus of Tiberias will not meet this requirement, for he wrote a history of the rebellion, which Josephus sought to rebut in his *Wars*, but Justus did not write a work like the *Antiquities*. The summary table (5.13, *Dating Acts*, 197) does not give a mark of high probability of dependence to any passage from the *Wars* alone. Arguments for Lukan dependence focus upon the last books of the *Antiquities*.

[19]See Pervo, *Dating Acts*, 149-99.

[20]For an illustration, see Pervo, *Dating Acts*, 102 (Rom 12:11 ‖ Acts 18:25).

[21]Another factor is the evolution of Luke as a writer. "Luke the Historian" *could* not have used the letters because they would have provided useful data and helped him evade some apparent difficulties. "Luke the Theologian" did not use the letters because he rejected their theology. "Luke the Author," his current instantiation, was free to use whatever sources he chose to use and as he wished. See Pervo, *Dating Acts*, 135-37.

attraction of the source theories under review is that they offer viable resolutions to a number of questions. This is particularly true of the problems generated by the claim that Luke was unaware of Paul's letters, a dogma that is utterly risible when subjected to even a cursory examination. Luke knew that Paul wrote letters and could scarcely have avoided hearing some read, even if he declined to peruse them.[22] This approach to problem solving is a corollary of the axiom that the preferable hypothesis is that which *best* accounts for the data. Granted that all things are possible, the scholar must seek to identify what is most probable.[23]

One patently anachronistic objection to these hypotheses is that Luke did not utilize the Pauline corpus or Josephus in ways that would conform to modern practice. Luke's use of unnamed sources does not fall outside the boundaries of ancient historiographical practice.[24] Scholars generally accept Luke's alterations of Mark, but have often bridled at the thought that he would do the same to Paul. Underlying this is the debate about the historical accuracy of Acts. It seems that Luke can do as he pleases to Jesus, but *not* to Paul.[25]

The propositions that Luke used Josephus and a *collection* of Paul's letters establish 100 CE as the earliest possible date. "Collection" is a key word. If Luke had used only Romans or 1 Corinthians, for instance, one could argue that these letters appear to have enjoyed independent circulation,[26] but Acts exhibits knowledge of 2 Corinthians (or at least a fragment thereof),[27] Romans (8 references), 1 Corinthians (14 references), Galatians

---

[22]For the practice of reading letters in Christian assemblies, see, e.g., 1 Thess 5:27, Col 4:16, *1 Clement* 47, and Pervo, *Dating Acts*, 235.

[23]Too much research on Acts has operated with the principle that any hypothesis that appears to account for the data is valid.

[24]Since Greco-Roman historiography belonged to the realm of literature, many genres participated in these standards.

[25]One impact of the recognition that Luke utilized Paul's letters is that the venerable pillar of "undersigned coincidences" between Acts and the epistles, long used to buttress claims for the historical reliability of Acts, has collapsed. See Pervo, *Dating Acts*, 388n.32.

[26]This can be confirmed from both utilization (e.g., *1 Clement*) and textual data. The latter is particularly clear in the case of Romans. See Pervo, *Dating Acts*, 387n.22.

[27]It is possible that Luke had access to the fragment of 2 Cor 10–13 (presum

(25 references), Ephesians (19 references), and 1 Thessalonians (13 references). Less well attested are Philippians (4 references) and Colossians (3/4 references).[28] These data point to a collection that included at least one deuteropauline letter (Ephesians, probably also Colossians) and one or two presumably composite letters (2 Corinthians; Philippians).[29] The alternative—that the author found copies of these documents by traveling to various Pauline sites (including [N.] Galatia!)—is too improbable to merit serious consideration. The data support the simpler hypothesis: Luke had access to a collection. They also show that Luke read Paul's words through a deuteropauline lens. The voice was Paul's voice, but the hands were those of deuteropauline.[30]

---

ably at Ephesus). The other possible allusions (2 Cor 2:4; 11:25) are not definitive. Nonetheless, the weight of data from other epistles suggests that his collection included the composite text known as 2 Corinthians. The editor of that text may have destroyed his sources—parts of which were not flattering to Paul—when he produced the composite. Acts and 2 Corinthians share a similar view of Paul's career (see Pervo, *Dating Acts*, 320-21).

[28]The parentheses include the number of allusions discussed in *Dating Acts*, 139-43.

[29]It is at least somewhat more probable that composites of Pauline correspondence were produced for inclusion within a collection than as freestanding texts. For a summary of what can be deduced about early editions of the letters see Harry Y. Gamble, *Books and Readers in the Early Church: A History of Early Christian Texts* (New Haven CT: Yale University Press, 1995) 59-62. Luke's edition of Romans included chapter 15, for he cites verses 29-31 and utilizes Paul's plans for his construction of the final journey to Jerusalem (*Dating Acts*, 119-20).

[30]See below.

Acts *may* be attested by Polycarp, ca. 130 CE.[31] Otherwise one must look to the *Acts of Paul* and to the *Epistula Apostolorum*, of roughly mid-second-century date.[32] The earliest secure date is Irenaeus, ca. 175 CE.[33] All in all, it is not possible to prove that Acts was written before 150 CE,[34] but

---

[31]Pervo, *Dating Acts*, 17-20. Although I think Polycarp's *Philippians* is a composite, that hypothesis is not crucial. The fundamental issue is the date of Ignatius's martyrdom. The Trajanic date (ca. 115) is based upon Eusebius (*Eccl. theol.* 3.36.1). That reference is extremely vague. Eusebius then claims that Polycarp, a "companion of the apostles," had been appointed bishop of Smyrna by the "eyewitnesses and ministers of the Lord" (cf. Luke 1:2). Contemporaries included Papias, bishop of Hierapolis, and Ignatius, the third bishop of Antioch in a succession that began with Peter. Eusebius has every interest in locating these people as early as possible, indeed, earlier than possible. Moreover, 3.33.3 cited the correspondence of Pliny with Trajan (Pliny, *Epistles* 10.96-97). It is reasonable to think that Eusebius viewed Trajan as an emperor under whom persecutions occurred and thus placed Ignatius's death within his reign. Eusebius's statements do not constitute chronological evidence. Papias is usually dated ca. 130, and this is a more viable date for the correspondence of Ignatius.

[32]These attestations are disputable. See the thorough analysis by Andrew Gregory, *The Reception of Luke and Acts in the Period before Irenaeus*, WUNT 169 (Tübingen: Mohr Siebeck, 2003). I am rather certain that both the *Acts of Paul* and the *Epistula Apostolorum* knew and used Acts, but their dating is uncertain, although probably anterior to 175.

[33]Pervo, *Dating Acts*, 23, observes that the citation of Acts 7:60 (prayer of Stephen) in the *Letter of the Churches in Vienne and Lyons* (*The Martyrs of Lyons* 2.5) could be a later insertion, since the text is first attested in Eusebius and was probably edited. This is valid, but since Irenaeus replaced the martyred bishop Pothinus, it is not improbable that Acts was known and read at Lyons prior to Irenaeus's accession (cf. also 1.9, which may be a reflection of Acts 18:25, or Rom 12:11, the source of Acts). The first absolutely certain reference to Acts is therefore from Gaul in the last quarter of the second century. Acts is not named in the letter, nor is it cited as Scripture. It is possible that the recipients in Asia and Phrygia were expected to recognize the source. The importance of the citations, if valid, is that Acts was read in Gaul for general edification and not only as a bulwark against heresy.

[34]Justin Martyr (d. ca. 165) knew Luke, in an uncertain form as he harmonized it with Matthew, but he cannot be proven to have known Acts. See Pervo, *Dating Acts*, 20-23. Justin may have known Acts and rejected it, which would indicate that he did not view Luke and Acts as inseparable. For Irenaeus the books do appear to

few, if any, would attempt to date it later.[35] By the final quarter of the century its utility in the conflict with Marcion and other "heretics" gave it an intellectual cachet hitherto lacking. This was due to the decision of some to claim Paul for the emerging catholic church rather than to let the heretics have him.[36] In more "popular" circles Acts was quite a success and gave rise to a number of sequels, parallels, and imitations.[37]

Refinement of this ca. 100–130 CE bracket involves a long and often tedious study of terms and concepts, including institutional organization, theologoumena, and polemical issues.[38] From this survey it transpires that Acts suits the world of the Apostolic Fathers, the Pastoral Epistles, and the beginnings of apologetic. Luke pursues some of the goals of the apologists with the methods of the evangelists (i.e., by telling stories about persons). The fragmentary *Kerygma Petri* appears to be a good parallel.[39] This tugs toward 130 CE. Pressure from the other direction can be seen from two texts with which Acts shares a good deal: Ephesians (c. 90-100)[40] and *1 Clement* (ca. 100).[41] A date of 110–120 CE, or ca. 115 CE, is therefore reasonable. A date of 120-25 CE is not excluded,[42] but is slightly less probable.[43] Here endeth the preface. What follows will look at Acts from the perspective of the second decade of the second century.

---

constitute a unity of sorts. (See the next essay in this volume by Gregory.)

[35]The latest date identified in the preparation of *Dating Acts*, appendix II, is 140 or later (John Townsend).

[36]Irenaeus knew and utilized Justin's antiheretical work, but took a different position on the place of Paul in emergent orthodoxy. He attempted a synthesis that embraced trends and texts from all parts of the empire save Alexandria.

[37]These include the Apocryphal Acts, hagiography (to a degree), and the *Epistula Apostolorum*. On "popular" see n. 60 below.

[38]Pervo, *Dating Acts*, 201-308.

[39]Pervo, *Dating Acts*, 341-42. For the text, see Michel Cambe, *Kerygma Petri: Textus et commentarius*, CCSA 15 (Turnhout: Brepols, 2003). Wilhelm Schneemelcher provides a translation and discussion in *New Testament Apocrypha*, 2 vols, trans R. McL. Wilson (Louisville: Westminster/John Knox, 1992) 2:34-41.

[40]Pervo, *Dating Acts*, 293-99.

[41]Pervo, *Dating Acts*, 301-305.

[42]Tyson prefers this date, *Marcion and Luke-Acts*, 78.

[43]A date of ca. 105–110 is even less probable.

II. And so . . .

I am on record as questioning a global approach to the unity of Luke and Acts.[44] This skepticism also applies to the date. The gospel could have been issued as much as a decade before Acts, and may have been revised when Acts was completed.[45] At least some of the differences between the two books are readily explained by allowing a difference in date.[46] One of the weaknesses of the global understanding is its implicit assumption that the gospel and its sequel were fully planned, then composed in rapid sequence (perhaps while Luke was on sabbatical in Heidelberg). Both Luke and Acts exhibit a plan, and the two volumes interrelate, but no one knows whether Acts was an afterthought or part of the initial plan or how long it took the author to write them.[47]

Luke and Acts regard the followers of Jesus as the legitimate inheritors of God's promises. They therefore possess Israel's sacred writings, all of which are understood as prophetic demonstrations of the correctness of Lukan christology.[48] The messiah had to die and be raised so that he could

---

[44]Mikeal C. Parsons and Richard I. Pervo, *Rethinking the Unity of Luke and Acts* (Minneapolis: Fortress Press, 1993).

[45]The best candidate for such revision would be Luke 1–2, which appear to have been written after Luke 3–24, but are evidently reflected in Acts. See Joseph A. Fitzmyer, *The Gospel according to Luke*, 2 vols., AB 28, 28A (Garden City NY: Doubleday, 1981, 1985) 1:310-11, and Raymond E. Brown, *The Birth of the Messiah: A Commentary on the Infancy Narratives in the Gospels of Matthew and Luke*, 2nd ed. (New York: Doubleday, 1993) 239-41, 624-25. Joseph B. Tyson argues that the "precanonical" edition of Luke was shorter than the current text (*Marcion and Luke-Acts*, 79-120). If this theory—which has much in its favor—is accepted, canonical Luke and Acts are best viewed as roughly simultaneous.

[46]See, e.g., Stephen G. Wilson, "Lucan Eschatology," *NTS* 14 (1970–1971): 330-47, 347, commenting upon the lack of imminent expectation of the end in Acts. For some hypotheses about the history of composition see, Alexander, *Acts in Its Ancient Literary Context*, 25.

[47]An earlier dating for Luke is not necessary to my hypothesis. The use of Mark in Acts (Pervo, *Dating Acts*, 35-49) excludes the possibility that Acts was written before Luke.

[48]Note Acts 3:18, which claims that all the prophets said that the Messiah would suffer. Historical criticism would change "all" to "none." Acts 3:18 states a hermeneutical presupposition rather than an inductive conclusion.

become a universal savior. Nothing else is of value, neither ethnic and national identity, nor the temple and its cultus, nor Torah and observance. One can see the roots of these claims in early Gentile Christianity, but they are no less remarkable for that. Acts says, in effect, "We take what we want, use it as we will, and declare the rest unimportant." If the Jewish people had lost their land and their sanctuary, that was further proof of their error. They threw out the baby and have boiled away the bath water.

Many fine scholars object to using the label "Christian" for believers in Acts, but it is appropriate.[49] Luke does not care for the word, to be sure, but he knows it. The term is not attested until the close of the first century. It reflects the recognition that Christianity was a religion distinct from Judaism.[50] That is how Acts views matters. It is not seeking to define the boundaries between followers of Jesus and adherents of nascent rabbinic Judaism, an observation that is somewhat valid for Matthew. Others maintained closer links to Israel for centuries,[51] but the interest of Acts is to expound and defend already established boundaries.

If it was at one time useful for Jesus-people to take shelter under the umbrella of Judaism, that became inconvenient under the Flavians, and rather more so under Trajan and Hadrian, whose reigns saw two additional revolts.[52] I think that Acts' treatment of the Jews as "the other" is due less to conflict with the contemporary synagogues than to exploitation of burgeoning anti-Semitism.[53] If nearly all of our problems are caused by "the

---

[49]See Pervo, *Dating Acts*, 320-21, and Paul R. Trebilco, *The Early Christians in Ephesus from Paul to Ignatius,* WUNT 166 (Tübingen: Mohr Siebeck, 2004) 554-60.

[50]The statement presumes that "Christian" was coined by outsiders. Insiders may speak about sects or parties (such as "Pharisees"), but for outsiders Jews were simply Jews.

[51]For a survey of texts and movements, see R. P. R. Murphy, "Jewish Christianity," in *A Dictionary of Biblical Interpretation*, ed. R. J. Coggins and J. L. Houlden (Philadelphia: Trinity Press International, 1990) 341-46.

[52]On the diaspora revolts, see Pervo, *Dating Acts*, appendix IV, 369-72. That appendix refers to W. Horbury's forthcoming chapter on these uprisings. In fact, Miriam Pucci Ben Zeev contributed the chapter, "The Uprisings in the Jewish Diaspora, 116–117," in *The Cambridge History of Judaism*, ed. Steven T. Katz (Cambridge UK and New York: Cambridge University Press, 2006) 4:93-104.

[53]This is not to deny any conflict with contemporary synagogues. Just as Christians were motivated to differentiate themselves from the increasingly

Jews," that is something to be said in our favor. One tactic of apologetic is to ask, "With enemies like this can we be that bad?"[54] In Acts "the Jews" are those who reject Jesus. Israelites by birth who accept him are no longer "Jews" (contrast Gal 2:13).

Acts is also aware of conflicts with polytheism *per se*, that is, not just with local or broader governments, but with particular cults. Those who regard "magic" as a threat to the social order will appreciate the Christians' success in exposing and repressing it.[55] Polytheistic opposition derives from some of its least reputable representatives, scoundrels who exploit people's beliefs for their own economic benefit.[56] Conflict with the ruler cult emerges at the end of the first century;[57] the need to attend to opposition from other cults fits the second century better than the first.[58] The method is vulgar apologetic, the ancient equivalent of the political "attack ad." Believers are opposed by the base and vile, while Christian theology can be framed in philosophical language. In Acts the "bad guys" are usually Jews, sometimes polytheists, but the values and methods of both are similar. Lukan apologetics routinely takes the form of melodrama. This is in accordance with its popular tone.[59]

---

despised Jews, so Jews probably wished to dissociate themselves from the equally despised Christians. This is a general statement. In some communities Christians and Jews may have abstained from mutual enmity.

[54]Cf. Robert F. Stoops, "Riot and Assembly: The Social Context of Acts 19:23-41," *JBL* 108 (1989): 73-91.

[55]Cf. Acts 8:9-24; 13:6-12; 19:18-19. The problem of defining "magic" in a nonprejudicial fashion is an issue for fruitful discussion among historians of religion, but for Luke magic is "bad religion" largely propelled by greed and self-aggrandizement. See Hans-Josef Klauck, *Magic and Paganism in Early Christianity: The World of the Acts of the Apostles* (Minneapolis: Fortress, 2003).

[56]Cf. Acts 16:16-21; 19:23-40. (Regarding the latter, note that no priests or other officials of the cult of Artemis are involved in the turbulence.)

[57]See Revelation. Competition with the ruler cult is apparent in the Pastorals, and, somewhat more subtly, in Luke and Acts (e.g. Luke 2:8-14).

[58]"Need to attend" is vital. Conflicts require that the number of Christians had grown to the point at which they could be perceived as a threat. See Pervo, *Dating Acts*, 317-19.

[59]The view of Acts as "popular" was the thesis of Richard I. Pervo, *Profit with Delight* (Philadelphia: Fortress Press, 1987). My most recent contribution to the subject is "Direct Speech in Acts and the Question of Genre," *JSNT* 28 (2006): 285-

The community organization in view belongs to the era of the apostolic fathers. Luke is aware of bishops, presbyters, and deacons. He is familiar enough with the office of bishop to have reservations about it (i.e., he does not endorse "one-man rule" of monepiscopacy). He prefers government by presbyters, for whom the term "bishops" is acceptable, so long as they are plural. The Ignatian ideal is on the horizon. Luke also knows of charitable ministers, and characterizes the seven in terms that suit deacons.[60] In general Luke prefers to describe what we call "ordained ministry" in functional terms. Acts lives in an "early catholic" world. The author is not an exponent of so-called "early catholicism." He is, however, a collaborator with it.[61] One noticeable deviation is his preference for celibacy,[62] which entails shelving the household model so dear to the Pastor and others. Although he will not bind the Spirit to office, Luke prefers to associate charismatic phenomena with the authorized officials of the community.[63] Rather than tell the tale of succession, he shows it taking place, in Jerusalem and Ephesus, for example. James succeeds Peter; presbyters take up where the apostles and Paul left off. His understanding is not unlike that of *1 Clement* or, for that matter, the Pastorals.

Emphasis upon well-organized communities is a phenomenon of "proto-orthodoxy" that gained strength from the late first century onward. Good leadership was essential for protection of the faithful from dishonest leaders, promotion of the claim that Christianity did not constitute a moral or political threat to the general society, and, above all, for the suppression of teachings deemed injurious or false. The church, like society in general,

---

307. For a definition of "popular literature" see William Hansen, *Anthology of Ancient Greek Popular Literature* (Bloomington: Indiana University Press, 1998) xi-xvii, and Oronzo Pecere, *La letteratura di consumo nel mondo greco-latino*, ed. Oronzo Pecere and A. Stramaglia (Cassino, Italy: Università degli studi di Cassino, 1996) 5-7.

[60]The view of the seven as "deacons" goes back at least to Irenaeus (*Haer.* 1.26.3; 3.12.10; 4.15.1).

[61]See Pervo, *Dating Acts*, 203-29.

[62]On Luke's lack of enthusiasm for marriage and child-bearing, see Pervo, *Profit with Delight*, 181n.179.

[63]Acts 2:1-41; 8:14-17; 10:44-47; 13:1-3; 19:1-7. Peter performs any required interpretation (2:14-36; 10:46b-47). Ecstatic prophecy apparently occurs in unison. Compare and contrast 1 Cor 14:20-33a.

was portrayed as hierarchical, an exponent of strong family life and values, and not prone to democratic excesses.[64] These concerns were apologetic and missionary. Of even greater importance was the role of leadership in combating false teaching.

The major function of leaders is care for the flock, and the primary pastoral task is teaching. Leaders must protect the faithful. Shepherds are needed because the wolves are out there, and, to be candid, inside the sheepfold. Greed is a problem, charity causes difficulties, and other issues doubtless existed, but Luke's major concern is the conflict with rival teachers, who, to complete the circle, exhibit greed.[65] Little can be gleaned about the specifics of the challenged doctrines, but one can at least hypothesize that they conflict with some of what has been expounded in Luke and Acts. Acts is also familiar with second century terminology, practice, and understanding of Christian initiation and ecclesiastical ordination.[66]

Lukan focus upon the continuity of salvation history was of use in refuting those who proclaimed the opposite. Luke was associated with a wing, "school,"[67] or element of deuteropaulinism that followed the line of Romans and Ephesians against tendencies that might be inferred from, for

---

[64]See Richard I. Pervo, "Meet Right—and Our Bounden Duty," *Forum* n.s. 4/1 (2001): 45-62.

[65]Acts 20:17-35, esp. vv. 28-31.

[66]For initiation note, in particular, 12:1-17. Acts 6:3-7 and 13:1-3 exhibit familiarity with what is later called "ordination." Note also 14:23 (and Tit 1:5). On initiation, see Pervo, *Dating Acts*, 278-80, and 214-16 on ordination.

[67]If Luke did not "belong to a school," he benefited from school activities. See Alexander, *Acts in Its Ancient Literary Context*, 47-48, with many references. Although there is probably some consensus about the existence of one or more "Pauline schools," their origin, nature, and scope are a matter of considerable debate and speculation. For a good discussion of the models proposed see Andreas Lindemann, *Paulus im Ältesten Christentum*, BHT 58 (Tübingen: J. C. B. Mohr, 1979) 36-38. Two relevant and seminal studies are Hans-Martin Schenke, "Das Weiterwirken des Paulus und die Pflege seines Erbes durch die Paulus-Schule," *NTS* 21 (1974–1975): 505-18, and Hans Conzelmann, "Die Schule des Paulus," in *Theologia Crucis-Signum Crucis: Festschrift E. Dinkler* (Tübingen: J. C. B. Mohr, 1979) 85-96. For a critique of "school-theories" as explanations of pseudonymity, with references to literature, see David G. Meade, *Pseudonymity and Canon* (Grand Rapids MI: Eerdmans, 1987) 6-9.

example, Galatians or Colossians. Acts lends no support to the speculative wisdom theology that appeared in Colossians, was continued (although blunted) in Ephesians, and would flourish in circles labeled "gnostic."[68] With this come Luke's overtures toward "natural theology," a fruitful field for later apologetics.[69] No one who wished to interpret Paul via strong discontinuity between Israel and Christ, or between nature and grace, or who found him an inspiration to cosmic speculation could gain so much as a toehold in Acts. The Lukan Paul is also a staunch opponent of antinomianism, a charge that plagued the historical Paul and some of his followers in later eras.[70] To this must be added the utter, dare one say crude, incompatibility of Lukan thought with anything verging upon Docetism.[71]

For Mark the novelty of the message about Jesus was fundamental.[72] Marcion also reveled in the new revelation of a hitherto unknown god.

---

[68]The quotation marks indicate that the term is a convenience for a number of movements.

[69]On Lukan "natural theology," see, e.g., David L. Balch, "The Areopagus Speech: An Appeal to the Stoic Historian Posidonius against Later Stoics and the Epicureans," in *Greeks, Romans, and Christians: Essays in Honor of Abraham J. Malherbe*, ed. David L. Balch, Everett Ferguson, and Wayne A. Meeks (Minneapolis: Fortress Press, 1990) 52-79, and, in the same volume, Jerome H. Neyrey, "Acts 17, Epicureans and Theodicy: A Study in Stereotypes," 118-34. The theme is closely bound to Luke's view of divine providence, on which see, e.g., John T. Squires, *The Plan of God in Luke-Acts*, SNTSMS 76 (Cambridge UK and New York: Cambridge University Press, 1993).

[70]Rom 3:8. In the Reformation and subsequent eras antinomianism was some-times defended as a logical consequence of the Pauline doctrine of justification. Acts 24:27 reveals the moral Paul expounding "correct behavior" (δικαιουσύνη, not in the Pauline sense) and "self-control" (ἐγκράτεια), on which values see Pervo, *Dating Acts*, 266-68. One strength of Maurice Wiles's *The Divine Apostle: The Interpretation of St Paul's Epistles in the Early Church* (Cambridge UK: Cambridge University Press, 1967) is his sensitive treatment of the moralistic orien-tation of many early interpreters of Paul; see, e.g., 132-39.

[71]If Charles Talbert's *Luke and the Gnostics* (New York: Abingdon, 1966) did not receive overwhelming approval, it does identify data that require attention.

[72]See Mark 2:21-22, which Luke effectively blunts by appending 5:39: "And no one after drinking old wine desires new wine, but says, 'The old is good.' " (Note that this verse is absent from D, many mss. of the Old Latin, and Eusebius.)

Matthew advocated the value of both new and old.[73] Antiquity tended to assign high value to . . . antiquity.[74] One of the most damaging charges that could be hurled against a movement or system was that it represented a departure from tradition. In due course apologetics had to address this matter.[75] At the head of this column stood the author of Luke and Acts, notably Acts 17:16-34, where Paul addresses the Areopagus.[76] The major plank in this platform, not mentioned in that address, was the claim that the Way represented the message of the Law and the Prophets. In addition to its general apologetic value, insistence upon the ancient character of the Christian faith was also a powerful tool for refutation of the radical Pauline tradition, which stressed the replacement of the old by the new.

One may counter that all of these positives do not prove the existence of a negative. That is a valid point, but it is also valid to observe how convenient Luke and Acts would be for refutation of Marcion[77] and others of a dualistic propensity. Here one need not rely upon conjecture. Irenaeus is proof positive. I do not think that these theological emphases were accidental. Consider what was going on at Ephesus during the period from ca. 90–125 CE. Helmut Koester identifies "several rival Christian groups," including

> the originally Pauline church, supported by the Qumran-influenced Paulinist who wrote Ephesians, but also represented by the author of Luke-Acts who in his own way accommodated the tradition of the great

---

[73]Note, in particular, Matthew 13:52.

[74]Hubert Cancik, "The History of Culture, Religion, and Institutions in Ancient Historiography: Philological Observations concerning Luke's History," *JBL* 116 (1997): 681-703, 692-93.

[75]Examples include Minucius Felix, *Octavius* 6.1-3; Origen, *Cels.* 5.25. For others see G. W. Clarke, *The Octavius of Marcus Minucius Felix*, ACW 39 (New York: Newman Press, 1974) 189-90, 195.

[76]See Abraham Malherbe, *Paul and the Popular Philosophers* (Minneapolis: Fortress, 1989) 151-52, with many references. See also Philip S. Esler, *Community and Gospel in Luke-Acts*, SNTSMS 57 (Cambridge UK: Cambridge University Press, 1987) 214-17, and, with many references to primary literature, Squires, *Plan of God in Luke-Acts*, 75n.195, 149n.158.

[77]See Tyson, *Marcion and Luke-Acts* and Christopher Mount, *Pauline Christianity: Luke-Acts and the Legacy of Paul*, NovTSup 104 (Leiden: E. J. Brill, 2002).

apostle to the expediencies of the church; a Jewish-Christian 'school' engaging in a daring interpretation of the Old Testament (an early Gnostic like Cerinthus would fit this description rather well); a heretical sect, called the Nicolaitans by the Apocalypse of John (Rev. 2:6); and finally, a Jewish-Christian conventicle which was led by the prophet John.[78]

Acts was probably written at Ephesus during the last third of this period.[79] It should also be noted that Luke could no more identify specific false teachers and teaching[80] than he could speak of the destruction of the temple, for he maintained that intra-Christian false teaching did not arise until after Paul and the apostles had left the scene (Acts 20:29), that is, after the dramatic date of Acts.

Luke may not have been particularly concerned about "Judaizers," but it is difficult to repress the suspicion that he was aware of believers who neither thought very highly of Paul (Luke's refusal as much as to mention Paul's letters speaks loudly, as does withholding of the title "apostle") nor, in all probability, of hyper-Paulinists who neglected, if they did not reject, the Israelite heritage and its Scriptures.[81] Luke's Paul comes down strongly

---

[78]Helmut Koester in *Trajectories through Early Christianity*, ed. James M. Robinson and Helmut Koester (Philadelphia: Fortress Press, 1971) 154-55. See also Koester in *Ephesos: Metropolis of Asia*, HTS 41 (Valley Forge PA: Trinity Press International, 1995) 119-140, and the thorough study of Trebilco, *Early Christians in Ephesus from Paul to Ignatius*.

[79]Arguments for locating Acts in Ephesus are made in my *Acts: A Commentary*. See Peder Borgen, *Philo, John, and Paul: New Perspectives on Judaism and Early Christianity*, BJS 131 (Atlanta: Scholars Press, 1987) 273-85, esp. 282, and Vernon K. Robbins, "The Social Location of the Implied Author of Luke-Acts," in *The Social World of Luke-Acts: Models for Interpretation*, ed. Jerome H. Neyrey (Peabody MA: Hendrickson, 1991) 305-32, 315-18.

[80]Hints exist. Acts speaks of persons who are not familiar with the fullness of Christian belief, e.g., Apollos (18:24-26) and disciples of John the Baptist (19:1-7). Ernst Haenchen interprets the latter as showing Paul's ability to refute deviant movements—*The Acts of the Apostles: A Commentary*, ed. and trans. Bernard Noble, Gerald Shinn, Hugh Anderson, and R. McL. Wilson (Oxford UK: Blackwell; Philadelphia: Westminster, 1971) 557—a view that C. K. Barrett regards as "probably right." Barrett, *The Acts of the Apostles*, 2 vols, ICC (Edinburgh: T.&T. Clark, 1994, 1998) 2:886.

[81]This category is rather inferential. It presumes—with John Knox, *Marcion and the New Testament* (Chicago: University of Chicago Press, 1942) 15-16—that

on the side of continuity. As for observance, it is noteworthy that Paul alone is depicted as engaging in the temple cult[82] and that neither James nor anyone else is portrayed as lifting even a finger to help extract Paul from his difficulties in Jerusalem, although their testimony would have been decisive. Luke tolerates the observant, so long as they do not create difficulties.[83] Those devoted to Torah would not have found in Acts a warm welcome.[84]

Familiarity with Josephus's *Antiquities* affects the study of genre.[85] The relationship between these authors passes from the realm of useful parallels in the analysis of literary types to the possibility of more direct imitation. This observation does not seek to invalidate Gregory E. Sterling's description of Luke and Acts as "apologetic historiography,"[86] but it will put the comparison upon a different footing. One far from unpromising avenue of research is to inquire whether Josephus did not simply serve as the source of useful data and the stimulation of certain themes, but whether the Jewish author inspired Luke, possibly motivated the composition of the second volume (and the revision of the first?). That, however, is a subject for another study, one that I, for better or worse, do not expect to write.

Marcion did not spring fully armed from Zeus's breast. For the deuteropaulines, Paul is, in essence, the only apostle. Colossians, which is probably the earliest deuteropauline letter, has no references to or citations of Scripture, indicating that in the first century there was a Paulinism detached from Israelite sacred writings. Mark does cite Scripture, but it represents a Gentile Christianity somewhat to the "left" of Paul.

[82]Acts 2:46 does not speak of participation in the sacrificial cult. In Acts 3:1, the narrator reports that Peter and John were on their way at the time of evening prayer. Peter preaches there (3:12-26). The rescuing angel directs the apostles to teach in the temple (5:20; cf. 5:42). For them, as for Jesus (Luke 19:47; 20:1) the temple was a place for teaching.

[83]Justin has a similar view (*Dial.* 47).

[84]The text preserved in the Pseudo-Clementine *Recognitions* 1.27-71 takes a hostile view of Acts. See F. Stanley Jones, *An Ancient Jewish Christian Source on the History of Christianity: Pseudo-Clementine Recognitions 1.21-71*, SBLTT 37 (Atlanta: Scholars Press, 1995).

[85]For a recent review of that discussion see Thomas E. Phillips, "The Genre of Acts: Moving toward a Consensus?" *CBR* 4 (2006): 365-96.

[86]Gregory E. Sterling, *Historiography and Self-Definition: Josephos, Luke-Acts, and Apologetic Historiography*, NovTSup 64 (Leiden: E. J. Brill, 1992).

Conclusion

Acts pursues a number of apologetic ends in narrative forms, defends the existence of Christianity as a separate (but not new) religion distinct from that of "the Jews," exhibits competition with polytheists, and reflects settled, organized communities defending their boundaries against competing forms of the Christian message. These rival interpretations have apparent affinities with persons and movements opposed in Revelation, the Pastorals, Polycarp, and Ignatius. Some of these items could, with prodigious effort and abundant speculation, be located in the 80s or, with slightly more comfort, in the 90s, but the arguments for locating all of them in the period between 110-130 are vastly more cogent. Dating Acts in the 80s requires a great deal of *explaining away*. A later date permits the interpreter to *explain from*. J. C. O'Neill was more than half right.[87] The home of Acts is in the suburbs of the apologists.

---

[87]J. C. O'Neill, *The Theology of Acts in Its Historical Setting* (London: SPCK, 1961) sought, in terms of my metaphor, to locate Acts in the city of the apologists. He wished to date Justin closer to 130, although his *Apology* (in two parts) belongs to the second half of the reign of Antoninus Pius (138-161), and concentrated upon one end of the spectrum, whereas, as the critique of Conzelmann ("Luke's Place," 302-04) indicated, both poles require attention.

Irenaeus and the Reception of Acts in the Second Century

Andrew Gregory

"Acts is not attested at all before Irenaeus." So concluded Hans von Campenhausen, writing in 1968.[1] That conclusion may stand as a bald statement, but it will benefit from some qualification. Thus we might note that Irenaeus is the first firmly dateable author who provides secure and incontrovertible evidence for the knowledge and use of Acts. Restating von Campenhausen's statement in this more nuanced way maintains the importance of Irenaeus as a witness to the early reception of Acts, but also prepares the way for two other observations. The first is that other traces of the earlier use of Acts have sometimes been suggested, although none of those traces is nearly as secure as is the evidence from Irenaeus. The second is that there is some evidence from other texts from the late second or early third centuries that may suggest that each of their authors knew Acts, even if none may be securely dated prior to Irenaeus.

This potential early evidence for the reception of Acts may be taken in at least two ways. One is that Irenaeus may not have been atypical in using Acts when he did. The other is that even if Irenaeus was atypical and innovative in his use of Acts, and was thereby instrumental in bringing it to greater prominence than it had ever received before, nevertheless other authors were quick to follow his example. Neither observation detracts from Irenaeus's significance in our attempts to uncover the early history of the book of Acts, but each reminds us that Irenaeus was himself a product of late-second century Christianity as well as someone who appears to have shaped the way in which Christianity subsequently developed.

In this chapter I propose therefore to look selectively at a range of other early evidence for the reception of Acts as well as that of Irenaeus. Since Irenaeus's evidence is clearest, I shall begin there in the hope that it will provide a point of contrast or comparison with that of other authors. I shall then conclude with some general observations.

---

[1]Hans von Campenhausen, "Die Apostelgeschichte finden wir vor Irenäus überhaupt nicht bezeugt," in *Die Entstehung der christlichen Bibel* (Tübingen: Mohr Siebeck, 1968) 152; ET: *The Formation of the Christian Bible*, trans. J. A. Baker (London: A & C Black, 1972) 128.

I. Irenaeus

Irenaeus's knowledge and use of Acts are incontrovertible. As André Benoit observed, not only does Irenaeus know its title, not only does he know its author, but also he cites the book often and recognizes it as Scripture.[2]

Irenaeus draws extensively on Acts in the early part of Book III of *Against Heresies*, but also refers to, quotes from, or alludes to it in all five books of this work. It is also likely that Irenaeus alludes to Acts in his later *Demonstration*, albeit on a more modest scale.[3] Here the allusions are so slight, however, that they could not be confidently identified as such were it not for Irenaeus's clear and extensive use of Acts in his earlier writing. This is an important observation: had the Latin translation of Irenaeus's *Against Heresies* been lost, as was the Greek original, then we would have no clear evidence of Irenaeus's use of Acts.

When Irenaeus draws on Acts in Book III of *Against Heresies*, he does so in order to refute his opponents (Valentinians, Marcionites and others) on the basis of the Scriptures. Thus his arguments here need to be understood in the context of the teachings of his opponents as he has previously presented them (Book I) and then set out to refute them on the basis of rational argument (Book II).

Acts is featured only very briefly at the beginning of *Against Heresies* 3.1, but it plays a very significant role at this point in his argument. Irenaeus's concern here is to demonstrate that it was to the apostles that the Lord gave the power of the gospel, and that it was through them that the truth has come down to the later true believers for whom Irenaeus writes. The first scriptural authority that he cites is Jesus' charge to his apostles, recorded only at Luke 10:16: "whoever listens to you listens to me, whoever rejects you rejects me, and whoever rejects me rejects the one who sent me." Irenaeus then draws on Luke again, but now in conjunction with Acts. He conflates the ending of Luke and beginning of Acts in a reference to the post-resurrection investment of the apostles with power from on high and their reception of perfect knowledge before—or because of which—they departed to the ends of the earth, preaching good news as they went. Here

---

[2]André Benoit, *Saint Irénée: Introduction à L'Étude de sa Théologie* (Paris: Presses Universitaires de France, 1960) 122.

[3]E.g. *Dem.* 36, cf. Acts 2:30; *Dem.* 41, cf. Acts 1:8-9 and 10:42; *Dem.* 71, cf. Acts 5:15; *Dem.* 74, cf. Acts 4:25; *Dem.* 83, cf. Acts 1:9-11; *Dem.* 96, cf. Acts 4:12.

Irenaeus uses Luke and Acts together, albeit allusively, in a way that draws upon the narrative links between the end of one volume and the beginning of the other.

Irenaeus states clearly why he gives such an emphatic place to the opening of Acts. Contrary to the claims of his opponents, there was never a time when the apostles did not possess perfect knowledge, because they received it at this early stage. Jesus' words in Luke 10:16 indicate the authority of the apostles, and the post-resurrection fulfilment in Acts 1 of the promise of Luke 24:49 demonstrates that Jesus' apostles were his Spirit-filled and authoritative representatives from the earliest time in the history of the church. Contrary to the claims of Irenaeus's opponents, Jesus' apostles did not possess only imperfect knowledge on which others might later improve. Thus Irenaeus uses the depiction of the apostles being filled with the Spirit (Acts 1:8, fulfilled at Acts 2) to claim that Acts provides the backdrop against which all the writings and teachings of the apostles must be understood. He suggests that there was no need for others to be given superior knowledge at another time. The Valentinians whom Irenaeus opposes might claim that Jesus offered post-resurrection instruction for a period of 18 months (*Haer.* 1.30.14), but Irenaeus uses Acts to show that such continuing teaching was not necessary and did not take place.

Two particular points about Irenaeus's use of Acts here should be noted, each of which provides a point of comparison with other early witnesses or possible witnesses to the reception of Acts. The first observation is that it is Acts on which Irenaeus draws when he wishes to underline the importance of Jesus' post-resurrection empowerment of his disciples. He could have used the commissioning scene at the end of Matthew or the scene in John in which the risen Jesus breathes his Spirit upon his disciples, but instead he used Luke and Acts. The second observation is not just that Irenaeus draws on Acts, but that he draws on Acts in conjunction with Luke rather than with any other part of his fourfold gospel tradition. Luke 10:16 is single tradition, so it is not possible to be confident whether Irenaeus uses it because he wishes to draw on Luke rather than another gospel, or simply because it is the single most apposite saying of Jesus that he could draw from any part of his fourfold gospel. In any case, it certainly suits his context. Thus it may be a coincidence rather than a conscious decision to read Luke and Acts together that prompted Irenaeus to cite Luke here. On either understanding, the way in which he conflates Luke 24:49 with Acts 1:8 makes it difficult to deny that he reads them together in the way that

Luke invited his readers to do. Thus Irenaeus treats Luke in two distinct but complementary ways. Luke is not only part of Irenaeus's fourfold gospel but is also the first of two consecutive volumes written by the same author, each of which exhibits narrative continuity with, and may be read in the light of, the other. Thus here we appear to have some evidence that Irenaeus recognized the literary unity of Luke-Acts, at least in an authorial and narrative sense.[4]

Having noted that Irenaeus used Luke and Acts together to explain how Jesus' teaching was transmitted to his followers at an early stage, it is important to be clear that Irenaeus turns next to all four canonical gospels as witnesses to the scriptural teaching that there is one creator God. Thus for the rest of 3.1-15 it is primarily on the testimony of these four apostolic witnesses that Irenaeus bases his argument about the existence of one creator God whose teaching has been transmitted securely in one Spirit-filled church. It is only in 3.16 that Irenaeus returns to Acts, as he seeks to show that the witnesses of other apostles besides the four evangelists testify to the same beliefs.

As Irenaeus's introduction to his use of Acts suggests, he is interested in Acts because it contains the teaching of other apostles besides Matthew, Mark, and John. Twice he refers to its contents as the teaching and acts of the apostles (*Haer.* 3.12.11, "they who wish may learn from the very words and acts of the apostles" [*ex ipsis sermonibus et actibus apostolorum*]; *Haer.* 3.15.1, "his subsequent testimony, which concerns the acts and the doctrine of the apostles" [*de actibus et doctrina apostolorum*]), and once he appears to use the phrase "Acts of the Apostles" as a title for the book (*Haer.* 3.13.3, "if therefore anyone shall research carefully from the Acts of the Apostles" [*ex Actibus Apostolorum*]). He also refers to Acts as Scripture (*Haer.* 3.12.5, *inquit Scriptura*, quoting Acts 4:32). Time and time again he emphasizes that the teaching in Acts states that there is one creator God, a claim that he substantiates by drawing at great length on the first half of Acts with particular reference to its presentation of the teaching of Peter, John, Philip, Paul, Stephen, James and the apostles as a group. Their

---

[4]I have tried to defend this position more fully elsewhere, in dialogue with Kavin Rowe. See C. Kavin Rowe, "History, Hermeneutics, and the Unity of Luke-Acts," *JSNT* 28 (2005): 131-57; "Literary Unity and Reception History: Reading Luke-Acts as Luke and Acts," *JSNT* 29 (2007): 449-57; and Andrew Gregory, "The Reception of Luke and Acts and the Unity of Luke-Acts," *JSNT* 29 (2007): 459-72.

teaching, as presented in Acts, is in accord with that of the evangelists, just as Paul's teaching, as presented in Acts, is in accord with his letters. Both as individuals, and as a body, the apostles whose words and deeds are recorded in Acts all proclaimed one creator God from whom came both Jesus and the Spirit:

> Thus the apostles did not preach another God, or another Fullness; nor that the Christ who suffered and rose again was one, while he who flew off on high was another, and remained impassible; but that there was one and the same God the Father, and Christ Jesus who rose from the dead; and they preached faith in him, to those who did not believe on the Son of God, and exhorted them out of the prophets, that the Christ whom God promised to send, he sent in Jesus, whom they crucified and God raised up. (*Haer.* 3.12.2)[5]

Irenaeus's argument from the apostolic teaching in Acts concludes and climaxes with an account of Acts 15. He follows Luke in emphasizing that the apostles were united in their teaching, but notes also that the scrupulous care with which the apostles followed the Mosaic Law is further evidence that there is but one God (*Haer.* 3.12.15). Had the apostles learned from Jesus that there was another God besides the one who gave the law, they would not have been so scrupulous about observing it themselves, even though they did not demand that Gentiles observed it too.

It is at this point that Irenaeus turns to refute the opinions of opponents who claim that Paul alone knew the truth, being the recipient of revelation that was not given to the others (*Haer.* 3.13.1). On the contrary, Irenaeus argues that Paul's teaching is consistent with Luke's testimony about the teaching of the other apostles, and that Luke is to be believed because he was present at many of the incidents that he recounts (*Haer.* 3.14.1). Thus Irenaeus returns to the narrative of Acts, concentrating now on the so-called we-passages and other parts of the predominantly Paul-focussed second half of Acts. Its content, says Irenaeus, Luke delivered to us (i.e. to the church, the successors of the apostles and the faithful guardians and transmitters of their teaching, not to his opponents who claim secret revelation), just as eye-witnesses and ministers of the word delivered it to Luke (*Haer.* 3.14.2).

---

[5]The translation is from Alexander Roberts and James Donaldson in vol. 1 of the *Ante-Nicene Fathers*, new edition, ed. Alexander Roberts, James Donaldson, Philip Schaff, and Henry Wace (Repr.: Peabody MA: Hendrickson, 1994).

The allusion to Luke's preface is clear, so once again Irenaeus reads Luke's second volume in the light of volume one. This is the immediate context in which Irenaeus goes on to note a great deal of uniquely Lukan tradition and to argue that those who accept part of what Luke has written must be prepared to accept it all. Here it is very tempting to find the strongest evidence yet for Irenaeus reading Luke and Acts as two parts of a literary whole, but it is actually very difficult to be certain exactly what he means. Previously, Irenaeus has read Acts through the lens of Luke 1:2 and at this particular point (*Haer*. 3.14.3) Irenaeus turns to castigate Marcion and Valentinus for using only certain parts of Luke's gospel and not others. In the immediate context here, Irenaeus states that these men must either receive the rest of Luke's narrative or reject the parts that they already accept. (*Necesse est igitur et reliqua quae ab eo dicta sunt recipere eos aut et his renuntiare, Haer*. 3.14.4). He is interested in all or nothing.

Irenaeus's use of both Luke and Acts in Book III of his *Against Heresies* makes it tempting to suppose that his reference to the other things that Luke has said[6] includes his second volume as well as his first, for Irenaeus is in no doubt that both are from Luke's hand. On the other hand, when he refers to the selective way in which he accuses Marcion and Valentinus of using Luke he refers only to the use that they make of Luke's Gospel. Neither here in Book III, nor in Book I where Irenaeus first refers to their selective use of Luke, does Irenaeus make any explicit reference to their knowledge or use of Acts.[7] Therefore the general tenor of Irenaeus's argument may make it more likely than not that he calls on his opponents to read the third gospel not only in its entirety but also in its entirety as part of a two-volume work. Nevertheless the immediate context in which his statement occurs is too ambiguous to allow any firm conclusion to rest upon it. Irenaeus's knowledge of the common authorship of Luke and Acts is

---

[6]Is it significant that Irenaeus refers to what Luke has *said* rather than to what he has written?

[7]Elaine Pagels suggests that at 3.12.6-7 Irenaeus is responding to gnostic exegesis of Acts's account of Peter's vision. See Elaine Pagels, "Visions, Appearances, and Apostolic Authority: Gnostic and Orthodox Tradition," in *Gnosis*, ed. Barbara Aland (Göttingen: Vandenhoeck & Ruprecht, 1978) 415-30, here 423. However I am uncertain whether Irenaeus is responding to prior Valentinian use of Acts or introducing Acts as a weapon against Valentinian claims that are made quite apart from Acts.

undisputed (*Haer.* 3.14.2, 3.15.1), and I think that it is meaningful to speak of his appreciation of the unity of Luke-Acts. Here, however, just where we might like him—and perhaps even expect him—to make more of the connection between Luke and Acts, and what that connection might mean, Irenaeus does not do so.

Three points about Irenaeus's use of Acts in this part of Book III may be noted. First, Irenaeus uses Acts as a source or compendium of the words and deeds of the apostles. He is interested in what they taught, and draws on Acts to show that all taught the same message that has come down to him through the open and unbroken tradition of the church. Thus Acts is a text on which Irenaeus draws to maintain his own theological position and the sociological and ecclesiological claims that his position entails. Second, Irenaeus also reads Acts as more than a source or compendium of the words and deeds of the apostles. Acts is not only a source on which he draws but also a normative text that Irenaeus commends to others and on which he offers comments of his own.[8] Third, he reads Acts in the light of the preface to Luke, thus showing that he recognizes their literary unity. Elsewhere, however, when he chides Marcion and Valentinus for using only some of Luke and tells them that they must use all of his writing or none, it is difficult to be clear whether he means that they must use Luke or Luke-Acts as a whole. If the latter, this might imply that Marcion[9] and Valentinus did not draw on Acts. If so, this could mean either that they consciously and actively rejected it, or simply that it was a book that they may not have known or used. Ongoing uncertainty about the extent to which Acts was used prior to Irenaeus means that we should draw no firm conclusions from our inability to demonstrate that a particular author knew Acts.

---

[8] I owe this distinction to François Bovon. See François Bovon, "The Reception and Use of the Gospel of Luke in the Second Century," in *Reading Luke: Interpretation, Reflection, Formation*, ed. Craig Bartholomew, Joel B. Green, and Anthony C. Thiselton (Grand Rapids MI: Zondervan, 2005) 379-97, esp. 382 and 396.

[9] For the view that Acts (and canonical Luke) was written in response to the challenge posed by Marcion, see John Knox, *Marcion and the New Testament: An Essay in the Early History of the Canon* (Chicago: University of Chicago Press, 1942) 119-40, and Joseph B. Tyson, *Marcion and Luke-Acts: A Defining Struggle* (Columbia: University of South Carolina Press, 2006), 76-78. The latter builds explicitly on the work of the former.

Finally, to conclude this overview of Irenaeus's use of Acts, three further observations of a more general nature than those noted above may also be made. The first is that Irenaeus finds in Acts one of the earliest foundations of the apostolic tradition, for it demonstrates that the apostles, who were taught by Jesus both during his life and after his resurrection, were Spirit-filled witnesses from the earliest possible time. Thus it provides the narrative foundation for the faithful transmission of Jesus' teaching first to his earliest followers and then through those who succeeded them in the Spirit-filled and Spirit-guided church. Second, it indicates that there is only one Creator God, the God of Moses, for this is what was taught both individually and collectively by those apostles. Third, Irenaeus appears to read Acts in two different but complementary ways. Sometimes he reads it in conjunction with, and in the light of, Luke. Sometimes, however, he reads Acts as continuing and providing the context for the teaching of all four of the gospels whose authority he defends, not just that according to Luke. Irenaeus can read Acts either in conjunction with Luke or in conjunction with the fourfold gospel, just as he can read Luke either in conjunction with Acts or in conjunction with the other elements of the fourfold gospel.

That we are able to make these observations is only because Irenaeus draws on Acts so much, and because he refers explicitly to the text by name and to Luke as its author. This is an extremely important point and its significance needs to be noted. Clement of Alexandria also refers to Luke as the author of Acts, as does Tertullian, but the only possibly pre-Irenaean text that does so is the Muratorian fragment. The author of the fragment identifies Luke as the author of both Luke and Acts and even appears to allow his knowledge of the preface to Luke's first volume influence his allusion to the preface to Luke's second volume.[10] This suggests that this author, like Irenaeus, could read Luke and Acts together as part of one literary narrative even if he could also refer to Luke as the third book of the gospel, a clear indication that he also read Luke as one element within the fourfold gospel.

---

[10]The author of the Muratorian Fragment writes that in Acts, Luke described for "most excellent Theophilus" (*optimo Theophilo*) things that happened in his presence, and refers to the death of Peter and Paul's departure from Rome. It is only in Luke 1:3, not in Acts 1:1-2, that Theophilus is addressed as κράτιστη, "most excellent."

Unlike Irenaeus, none of the potential pre-Irenaean sources for the reception of Acts explicitly treats it as an identifiable literary text in this way. Their authors may know Acts as a text, and may even know that it was written by Luke, but such use as they may betray allows us to infer little more than that they may have used it as a source from which they could mine information about the early apostles to then use for their particular ends—as also, of course, did Irenaeus. That these other texts make no explicit reference to Acts, and contain fewer parallels to Acts than does Irenaeus, means that we can only be sure that parallels with Acts depend on Acts if those parallels include material that shows signs of Lukan redaction.[11] This of course is very difficult to establish, since there is little agreement on the extent to which Luke drew on earlier sources and traditions when he wrote Acts.[12] The more likely that it is that Luke drew on earlier sources or traditions that others may also have used, and/or the more likely it is that his narrative is a faithful representation of such episodes in the early church that he narrates, then the more difficult it is to be confident that later parallels with Acts are evidence of literary dependence on his text.

This methodological difficulty affects our assessment of the three other texts that I shall briefly discuss in what follows. These are: the *First Apology of Justin Martyr*, the *Epistula Apostolorum* and the *Letter of Peter to Philip*. Polycarp and Justin are certainly earlier than Irenaeus, and each of the other texts might also antedate the writings of Irenaeus.

---

[11]For a fuller discussion of this methodological point, see Andrew Gregory and Christopher Tuckett, "What Constitutes the Use of the New Testament in the Apostolic Fathers? Reflections on the Methodological Issues," in *The Reception of the New Testament in the Apostolic Fathers*, ed. Andrew Gregory and Christopher Tuckett (Oxford UK: Oxford University Press, 2005) 61-82, esp. 78-79, and Andrew Gregory, *The Reception of Luke and Acts in the Period before Irenaeus*, WUNT 2.169 (Tübingen: Mohr Siebeck, 2003) 5-20, esp. 7 and 13-20.

[12]On the question of sources on which Luke may have drawn for Acts, see Jacques Dupont, *The Sources of Acts* (London: DLT, 1964); Jacob Jervell, "The Problem of Tradition in Acts," in *Luke and the People of God* (Minneapolis: Augsburg, 1972) 19-39; and François Bovon, "L'Origine des récits concernant les apôtres," *RTP* 3.17 (1967): 345-50, reprinted in *L'Oeuvre de Luc: Études d'exégèse et de théologie*, LD 130 (Paris: Cerf, 1987) 155-62.

II. Justin Martyr

There are a number of parallels between the writings of Justin Martyr and Luke-Acts. Justin's use of Luke is all but certain, but scholars differ greatly on the question of whether Justin knew and used Acts. Among recent commentators on Acts, Fitzmyer[13] and Barrett[14] are very cautious in their conclusions about Justin's knowledge of Acts. Ernst Haenchen is much more confident, and finds the first decisive reference to Acts at 1 *Apology* 50.12.[15] This is an important passage, so I shall take it as the focus for this brief discussion of Justin as a potential witness to Acts. Here Justin refers to the ascension in terms very similar to those found at the end of Luke, and his demonstrable use of Luke elsewhere makes it likely that he draws on it here. A number of details may be noted. Luke refers to those who are with Jesus (1) seeing him ascend into heaven; (2) receiving power which Jesus sent from heaven; (3) going to every race of men and women; (4) teaching; and (5) being called apostles.

Much of this may be paralleled from Luke rather than from Acts. Justin's account appears to presuppose that the ascension took place on the same day as the resurrection, suggesting the chronology of Luke rather than of Acts. However there are two statements that may reflect Acts rather than Luke. The first is Justin's statement that those with Jesus saw him ascending into heaven, for only in Acts are we told explicitly that Jesus' disciples were watching as he was taken up (1:9) and that the disciples were gazing up toward heaven as he was going (1:10). Yet this evidence is far

---

[13]Joseph A. Fitzmyer, *The Acts of the Apostles: A New Translation with Introduction and Commentary*, AB 31 (New York: Doubleday, 1998) 53. Fitzmyer notes that "the relation of Acts . . . to Justin is far from clear."

[14]C. K. Barrett, *A Critical and Exegetical Commentary on the Acts of the Apostles*, 2 vols., ICC (Edinburgh: T.&T. Clark, 1994, 1998) 1:44. Barrett notes: "To prove the negative assertion, that Justin was totally unfamiliar with Acts, is impossible; but if he knew it he made little use of it, and made some statements that cannot easily be harmonized with it." Similarly in the second volume of the same work, Barrett notes: "It cannot be proved either that Justin did or that he did not know Acts" (2:lxiv-lxv).

[15]Ernst Haenchen, *The Acts of the Apostles: A Commentary*, ed. and trans. Bernard Noble, Gerald Shinn, Hugh Anderson, and R. McL. Wilson (Oxford UK: Blackwell; Philadelphia: Westminster, 1971) 8.

from decisive. Luke's stress on a visible ascension is probably an allusion to Elijah's stipulation that Elisha must see him taken away if he is to inherit a double share of his spirit (2 Kgs 2:9-12) and others besides Luke may have made a connection with this story. Further, as Barrett observes, belief in the ascension was widespread by Justin's time, "and it could hardly be asserted that it happened without the implication that some had seen it happen; and if not the apostles, who?"[16]

The second parallel that might be taken to depend on Acts rather than on Luke is Justin's reference to the apostles receiving power. The verbal echo with Acts 1:8 is clear, but the question of what we are to make of this is complicated by a conceptual and partial verbal parallel at Luke 24:49, where Jesus tells his disciples to wait in the city until they are clothed with power from on high. Justin certainly uses the same verb that is found at Acts 1:8, but this is hardly convincing proof that he alludes to Acts rather than to Luke.

Of course, the case that can be made for Justin's use of Acts does not rely on this passage alone, even if Haenchen rests a great deal upon Justin's parallel to Acts 1:8. Oskar Skarsaune has paid great attention to the proof-text tradition that he finds behind Justin's writings, and has shown that it contains significant parallels with the thought of Luke as that thought is expressed in each of Luke's two volumes. Thus Justin uses scriptural proofs in a way that is similar to that of the missionary speeches in Acts, and the setting of Justin's *Dialogue with Trypho* is broadly similar to that of Paul's missionary teaching and preaching in Acts.[17] Yet these parallels might be explained not on the basis of literary dependence, direct or indirect, on Acts, but on the basis of a common *Sitz im Leben*.

Similarly, the fact that Justin shares with Luke the belief that he "carries on an exegetical tradition handed down to the Church from the risen Christ via the apostles"[18] does not mean that he depends on Luke for that idea. Further, even if Justin did draw on Luke for that belief, Justin could just as easily take such an idea from Luke's first volume as from his second,[19]

---

[16]Barrett, *Acts of the Apostles*, 1:40.

[17]Oskar Skarsaune, *The Proof from Prophecy*, NovTSup 56 (Leiden: Brill, 1987) 256-69.

[18]Skarsaune, *Proof from Prophecy*, 256, 11-13.

[19]Luke 24 refers to the postresurrection teaching of Jesus, and looks forward to the life of the church.

particularly if he harmonized and conflated the end of Luke with the end of Matthew. Justin frequently conflates Matthew and Luke, so it may be much easier to view this passage as yet another instance of Justin's conflation of these two texts than as the single instance of his use of Acts. Thus Justin's reference at *1 Apology* 50.12 to apostles going to every race of men and women might be associated just as easily with Matthew 28:19 as with Acts 1:8. Certainly neither Matthew nor Luke use the word apostle at the end of their gospels, but it does not appear in Acts until the end of chapter one, long after the ascension scene and Jesus' commission of his disciples is complete.

Modern readers accustomed to reading Luke and Acts as Luke-Acts may well find it easy to see the way that Justin mirrors the continuity that exists between Luke 24 and Acts 1 and beyond, but this is far from proof that Justin knew Acts or that he read it as part of Luke-Acts. He may have known Acts, but we cannot be certain. *First Apology* 50.12 can be explained adequately on the basis of Justin's conflation of Matthew and Luke. We may be reasonably certain that he used both Matthew and Luke, but the evidence for his use of Acts remains unclear.[20]

III. The *Epistula Apostolorum*

Two other texts show an interest in the apostles and include clear parallels to Acts and may therefore reflect literary dependence upon it: the *Epistula Apostolorum* and the *Letter of Peter to Philip*. Each may be classified as a dialogue in which the risen Christ appears to and instructs his disciples. The date at which such texts were first circulated is far from clear. Elaine Pagels notes Morton Smith's suggestion that in Acts Jesus refuses to enter into dialogue with his apostles, which may mean that Acts is at least in part a response to such writings.[21] However there is a general tendency to see such writings as presupposing and developing rather than anticipating canonical accounts of the risen Jesus' encounters with his disciples. If so, any literary dependence between these texts and Acts is more likely to be explained on the hypothesis that they are dependent on and perhaps reacting to Acts rather than vice versa.

---

[20]For a fuller discussion of the relationship of *1 Apology* 50.12 to Luke and Acts, see Andrew Gregory, *The Reception of Luke and Acts in the Period before Irenaeus*, WUNT 2.169 (Tübingen: Mohr Siebeck, 2003) 287-91, 317-21.

[21]Pagels, "Visions, Appearances, and Apostolic Authority," 415-30, here 419.

The *Epistula Apostolorum* has been considered the earliest extant witness to Acts,[22] but continuing uncertainty about its date makes this claim difficult to sustain. Leaving aside a number of minor parallels, two groups of parallels warrant brief attention. The first group concerns Jesus' ascension. The ascension is depicted at *Epistula* 51, when Jesus is taken away from the presence of his disciples. The presence of a cloud, and the implication that they see him go (although the text emphasizes what they hear, not what they see) may each reflect dependence on Acts, but uncertainty as to whether Luke drew on earlier traditions for his own ascension account means that dependence remains uncertain. The same caution applies to *Epistula* 18, where Jesus predicts that the disciples will see him go into heaven, and to *Epistula* 34, where the disciples ask about eschatology in a manner similar to Acts 1:6. These passages do not demand dependence between Acts and the *Epistula Apostolorum*, but they do show that each text shows a strong interest in the ascension of Jesus as a watershed moment in the lives of his apostles.

This interest in the apostles may also be seen in the second group of parallels. The first, *Epistula* 15, concerns the imprisonment of an unnamed apostle at Passover, his miraculous night-time release by an angel and his subsequent reimprisonment. There are both similarities and differences with the account of Peter's imprisonment and release in Acts 12. The second, *Epistula* 31, tells the story of the conversion of Paul in a manner that is reminiscent of Acts. The third, *Epistula* 33, has Jesus speak to the other apostles about Paul and tell them how he will speak with him from heaven. Again, there are parallels with Acts as well as elements that are not present in Acts and that might reflect another source. Neither these three parallels nor any others demonstrate dependence on Acts. Therefore, since we cannot be confident that the *Epistula* draws on Acts, we cannot draw any conclusions about how its author might have treated Acts. We may note only that these parallels are evidence of an interest in the sort of stories told about apostles that are found in Acts.

A final comment on this text concerns the possibility that its author knew Luke as well as Acts. Various parallels with Luke may be noted, but

---

[22]Julian V. Hills, *Tradition and Composition in the Epistula Apostolorum*, HDR 24 (Minneapolis: Fortress Press, 1994) 4, citing Arthur D. Nock, "The Apocryphal Gospels," *JTS* n.s. 11 (1960): 63, and Philip Vielhauer, *Geschichte der urchristlichen Literatur* (Berlin: de Gruyter, 1975) 407.

it is not clear that they demand dependence on that gospel.[23] Even if the author of the *Epistula* did draw on both Luke and Acts, the allusive way in which he did so does not allow us to adduce him as evidence for someone who read Luke and Acts as part of one literary whole.

IV. The *Letter of Peter to Philip*

The *Letter of Peter to Philip*, part of Nag Hammadi Codex 8, was not published until 1976. It was therefore not known to Hans von Campenhausen. The likely date of its composition is unclear. Pheme Perkins notes that it appears to respond to anti-gnostic arguments of the sort that Irenaeus presents.[24] This is not conclusive proof that it is therefore later than Irenaeus (and Perkins does not present it as such), but may suggest that a later date is likely. There is widespread agreement that it shows signs of literary dependence on Acts.[25] Marvin Meyer is commendably cautious in noting that parallels do not themselves constitute firm evidence of literary

---

[23]Probably the strongest evidence in favor of the text's use of Luke is *Epistula* 5, which is parallel to the story of the healing of the woman with a hemorrhage that is found in triple-tradition at Luke 8:43-48 and the Markan and Matthean parallels. Of the canonical gospels, only Luke has Jesus state that he noticed that power had gone forth from him, so the use of this phrase in the *Epistula* may suggest dependence on Luke. Also important is *Epistula* 3, where in the space of only eight words in the Ethiopic, the *Epistula* refers to three details (Bethlehem, swaddling clothes, and the child growing up) that are found in Luke 2. I am grateful for these observations to Dr. Darrell Hannah, who is working on a new translation, introduction, and commentary on the *Epistula Apostolorum* for the series Oxford Early Christian Gospel Texts.

[24]Pheme Perkins, *Gnosticism and the New Testament* (Minneapolis: Fortress, 1993) 182, and *The Gnostic Dialogue: The Early Church and the Crisis of Gnosticism* (New York: Paulist Press, 1980) 115.

[25]For further details, see Klaus Koschorke, "Eine gnostische Pfingspredigt: Zur Auseindandersetzung zwischen gnostischem und kirchlichem Christentum am Beispiel der 'Epistula Petri ad Philippum' (NHC VIII, 2)," *ZTK* 74 (1977): 323-43, esp. 326-27; Gerard P. Luttikhuizen, "The Letter of Peter to Philip and the New Testament," in *Nag Hammadi and Gnosis*, ed. R. McL. Wilson (Leiden: Brill, 1979) 96-102; Pheme Perkins, *The Gnostic Dialogue: The Early Church and the Crisis of Gnosticism* (New York: Paulist Press, 1980) 122-23; and Craig A. Evans, Robert L. Webb, and Richard A. Wiebe, eds., *Nag Hammadi Texts and the Bible: A Synopsis and Index*, NTTS XVIII (Leiden: Brill, 1993) 341-50.

dependence,[26] but his note that this text includes parallels to material that is very likely the result of Lukan redaction[27] suggests that literary dependence is the most likely explanation for these parallels. Certainly the text differs from Acts on a number of key points, but such differences may be easily accounted for on the grounds that the author of the *Letter of Peter to Philip* held different views from those presented in Acts. Further, the later that the text is dated, the more likely its dependence on Acts becomes. There is little reason to dispute Perkins's description of the text as "a take-off of the early chapters of Acts,"[28] even if Hans-Gebhard Bethge's observation that its dependence on Acts is "completely obvious" perhaps goes too far.[29] Nevertheless, the numerous parallels between this text and the first part of Acts are significant. As Meyer notes, "Even the genre of texts they [Acts and the *Letter of Peter to Philip*] represent—a narrative on Peter and the apostles within which are included revelatory, liturgical and edificatory materials—is similar."[30]

As is also the case with the *Epistula Apostolorum*, the *Letter of Peter to Philip* includes some parallels with Luke as well as with Acts. These include elements that probably originate in Lukan redaction,[31] so there is

---

[26]Marvin Meyer, *The Letter of Peter to Philip*, SBLDS 53 (Chico CA: Scholars Press, 1981) 190-91, and "NHC VII, 2: The Letter of Peter to Philip, Introduction," in *Nag Hammadi Codex VIII*, ed. John H. Sieber, NHS 31 (Leiden: Brill, 1991) 229.

[27]Meyer, *Letter of Peter to Philip*, 199n.4.

[28]Perkins, *The Gnostic Dialogue*, 122.

[29]"Ganz offenkundig kennt der Autor das lukanische Doppelwerk, denn es liegt Vielzahl von Bezügen vor." Hans-Gebhard Bethge, "Der Brief des Petrus an Philippus (NHC VIII, 2)," in *Nag Hammadi Deutsch* II, ed. Hans-Martin Schenke, Hans-Gebhard Bethge, and Ursula Kaiser, Koptisch-Gnostische Schriften 3 (Berlin: Walter de Gruyter, 2003) 663-76, quote on 667. The evidence for the use of Luke is more easily demonstrated than the evidence for the use of Acts, but that is because we have parallel texts with which we may compare Luke but not Acts.

[30]Meyer, "NHC VII, 2," 229. Meyer goes on to note that the prefixing of a letter to the *Letter of Peter to Philip* distinguishes it from Acts. This is correct, but it may be significant to note that Acts contains a letter within its text, so even the juxtaposition of a letter and a narrative has a Lukan precedent.

[31]E.g. 139.9-14, the account of the transfiguration, where Jesus is said to pray, and that his appearance changed as he was praying. Cf. Luke 9:28b-29 and parallels. This is clear evidence of Lukan redactional material in triple tradition. Also, the *Letter of Peter to Philip* includes two forms of the heavenly saying: the

good reason to believe that the author of this text knew Luke as well as Acts. However he shows no explicit interest in either writing as a text rather than as a source, so we are unable to draw any conclusions about whether he read Luke and Acts as two parts of one literary whole. As before, what we see is clear evidence of interest in apostles, now marshalled in support of gnostic claims to apostolic authority for their teaching. The density of parallels between the *Letter* and canonical writings suggests that its author stands within a particular exegetical tradition that draws on a range of Christian texts, but it is difficult to say more about Acts than that it appears to be used as a source for information about the early apostles. However, the way in which the *Letter* stresses apostolic unity is clearly important, as is its stress on continuity between what Jesus is said to have taught both before and after his resurrection. These features are also present in Luke-Acts, of course, but the way in which the *Letter* puts such emphasis on the involvement of all the apostles alongside Peter may be compared to the Muratorian fragment's reference to Acts as "The Acts of all the Apostles."

Other sources that might profitably be considered[32] include the *Letter from the Churches of Lyons and Vienne*, the source that may be isolated behind *Pseudo-Clementine Recognitions* 1.27-71, and Eusebius's testimony (*Eccl. theol.* 5.17.3) concerning an anonymous opponent of the new prophecy in Phrygia. Each includes parallels with Acts that may be taken as evidence of literary dependence on Acts as a source, although it is difficult to see how any one of these offers any evidence that allows us to comment on whether Acts was considered an authoritative and normative text rather than a source that later authors could mine, each for his own purpose. Also important are the Apocryphal Acts. The earlier Acts may have some claim to antedate Irenaeus, or at least to come from the early third century, and the fact that these texts complement rather than overlap with their canonical counterpart may suggest that their authors were familiar with the whole of Acts, and that they set out to supplement rather than to supplant it. If so, that in itself may suggest that they considered it in some sense a given and that they had no reason to change Acts even if they

---

form found in Matthew and Mark, and the form found in Luke. With 134.15-16 cf. Luke 9:35b and parallels.

[32]For an extended discussion of these texts, see Gregory, *Reception*, 326-49.

wished to compose other texts that might stand alongside Luke's second volume.

Conclusion

The main thing to be said is widely accepted: that the evidence of Irenaeus marks a watershed in what we are able to say about the early reception of Acts. However this does not mean that Irenaeus was the first to use Acts, or that his use of this text was necessarily innovative. Irenaeus was certainly of enormous influence in the way in which the Christianity of the Great Church developed. Nevertheless, it may be too much to ascribe to his influence the not insignificant number of other texts from the late second and/or early third centuries that may also indicate the use of Acts. Further, the well-known phenomenon of the divergent forms in which the text of Acts appears suggests that Acts may already have been circulating in both its so-called Western and Alexandrian forms from the time of Irenaeus and possibly before.[33]

This too suggests that Acts will have been known to other authors besides Irenaeus. François Bovon has argued elsewhere that it was perfectly natural for early Christians to be interested in their founders,[34] so Acts could have helped to meet such an interest from an early period, even if there is no clear evidence that it had a liturgical use.[35] The fact that Acts shows significant theological affinities with a number of texts from the early second century, as demonstrated by Richard Pervo,[36] by Joseph Tyson,[37]

---

[33]This conclusion has been disputed by Barbara Aland. For bibliography and a response to Aland's critique, see Christopher M. Tuckett, "How Early Is the 'Western' Text of Acts?" in *The Book of Acts as Church History. Apostelgeschichte als Kirchengeschichte: Text, Texttraditionen, und antike Auslegungen*, ed. Tobias Nicklas, BZNW 120 (Berlin: de Gruyter, 2003) 69-86.

[34]François Bovon, "The Apostolic Memories in Ancient Christianity," in *Studies in Early Christianity*, WUNT 161 (Tübingen: Mohr Siebeck, 2003) 1-16.

[35]But could Justin have included it among the "Memoirs of the Apostles?" This title is often taken to have been synonymous with the four gospels. Even if it included them, could it not have included other gospels as well as Acts or similar narratives?

[36]See Richard I. Pervo's essay in this volume and his *Dating Acts: Between the Evangelists and the Apologists* (Santa Rosa CA: Polebridge Press, 2006).

[37]See Joseph B. Tyson's essay in this book and his *Marcion and Luke-Acts: A*

and others,[38] may mean that there were readers from this stage who would have been favourably disposed to it. Certainly this could be used to support an argument that Acts was not written until then.[39] But, if (and I accept that this is a big "if") there are other arguments that may be used to defend the more customary date of c. 80-90, such theological affinities should alert us not to the likelihood that Acts was written in the early second century but to the likelihood that it was read in the early second century, even if no external evidence for its use survives.

Much else from this period has been lost. The fact that our extant texts do not answer our questions of when and how Acts was first used does not mean that we should base any conclusions on their silences. Presumably Acts was read by Theophilus and by at least some members of his

------

Defining Struggle (Columbia: University of South Carolina Press, 2006).

[38]E.g., J. C. O'Neill, *The Theology of Acts in its Historical Setting*, 2nd rev. ed. (London: SPCK, 1970) esp. 1-28, and John T. Townsend, "The Date of Luke-Acts" in *Luke-Acts: New Perspectives from the Society of Biblical Literature Seminar*, ed. Charles H. Talbert (New York: Crossroad, 1984) 47-62. Charles Talbert expressly denies a second-century date for Luke-Acts, but notes interesting parallels between the concerns of the author of Acts and those of second- and third-century authors such as Ignatius, Hegesippus, and Tertullian. See *Luke and the Gnostics* (Nashville: Abingdon, 1966). Most recently, see Matthias Klingenhardt, "Markion vs. Lukas: Plädoyer für Wiederaufnahme eines alten Falles," *NTS* 52 (2006): 484-513.

[39]For a brief discussion of this matter, see Gregory, *Reception*, 353. I am cautiously inclined toward a date in the late first century, but recognize that the evidence on which this conclusion is reached is at best ambiguous. If the "we-passages" can be taken as evidence that Luke was a companion of Paul, this would mean that Acts (and therefore Luke, since each is written by the same author) could hardly have been written later than the 90s. It is not inconceivable that this could allow that Luke had access to Josephus and to a collection of the letters of Paul, although I have not yet seen evidence that makes me think that Luke had access to a collection of Paul's letters (if by collection we mean some sort of formally constituted corpus) rather than simply to a number of them. On the question of which of Paul's letters were known to the Apostolic Fathers, and whether knowledge of one or more letters constitutes knowledge of a collection, see the assessment of various contributors in Andrew Gregory and Christopher Tuckett, eds., *The Reception of the New Testament in the Apostolic Fathers* (Oxford UK: Oxford University Press, 2005) esp. 156-57, 185, 226-27, 245, 292. Cf. Pervo, *Dating Acts*, 51-147.

immediate circle. Perhaps too it remained in use from Theophilus to Irenaeus, even if we find no early attestation for it. As has often been noted, the absence of evidence is not evidence of absence.

The Reception of the Book of Acts in Late Antiquity

François Bovon

My intention in this paper is not to offer a definitive survey, but to open some doors of thought as a way of inviting scholars to further research and inquiry. I will begin with a few remarks on the second century CE, the most obscure period with respect to our topic. I then move to three witnesses from the third century CE: Tertullian and Cyprian in the West, Origen in the East. Following these I move into the fourth and fifth centuries, the golden era of the Patristic Period, which is also the time when the book of Acts, now canonized, becomes part of the Christian narrative heritage. At the end of my *invitation au voyage*, I introduce two figures from the sixth century CE, the little known Roman poet Arator and the encyclopedist Cassiodorus.

Few modern names are mentioned in this paper, first because I prefer to insist on the primary sources, and second because only a few scholars have devoted deliberate interest in our particular topic. The New Testament scholar, Nikolaus Adler, writing on Pentecost, devoted a chapter on the history of interpretation of Acts 2.[1] I could add the Yale dissertation by Kenneth Bruce Welliver on the same topic.[2] The historian of mission Werner Bieder wrote a little book half a century ago.[3] Lucien Cerfaux and, more recently, Gianfranco Ferrarese have published studies on the history of the reception of Acts 15, the account of the Jerusalem conference.[4] A. L.

---

[1]Nikolaus Adler, *Das erste christliche Pfingstfest: Sinn und Bedeutung des Pfingstberichtes Apg 2,1–13*, NTAbh 18.1 (Münster i. W.: Aschendorff, 1938) 65-132.

[2]Kenneth Bruce Welliver, "Pentecost and the Early Church: Patristic Interpretation of Acts 2" (Ph.D. diss., Yale, 1961).

[3]Werner Bieder, *Die Apostelgeschichte in der Historie: Ein Beitrag zur Auslegungsgeschichte des Missionsbuches der Kirche*, ThSt 61 (Zurich: Theologischer Verlag Zürich, 1960).

[4]Lucien Cerfaux, "Le chapitre XVe du Livre des Actes à la lumière de la littérature ancienne," in *Miscellanea Giovanni Mercati*, Studi e Testi 121 (Vatican City: Biblioteca Apostolica Vaticana, 1946) 107-26; reprinted in Lucien Cerfaux, *Recueil: Études d'exégèse et d'histoire religieuse*, 3 vols., BETL 6, 7, 71 (Gembloux: Duculot, then Leuven: Leuven University Press and Peeters, 1954–1985) 2:105-24; Gianfranco Ferrarese, *Il concilio di Gerusalemme in Ireneo di Lione. Ricerche sulla storia dell'esegesi di Atti 15,1-29 (e Galati 2,1-10) nell II*

B. Wylie wrote a dissertation on John Chrysostom's *Homilies on Acts* in 1992.[5] My own dissertation dealt with the story of Cornelius (Acts 10:1–11:18) in the first six centuries.[6]

I must also mention some tools that have been useful in my inquiry. These include the volumes of the *Biblia Patristica*,[7] with their many references to *Wirkungsgeschichte* [history of effect]. Also the *Nag Hammadi Texts and the Bible*, edited by Craig Evans, R. L. Webb and R. A. Wiebe;[8] a regular section of the *Bibliographia Patristica*;[9] Anne-Marie La Bonnardière's *Biblia Augustiniana*[10] even if the book of Acts remains missing; James W. Wiles, *A Scripture Index to the Works of St. Augustine in English Translation* published in 1995;[11] and Hermann Josef Sieben's

---

secolo, Testi e ricerche di scienze religiose 17 (Brescia: Paideia, 1979).

[5]A. L. B. Wylie, "John Chrysostom and his Homilies on the Acts of the Apostles: Reclaiming Ancestral Models for the Christian People" (Ph.D. diss., Princeton Theological Seminary, 1992). Also see A. L. B. Wylie, "John Chrysostom's Homilies on Acts," in *Biblical Hermeneutics in Historical Perspective: Studies in Honor of Karlfried Froelich on his Sixtieth Birthday*, ed. Mark S. Burrow and Paul Rorem (Grand Rapids MI: Eerdmans, 1991) 59-72.

[6]François Bovon, *De Vocatione Gentium: Histoire de l'interprétation d'Act. 10,1–11,18 dans les six premieres siècles*, BGBE 8 (Tübingen: Mohr Siebeck, 1967).

[7]Prepared by the Centre d'analyse et de documentation patristiques (Strasbourg); see J. Allenbach et al., *Biblia Patristica*, 7 vols. (Paris: Centre National de la Recherche Scientifique, 1975–2000).

[8]*Nag Hammadi Texts and the Bible*, ed. Craig A. Evans, R. L. Webb, and R. A. Wiebe (Leiden: Brill, 1993).

[9]*Bibliographia Patristica*, 35 vols., ed. Wilhelm Schneemelcher (Berlin: de Gruyter, 1956–1990).

[10]Anne-Marie La Bonnardière, *Biblia Augustiniana*, 7 vols., Antiquité 11, 18, 21, 26, 42, 49, 67 (Paris: Études augustiniennes, 1960–1975). (The work is not complete.)

[11]James W. Wiles, *A Scripture Index to the Works of St. Augustine in English Translation* (Lanham MD: University Press of America, 1995).

Kirchenväterhomilien zum Neuen Testament.[12] Finally, I also acknowledge
a recent article by Susanne Müller-Abels.[13]

I. The Second Century CE

The first question I would ask is this: What is the first, and by this I mean
the oldest, indisputable mention of the book of Acts? I do not think that the
kerygmatic expressions found in the so-called Apostolic Fathers and in the
writings of the apologists constitute proof of their acquaintance with the
book of Acts. The first two indisputable references lead us surprisingly to
Lyon in Gaul: Irenaeus knows, likes, and considers the book of Acts as an
apostolic authority.[14] The bishop of Lyon, who is the first one to mention
the title of the book (*Haer.* 3.13.3), summarizes several parts of the second
Lukan book (*Haer.* 3.12.1ff) and uses the book without any reservation (he
defends Luke as an authority in *Haer.* 3.14.1–4). Irenaeus uses the book of
Acts also in the *Demonstration of the Apostolic Preaching* (for example the
ascension story in 83.5). The second testimomy, the account of the
martyrdoms at Lyon and Vienna, ends with an explicit reference to
Stephen's death: the martyrs of Gaul died with the same piety manifested
in Stephen and they prayed that the Lord forgive those who were
persecuting them.[15] These are two witnesses of an early orthodox reception
of the book of Acts in the second century, perhaps by the same author.[16]

---

[12]Hermann Josef Sieben, *Kirchenväterhomilien zum Neuen Testament: Ein
Repertorium der Textausgaben und Übersetzungen. Mit einem Anhang der Kirchen-
väterkommentare*, Instrumenta Patristica 11 (The Hague: Martinus Nijhoff International, 1991).

[13]Susanne Müller-Abels, "Der Umgang mit 'schwierigen' Texten der Apostel-
geschichte in der Alten Kirche," in *Apostelgeschichte als Kirchengeschichte: Text,
Texttraditionen und antike Auslegungen*, ed. Tobias Nicklas and Michael Tilly,
BZNW 120 (Berlin: de Gruyter, 2003) 347–71.

[14]As Andrew Gregory presents a paper on the book of Acts in Irenaeus in this
volume, my comments here are brief. See Gregory, "Irenaeus and the Reception of
Acts in the Second Century" in this volume.

[15]Eusebius, *Hist. eccl.* 5.2.5.

[16]On the earliest attestations of the book of Acts, see Ernst Haenchen, *Die
Apostelgeschichte, neu übersetzt und erklärt*, 6th ed., KEK 3 (Göttingen: Vandenhoeck und Ruprecht, 1968) 1-13.

As I have recently demonstrated there was another reception of the Third Gospel in addition to the proto-Orthodox, namely in popular, or apocryphal, literature.[17] Can we affirm the same survival of the book of Acts? It seems that the answer should be yes, since the *Epistula apostolorum*, written probably in the middle of the second century CE, alludes clearly to the episode of Acts 12:1-17, Peter's miraculous liberation from prison at the time of Passover.[18] The answer to this question depends also on the answer to another question that was ardently debated ten years ago: Were the apocryphal Acts of the Apostles dependent on the canonical Acts? Willy Rordorf said no.[19] Julian V. Hills, Richard Bauckham, Richard I. Pervo, and Daniel Marguerat took the position that they were dependent on the second book of Luke.[20] I myself consider that the authors of the *Acts of Paul* and the *Acts of Peter* may have known the Lukan Acts of the Apostles, but that they created their literary works independently of them. The Ephesus episode in the *Acts of Paul* is built on an oral tradition used also by Luke in Acts 19, and not on the second book of Luke.[21] The same is true *a fortiori* for the *Acts of John*, the *Acts of Andrew*, and the *Acts of Thomas*. The authors of these works did not consider it their primary purpose to rival, marginalize, or supplement the Lukan book of Acts. In the forms we have them—and these are without doubt more recent than the second century—

---

[17]Bovon, "Gospel of Luke in the Second Century," 379-97.

[18]*Epistula apostolorum* 15 [26].

[19]Willy Rordorf, "Paul's Conversion in the Canonical Acts and in the *Acts of Paul*," trans. Peter Dunn, *Semeia* 80 (1997): 137-44.

[20]Julian V. Hills, "The *Acts of Paul* and the Legacy of the Lukan Acts," *Semeia* 80 (1997): 145-58; idem, "The Acts of the Apostles and the *Acts of Paul*," in SBLSP, ed. Eugene Lovering (Atlanta: Scholars Press, 1994) 24-54; Richard Bauckham, "The *Acts of Paul* as a Sequel of Acts," in *The Book of Acts in Its Ancient Literary Setting*, BAFCS 1, ed. Bruce W. Winter and Andrew D. Clarke (Grand Rapids MI: Eerdmans, 1993) l05-52; Richard Bauckham, "The *Acts of Paul*: Replacement of Acts or Sequel to Acts?" *Semeia* 80 (1997): 159-68; Richard I. Pervo, "A Hard Act to Follow: The *Acts of Paul* and the Canonical Acts," *JHC* 2/2 (1995): 3-32; and Daniel Marguerat, "The 'Acts of Paul' and the Canonical Acts: A Phenomenon of Rereading," trans. Ken McKinney, *Semeia* 80 (1997): 169-83.

[21]*Acts of Paul* 9.1-28 (Coptic Bodmer Papyrus 41, 1-8, and Greek Hamburg Papyrus, 1-5).

the *Acts of Philip*, in an effort of mimesis, used and adapted Acts 17 (Paul's presence in Athens and his speech before the Areopagus).[22]

That there may have been some competition between Luke-Acts and the non-canonical Acts of apostles is supported by evidence from the *Muratori Canon* (a document that, despite a Harvard tradition, I consider to reflect the Roman community in the second, not the fourth, century CE): that the canon calls the book of Acts the "Acts of all the apostles" suggests that the author of the canon knew of the existence of other Acts of apostles and was eager to discredit them.

As such, the *Muratori Canon* is also an important witness to the reception of the book of Acts in the West, this time in Rome and not in Gaul.[23] This knowledge of Acts in the second century is attested in another way through textual criticism. The famous two forms of the texts of Acts, the Egyptian and the so-called Western, constitute a double witness: first to the distribution of the book in the Roman Empire and also to its flexibility, due to its lack of canonicity. It is not impossible that those two forms are the result of conscious revisions and that these recensions were produced in the second century CE by emerging Christian schools. The location of such grammatical, stylistic, and theological efforts is uncertain: Alexandria, Ephesus, and Rome have been suggested.[24]

---

[22]*Acts of Philip* 2; see François Bovon, Bertrand Bouvier, and Frédéric Amsler, *Acta Philippi. Textus*, CCSA 11 (Turnhout: Brepols, 1999) 40-75. This act 2 seems to be written on the basis of a similar plot in *Acts of Philip* 6 and in *Acts of Philip Martyrdom*. Some later summaries of the *Acts of Philip* place this act 2 at a different location, after *Acts of Philip* 7. These facts suggest that *Acts of Philip* 2 is the youngest element in the large composition of the *Acts of Philip*.

[23]See Marie-Joseph Lagrange, *Histoire ancienne du canon du Nouveau Testament* (Paris: Gabalda, 1933); *The Canon Debate*, ed. Lee Martin McDonald and James A. Sanders (Peabody MA: Hendrickson, 2002); and Martin Meiser, "Texttraditionen des Aposteldekrets—Textkritik und Rezeptionsgeschichte," in *Apostelgeschichte als Kirchengeschichte*, 373-98.

[24]See Christian-Bernard Amphoux, "Les premières éditions de Luc, I: Le texte de Luc 5," *ETL* 67 (1991): 312-27; idem, "Les premières éditions des Luc, II: l'histoire du texts au II siècle," *ETL* 68 (1992): 38-48; see also Eldon J. Epp, *Theological Tendency of Codex Bezae Cantabrigiensis in Acts*, SNTSMS 3 (Cambridge UK: Cambridge University Press, 1966) and Marie-Émile Boismard and André Lamouille, *Le texte occidental des Actes des apôtres: Reconstitution et réhabilitation*, 2 vols., Synthèse 17 (Paris: Recherches sur les civilisations, 1984).

It should be noted that the presence of the book of Acts does not mean *ipso facto* its recognition as a canonical document. It would have been read, then respected for its authority and finally recognized as a holy book inspired by God. This process took time and did not unfold everywhere at the same rate. On the whole, the knowledge and canonization of the book of Acts took longer than the reception of the gospels.

The question remains: What about Marcion? If he likes the Gospel of Luke, what did he do with the Acts of the Apostles? Marcion does not seem to be sensitive to the literary and doctrinal unity of the two works since, according to Pseudo-Tertullian (*Adversus omnes haereses* 6), Marcion "Acta Apostolorum et Apocalypsin quasi falsa reicit,"[25] which means that Marcion not only remains silent concerning the book of Acts, but he in fact explicitly rejects it. Probably, as Adolf Harnack puts it, Marcion shook down "seine [Luke's] ganze dogmatisch-historische Konstruktion."[26] It is probable that Tertullian alludes to Marcion's position when he says in *De praescr.* 22.10-11:

> He [Christ] (thus) shows that there was nothing of which they [the disciples] were ignorant, to whom He had promised the future attainment of all truth by help of the Spirit of truth. And assuredly He fulfilled His promise, since it is proved in the Acts of the Apostles that the Holy Ghost did come down. Now they who reject that Scripture can neither belong to the Holy Spirit, seeing that they cannot acknowledge that the Holy Ghost has been sent as yet to the disciples, nor can they presume to claim to be a church themselves.[27]

If the motto is clear with respect to the Marcionites, what about the Jewish-Christian position? Epiphanius's *Panarion* reserves a surprise for us

---

[25]Pseudo-Tertullian, *Adversus omnes haereses* 6 (CSEL 47).

[26]Adolf Harnack, *Marcion: Das Evangelium vom fremden Gott*, 2nd ed. (Leipzig: J. C. Hinrichs'sche Buchhandlung, 1924) 173. More recently, see Joseph B. Tyson, *Marcion and Luke-Acts: A Defining Struggle* (Columbia: University of South Carolina Press, 2006) and Matthias Klingenhardt, "Markion vs. Lukas: Plädoyer für Wiederaufnahme eines alten Falles," *NTS* 52 (2006): 484-513.

[27]*Preascr.* 22:10-11 (*ANF* 3:253). See also *Marc.* 5.2, where Tertullian writes: "Now, if even to this degree the Acts of the Apostles are in agreement with Paul, it becomes evident why you reject them: for they peach no other god than the Creator, nor the Christ of any god but the Creator." *Tertullian Adversus Marcionem*, trans. Ernest Evans (Oxford UK: Clarendon Press, 1972) 2:519.

here. In book 30 of his *Panarion* on Jewish-Christian sects, the bishop of Salamis on Cyprus says that the Ebionites were not reading the canonical Acts of the Apostles but instead other Acts: "They say that there are other Acts of Apostles; and these contain much utterly impious material, with which they deliberately arm themselves against the truth."[28] Epiphanius then mentions the *Degrees of James*. As it is known to us, this Jewish-Christian document is probably preserved in the first book of the Pseudo-Clementine *Recognitions* 1.27–71.[29] We may conclude that the Ebionites not only had a different memory of Jesus through their own gospel but they also had a different story of the origins of Christianity. The *Degrees of James* (*Ps.-Clem., Rec.* 1. 43–44) recounts another story of the Twelve in Jerusalem; they insist on the leadership of James and mention the dialogues with the Jewish priests.

The discovery of the Nag Hammadi Library leads us to ask again, now more astutely: What was the position of the several gnostic movements regarding the book of Acts, and what was their reconstruction of Christian origins? As for the apologists, we find in the Nag Hammadi Codices (NHC) some similarity of expression to the book of Acts, but most of the references established by Craig A. Evans, R. L. Webb, and R. A. Wiebe do not compel one to speak in terms of literary dependence.[30] In my view the only treatise where the situation is different is the *Letter of Peter to Philip* (NHC

---

[28] Epiphanius, *Pan.* 30.16.6 (trans. Frank Williams). See A. F. J. Klijn, "The Apocryphal Acts of the Apostles," *VC* 37 (1983): 195: "Epiphanius seems to be better informed about the use of these Acts. He writes that the Origenians (ωριγένιοι) use apocryphal Acts 'especially the Acts of Andrew and of others', the Encratites use those of Andrew, John, Thomas, and of others and the *Apostolici* (ἀποστολικοῖ) or Apotactici (ἀποτακτικοῖ) especially use the Acts of Andrew and Thomas. These various groups are related to the Encratites and are located mainly in Asia Minor. It can be seen that especially the Acts of Andrew, John, and Thomas were assumed to be heretical."

[29] See André Schneider and Luigi Cirillo, "Roman pseudo-clémentin, Reconnaissances," in *Écrits apocryphes chrétiens*, 2 vols., ed. François Bovon, Pierre Geoltrain, and Jean-Daniel Kaestli, La Pléiade 442, 516 (Paris: Gallimard, 1997-2005) 2:1602-1605.

[30] *Nag Hammadi Texts and the Bible*, 21, 50, 119-120, 186, 215, 239, 251-52, 278, 298, 300, 333, 382, and 416.

VIII.2).[31] It is evident first that the author knows the book of Acts, the story of Pentecost in particular; [32]and second, that he disagrees with the Lukan report and tries to elaborate his own vision of the origin of the church and the first distribution of the Holy Spirit.[33] It is also possible that the Nag Hammadi *Apocalypse of Paul* (NHC V.2) or the Nag Hammadi *Apocalypse of Peter* (NHC VII.3) is in some kind of conversation with the canonical Acts of the Apostles.

II. The Third Century

Tertullian knows and appreciates the book of Acts.[34] It is interesting to note that he nearly always indicates "in the Acts of the Apostles" when he refers to it, while he does not mention the gospels' names when quoting sayings of Jesus. It was an early Christian tradition to refer to Jesus' voice and authorship when quoting one of his sayings. In the case of stories from the book of Acts no such tradition existed. As the book was not so well known and rather slow to be canonized, Tertullian's precision is motivated by his desire to let it be better known and through its authority be venerated. In his treatise *On Baptism* 10, for example, Acts is the only work he refers to by name amidst a slew of quotations from the gospels and some Pauline epistles.[35]

There are however cases where Tertullian does not make any explicit reference to the source of his knowledge. For instance, he makes a handful of references to Stephen and his martyrdom, but does so without referring

---

[31]*Nag Hammadi Texts and the Bible*, 341-50.

[32]Here as there Jesus appeared to the disciples before he was taken up into heaven while the disciples return to Jerusalem, again gathering together where they spent time in the temple healing a multitude.

[33]See Klaus Koschorke, "Eine gnostische Pfingstpredigt: Zur Auseinandersetzung zwischen gnostischem und kirchlichem Christentum am Beispiel der 'Epistula Petri ad Philippum' (NHC VIII,2)," *ZTK* 74 (1977): 323-43.

[34]See J. H. Petzer, "Tertullian's Text of Acts," *SecCent* 8 (1991): 201-15.

[35]Another example: in *Against Praxeas* 28, Tertullian counters a false conclusion regarding the Trinity by claiming that "But that is not the teaching of the Acts of the Apostles in that cry of the church to God." ET: *Tertullian's Treatise against Praxeas*, trans. Ernest Evans (London: SPCK, 1948). Acts 4:27 is then quoted. I would like to thank Matt Sullivan who made an inquiry for me in the work of Tertullian in November 2006.

to Acts (*Res.* 55; *Prax.* 30; *Pat.* 14). The same holds true for some references to Paul's conversion (*Bapt.* 13), the account of Philip and the eunuch (*Bapt.* 4, 18), and the ascension of Christ and the words of the angels to the apostles immediately thereafter (*Bapt.* 19; *Res.* 51; *Carn. Chr.* 24.4). In such cases Tertullian refers more to the story than to the book and these stories, more than others contained in the book of Acts, were well known among Christians of Tertullian's day.

One should note finally that Tertullian uses the Acts of the Apostles in a polemical way in his larger work *Against Marcion*. It is clear that the book of Acts had little place in early Christian communities and only became important later, when it was necessary to base correct doctrine on the teaching and career of some of the apostles. If so, then the following passage (5.2.7) becomes particularly telling.

> After that, as he [Paul] then briefly describes the course of his conversion from persecutor to apostle he confirms what is written in the Acts of the Apostles, in which the substance of this epistle is reviewed; namely, that certain persons intervened who said that men ought to be circumcised, and that Moses' law must be kept, and that then the apostles, when asked for advice on this question, reported on the authority of the Holy Spirit that they ought not to lay burdens upon men which not even their fathers had been able to bear [Acts 15:10]. Now, if even to this degree the Acts of the Apostles are in agreement with Paul, it becomes evident why you reject them; for they preach no other god than the Creator, nor the Christ of any god but the Creator, since neither is the promise of the Holy Spirit proved to have been fulfilled on any other testimony than the documentary evidence of the Acts. And it is by no means reasonable that that writing should in part agree with the apostle, when it relates his history in accordance with the evidence he supplies, and in part disagree, when it proclaims in Christ the godhead of the Creator, with intent to make out that Paul did not follow the preaching of the apostles, though in fact he did receive from them the pattern of teaching how the law need not be kept.[36]

---

[36]"Exinde decurrens ordinem conuersionis suae de persecutore in apostolum scripturam Apostolicorum confirmat, apud quam ipsa etiam epistulae istius materia recognoscitur, intercessisse quosdam qui dicerent circumcidi oportere et obseruandam esse Moysi legem, tunc apostolos de ista quaestione consultos ex auctoritate spiritus renuntiasse non esse imponenda onera hominibus quae patres ipsi non potuissent sustinere. Quodsi et ex hoc congruunt Paulo Apostolorum Acta, cur ea respuatis iam apparet, ut deum scilicet non alium praedicantia quam

In the middle of the third century CE, Cyprian, following in the footsteps of Tertullian, regularly uses the expression "in the Acts of the Apostles;" only once does he consider a quotation from Acts to be taken from "Scripture."[37] If I may use very elementary statistics, the book of Acts is quoted twice less than the Gospel of Luke, three times less than the Epistle to the Romans and four times less than the Gospel of John.

Most of the time the bishop of Carthage considers the book of Acts a source of examples: the unanimity of the first Christians (Acts 4:32) is mentioned as a model over and against the present bad situation;[38] the good works of Cornelius are an example of reward;[39] Tabitha's almsgiving is an example of the generosity of the first Christians selling their properties;[40] Stephen's prayer for his persecutors an example of forgiveness.[41] The book of Acts serves also as quarry to be mined for the multiple quotations found in his book *Testimonia against the Jews*. For instance, in *Test.* 1.21 he uses Paul's famous exclamation, "Since you the Jews do not accept the Gospel I will turn to the Gentiles," which is taken from Acts 13:46 (he quotes actually Acts 13:46b-47). In *Test.* 3:3 he uses Acts 4:32—evidently one of Cyprian's favorite verses—as an example of generosity; in *Test.* 3:61 he uses Acts 3:6 (Peter stating that he has neither gold nor silver) as an admonition against greed. The point "that what any one has vowed to God, he must quickly repay" is made in *Test.* 3:30 by the negative example of Ananias and Sapphira (Acts 5:3-4).

In addition to the moral dimension (examples) and the apologetic usage (*testimonia*) Cyprian adds a *tertius usus*: to refer to Acts as a "scriptural" authority in a controversy that is at the same time practical, pastoral, and

---

creatorem, nec Christum alterius quam creatoris, quando nec promissio spiritus sancti aliunde probetur exhibita quam de instrumento Actorum. Quae utique uerisimile non est ex parte quidem apostolo conuenire, cum ordinem eius secundum ipsius testimonium ostendunt, ex parte uero dissidere, cum diuinitatem in Christo creatoris annuntiant, ut praedicationem quidem apostolorum non sit secutus Paulus, qui formam ab eis dedocendae legis accepit." Tertullian, *Against Marcion*, 5.2.7. Translation above from Evans, *Tertullian Adversus Marcionem*, 517-19.

[37]Cyprian, *Unit. eccl.* 25. One manuscript adds "divine" before "Scripture."

[38]Cyprian, *Epist.* 11 (7).3.1; *Unit. eccl.* 25.

[39]Cyprian, *Dom. or.* 32.

[40]Cyprian, *Eleem.* 6.25.

[41]Cyrpian, *Pat.* 16.

doctrinal. I am referring here to the controversy that set up the opposition between Cyprian, the "pope" at Carthage, and Stephen, the "pope" at Rome, regarding the validity or invalidity of the baptism received by the heretics wishing to join the catholica. The lines were clearly drawn: for Cyprian, the baptism received by those involved in the heresy is not a true Christian baptism. It has no validity. Therefore, it is necessary to re-baptize the heretics (which for Cyprian is not really re-baptism, since the first was not a true baptism). For Stephen, bishop of Rome, since the formula "in the name of the Father, and the Son, and the Holy Spirit" has been used, it is wrong to redo a sacrament that, according to Scripture, is valid and should never be renewed. The examples of baptism preserved in the book of Acts were used by both sides.[42]

Actually the author who used them with the greatest vehemence and success is an anonymous author who, even if located in Africa, defended the Roman position. I am referring here to the author of *De rebaptismate*, which is strangely preserved among the spuria of Cyprian even as he defends just the opposite of the bishop of Carthage.[43] This author likes, as he says, to bring together relevant biblical texts and—showing his herme-neutic expertise—explain the obscure passages by using clear and evident ones. Matthew 3:11; Acts 1:4–5 and 11:15–17 are his favorite texts for the decisive separation of water baptism from Spirit baptism. For him, the gift of the Spirit is the important part, which has liturgical representation in the laying on of hands. The exceptions preserved in the book of Acts (where the gift of the Spirit is separated from water baptism) are the strongest argument in favor of the laying on of hands as sufficient ritual for the reintegration of baptized heretics into the church. Even if the author is often confused, it is significant that he, even more than Cyprian, was among the first to systematically use the examples of baptism mentioned in the book of Acts to solve a disciplinary and doctrinal question of his day.

---

[42]In 256 CE, the African bishops, including Cyprian, held a synod and com-municated in a famous letter (Cyprian's *Epist.* 72) to the bishop at Rome their deci-sion to require a new baptism. John 3:5 (on the need of water baptism for salvation) and Acts 10:44–48 (Cornelius's baptism even after the gift of the Spirit) are the primary and only biblical quotations mentioned in the cover letter to their doctrinal demonstration. See Bovon, *De Vocatione Gentium*, 268–80.

[43]See Pseudo-Cyprian, *De rebaptismate*, ed. G. Rauschen, Florilegium Patristicum 11 (Bonn: Hanstein, 1916).

Origen of course plays a major role in the history of interpretation and reception of the Acts of the Apostles; thus he merits special inquiry. What I can state at this point is the following: the majority of references to Acts concerns Origen's *Commentary on Matthew* and his *Contra Celsum*, even if references are also scattered in his homiletical works and *De principiis*.[44] It appears also that some chapters in Acts (the account of the ascension in Acts 1; Pentecost, Acts 2; Cornelius as the first Gentile accepted into the church, Acts 10) were more successful, I mean more often quoted than others (the choice of the Seven, Acts 6; Peter in prison, Acts 12; Barnabas and Paul missionary travel, Acts 13-14). Acts is for Origen a true account of the history of the early church and the teaching of some of its key figures: it plays an important role in Origen's refutation of Celsus and Celsus' Jewish "informateur" (*Cels.* 1.57; 2.1; 2.17; 2.45). Acts is more than a historical witness to the past of the apostles and the early church; it is a normative document relying correctly on the Old Testament and is even a teaching telling how to read the Scriptures (*Cels.* 3.46; 5.8; 8.26) as is shown by observing the literal and moral understanding of the story of Ananias and Sapphira (Acts 5:1-11) in the context of Origen's exegesis of the story of the rich man (Matt 19:16-22).[45]

Taking the story of Cornelius (Acts 10:1-11:18) as an example, Origen first insists on the notion of merits: if Cornelius receives the visit of the angel, it is because of his alms and good works mentioned explicitly by Luke (Augustine, in the Semipelagian controversy, will have a very different interpretation: for the bishop of Hippo, the Roman officer's good works are to be attributed to the *gratia praeueniens*[46]). Therefore, according to Numbers 18:8-14, Origen explains, Cornelius can be called the "first fruits" of the church of Caesarea and even of the church of all the nations.[47]

When dealing with Peter's vision of the tablecloth and the pure and impure animals, Origen surprises us by first offering a literal interpretation: the Alexandrian theologian considers Peter's vision in its historical

---

[44]See the volume prepared by the Centre d'analyse et de documentation patristiques: J. Allenbach et al., *Biblia Patristica*, vol. 3: *Origène* (Paris: Centre National de la Recherche Scientifique, 1980) 347–52.

[45]Origen, *Com. Matt.* 15.14-15. I am relying here again on a preliminary work by my research assistant Matt Sullivan.

[46]See Augustine, *Praed.* 7.12; Bovon, *De Vocatione Gentium* 74-75.

[47]See Origen, *Hom. Num.* 11.3; Bovon, *De Vocatione Gentium* 39-43.

dimension as someone learning from God how to understand in a new way, in the true spiritual way, the requirements of the law. For Origen the vision has to do with the end of Jewish dietary restrictions. Acts 10:15 ("What God made pure . . . ") has the favor of the Alexandrian scholar who relies on it and likes it.[48] While Origen, the Alexandrian, is a true representative of the literal meaning of Peter's vision (for him the animals remain animals and represent potential food), some Antiochian theologians chose on the contrary the spiritual and allegorical interpretation (the vision being here connected with the calling of the nations and the animals being figures of potential Gentiles).

III. The Fourth and Fifth Centuries

By the fourth and fifth centuries the book of Acts had been canonized. It is mentioned in the lists preserved in particular in Athanasius's Thirty-Ninth Easter Letter.[49] We even have some information concerning its liturgical use as part of the lectionary. It appears that the book of Acts was read in the liturgy of the churches and that logically, according to the calendar of the liturgical year, this reading took place after remembrance of the great celebrations of Jesus Christ's redemptive acts on the cross and resurrection. But as always happens when innovation occurs, hesitations, differences and oppositions arose at the same time. We have good reason to believe that two different solutions were chosen: in the Eastern, Byzantine part of the empire, in Armenia and in Africa,[50] in Spain and in Gaul, as well as in Milan, the book of Acts was read after Easter, since Jesus' resurrection constitutes the birth of the Christian faith and the Christian church.[51] In Rome, on the contrary, reading the book of Acts seems to have begun at Pentecost

---

[48]Origen, *Cels.* 2.1; Bovon, *De Vocatione Gentium* 93-103.

[49]See Daryl D. Schmidt, "The Greek New Testament as a Codex," in *Canon Debate*, 469-84, esp. 476-78. Also see Harry Y. Gamble, "The New Testament Canon: Recent Research and the Status Quaestionis," in *Canon Debate*, 296-94, esp. 291; and Everett Ferguson, "Factors Leading to the Selection and Closure of the New Testament Canon: A Survey of Some Recent Studies," in *Canon Debate*, 295-320, esp. 319.

[50]For Africa, according to Augustine, *Serm.* 315.1 (PL 38.1426).

[51]See G. Godu, "Épîtres," in *DACL* 5.1, col. 273 and 293; see also Robert Cabié, *La Pentecôte: L'évolution de la Cinquantaine pascale au cours des cinq premiers siècles*, Bibliothèque de liturgie (Paris: Desclée, 1965) 97–100.

since—and this is also a good theological justification—the outpouring of the Spirit on the day of Pentecost constitutes the birth of the church.[52]

Now that every community possessed at least one copy of the book of Acts, its diffusion—material and spiritual—began. The first attestation of the success of this book is the collection of homilies. Most of the time these were not part of a *lectio continua*, but related to a feast day. As soon as the Feast of Pentecost became a special day, apart from the long fifty days of the great Easter celebration (the long Feast of Joy), sermons appear for this feast. The miracles at Pentecost were a particular focus of the debates. Gregory of Nazianzus[53] considered this a wonderful episode of speaking in foreign tongues and not a miraculous audition, since the miracle is connected with the disciples and not the audience. Cyril of Jerusalem shared this opinion, since the mockery mentioned in Acts 2:13 refers to the disciples.[54] Certainly, if they were full it was not with wine, but with the Holy Spirit of God.[55]

Sermons were also devoted to the feast days of apostles and martyrs. While sermons on Peter and Paul include references to the book of Acts— Peter's healing power, for example, or Paul's conversion—it is the number and variety of sermons devoted to Stephen as the first martyr that holds the attention of the historian. Gregory of Nyssa, Augustine of Hippo, and Hesychius of Jerusalem all preached—often more than once—on the first martyr.[56] They insist on his service as a deacon, his polemical wit against

---

[52]See G. Godu, "Épîtres," col. 331; see also Stephan Beissel, *Entstehung der Perikopen des römischen Meßbuches: Zur Geschichte der Evangelienbücher in der ersten Hälfte des Mittelalters* (Repr.: Rome: Herder, 1967; 1st ed., 1907).

[53]Gregory of Nyssa, *Oratio in Pentecosten* 41.11 (SC 358, 338-41); Adler, *Das erste christliche Pfingstfest*, 3.

[54]Cyril of Jerusalem, *Catech.* 17.16-19 (PG 33, 988-92); Adler, *Das erste christliche Pfingstfest*, 3.

[55]On Acts 2:1–13, the story of Pentecost, and its patristic interpretation see Adler, *Das erste christliche Pfingstfest*, 1-13, and Susanne Müller-Abels, "Der Umgang mit 'schwierigen' Texten der Apostelgeschichte in der Alten Kirche," in *Apostelgeschichte als Kirchengeschichte*, 347-72.

[56]See, e.g., Gregory of Nyssa, *Encomium in sanctum Stephanum protomartyrem* in *Gregorius Nyssenus: Encomium in sanctum Stephanum protomartyrem. Griechischer Text, eingeleitet und herausgegeben mit Apparatus criticus und Übersetzung*, ed. Otto Lendle (Leiden: Brill, 1968); Augustine of Hippo, *Sermones*, 320-24; Hesychius of Jerusalem, *Homilia in s. Stephanum* 9 in *Les Homélies festales*

the Jewish authorities, and his patience during his martyrdom. After 415 CE and the revelation of his relics, they underscore the power of the martyr and his relics for sisters and brothers.

Just as the book of Acts became a quarry of examples for Cyprian, so also it became a collection of virtues (and vices) for later preachers. Maximus of Turin in the fourth century, when preaching on greed, recounts the story of Ananias and Sapphira as a bad example.[57]

But the reality that the book of Acts took longer than the gospels to be accepted and canonized is reflected in the fact that no one offered a series of sermons on the book of Acts, considered as *lectio continua*. During a time when sermons on the earliest Bible for Christians, the Hebrew Bible, particularly the Septuagint, were frequent and during a time when homilies on the gospels, particularly on Matthew, were common, no one dared or even thought about explaining all the chapters of Acts. It is difficult to find a sermon about Paul on Cyprus or about Paul's appearance before Felix; Sieben's index of Church Fathers' Homilies is eloquent here by its silence.[58]

There is however one exception, a famous exception: John Chrysostom, who around 400 CE, while he was bishop of Constantinople, decided to preach on the book of Acts in its entirety. But it is indicative and sympto-matic of the situation that the Golden Mouth began his first homily by com-plaining that the book of Acts was ignored by many Christians. I quote: "To many persons this Book is so little known, both it and its author, that they are not even aware that there is such a book in existence. For this reason especially, I have taken this narrative for my subject, that I may draw to it such as do not know it, and not let such a treasure as this remain hidden out of sight."[59]

We still do not have a critical edition of this series of homilies. It has been edited several times since the first Latin translation by Erasmus and others, printed in Basel by Frobenius. The first edition of the Greek text by Hieromynus Commelin was published in 1603 in Heidelberg. It was then reissued again by Henry Savile in his superb edition of John Chrysostom

---

d'Hésychius de Jérusalem, 2 vols., ed. Michel Aubineau, Subsidia Hagiographica 59 (Brussels: Société des Bollandistes, 1978–1980) 1: 289-350.

[57]Maximus of Turin, *Sermo Sequentia de avaritia et de Anania* 18, CCSL 23 (Turnhout: Brepols, 1962) 67–69.

[58]Sieben, *Kirchenväterhomilien zum Neuen Testament*, 133.

[59]John Chrysostom, *Hom. Act.* 1.1, trans. H. Browne.

works (Eton, 1613). Savile was the first to notice the existence of two recensions, one rough and one smooth with frequent merging of the two, creating a third version! But all of the editions until Migne's *Patrologia Graeca* presented an eclectic text; we are still waiting for an edition of the rough recension, the original being rough because John—very busy and worried that he had no time to prepare them—improvised them and tachygraphs tried to grasp as much as they could.

Our good fortune from that unfortunate situation is that the British scholar, Henry Browne, translated for the Oxford Library of the Fathers (then for the Nicean and Post-Nicean Fathers, first series, vol. 11) the reconstruction he had made for himself of the rough text. Our best access to Chrysostom's *Homily on Acts* is therefore still the English translation.[60]

In the first homily, after the passage I quoted, Chrysostom says that the value of Acts is equal to the value of the gospels. Acts abounds in good philosophy, doctrinal truth, and powerful deeds of the Spirit. The preacher then explains that Luke, Paul's disciple, is the author of both volumes, and that Luke divided his work into two sections in order to avoid the reader's fatigue and because the topics were different. The book of Acts focuses on the miracles performed by the Holy Spirit while the gospel presents Jesus' powerful deeds. While Chrysostom admits that Lukan christology is often low christology, he explains this surprising fact in terms of the religious circumstances of Luke's time. What is more important is the divine economy: the book of Acts fulfills Jesus' numerous prophecies just as the gospel fulfills the prophecies contained in the Holy Scriptures of the Old Testament. Another important aspect is Chrysostom's nostalgia for the primitive church, which takes the famous summaries of the *vita apostolica* as historically true and regrets that such unanimity and generosity are no longer available. But nostalgia is not the last word of this comparison. In

---

[60]On the efforts of Henry Browne and Edgar R. Smothers, see Bovon, *De Vocatione Gentium*, 6-12; it is now Francis T. Gignac who has taken over the task of editing these homilies; see Gignac, "The New Critical Edition of Chrysostom's *Homilies on Acts*: A Progress Report," in *Text und Textkritik: Eine Aufsatzsammlung*, ed. Jürgen Dummer, TU 133 (Berlin: Akademie Verlag, 1987) 165-68; idem, "Evidence for Deliberate Scribal Revision in Chrysostom's *Homilies on the Acts of the Apostles*," in *Nova et Vetera: Patristic Studies in Honor of Thomas Patrick Halton*, ed. John Petruccione (Washington DC: Catholic University of America Press, 1998) 209-25.

preaching on Acts, Chrysostom hopes for a hermeneutical miracle: that the paradisiacal situation of the primitive church will be re-actualized in the Constantinople of his own day.

Each homily comments on approximately twenty verses of Scripture and is divided into three parts. In the first, Luke, like a docent at the Boston Museum of Fine Arts, draws attention to the story, conceived as a piece of art that the eye more than the ear must contemplate. The second part begins with a regular formula: "But let us revisit what we have just said." Chrysostom chooses some aspects of the biblical passage he considers particularly important (for example, see *Hom. Act.* 5.2 on Acts 2:14 following; in the second part he goes over v. 14, the expressions the "third hour," the Joel quotation and other details). This second part is unique in Chrysostom's preaching production and may be explained by his wish to implement a particular awareness of this little known book.[61] The third part is most often—surprisingly—completely detached from the Lukan text and from John's interpretation up to this point: it refers to a special concern of the bishop at that particular moment. In a homily on Peter's visit to Cornelius, for example, Chrysostom develops in this third part a kind of theodicy (God is not the origin of evil) and criticizes those who postpone their baptism.[62]

If Chrysostom has little interest in any specific exegetical problem (no grammatical solution, alas!), he often makes a psychological remark. For example, concerning Acts 10:17 Chrysostom says that Cornelius's embassy arrived at just the right moment to help Peter resolve his hesitation over the vision of the tablecloth containing all of the animals.[63] More often, he prefers to comment on Christian ethics: Peter—apart from God—had a moral responsibility to open the doors of the church to the Gentiles: the apostle was simultaneously strong and diplomatic in Jerusalem (Acts 11) when he had to justify his actions, his decision to welcome Cornelius into the Christian community, and to baptize him (Acts 10).[64]

Parallels to these homilies appear in this golden period of patristic literature in the first commentaries on Acts. The beginning is modest,

---

[61]It is already the suggestion furnished by Bernard de Montfaucon according to Edgar R. Smothers, "Le texte des Homélies de saint Jean Chrysostome sur les Actes des apôtres," *RechSR* 27 (1937): 514.

[62]John Chrysostom, *Hom. Act.* 23.3-4.

[63]Chrysostom, *Hom. Act.* 22.2.

[64]Chrysostom, *Hom. Act.* 24.1-2.

starting in Syria and Egypt. Ephrem's commentary, discovered in an Armenian version and published in 1921, is little more than a summary and a rewriting of the book of Acts.[65] Ephrem's interpretation appears to be implicit and discreet. The Syrian theologian insists on the activity of the Holy Spirit and liberation from the law through the gospel of Christ.[66] In Alexandria, Didymus the Blind also summarizes the book of Acts but, more than Ephrem, his inclusion of polemic and theological interpretation constitutes a true commentary. This work is only preserved in fragments scattered in chains (*catenae*).[67] Some fragments, confirmed by Didymus's *Treatise on the Trinity*, reveal his particular interest in Peter's christological speeches. Didymus quotes practically all the verses of Acts 10:34–43 in his work on the Trinity.[68] His fragments on the story of Cornelius deal in particular with Peter's vision. Two points should be mentioned here: a) following a correct understanding of parables, one could see human beings behind the animals shown to the apostles; b) the Petrine *extasis* allows Didymus to contradict the Montanists, since the apostle remained awake and could use his ability to reason during his religious experience. Didymus is perhaps the first to realize that the *narratives* of Acts can be read and interpreted in a *theological* exegesis.

More mysterious is the work of another scholar from Alexandria who appears between the fourth and sixth centuries CE, a certain Ammonios.[69] Only fragments of his work on Acts are preserved in the chains. The literary genres of his commentary are the gloss and scholia; he uses a recurrent introductory formula: "It is characteristic that. . . . " For the most part his comments concern moral character. He also emphasizes piety and faith.

---

[65]F. C. Conybeare, "The Commentary of Ephrem on Acts," in *The Beginnings of Christianity*, part 1: *The Acts of the Apostles*, 5 vols., ed. F. J. Foakes-Jackson and Kirsopp Lake (London: Macmillan, 1920–1933) 3:380-453; see Bovon, *De Vocatione Gentium*, 2-5.

[66]See A. Merk, "Der neuentdeckte Kommentar des hl. Ephraim zur Apostelgeschichte," *ZTK* 48 (1924): 52–53.

[67]On these fragments see Bovon, *De Vocatione Gentium* 5-6, 107-10, 142, and 145-47.

[68]Didymus the Blind, *De Trinitate* 1.27; 1.29; 2.6.23; 2.7.2; 3.2.22. The authenticity of this is uncertain.

[69]See Bovon, *De Vocatione Gentium* 12-14.

The fourth and fifth centuries were also a time of intense doctrinal controversies on the nature of Christ, on the divinity of the Holy Spirit, on
human freedom and divine election. The great theologians of that time all
make use of scriptural arguments from the book of Acts or contradict their
opponents who sometimes base their opinions on the naïve morality of Luke
or the undeveloped christology of Acts.

Acts 10:38, a passage concerning Christ's unction, became one of the
most debated verses.[70] It was probably first used by those who doubted the
total equality of the Son with the Father. Most likely it was Paul of
Samosata who, even before the western adoptionists, quoted this verse to
support his christology: "Jesus, from Nazareth that God anointed with the
Holy Spirit and power, who went through the land doing good works, etc."
Psalm 45 (44): 7(8) can also be read from an adoptionist perspective:
"Therefore God, your God, has anointed you with the oil of gladness
beyond your companions." These two texts were passionately debated: the
orthodox view, on the defensive side here, attempted to minimize the sub-
ordination of the Son.

We have long apologetic explanations of these two passages in
Athanasius, *Oratio contra Arianos* 1.37 and 1.46–52.[71] And it comes as no
surprise that we read quotations of Acts 10:38 and Ps 45 (44):7(8) in the
Arian *Tractatus in Lucae Euangelium* (dated the end of the fourth century)
as the author explains Luke 4:18 (Jesus, preaching in Nazareth, claims that
the Spirit of the Lord is upon him).[72] The same controversy appears in
Africa, where we find Augustine opposing the Arian bishop Maximinus,
claiming that the unction in Ps 45 (44):7(8), like the unction in Acts 10:38,
has nothing to do with the begetting of the Son in the supposed time
imagined by the Arians, but refers instead to the incarnation.[73] In Gaul,
Hilarius of Poitiers also proposed an interpretation of Acts 10:38 and Ps 45
(44):7(8) along the line of Athanasius.[74] From the four corners of the earth
the orthodox theologians of the fourth and fifth centuries developed what

---

[70]See Bovon, *De Vocatione Gentium*, 224-46.

[71]See Athanase d'Alexandrie, *Les Trois Discours contre les Ariens*, Donner
raison 15, Traduction et notes Adelin Rousseau, ouverture et guide de lecture René
Lafontaine (Bruxelles: Lessius, 2004) 83-84 and 94-103.

[72]See the Arian, *Tractatus in Lucae Euangelium* 4.18 (PL Suppl 1:335-36).

[73]Augustine of Hippo, *Contra Maximinum* 2.16.3 (PL 42,782-83).

[74]Hilarius of Poitiers, *De Trinitate* 11.18 (SC 462, 328-30).

eventually became the correct interpretation of Jesus' unction: a) there is a necessity, an economical necessity for this unction and b) it concerns not the divine nature of Christ, but his humanity.

Once the orthodox interpretation was secured, the same verse, Acts 10:38, served as support for arguments in the subsequent controversy on the divinity of the Spirit: if the Son is as divine as the Father, then the Spirit who anoints the Son cannot be of an inferior nature. All three are God: the Father who is the subject (the one who anoints), the Son who is anointed and the Spirit who is the agent of the anointing. It would be unacceptable to believe that the Spirit who has anointed the Son was less important than the Son was.[75]

The intense activity of the Holy Spirit in Acts provided ample support for theologians such as Basil the Great, who some years before the Ecumenical Council of Constantinople (381 CE) searched out every witness he could find to support the authority and independence of the Holy Spirit. The πνεῦμα, being subject of the verb, urging Peter to follow Cornelius's embassy (Acts 10:19), is at once considered in his divine nature and autonomy.[76]

There are four other settings, and consequently four other genres, that were favorable for an appropriation of the book of Acts.

(a) Monasticism understood itself as a faithful representation of early Christian ethical ideals: the summaries of Acts, describing what the Middle Ages would call the *uita apostolica*, served as the model and norm for the monastic movement.[77] Passages from Acts 2 and 4, particularly Acts 2:44; 2:45; 4:32 and 4:35, appear as scriptural authority in the *Rules* of Basil the

---

[75]See Bovon, *De Vocatione Gentium* 231-33.

[76]See Basil of Caesarea, *De Spiritu Sancto* 19.49.

[77]See Pier Cesare Bori, *Chiesa primitiva. L'immagine della comunità delle origini: "Atti 2,42-47; 4,32-37" nella storia della chiesa antica*, Testi e ricerche di scienze religiose 10 (Brescia: Paideia, 1974).

Great[78] as well as the rules of the West, the *Regula Magistri*,[79] and the Benedictine *Regula*[80].

(b) From the time of Eusebius, when Christian historiography was born, no one could write the origins of the church without reference to the book of Acts.[81] Even if Eusebius used other material (such as the apocryphal story of King Abgar) and, referring to the succession of bishops, framed the origins of the church differently from Luke, all the historians if they are describing the origin of Christianity in their *Ecclesiastical Histories* depend heavily on Acts. This remained true until deep into the Byzantine period, for example in the case of Nicephoros Callixtos Xanthopoulos who writes in the 14th century.[82]

(c) The fourth century was also a century of Christian poetry, written in Greek, Latin, and Syriac. It is enough to mention Prudentius, who in a short poem of four verses tells the story of Peter's vision and interprets it as the calling of all nations:

Peter sees in a dream a vessel descending from heaven,
Filled with all kinds of animals, he refuses to eat them

---

[78]Basil of Caesarea, *Reg. fus. tract.* 7.4; 19.1; 35.3 (PG 31, 933, 968 and 1008) and *Reg. breu. tract.* 93; 131; 135; 148; 183; 187 (PG 31, 1148, 1169, 1172, 1180, 1204-1205 and 1208).

[79]See *Regula magistri* 13.12 (Judas's fault, Acts 1:15, as a bad example); 20.5 (pray for those who are absent as in Acts 12:5 for the absent Peter); 53.26 (abstain from red and bloody meat, allusion to Acts 15:29); 82.20–21 (do not possess anything and do not follow Ananias and Sapphira's bad example, Acts 5:1–11); 87.14 (allusion to Acts 4:34); 87.15 (allusion to Acts 4:35); and 87.34 (when entering the monastery the future monk should not hide anything in order to be different from Ananias and Sapphira, Acts 5:1–11).

[80]Benedictine Rule 33–34 (Acts 4:32 for the requirement of poverty; Acts 4:35 for a fair and equitable repartition among all); 55 (responsibility of the abbot to care for the well-being of every monk, that no one lacks what he needs); and 55 (avoid fraud and do not follow Ananias and Sapphira's bad example, Acts 5:1–11).

[81]On Eusebius and Luke, see Francois Bovon, "The Apostolic Memories in Ancient Christianity," and "Eusebius of Caesarea's Ecclesiastical History and the History of Salvation," both in *Studies in Early Christianity* (Grand Rapids MI: Baker Academic, 2003) 1-15, 271-83, and the bibliography supplied there.

[82]See Nicephoros Callixtos Xanthopoulos, *Historia ecclesiastica* 1.37-2.46 (PG 145, 714-889).

But the Lord commands him to look on all things as wholesome,
He arises and calls unclean tribes to the heavenly mysteries.[83]

In this same work, *Dittochaeus*, one finds three other poems based on the book of Acts: *Ditt.* 44 (45) on the story of Stephen; *Ditt.* 45 (46) Peter at the Golden Door; and *Ditt.* 47 (48) Paul's conversion. This work is dated 400 CE, that is, the same year as, at the other end of the empire, Chrysostom preached on Acts.[84]

(d) Christian art began with Old Testament scenes, then welcomed the gospel story of Jesus as a young and powerful man. We have to wait until the fourth century to see illustrations from the book of Acts. Fourth century CE sarcophagi and early fifth century CE ivories display scenes from stories related to the canonical Acts of the Apostles, while others have their origin in the apocryphal *Acts of Peter* and *Acts of Paul*.[85] Peter's denial of Jesus derives of course from the canonical gospels as Peter's arrest is likely based on the apocryphal *Acts of Peter*.

While few works of art themselves have been preserved, we have literary sources that bear witness to their existence: The *Liber pontificalis ecclesiae Ravennatis* compiled by Agnellus in the ninth century tells us that Neon, bishop of Ravenna in the fifth century, had several biblical episodes painted on the walls of his episcopal palace in Ravenna.[86] One wall was devoted to Peter, and Agnellus transcribed for us the hexameters that accompanied this painting, which he was still able to read in the ninth century: from these verses it appears that Peter's vision of the pure and

---

[83]Somniat inlapsum Petrus alto ex aethere discum Confertum omnigenis animalibus: Ille recusat Mandere, sed dominus iubet omnia munda putare. Surgit et inmundas uocat ad mysteria gentes. *Dittochaeus* 46 (47 in the English translation; CCSL 126, 399); see *The Poems of Prudentius*, 2 vols., trans. M. Clement Eagan, The Fathers of the Church (Washington DC: Catholic University of America Press, 1965) 2:194.

[84]On Prudentius, see Pierre de Labriolle, *Histoire de la littérature latine chrétienne*, 2 vols., 3rd ed., revue et augmentée par Gustave Bardy, Études anciennes (Paris: Belles Lettres, 1947) 327-417.

[85]See Herbert L. Kessler, "Scenes from the Acts of the Apostles on Some Early Christian Ivories," *Gesta* 18 (1979): 109-19. I am grateful to Mikeal C. Parsons who drew my attention to this article.

[86]Agnellus of Ravenna, *Liber pontificalis ecclesiae Rauennatis*, ed. Deborah Mauskopf Deliyannis, CCCM 199 (Turnhout: Brepols, 2006) 177.

impure animals was represented on one wall.[87] It is certain that other stories from the canonized Acts of the Apostles were represented in mosaics and painted on walls, ceilings, and the floors of churches and bishops' palaces. The ascension (Luke 24:50-53 and Acts 1:9-11) appears on the upper right of a Munich plaque.[88] Sapphira and Ananias's punishment (Acts 5:1-11) is represented on an ivory lipsanotheca in Brescia.[89] The earliest representation of the Pentecost that I know is the one preserved in the *Rabbula Codex*, a manuscript of the end of the sixth century CE.[90]

A point to be made is that the apostles are very much present in Christian art from the fourth century on, but they often represent a collegium, a group of the twelve disciples establishing the foundation of the church from a dogmatic position that existed independently from the narrative of the book of Acts. The same is true of the *Traditio legis*: Jesus giving the new law of the gospel to Peter at his right side and to Paul at his left.[91] These are doctrinal representations. In the less numerous cases of narrative representation, to our surprise the non-canonical scenes (Peter before Nero, Paul and Thecla, etc.) are as numerous as the canonical acts.[92] This observation may confirm Chrysostom's judgment that the book of Acts was not popular in late antiquity.

By way of summarizing the presence of representations from the book of Acts in Christian art, we may say the following: (a) pictorial representations of the book of Acts are late, for knowledge of this book spread slowly; (b) these representations were threatened by the success of apocryphal stories on the apostles; (c) these images were also marginalized by the presence of a collective and abstract image of the apostles as

---

[87]See Bovon, *De Vocatione Gentium*, 164-65.

[88]See Kessler, "Scenes," 109-10.

[89]See Kessler, "Scenes," 110.

[90]On the *Rabbula Codex*, see Robert S. Nelson, "Rabbula Gospels," in *The Oxford Dictionary of Byzantium*, 3 vols. (Oxford UK: Oxford University Press, 1991) 3:1769.

[91]On the *Traditio legis*, see Yves Christe, "Apocalypse et 'Traditio legis'," *Römische Quartalschrift für christliche Altertumskunde und Kirchengeschichte* 71 (1976): 42-55.

[92]See Georg Stuhlfauth, *Die apokryphen Petrusgeschichten in der altchristlichen Kunst* (Berlin: de Gruyter, 1925) and Bovon, *De Vocatione Gentium*, 292-95.

collegium (the Twelve Apostles) and the emblematic dual authority of Peter and Paul.

IV. The Sixth Century

It is well known that from the fourth century CE on, the Roman church insisted on the *concordia* of Peter and Paul as the two founders, the two pillars of the Christian community of the capital, of the Roman episcopal see, of the Roman city and its imperial ambition.[93] The scene of the *Traditio legis* on so many sarcophagi as well as the mosaic representations of the two apostles are the visible traces of this ambition. The evolution and rewritings of the *Acts of Peter* under the form of the Pseudo-Marcellus confirm this harmony and coordination of the two apostles of the Western world.[94]

It is in this context that we situate the attempt by a Roman subdeacon, living in the middle of the sixth century, Arator by name, who wanted to salute Pope Vigilius (537–555) and, at the same time, reaffirm the book of Acts as normative authority for the Roman church and its apostolic see. His ambition finds its expression in a long poem recorded in two books. The first book (1076 verses) deals with Acts 1–12 and is devoted to Peter. The second book (1250 verses) deals with Acts 13–28 and is devoted to Paul. Arator chose this division of the book of Acts, while many modern authors prefer to locate the main division at the end of the Jerusalem conference in Acts 15. Arator's diptych is not surprising: it insists on the two heroes, Peter and Paul, of the Roman *concordia* tradition.

In recent decades, there has been a renewed interest in this neglected Christian poet. After a critical edition by A. P. McKinlay in 1951,[95] an article by Klaus Thraede provided an analysis of the structure of the work, its location in Christian Latin poetry of late antiquity, the literary genre of

---

[93]See Hans Lietzmann, *Petrus und Paulus in Rom*, 2nd ed., Arbeiten zur Kirchengeschichte 1 (Berlin-Leipzig: de Gruyter, 1927) and Charles Pietri, "Concordia apostolorum et renovatio urbis," *Mélanges d'archéologie et d'histoire* 73 (1961): 275-322.

[94]See Gérard Poupon, "Fiche signalétique: Les Actes de Pierre," in *Les Actes apocryphes des apôtres: Christianisme et monde païen*, Publications de la Faculté de théologie de l'Université de Genève 4 (Geneva: Labor et Fides, 1981) 299-301.

[95]*Aratoris subdiaconi de Actibus apostolorum*, ed. A. P. McKinlay, CSEL 72 (Vienna: Hoelder-Pichler-Tempski, 1951).

the two books, its motifs and topics, its exegetical method, its general tendency, and its dependence on Latin epic literature.[96] In 1987, Richard J. Schrader, Joseph L. Roberts III, and John F. Makowski offered an English translation with an introduction.[97] In 1993 Richard Hillier presented a monograph that particularly treated the baptismal context of Arator's focus.[98] Finally, in 2006 the Corpus Christianorum Series Latina published an exhaustive critical edition of the 27 Latin manuscripts by A. P. Orbán.[99] Arator's success in the Middle Ages is particularly impressive. While many modern philologists take the position that Arator's poem is the "worst of poems on an excellent subject,"[100] Cassiodorus, Beda Venerabilis, Rabanus Maurus, and many other medieval writers appreciated and used his work extensively. The age, number, and quality of the manuscripts are also indicative of his success. Bede, for example, says that "[Arator] has aided me most, who going through the same book chapter by chapter in heroic poetry, added not a few flowers of allegory in the same meter."[101] Arator himself presents his work to Pope Vigilius in this way:

> There is a burning in my mind to celebrate the labors of those [Apostles] by whose voice faith obtains a path in the world. Therefore, I shall sing in verses the Acts that Luke related, and following his account I shall speak true poetry. [And he adds in a significant way:] I shall disclose alternately what the letter makes known and whatever mystical sense is revealed in my heart.[102]

---

[96]Klaus Thraede, "Arator. Nachtrag zum RAC," *JAC* 4 (1961): 187–96.

[97]Richard J. Schrader, Joseph L. Roberts III, and John F. Makowski, *Arator's on the Acts of the Apostles* (Atlanta: Scholars Press, 1987).

[98]Richard Hillier, *Arator on the Acts of the Apostles: A Baptismal Commentary* (Oxford UK: Clarendon, 1993). See also Bruno Bureau, *Lettre et sens mystique dans l'"Historia apostolica" d'Arator: Exégèse et épopée*, Études augustiniennes: Antiquité 153 (Paris: Études augustiniennes, 1997).

[99]*Aratoris subdiaconi: Historia apostolica*, ed. A. P. Orbán, CCSL 130, 130A (Turnhout, Belgium: Brepols, 2006).

[100]According to Eleanor S. Duckett, quoted by R. Schrader et al., *Arator's on the Acts of the Apostles*, 3.

[101]Bede The Venerable, *Expositio Actuum apostolorum*, Praefatio 19-22 (CCSL 121, 4); see R. Schrader et al., *Arator's on the Acts of the Apostles*, 3.

[102]*Epistula ad Vigilium* 17-22 (CCSL 130, 214); trans. R. Schrader et al., *Arator's on the Acts of the Apostles*, 22.

This quotation, as well as Bede's witness, make it clear that Arator's poem tends to trespass the literal understanding of the Lukan text of Acts and uncover spiritual meanings. At the end of his rewriting of the story of Cornelius, Arator focuses less on the calling of the Gentiles and more on Peter, who is understood allegorically not as a fisherman, but as a hunter eager to catch the Gentiles as spoils. This passage also helps us understand that—besides the allegorical tendency—Arator's primary intention is to offer a panegyricum of the first apostle to Pope Vigilius, who was Peter's worthy successor.

I must add that the poet, before displaying a section of his hexameters, offers a summary in prose of the biblical passage from Acts he intends to reframe in poetic form. For example, the introduction to verses 552–85 (on the ordination of the Seven, Acts 6) reads as follows: "Concerning the occasion on which seven deacons were ordained—among them Stephen was chosen—because the Apostles had said that it was fitting for them to devote themselves rather to the word of preaching than to waiting on tables for the people."[103] He then continues in a poetic manner:

> The powers of the ministry appropriate to the holy altars were established in seven men, chosen from everywhere, whom it was decided to call Levites [deacons]. How gloriously in the band of the Church began to shine, so as to mix the cup of life and offer the water with the blood of the Lamb! The glory conferred by this number [seven] carries along with it sublime mysteries, which the dimensions of my [poetic] journey do not allow me to pursue further now, lest speaking more I be found to have said less.[104]

Let me conclude that later on, erudite theologians tried to collect and preserve the Christian heritage during a time of war and decline. One of them, Cassiodorus (ca. 580 CE), a former member of the Roman senate, in his retreat at the Vivarium presents and summarizes the book of Acts.[105] His intention is to transmit this heritage of the origins of Christianity to his

---

[103]Trans. R. Schrader et al., *Arator's on the Acts of the Apostles*, 41.

[104]Trans. R. Schrader et al., *Arator's on the Acts of the Apostles*, 41; on Arator's work see also Bovon, *De Vocatione Gentium*, 14-18. ·

[105]See Cassiodorus, *Complexiones Actuum apostolorum* (PL 70, 1381-1406); see Bovon, *De Vocatione Gentium*, 18-20.

brothers, the monks. In simplifying the biblical text, he helps the monks exercise their memory and remember the essentials of the biblical books.[106]

If this work constitutes the protective ending of late antiquity, one century later Bede's commentary on Acts, followed by a *Liber retractationis in Actus apostolorum* (PL 92, 995–1032), mark a renewal, the beginning of the medieval interpretation of Acts. But this is another topic.[107]

---

[106]Cassiodorus, *De institutione diuinarum litterarum* 1.9.1 (PL 70, 1122) refers to John Chrysostom's collection of fifty-five homilies on Acts and its translation in Latin.

[107]Bede The Venerable, *Super Acta apostolorum Expostio* (PL 92, 937–96); *Liber retractationis in Actus apostolorum* (PL 92, 995–1032); see Bovon, *De Vocatione Gentium*, 20.

Acts and the Structure
of the Christian Bible

David E. Smith

It is easy to assume that the book of Acts was canonized because of the
association of its traditional author, Luke, with the apostle Paul, and/or because of the canonical status of Luke's Gospel. But is this a sufficient explanation for the canonization of Acts? It is necessary to examine both the
text of Acts itself and the patristic use of Acts to determine the reason for
its canonization, its influence on the structure of the Bible, and its function
vis-a-vis the other biblical texts. The latest method used by canon scholars
to answer these kinds of questions is canon criticism, or the canonical-criti-
cal method. The primary operative principle for canon critics is the principle
of value.[1] Texts were canonized by the Jews and Christians of antiquity
because they held significant value for the canonizing communities. Why
was the book of Acts canonized? Of what value was it to the church fathers
who recognized its authority? It is my thesis that Acts functioned for the
fathers as the literary unifier of Scripture and that this function was a major
factor in its canonization.[2] As such, it provided a basis for the appropriation

---

[1]James Sanders has articulated this principle most explicitly and convincingly
in his works on the canon. See, e.g., his *Canon and Community: A Guide to Canonical Criticism* (Philadelphia: Fortress Press, 1984).

[2]For a fuller treatment of this thesis, see David E. Smith, *The Canonical Function of Acts: A Comparative Analysis* (Collegeville MN: Liturgical Press, 2002).
Acts was also used in the late patristic age to support the notion of apostolic succession (cf. Acts 20), something which had been defended primarily on the basis of
oral tradition during the second century. Other canon scholars have recognized a
limited unifying role for Acts in early Christianity, without fully developing the
thesis. For example, F. F. Bruce, drawing on the work of Harnack, acknowledged
that for the early Christians, Acts bridged the gap between the gospels and the
epistles. Bruce, *The Canon of Scripture* (Downers Grove IL: InterVarsity Press,
1988) 132-33. Likewise, Harry Gamble concluded that Irenaeus's use of Acts *suggests* that he valued it as evidence of the unity of the apostles, but then claims that
for Irenaeus, "authority of Acts . . . rests on the belief that its author was an inseparable companion of Paul and a disciple of the other apostles." Gamble, *The New Testament Canon: Its Making and Meaning* (Philadelphia: Fortress Press, 1985) 47.
And while hinting that there was some unifying value in Acts, Ernst Haenchen
claimed that "only because of its connection with the third gospel . . . was Acts
allowed to cross the threshold of the Canon." Haenchen, *The Acts of the Apostles:*

of *all* the texts of the developing biblical canon by the church fathers in their disputes with various gnostic opponents, including the Marcionites, and helped the patristic church to weave a fabric of unity with diverse texts.

I. Historical Context

One of the fundamental elements in the gnostic-catholic disputes of the second century and beyond was the issue of theological authority. The nature, extent, and interpretation of the biblical canon were all debated during this time. Was the God of the Old Testament the same God who had displayed divine love in Christ?[3] Were the Scriptures of ancient Israel and Judaism authoritative for the church? Did the apostles possess and publicly proclaim a complete divine revelation? Should "apostolic" writings be placed alongside the Old Testament texts as Scripture? Should they replace the Old Testament? Should there be any written canon at all in the church, and if so, which writings qualified? Debates over these and other issues related to theological authority were front and center during the early centuries of Christianity and they forced the church to clearly define the structure of its canon and creed.

II. The Structure of Acts

It is in this historical context that Acts is first used by the church fathers to argue for the *unity* of the Old Testament and the teachings of Jesus, the Jerusalem apostles, and Paul. That is, Acts seems to function for the fathers as a sort of "miniature Bible"—an organizing centerpiece. When the structure of the Bible is identified, clues to the role of Acts as a unifier of Scripture begin to emerge. If the key authoritative figures in biblical history are identified as the Israelite prophets, Jesus, the Jerusalem apostles (that is, Peter, John, and James the brother of Jesus [Gal 2:9]), and Paul, then we have a corresponding representation in the canon. The Old Testament represents the prophets, the Gospels represent Jesus, Paul's Epistles represent

---

A Commentary, ed. and trans. Bernard Noble, Gerald Shinn, Hugh Anderson, and R. McL. Wilson (Philadelphia: Westminster, 1971) 9.

[3]I use the designation "Old Testament" rather than "Hebrew Bible" in this essay for two reasons. First, I am looking at Scripture from a patristic (Christian) perspective. Second, because of the widespread use of the LXX during the patristic age, the use of "Hebrew Bible" to designate the pre-Christian Scriptures of the church in this period seems somewhat inaccurate.

Paul, and the General Epistles and Revelation represent the Jerusalem apostles.[4] But how does Acts fit into this canonical structure? It functions as the "glue" which holds all the pieces together; that is, as the unifier of all the writings. It takes in hand, so to speak, the pronouncements of the prophets of Israel, the ministry of Christ, the preaching of the Jerusalem apostles, and the preaching of Paul, and ties them all together by uniting the *texts* of the Old Testament with the authoritative *persons* of the New Testament—namely, Jesus, the Jerusalem apostles, and Paul—and their teaching ministries. Luke does this by associating the Holy Spirit with each of these canonical authorities.[5]

In Acts the prophets of ancient Israel are credited with speaking by the Holy Spirit and with predicting the outpouring of the Spirit in the last days (1:16; 2:16f; 28:25). Luke claims that Jesus too had been anointed with the Holy Spirit, had given commands through the Holy Spirit, and had promised the outpouring of the Spirit after his ascension (1:2; 1:5; 10:38). Furthermore, the Jerusalem apostles receive the Holy Spirit, speak by the Spirit, and confer the Spirit on others (2:4; 4:31; 5:32; 8:17; 11:28). Paul also is filled with the Spirit after his conversion, preaches by the Spirit, and confers the Spirit on others *like the Jerusalem apostles do* (9:17; 13:2; 13:9; 16:6-7;

---

[4]While technically the Hebrew Bible was structured in a threefold manner (Law, Prophets, Writings), the early Christians tended to read the whole corpus as prophetic literature. This was due largely to the Christological interpretation that they gave to the texts. That is, for them, the entire collection pointed to the coming of Christ. This is seen in the New Testament itself and in the patristic writings. Even in the writings of Luke—where the technical structure is affirmed (Luke 24)—one gets this sense. E.g., in Acts 2, Peter quoted from a psalm, calling David a "prophet," and applied the text to Christ (vv. 25-31). For an analysis of this phenomenon, see Jack T. Sanders, "The Prophetic Use of the Scriptures in Luke-Acts," in *Early Jewish and Christian Exegesis*, ed. Craig A. Evans and William F. Stinespring (Atlanta: Scholars Press, 1987) 191-93.

[5]For an interesting analysis of Luke's use of the Holy Spirit motif in shaping the characters of Acts, see Luke Timothy Johnson, *The Literary Function of Possessions in Luke-Acts* (Missoula MT: Scholars Press, 1977) 38-60. E.g., Johnson notes that the Paul of Acts looks very much like the Peter of Acts (40). Johnson attributes this to a "more basic understanding of spiritual authority which has shaped his presentation of both figures"—that is, the Holy Spirit, who both initiates and gives shape to the mission and who intervenes at every critical stage of that mission (40-41).

19:6; 20:23; 21:4; 21:11). All of these canonical authorities—prophets, Jesus, Jerusalem apostles, and Paul—are joined together by the Spirit and are thereby connected by Luke to the story of God's ancient and recent self-revelation in human history. *The church fathers inferred from this a theological unity within the writings attributed to these prophetic and apostolic persons, and claimed that a summary of this theology could be found within the book of Acts itself.*

III. Acts and Irenaeus

The first significant use of Acts in the early church is found in the writings of Irenaeus, late second century bishop of Lyons.[6] In his *Against Heresies*, Irenaeus quotes extensively from the book of Acts in an effort to demonstrate the sameness of the God of Israel and the God of the Christians, and the unity of the Old Testament and the preaching of the apostles (including that of Peter, John, James, and Paul). Throughout Book 3, Irenaeus attempts to refute the gnostics in general and Marcion in particular. They denied the validity of the Old Testament and the ministry of some of the apostles who, in their judgment, were too "Jewish" in their understanding of God. Irenaeus makes his case by establishing both the content of and the historical basis for the Rule of Faith. He argues from both oral tradition and Christian texts that were increasingly being recognized as authoritative within the church. Irenaeus is primarily arguing that the Creator—the God of the Old Testament—is also the Redeemer, in opposition to the gnostic bifurcation of the two.

In arguing for the sole legitimacy of catholic beliefs and practices from the texts of the developing New Testament canon, Irenaeus uses the Gospels, then Acts, and finally the Epistles. But he *begins* his biblical case by arguing on the basis of Acts chapter two that *all* the apostles were granted "perfect knowledge" by the Holy Spirit beginning on the day of Pentecost (*Haer.* 3.1.1).[7] He claims this *before* he systematically moves through the

---

[6]Gamble, *New Testament Canon*, 47.

[7]All English Ante-Nicene patristic quotations are taken from *The Ante-Nicene Fathers*, ed. Alexander Roberts and James Donaldson (Repr.: Peabody MA: Hendrickson, 2004). English post-Nicene quotations are taken from *Nicene and Post-Nicene Fathers*, 1st ser., ed. Philip Schaff (Repr.: Peabody MA: Hendrickson, 2004); and *Nicene and Post-Nicene Fathers*, 2nd ser., ed. Philip Schaff and Henry Wace (Repr.: Peabody MA: Hendrickson, 2004). All Greek patristic quotations are

Gospels, Acts, and Epistles adducing evidence against the gnostics. The experience of Pentecost is historically and theologically foundational for Irenaeus, and his use of the episode here gives us a glimpse of the canonically foundational nature of Acts for him. Furthermore, Irenaeus makes it clear that the apostles received the same Holy Spirit as the one predicted by the Old Testament. The result is the *linking* of the oracles of the Old Testament prophets with the preaching of the apostles on the basis of Acts 2.

Later in Book 3, Irenaeus continues to argue from the book of Acts for the unity of the preaching of *all* the apostles. He notes that "Peter, together with John, preached to [the multitude] this plain message of glad tidings" (*Haer.* 3.12.3). Furthermore, when Peter speaks, he speaks as a representative of all the apostles and the Jerusalem church. Irenaeus claims that from the words of Peter *in Acts* we can understand what (all) "the apostles" used to preach, the nature of their preaching, and their doctrine of God (*Haer.* 3.12.7). In essence, Acts functions here as a miniature New Testament.

After briefly arguing from the preaching of Philip, Irenaeus continues his case by arguing from Acts that Paul was in agreement with the Jerusalem church and the Twelve in his doctrine. Then Irenaeus boldly declares that from the book of Acts (which here he calls "the very words and acts of the apostles") one can learn that the "whole range" of the apostolic teaching proclaimed one God, who was both Creator and Redeemer (*Haer.* 3.12.11).

After arguing for the unity of the teaching of Paul and that of the Jerusalem church from the account of Paul's sermon at Lystra (in Acts 14), Irenaeus declares that "all [Paul's] Epistles are consonant to these declarations" (*Haer.* 3.12.9). Here we see the important early Christian concept of the New Testament Epistles as *extensions* of the apostolic preaching in Acts, a concept seen in the writings of other fathers like Tertullian, Eusebius, and John Chrysostom as well. For the church fathers, if Acts demonstrates the unified preaching of the apostles, it demonstrates the unity of their writings as well, their writings being extensions of their preaching.

IV. Acts and Tertullian

Tertullian of Carthage, writing in the early third century, reinforces the work of his older contemporary in a number of ways. In his work, *The Pre-*

---

from *Patrologia graeca*, 167 vols., ed. J.-P. Migne (Paris, 1857–1886). Italics are mine and are added for emphasis.

scription, he argues that Peter, James (son of Zebedee), John, and the rest of the apostles did, in fact, "know all things," contrary to the claims of some gnostics. Tertullian claims to know this on the basis of Jesus' promise to the apostles of the Holy Spirit, who would lead them into all truth and, Tertullian says, "assuredly He fulfilled His promise, since it is proved in the Acts of the Apostles that the Holy [Spirit] did come down" (*Praescr.* 22). He asserts that those who reject the book of Acts can neither belong to the Holy Spirit (since they cannot prove that the Spirit had been given) nor can they show when the church was first established. And in his work, *Against Marcion*, he similarly maintains that the promise of the Holy Spirit is shown to have been fulfilled "in *no other* document than the Acts of the Apostles" (*Marc.* 5.2). But because of Acts, Tertullian believes that the promise of the Spirit which was predicted by the prophet Joel was "absolutely fulfilled" (*Marc.* 5.8). For Tertullian, theological and canonical claims are difficult to make without the book of Acts because only Luke created a narrative account of the outpouring of the Spirit—a narrative which for Tertullian proves the theological credibility of the apostles and their unity with the prophets of ancient Israel.

V. Acts and Cyril of Jerusalem

The foundational work done by Irenaeus and Tertullian with regard to the canonically unifying function of Acts was incorporated into the works of subsequent church fathers. Next I examine the works of two fourth-century writers—Cyril of Jerusalem and John Chrysostom—as testimony to this. These two fathers are representative of catholic thought during the century when the New Testament canon took its final form. Furthermore, they provide the contemporary scholar with two different genres for analysis: the catechism and the commentary.

Cyril's *Catechetical Lectures* provides a rather comprehensive overview of catholic doctrine during the mid-fourth century. In his lecture on the Holy Spirit, Cyril finds great value in Acts as a source for pneumatology. In this context he asserts, "There is [only] One . . . Holy [Spirit] . . . He was in the Prophets, He was also in the Apostles in the New Testament" (*Catech.* 16.3). He goes on to say:

> Let no one therefore separate the Old from the New Testament; let no one
> say that the Spirit in the former is one, and in the latter another; since thus
> he offends against the Holy [Spirit] Himself . . . let the Marcionites be
> silenced . . . we know the Holy [Spirit], who [spoke] in the Prophets, and

who on the day of Pentecost descended on the Apostles in the form of
fiery tongues, here, in Jerusalem, in the Upper Church of the Apostles.
(*Catech.* 16.3)

Here Cyril implies that Acts 2 is evidence that the two Testaments must be
united into one canon. Furthermore, his specific denunciation of the
Marcionites in this context provides testimony to the continuing influence
of the sect and its philosophy of canon in the century normally associated
with the Arian controversy. The polemical use of Acts against Marcion,
inherited from the earlier fathers, has become a part of Cyril's theological
system and his catechetical rhetoric.

Throughout lecture 16, Cyril adduces evidence from various biblical
texts to support his general pneumatology, primarily from the Old
Testament. He ends by stating his intention to use the New Testament in the
next lecture. *In fact*, though, throughout lecture 17 it is *Acts* which functions
as the primary text for his exposition, and the experience of Pentecost is
central. Referring to the account of Jesus' breathing the Spirit on the
apostles in John 20, Cyril asserts that this episode bestowed divine grace
only partially because the apostles were not ready to receive it in full
measure. Cyril notes that Jesus instructs them to wait in Jerusalem for the
outpouring of the Spirit. Then he observes,

So they were sitting, looking for the coming of the Holy [Spirit]; and when
the day of Pentecost was fully come, here, in this city of Jerusalem . . . the
Comforter came down from heaven . . . He came down to clothe the
Apostles with power . . . His power was in full perfection . . . so were they
also baptized completely by the Holy [Spirit] (*Catech.* 17.13-14).

He goes on to contrast the experience of the tower of Babel with the
experience of Pentecost and claims that at Pentecost "minds were restored
and united (ἀποκατάστασις καὶ ἕνωσις τῶν γνώμων[8]), because . . . the self-
same Spirit, continuing what He is, as He had often wrought in Prophets,
now manifested a new and marvellous work" (*Catech.* 17.17-18).

After discussing Peter's Pentecostal sermon, Cyril then says that many
passages are still to come from the Acts of the Apostles in which the grace
of the Holy Spirit wrought mightily "in Peter and in all the Apostles
together;" many others are also promised from the Catholic Epistles and the
Epistles of Paul (*Catech.* 17.20). *In fact*, however, he only touches briefly

---

[8]Literally, "reversal and union of the thoughts."

on the Pauline Epistles and never uses the Catholic Epistles because, he says, "time would fail" him if he did (*Catech.* 17.34). What he does, instead, is continue to use *Acts* to claim that "with this Holy Spirit Paul also had been filled after his calling" (*Catech.* 17.26) and "in the power of the same Holy Spirit Peter also, the chief of the Apostles" conducted his ministry (*Catech.* 17.27). The reader gets the impression that for Cyril, Acts is a sort of "mini-canon" by which he can demonstrate the doctrine of all the apostles.

VI. Acts and John Chrysostom

In his commentary on Acts, John Chrysostom provides evidence of his understanding of the function of Acts within the Christian canon. Commenting on Acts 1-2, he declares, "so replete is [the book of Acts] with Christian wisdom and sound doctrine, *especially* in what is said concerning the Holy [Spirit]" (*Hom. Act.* 1). He goes on to argue that great change took place in the apostles because of the outpouring of the Spirit upon them. Before Pentecost, he exclaims, the apostles were ignorant, fearful, and *divisive*. But after the Spirit was poured out upon them, they became humble and *united*. In fact, he claims that Peter spoke for all twelve apostles in order that they might express themselves "through one common voice" (*Hom. Act.* 4).

But the strongest evidence that Chrysostom regarded Acts as the literary unifier of the canon comes from his comments on Acts 15 (the Jerusalem council). He argues that what *Peter said* at the council regarding salvation by grace through faith agrees with what *Paul wrote* in Romans: "The same that Paul says at large in the Epistle to the Romans, the same says Peter here" (*Hom. Act.* 32). And with regard to Paul's doctrine in 1 Corinthians and Ephesians, Chrysostom declares, "Of all these the seeds lie in Peter's discourse" (*Hom. Act.* 32). So for Chrysostom, the preaching of Peter in Acts *is expanded* in the Epistles of Paul. In a similar manner Chrysostom claims in his comments on Acts 20:32 that what Paul does when writing an epistle he also does when speaking in council (*Hom. Act.* 45). The unity of the apostolic oral proclamation in Acts is, for Chrysostom, extended throughout the writings of the New Testament. Furthermore, he claims that James (the brother of Jesus) "is not divided from [Peter and Paul] in opinion" and that John and the other apostles could have spoken at the Jerusalem council but chose to hold their peace because their souls were free from the "love of glory" (*Hom. Act.* 33). Furthermore, the decree "made in common" stood in agreement with the words of the Old Testament prophets (*Hom. Act.* 33). For Chrysostom, the united apostolic witness in Acts is linked to the oracles of the Old Testament and is extended throughout the writings of the New Testament. He reaches this conclusion from a reading of Acts 2 and 15. Acts clearly functions for him as the literary unifier of the canon.

This canonical function assigned by Chrysostom to Acts is strengthened by a contrast with his commentary on Galatians. The comparison is interesting because Paul does claim in this epistle that the "pillar" apostles (James, Peter, and John) gave him the "right hand of fellowship" (2:9). By this statement (and a few others in Galatians) Chrysostom is able to assert the unity of the apostolic preaching. However, the ambiguity of Paul's relationship with the Jerusalem apostles reflected in Galatians is also clearly a problem for Chrysostom. In his comments on 1:1-3 he observes, "that this Epistle breathes an indignant spirit, is obvious to every one even on the first perusal" (*Hom. Gal.* 1.1-3). With regard to the question of the lateness of Paul's apostolic call (1:15-16), Chrysostom admits that although he knows that his hearers desire an answer, he cannot provide one; they must beg God to reveal it to them (*Hom. Gal.* 1.15-16). In his comments on Galatians 1:17 ("nor did I go up to Jerusalem to those who were already apostles before me"), Chrysostom acknowledges that these words do seem to display "an arrogant spirit" (*Hom. Gal.* 1.17). In fact, though he argues for apostolic unity, he must go to great lengths throughout the commentary on chapters one and two to demonstrate this, even arguing that Paul's rebuke of Peter at Antioch was a prearranged charade which the apostles carried out for educational reasons, and admitting that "many, on a superficial reading of this part of the Epistle, suppose that Paul accused Peter of hypocrisy"— something which Chrysostom denies (*Hom. Gal.* 2.11-12). It is evident that for the archbishop (and for the "many" who read the letter otherwise), Galatians could not function as the unifier of the canon, notwithstanding the scattered comments on the unity of the apostles which it contains. This role was reserved for Acts, whose function—along with the structure of the entire Christian Bible—can be illustrated as follows.

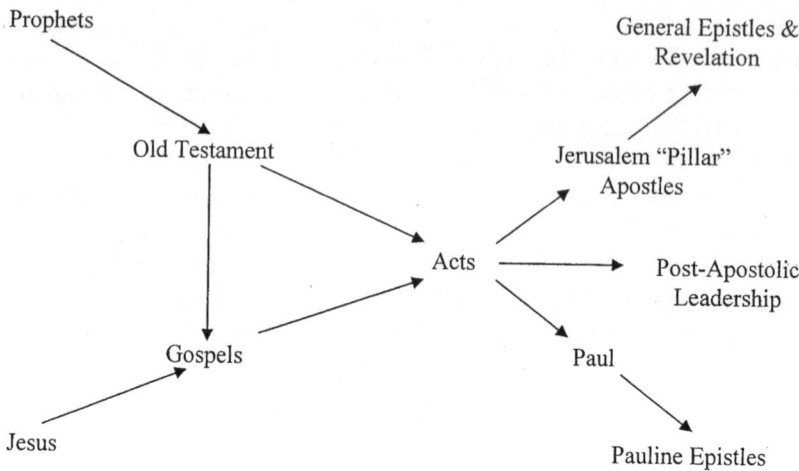

Conclusion

It is no coincidence that the canonical status of Acts was never seriously questioned by great church leaders throughout the Mediterranean world after the early third century. While the association of its author Luke with the apostle Paul gave the text *a priori* authority, it was the value of the content of Acts that seems to have thrust it into the heart of the biblical canon. By uniting the ministries of the prophets, Jesus, the Jerusalem apostles, and Paul, Luke provided a paradigm that would help the church to weave a fabric of unity with texts as diverse as Leviticus and Romans, Job and Proverbs, Galatians and James, the Synoptics and John. And, perhaps unwittingly, Luke and those who canonized his work thereby sanctioned a measure of diversity within Christianity itself.

The Rhetorical Function of Refutation in Acts 6–7 and 10–15[1]

Julien C. H. Smith

En route to becoming an orator in antiquity, one progressed through the *progymnasmata*, preliminary exercises whose goal was to inculcate the basics of compositional style in the student. Central to the *progymnasmata* was the exercise of refutation (ἀνασκευή), by which one was taught to overturn and demolish the arguments of an opponent. While the extent of Luke's rhetorical training cannot be ascertained, it seems more than likely that he cut his literary teeth on at least these preliminary exercises.[2] The ubiquity of refutation in Acts strongly suggests that his compositional training left an indelible mark on his literary style.[3] While many instances of refutation may be of limited exegetical significance, one may observe passages in which refutation appears to be playing a rhetorically significant role. This paper argues that Acts 6–7 and 10–15 must be read in the context of Luke's larger apologetic aim of defending Christian messianists as legitimate heirs of the traditions of Israel. As such, these sections of the

---

[1] I thank Charles Talbert and Mikeal Parsons for reading this paper and offering suggestions. In addition, I am grateful to Dr. Parsons for introducing me to the world of ancient rhetoric.

[2] On "the fruitfulness of looking to the *progymnasmata* for clues to the rhetorical strategies Luke employed in communicating his story," see Mikeal C. Parsons, "Luke and the *Progymnasmata*: A Preliminary Investigation into the Preliminary Excercises," in *Contextualizing Acts: Lukan Narrative and Greco-Roman Discourse*, ed. Todd C. Penner and Caroline Vander Stichele, SBLSymS (Atlanta: Society of Biblical Literature, 2003) 43–64. The lifelong effect of *paideia* upon both the literary ability and moral character of a person is helpfully discussed in Raffaella Cribiore, *Gymnastics of the Mind: Greek Education in Hellenistic and Roman Egypt* (Princeton NJ: Princeton University Press, 2001) 220.

[3] Statements and accusations are overturned in nearly every chapter of Acts. The following examples should suffice to illustrate this fact: Peter refutes the claim that the disciples are drunk (2:13–17); Peter and John refute the command to remain silent (4:18–20; cf. similar refutation in 5:27–29); the twelve refute the implied suggestion that the apostles should have a direct hand in remedying the inequitable food distribution (6:1–2); Peter refutes the divine command to eat unclean food; the divine voice in turn refutes Peter (10:13–15); and Peter refutes the implication of his divinity by Cornelius (10:25–26; cf. 14:12–15).

narrative are principally concerned to refute claims to the contrary, with which the authorial audience of Acts may have been familiar.

The concern to legitimate the messianist community in the face of accusations is a feature consistent with Greco-Roman and Jewish succession narratives, with which Luke-Acts shares many similarities.[4] Acts 6–7 will be shown to refute the claim that the messianists are illegitimate claimants to Israel's traditions because they speak against the temple and the customs of Moses. Acts 10–15 will be shown to refute the accusation of illegitimacy against the messianists on the grounds that they welcome uncircumcised Gentiles as full members into their community. The primary goal of this essay is to demonstrate the role that refutation plays within the rhetoric of these passages and within the larger argument of Acts. Secondarily, an understanding of these passages as argumentative discourse concerning the legitimacy of the messianists may challenge any reading that sees them as merely reflective of what has been referred to as Luke's "fundamental and systematic hostility towards Jews."[5]

Refutation in Ancient Rhetoric

Writers of *progymnasmata* considered the exercise of refutation (ἀνασκευή) to be crucial to the art of rhetoric.[6] In simplest terms, "Refutation is an

---

[4]A succession narrative "serves a variety of goals but is usually associated with the desire to show continuity in a given area, to guarantee preservation of something, *to legitimate* or authenticate." Charles H. Talbert, *Reading Luke-Acts in Its Mediterranean Milieu*, NovTSup 107 (Leiden: Brill, 2003) 42, emphasis added.

[5]This is the appraisal of Luke-Acts in general by Jack T. Sanders, *The Jews in Luke-Acts* (Philadelphia: Fortress, 1987) xvi. A more positive reading of Luke's treatment of the Jews can be found in Jacob Jervell, *Luke and the People of God: A New Look at Luke-Acts* (Minneapolis: Augsburg, 1972). The contours of this debate may be found in Joseph B. Tyson, *Luke, Judaism, and the Scholars: Critical Approaches to Luke-Acts* (Columbia: University of South Carolina Press, 1999).

[6]According to Aphthonius, "This progymnasmata includes in itself all the power of the art [of rhetoric]" (*Prog.* 28.3–4). The Greek text of the various *progymnasmata* may be found in *Rhetores Graeci*, 3 vols., ed. Leonard Spengel (Leipzig: Teubner, 1853–1856). Line citations are from this edition (vol. 2: Theon, Hermogenes, Aphthonius; vol. 3: Nicolaus). English translations are taken from *Progymnasmata: Greek Textbooks of Prose Composition and Rhetoric*, ed. and trans. George Alexander Kennedy, Writings from the Greco-Roman World 10 (Atlanta: Society of Biblical Literature, 2003).

overturning of some matter at hand" (Aphthonius, *Prog.* 27.25). As described by Theon, the exercise is deceptively simple: one refutes a statement by asserting that the opposite is true, *or* by demonstrating that similar things are equally false (*Prog.* 121.18–123.2). Refutation is not, however, simply a matter of saying "not X," but rather of skillfully demonstrating the variety of bases upon which "not X" is seen to be true. Students were taught to refute claims, for example, on the basis of what was in accordance with "common manners and customs," or what was considered "reverent . . . either pleasing to the gods or to the dead" (Theon, *Prog.* 122.4–5; cf. Hermogenes, *Prog.* 8.29–9.16). Later composers of *progymnasmata* stress that only *credible* claims need be refuted: "No attempt should be made to argue against or for things that are entirely false, like fables, but clearly there is need to compose refutations and confirmations of things open to argument on either side" (Hermogenes, *Prog.* 8.30–9.4). Nicolaus explains the rationale behind this strategy: "for by (attempted) refutation of acknowledged truths we shall not seem truthful—for no one will pay attention—nor by refuting falsehoods either—for no one needs to be persuaded" (*Prog.* 466.18–22).[7]

The remarks of Quintilian suggest that with regard to arrangement and style, a student would have felt considerable latitude to freely compose a refutation in such manner as to be persuasive to the audience.[8] The order in which one structured the refutation was not critical, since one needed to be flexible to respond to repeated and varied objections (*Inst.* 5.13.53). Those who devise a strict order for refutation "are thrown into confusion by the necessities of real conflict" (*Inst.* 5.13.59). Quintilian scoffs at rigid adherence to "these petty rules, which make us behave like little children tracing the shapes of the letters or (as the Greeks say) carefully keeping to

---

[7]Cf. Aphthonius, *Prog.* 27.26–27; John of Sardis, *Prog.* 67–71. In a similar vein, Quintilian advises that, when faced with an irrefutable argument, it may be "best treated with contempt as trivial or irrelevant to the Cause . . . and the pretense sometimes succeeds to the point that we trample down, as it were, by showing our distaste for them, Arguments which we cannot refute" (*Inst.* 5.13.22).

[8]Such freedom of composition may be detected in Luke's use of *prosopopoieia* (speech in character) in the speeches in Acts, a common literary technique among Greek·historians, George Alexander Kennedy, *New Testament Interpretation Through Rhetorical Criticism* (Chapel Hill: University of North Carolina Press, 1984) 114.

the clothes that mother gave" (*Inst.* 5.14.31). The key consideration in composing an argument was its potential to persuade a given audience rather than its slavish conformity to the rules of rhetoric as found in rhetorical handbooks.[9]

Quintilian also helps one understand the strategic concerns underlying the sometimes sharp tone of ancient rhetoric. In responding to the one leveling the accusation, "occasionally it may be right to criticize not only their speech, but their way of life, their expression, their walk, or their bearing. . . . This move is more permissible against the accusers, whom one's duty as defense advocate sometimes obliges one to insult" (*Inst.* 5.13.39–40). Quintilian's instructions lend further support to the study by Luke Timothy Johnson, which demonstrates that the caustic tone of intra-Jewish polemic in the ancient world is to be understood in the context of Hellenistic philosophical rhetoric.[10]

By way of summary, one notes the following: (1) The exercise of refutation was an essential component of argumentative discourse. (2) Among later progymnasmatists, only credible accusations were considered worthy of refutation. (3) With regard to style and order, the actual composition of a refutation was dependent upon the exigencies of the situation. (4) When faced with an irrefutable argument, insult and contempt were considered fair game. The following analysis of Acts 6–7 and 10–15 will focus on evidence of refutation as a marker of argumentative discourse,

---

[9]That actual speeches deviated from the guidelines of rhetorical handbooks has been amply demonstrated. See Margaret M. Mitchell, *Paul and the Rhetoric of Reconciliation: An Exegetical Investigation of the Language and Composition of 1 Corinthians* (Louisville: Westminster/John Knox, 1991).

[10]One should add that Luke's polemical language directed toward Jews is fairly mild in contrast to the hostility sometimes expressed between rival Jewish groups. At Qumran, for example, the "rule of thumb is that you cannot say enough bad things about outsiders." Luke Timothy Johnson, "The New Testament's Anti-Jewish Slander and the Conventions of Ancient Polemic," *JBL* 108 (1989): 430. This is not to bestow a moral stamp of approval on such expression simply because it was conventional. It does, however, help one understand Luke's rhetoric (and that of the New Testament more broadly) vis-à-vis the Jews as primarily connotative, rather than denotative.

which sheds light on the function of these passages in the larger context of group legitimation.

Refutation in the Rhetoric of Acts

A. Acts 6–7. Acts 6:8–7:60 narrates the charges brought before Stephen in the council, his lengthy response, and subsequent death by stoning. Stephen is accused both of speaking against the temple, which Jesus will supposedly destroy, and against the customs of Moses, which Jesus will supposedly alter (6:13, 14). The purpose of the speech, as Howard Clark Kee has observed, is to assure the readers/hearers that the good news which is being proclaimed in no way undermines Mosaic custom.[11] It has been remarked, however, that Stephen's speech bears little relation to the charges brought against him.[12] On the contrary, it may be seen how Stephen masterfully refutes both of these accusations in 7:2–53, by means of a selective rehearsal of Israelite history, in which he weaves the themes of "place" (τόπος, 6:13) and "law/custom" (νόμος/ἔθος, 6:13-14). He begins with Abraham, establishing first that God indeed planned to bring the descendants of Abraham to serve God "in this place" (7:2–7). His concluding mention of the "covenant of circumcision" links law/custom with place (7:8).

In his narration of the sojourn in Egypt (the foreign land in 7:6–7), Stephen notes that Joseph is betrayed by his brothers, yet thanks to God's presence with him, is able to save his people (7:9–16). Similarly, Moses is

---

[11]Howard Clark Kee, *To Every Nation under Heaven: The Acts of the Apostles* (Harrisburg PA: Trinity Press International, 1997) 95–96.

[12]So Hans Conzelmann, *Acts of the Apostles: A Commentary on the Acts of the Apostles*, trans. James Limburg et al., ed. Eldon Jay Epp and Christopher R. Matthews, Hermeneia (Philadelphia: Fortress, 1987) 57; F. F. Bruce, "Stephen's Apologia," in *Scripture: Meaning and Method*, ed. Barry P. Thompson (Hull, England: Hull University Press, 1987) 39; Sanders, *Jews*, 247; Ernst Haenchen, *The Acts of the Apostles: A Commentary*, ed. and trans. Bernard Noble et al. (Oxford UK: Blackwell; Philadelphia: Westminster, 1971) 286. By contrast, it has been noted that while Stephen's line of thought is not determined by the charges, he does not ignore them. Robert C. Tannehill, *The Acts of the Apostles*, vol. 2 of *The Narrative Unity of Luke-Acts: A Literary Interpretation* (Minneapolis: Fortress, 1990) 85, and John J. Kilgallen, "The Function of Stephen's Speech (Acts 7,2–53)," *Bib* 70 (1989): 185.

rejected by his people (7:27–28), and later becomes their ruler and deliverer (7:34). Tucked in between Moses's rejection by his people and his deliverance of them, is an excursus on sacred place. Fleeing his people who suffer as aliens in Egypt, Moses himself becomes an alien in Midian (7:29). It is here, when Moses is seemingly twice removed from the land of promise (that is, doubly an alien), that God appears to him in a holy place (7:33). Concerning Moses, Stephen informs his accusers that (1) he prophesied the coming of a prophet like himself (that is, Jesus, 7:37); (2) he did indeed receive living oracles to pass on to the Israelites (7:38); but (3) the Israelites were disobedient, repudiating Moses (7:39). As a result of the Israelites' idolatry (7:40–41, 43), God declared that it was not in fact God whom they were worshipping (7:42), and God vowed to remove them to a foreign place, beyond Babylon (7:43). Thus, God's removal of Israel to a foreign place is the result of their rejecting God's law delivered through Moses (that is, the customs of Moses).[13]

Stephen then turns to the topic of God's dwelling place, tracing its history from the tabernacle in the wilderness (7:44–45) to the temple built by Solomon (7:46–47). Addressing directly the first accusation (speaking against the temple), he concludes that God does not dwell in a temple built by human hands, but rather in heaven. God, whose hand made everything, inquires through the prophet: "What is the place of my resting?" (7:48–50, citing Isaiah 66:1).[14] The accusation that Stephen has spoken against the

---

[13]Luke Timothy Johnson terms this speech a "septuagintal targum" and considers it representative of a class of writings which present a "reworking of the biblical tradition to propagate or defend a specific perspective on that tradition." Johnson, *Septuagintal Midrash in the Speeches of Acts*, the Père Marquette Lecture in Theology (Milwaukee: Marquette University Press, 2002) 25. With regard to the traditions of Joseph and Moses, Johnson notes that "Luke has edited his account in such fashion as to show how each fits into a pattern of twofold sending and rejection, so that these biblical *exempla* point forward to the twofold sending and rejection of the prophet Jesus" (29). Stephen is underlining the prophetic character of Scripture and supporting "the ideological position of his community that Scripture is best understood when read as pointing toward the risen prophet Jesus" (29).

[14]Concerning Luke's treatment of the temple through the mouth of Stephen, Sanders concludes: "Stephen and, indeed, all Christianity à la Luke oppose the Temple and Mosaic custom. Stephen's sermon in the Sanhedrin allows Luke to express his objections to Judaism and to put clearly before his readers the nature of

temple is thus refuted with an argument from the opposite (cf. Theon, *Prog.* 121.18–21): despite the existence of the tabernacle and the temple, God does not dwell in a temple made by human hands. It is important to note that Stephen's refutation does not signify God's replacement or rejection of the temple, but rather God's transcendence of the temple.[15] The implication is that God is not present where one would expect God to be, but is now present where Stephen's accusers least expect (indeed, cannot conceive) God to be. That is, as Luke has already demonstrated in 2:4 and 4:31, God is present through the Holy Spirit in the community of messianists.

Finally, Stephen concludes by addressing the second accusation: speaking against the law. While his accusers may keep the customs of Moses, they are "uncircumcised in heart and ears" (7:51) because they have persecuted and murdered the prophets (7:52) and "rejected the law ordained by angels" (7:53).[16] The further accusation that Stephen has spoken against the customs of Moses is refuted with an argument from the similar (cf.

---

the rift between Judaism and Christianity" (*Jews*, 248). However, one finds a more balanced perspective, which preserves the tension in Stephen's speech, in Robert L. Brawley, "The God of Promises and the Jews in Luke-Acts," in *Literary Studies in Luke-Acts: Essays in Honor of Joseph B. Tyson*, ed. Richard P. Thompson and Thomas E. Phillips (Macon GA: Mercer University Press, 1998) 290: "Stephen upholds Moses and the temple, but finds fault with people who disobeyed the revelation at Sinai and misconstrued the temple as God's residence in the house of Jacob alone (7:46). The citation of Isaiah 66:1–2 is then not an attack on the temple but a proclamation of God's universality. Stephen's speech claims the Abrahamic heritage not only for Israel but for the whole earth."

[15]So Dennis D. Sylva, "The Meaning and Function of Acts 7:46–50," *JBL* 106 (1987): 261–75.

[16]Kennedy (*Interpretation*, 121–22) considers the speech incomplete, in that it lacks an explicit rejection of the council's right to try him, or an epilogue in which he calls for repentance—as is common in Peter's speeches. Kennedy does note, however, that the concluding vision may be seen to function as an epilogue, which would suggest that God, not the council, is the real judge. (Compare Quintilian's discussion of the possibility that one may have to plead for mercy before the judge [*Inst.* 5.13.7].) Kennedy may be correct here, but it should also be noted that Stephen is speaking before yet another judge, the readers of Acts. Thus, while Stephen's speech may be considered incomplete on formal rhetorical-critical grounds, this observation has little bearing on whether Stephen's speech achieves its purpose from the perspective of the reader.

Theon, *Prog.* 122.13–14): just like your fathers, you have rejected God's law and are killing God's prophets. In essence, Stephen is saying, "*We* are not rejecting the customs of Moses; *you* are." It may be asked why Stephen (or Luke) found it necessary to refute the two rather straightforward claims by means of a convoluted narrative rehearsal of Israel's history. One may be helped in answering this question by use of popular idiom: Stephen was "telling his side of the *story*." The story, so to speak, being told about the messianists by their non-messianist co-religionists may have sounded like this: "These folks *claim* to inherit the customs of Moses, but of course this is nonsense, since we are the true inheritors of Moses's customs. We worship God in the temple and observe the law, but these folks wish to destroy the temple and negate the law." It was not only necessary for Luke's audience to understand that this version of the story was false; they needed to be supplied with a competing version of the story that made sense.[17]

B. *Acts 10–15.* Two events concerning the entrance requirements of Gentiles into the messianist community function as bookends to this section of the narrative. These events are related to Stephen's speech in that they touch upon the larger issue of the legitimacy of the messianist community. The first of these is the encounter between Peter and Cornelius (10:1–48), which is followed by Peter's subsequent report to the church in Jerusalem (11:1–19). The second is the council in Jerusalem, which is convened to decide the requirements of Gentile believers vis-à-vis the law (15:1–35). Two significant accusations are refuted within this large section of text. In 11:3, Peter is accused of having eaten with uncircumcised men, and in 15:5, some messianist Pharisees assert that the Gentile messianists in Antioch must be circumcised and must obey the law of Moses. The events of chapter 10 set the stage for both of these later refutations.

In contrast to chapters 6–7, which present the refutation of two specific accusations, chapters 10–15 present an extended argument incorporating refutation at various points. Chapters 10, 11, and 15 are tied together

---

[17]Luke's competing interpretation of the biblical narrative resembles an advanced exercise, in which the student refutes an incredible narrative, while at the same time demonstrating the reason such a narrative came to be regarded as credible. Theon thus writes: "Not only to refute such mythologies, but also to show how such a distorted story originated, is a matter for a more mature skill than most have" (*Prog.* 95.8–11).

thematically by the question, "Is the distinction made between Jews and Gentiles a valid one for determining membership in the community?" These chapters are also tied together lexically, through the use of the verb, διακρίνω, which occurs in Luke-Acts only at 10:20, 11:2, 11:12 and 15:9. Although the basic meaning of the verb is "to make a distinction," its usage in this section of the narrative covers a broad semantic range.[18] Such varied use of a word occurring only here in the Lukan corpus suggests that the reader's attention is to be drawn precisely to this question of making distinctions.[19]

C. Acts 10. The narrative describing Peter's vision (10:9–16) and subsequent encounter with Cornelius (10:17–48) raises the questions of both *how* and *when* Peter understood the vision. In response to the divine voice commanding him to eat from the animals on the sheet, Peter responds, "By no means, Lord, for never have I eaten anything defiled *and* unclean" (μηδαμῶς, κύριε, ὅτι οὐδέποτε ἔφαγον πᾶν κοινὸν καὶ ἀκάθαρτον, 10:14).[20] This may be understood, according to Theon, as a refutation from what is "in accordance with nature and according to the common manners and customs of all [hu]mankind" (*Prog.* 121.26–29). The divine voice responds, "What God has cleansed, you must not consider defiled" (ἃ ὁ θεὸς ἐκαθάρισεν, σὺ μὴ κοίνου, 10:15). This may be understood as a refutation

---

[18]BDAG, s.v. διακρίνω, gives six basic definitions of this verb: (1) to differentiate by separating; (2) to make a distinction; (3) to evaluate, judge; (4) to render a legal decision; (5) to dispute, take issue; (6) to doubt, waver. In 10:20 διακρίνω probably means "to doubt"; in 11:2, "to dispute"; in 11:12, either "to doubt" or "to make a distinction"; and in 15:9, "to make a distinction."

[19]Parsons, "*Progymnasmata*," 56–61, has drawn attention to the rhetorical function of inflection as a way to emphasize the main subject of a fable or narrative. Luke's use of the verb διακρίνω here may be analogous to this rhetorical function.

[20]BDAG, s.v. κοινός, gives one meaning as "common, ordinary, profane," either in a general sense, or in reference to "that which is ceremonially impure" (2b). That the latter meaning is intended is suggested by Luke's use of the related verb κοινόω elsewhere in Acts (10:15; 11:9; 21:28). In 21:28, the verb clearly refers to Paul's alleged defilement of the temple: "he has actually brought Greeks into the temple and has defiled this holy place (κεκοίνωκεν τὸν ἅγιον τόπον τοῦτον)" (NRSV). See further the discussion of "defiled/unclean" terminology elsewhere in Luke-Acts in Mikeal C. Parsons, "'Nothing Defiled AND Unclean': The Conjunction's Function in Acts 10:14," *PRS* 27 (2000): 270.

from what is "reverent; this is two-fold, either pleasing to gods or to the dead" (*Prog.* 122.4–5). In short, the divine voice refutes Peter's refutation.

Mikeal Parsons convincingly makes the case that Peter only progressively understands the vision. Initially, he understands the significance of the vision to be that the clean animals, although made unclean by association with the unclean animals, have been cleansed by God. Yet by the time he speaks to Cornelius, Peter has figured out both that the vision applies to social interactions as well as food, and that κοινόν (defiled) is not the same as ἀκάθαρτον (unclean). The implications of this development are: (1) Jews will be cleansed by God from the ritual impurity of associating with Gentiles; and (2) Gentiles, who are unclean by nature, are now made clean. This is made clear in his explanation to Cornelius in 10:28, "God showed me not to call any person defiled *or* unclean" (κἀμοὶ ὁ θεὸς ἔδειχεν μηδένα κοινὸν ἢ ἀκάθαρτον λέγειν ἄνθρωπον).[21]

Peter's difficulty in interpreting the vision may be signalled by the appearance of διακρίνω in 10:20. The divine voice instructs him to "go with them, *not doubting*, because I have sent them" (πορεύου σὺν αὐτοῖς μηδὲν διακρινόμενος ὅτι ἐγὼ ἀπέσταλκα αὐτούς). Without exception, English translations take the meaning of διακρίνω here to refer to doubting. Although the context does not necessarily require it, there is a further clue in the passage to suggest that "not doubting" is the intended meaning here.[22] In verses 17–20, four verbs with the prefix δια- are used to describe the pondering, inquiring, or doubting of both Peter and the men sent from Cornelius.[23] Thus, while Peter is wondering confusedly about the vision (διηπόρει, 10:17a), the men from Cornelius are inquiring where Simon the tanner's house is (διερωτήσαντες, 10:17b). While Peter continues to ponder the vision (διενθυμουμένου, 10:19), the Spirit tells him that three men are

----

[21]Parsons, "'Nothing Defiled AND Unclean," 263–74. Central to his argument is the rendering of καί in 10:14 as "and," which yields an understanding of κοινόν καὶ ἀκάθαρτον as a hendiadys meaning "impure."

[22]The command would still make sense using definition (3) "go without evaluating, or judging," in which case the emphasis would be upon Peter's trusting the divine voice rather than his own faculty of judgment. Similarly definition (5) "go without disputing, or arguing," would make sense. In this case, presumably Peter would have been told not to argue with the divine voice.

[23]A fifth verb, πυνθάνομαι (inquire, ask, question; learn [by inquiry]), is also used to refer to the envoys' inquiring after Peter (v. 18).

looking for him, and that he is to go with them without doubting (διακρινόμενος, 10:20). The occurrence in proximity of these four verbs with the same prefix and similar semantic range hardly strikes one as accidental. While not corresponding precisely to figures of speech such as reduplication (ἀναδίπλωσις) or synonymy (συνωνυμία), the use of these verbs seems to focus the attention of the reader upon the confusing nature of this unfolding experience, both for Peter and for the envoys of Cornelius.[24] Peter's wondering and pondering is matched by the envoys' inquiring. This lends support to Parsons's argument that Peter did not comprehend the full import of the vision until face to face with Cornelius.

D. *Acts 11*. The encounter between Peter and Cornelius's household makes clear to both Peter and the reader that the distinctions between Jews and Gentiles are no longer to be considered valid for determining membership in the messianist community. This is what Peter must communicate to the circumcised believers in Jerusalem in chapter 11. When Peter enters Jerusalem, these believers begin to dispute with him (διεκρίνοντο, 11:2). They accuse him of having gone into (the house of) uncircumcised men and having eaten with them (11:3). It may strike the reader as odd that the circumcised believers are concerned about the observance of dietary custom, while the preceding narrative has been concerned about the stunning development that the Gentiles have received the Holy Spirit.

Peter too seems to regard the accusation as missing the point, and in fact, does not respond to it. He neither denies it, nor seeks to justify his actions; he simply ignores it.[25] This is in accordance with Hermogenes (*Prog.* 8.30–9.4) and Nicolaus (*Prog.* 466.13–24), who stress that only *credible* accusations need be refuted, and with Quintilian (*Inst.* 5.13.22), who allows that some arguments may be treated with contempt.[26] Peter's

---

[24]Reduplication (ἀναδίπλωσις) is the repetition of one or more words for amplification or appeal to pity. Synonymy (συνωνυμία) is the replacement of a word by another of the same meaning, to impress upon the hearer the force of the expression through variation. Ps-Cicero, *Rhet. Her.* 4.28.38.

[25]Kennedy claims that Peter is employing *metastasis*, the shifting of responsibility to God (*Interpretation*, 123). On this view, Peter's basic argument would be that "the order of God takes precedence over the law" (cf. Quintilian, *Inst.* 3.6.53; Ps-Cicero, *Rhet. Her.* 1.14.24). However, Peter does not shift responsibility for his having eaten with Gentiles onto God; he simply ignores the accusation.

[26]Cf. Aphthonius, *Prog.* 27.30–28.2; John of Sardis, *Prog.* 67–71.

retelling of the vision would have been a golden opportunity to refute his accusers on the basis of claiming to have done what was reverent (that is, pleasing to God; cf. Theon, *Prog.* 122.4–5). Instead, Peter begins to recount his encounter with Cornelius "step by step" (καθεχῆς, 11:4), although it becomes clear that this term denotes more than mere chronological order. Rather, καθεχῆς signals that the narrative will proceed "in a manner that his audience will find convincing,"[27] as borne out by the fact that certain elements within the sequence of the two visions are omitted (10:21–23a, 25–26), condensed (compare 10:34–44 with 11:15a) or conflated (compare 10:22, 30–33 with 11:13–14). It is thus important to note Peter's repetition of a seemingly insignificant detail—the Spirit's instruction to go with Cornelius's men μηδὲν διακρίναντα (11:12). It is unclear, however, whether this phrase should it be read, "without doubting," or "without making a distinction." If Luke's goal is simply to have Peter straightforwardly recount the events of chapter 10, it would be most natural to give the phrase the same semantic value it possessed in 10:20, "without doubting." However, the fact that Luke reshapes the narration of these events for rhetorical emphasis suggests another possibility, a double entendre.[28] Peter, in advance of the circumcised believers, and perhaps also in advance of the reader, has realized that the gift of the Holy Spirit to the Gentiles relates not just to

---

[27]Parsons, *"Progymnasmata,"* 52. Luke's use of καθεχῆς in the prologue to his gospel (Luke 1:3) and elsewhere (Luke 8:1; Acts 3:24; 11:4; 18:23) suggests that the term should be understood as referring to a narrative order which is rhetorically persuasive rather than strictly chronological. This is in accord with Theon's claim that clarity in narrative is achieved by the proper ordering (τάχις) of elements (*Prog.* 86.7-87.12). Parsons concludes: "For Luke, then, καθεχῆς here has rather everything to do with a rhetorically persuasive presentation that displays the virtue of clarity" (52-53).

[28]The possibility of a double entendre is raised in 15:9, when Peter makes clear that God οὐθὲν διέκρινεν μεταξὺ ἡμῶν τε καὶ αὐτῶν (did not make a distinction between us and them). Looking back from this perspective, the reader is led to ponder whether μηδὲν διακρίναντα in 11:12 should be interpreted in light of what follows (i.e., "not making a distinction," 15:9) rather than what precedes (i.e., "not doubting," 10:20). Or perhaps, a double meaning is intended: Peter was instructed to go to Cornelius without doubting the divine voice, and "without making a distinction," that is, without deciding that Gentiles *qua* Gentiles were necessarily precluded from the community.

commensality, but to membership in the community. Indeed, the account climaxes with the retelling of the Holy Spirit falling upon Cornelius's household, just as he had done upon the present company at Pentecost (v. 15). Peter concludes in verse 17, "If then God gave them the same gift that he gave us when we believed in the Lord Jesus Christ, who was I that I could hinder God?" Again one notes that, had he wanted to, Peter could have at this point easily refuted the original accusation regarding commensality. He might have said something to the effect that, "Since God makes no distinction in giving the Holy Spirit, we should make no distinction with whom we eat."

The absence of a refutation, coupled with the substance of Peter's narration of events suggests the following: (1) Peter does not refute the accusation because he deems it unworthy of refutation. It so far misses the significance of the preceding events that it can be dismissed. The absence of a refutation where it might be expected should not be construed as a rhetorical deficiency, however. On the contrary, (2) Peter's dismissal of the accusation provides the opportunity for him to redefine the parameters of the discussion. By avoiding the topic of commensality altogether, he is claiming that what is at issue is the reception of the Holy Spirit by Gentiles, not dietary customs. The circumcised believers are concerned that Peter has not properly made the distinction between Jew and Gentile for the purpose of determining with whom he can eat. Peter responds by claiming that such a distinction is no longer valid: it is not valid for the purpose of determining commensality, but more importantly, it is not valid for the purpose of determining membership in the messianist community.[29]

E. Acts 15. Did the Jewish messianists understand the implications of Peter's speech in chapter 11? The necessity of the council in chapter 15 strongly suggests that they did not.[30] Peter had come to understand the implication of the vision to be that the distinction between Jew and Gentile was no longer a valid criterion for membership in the community. The Jerusalem believers, however, apparently had construed Peter's words to

---

[29]Jervell claims that, of the two themes in the Cornelius account—table fellowship and admission to the church—the stress is on the latter (*People of God*, 66–67). So also Jacques Dupont, "Le salut des Gentils et la signification théologique du Livre des Actes," *NTS* 6 (1960): 148.

[30]Parsons concludes: "Peter is forced to make explicit the implications of the Cornelius episode" ("Defiled AND Unclean," 269).

indicate that the Jew-Gentile distinction was no longer valid *only* vis-à-vis commensality. So, after tensions in the Antioch community prompt the sending of Paul and Barnabus to Jerusalem (v. 2), messianist Pharisees claim that Gentile messianists must be circumcised and observe the law of Moses (v. 5). Peter's refutation of this claim takes the following form: (1) God gave the Gentiles the Holy Spirit, just as he did to us (v. 8); (2) God made no distinction (οὐθὲν διέκρινεν) between us and them (v. 9); therefore (3) why test God by burdening them with a burden we ourselves cannot bear (v. 10)?[31]

We may note the correlation between Peter's words here and in chapter 11: (1) Peter makes the point that what God gave to the messianist Jews, God has now given to the Gentiles, namely the Holy Spirit (11:15, 17a; 15:8). (2) Peter either implies or expresses that God does not make a distinction between Gentiles and Jews (implied in the Holy Spirit's statements to Peter—11:9, 12; expressly stated—15:9). (3) Peter concludes with a rhetorical question, implying that in view of the above points, to deny Gentiles *qua* Gentiles membership in the messianist community would be to stand in God's way (11:17), or put God to the test (15:10). In chapter 11, Peter did not refute the claim that he ate with uncircumcised men. To do so (either by denying the fact or justifying his rationale for doing so) would have been implicitly to acknowledge that the distinction between Jews and

----

[31]Amy-Jill Levine, *The Misunderstood Jew: The Church and the Scandal of the Jewish Jesus* (San Francisco: HarperSanFrancisco, 2006) 77, 126, claims that Peter's description of the law as "a yoke that neither our ancestors nor we have been able to bear" makes no sense whatsoever on the lips of Peter, a law observant Jew (cf. his response to the divine voice in 10:14, in which he claims to have perfectly followed Mosaic dietary regulations). These words, she argues, only make sense coming from Luke, a Gentile, and thus point to the author's apologetic purpose (so also Conzelmann, *Acts*, 117). Nevertheless, Peter's comments do make sense on the lips of an observant Jew inasmuch as they reflect the experience of moral impotence that Charles H. Talbert describes as "pessimistic anthropology." Talbert, *Romans*, Smyth & Helwys Bible Commentary (Macon GA: Smyth & Helwys, 2002) 190–205. Although this outlook did not characterize all observant Jews, it is reflected in 4 Ezra 3:19–22, 25–26; 9:36–37; and 1 QS 11.9–10. That such a pessimistic anthropology could have been derived from the Old Testament itself is demonstrated (as in the case of Paul, in Rom 7:7–25) by Francis Watson, *Paul and the Hermeneutics of Faith* (New York: T.&T. Clark, 2004) 377–80.

Gentiles vis-à-vis commensality was at the heart of the vision and encounter with Cornelius. Peter instead sought to change the parameters of the discussion by emphasizing that the central issue was the admittance of Gentiles into the messianist community on the basis of their having received the Holy Spirit. This apparently was not understood by the Jerusalem messianists, thus requiring the council in chapter 15. The correlation between Peter's refutation in chapter 15 and his earlier speech in chapter 11 further confirms that the issue all along had been the admission of Gentiles *qua* Gentiles into the community.

According to Jervell, those zealous for circumcision do not question the salvation of the Gentiles, but only their status as uncircumcised.[32] The narrative of chapters 10–15 shows the progressive refutation of this idea. In chapter 10, Peter regards the Gentiles as unclean by nature, and thus unfit for membership in the messianist community. This conception is refuted by the divine voice (10:13–15), although the full implication of the vision is perhaps only made clear to Peter progressively, through the course of his encounter with Cornelius. When Peter speaks before the circumcised messianists in chapter 11, he wishes to communicate the full import of the vision, namely that Gentiles *qua* Gentiles should be admitted to the community without regard to their uncircumcised status. As is made clear by the very nature of the accusation brought against Peter, the Jerusalem messianists do not perceive the significance of Peter's words; they believe that the issue is merely about commensality. Finally, in chapter 15, the issue comes to a head, and Peter makes explicit what had been implied in chapter 11. Yet, from the perspective of Peter's speech in chapter 15, his earlier insistence that the Spirit had instructed him to accompany Cornelius's men μηδὲν διακρίναντα (11:12) suggests a double entendre. While the Jerusalem messianists (and readers) heard "without doubting," Peter may have intended to convey, "without making a distinction."

Conclusion

Luke's skill in the composition and integration of refutation within a narrative framework is apparent. In chapters 6–7, he weaves the themes of place (τόπος), law (νόμος), and custom (ἔθος) into a complex reworking of scriptural tradition, in order to refute the claim that Stephen (and the

---

[32]Jervell, *People of God*, 67.

messianists) were abnegating Mosaic customs and speaking against the temple. Not only does Stephen refute the claim, but he implies that his own version of the story is the correct one: the messianists are the true inheritors of Mosaic customs, and in the midst of the messianists, God dwells by the Spirit. In chapters 10–15, Luke crafts a progressive refutation of the view that Gentiles should not be admitted to the messianist community unless they observe the customs of Moses. The progressive refutation is woven together thematically and lexically. Certainly, the language of these refutations is at times sharply polemical, but this must be understood within the conventions of Hellenistic philosophical discourse, as well as within the context of rhetorical strategy. This examination finds Luke's rhetoric to be shaped by the need to address both the perception of the messianists by non-messianist Jews, and the admission of Gentile messianists into the community. But it finds little in Luke's rhetoric that is as categorically anti-Jewish as some have thought.

Tabernacle and Temple: Rethinking the Rhetorical Function of Acts 7:44-50

James N. Rhodes

Few New Testament passages have received as much sustained scholarly attention as has the speech attributed to Stephen in Acts 7:2-53. Verses 44-50 of this speech—which focus on two historic sanctuaries of the people of Israel, the tabernacle and the Solomonic temple—have been of particular interest to scholars. According to a once-dominant and still widely held view, these verses offer a radical critique of the temple in Jerusalem. In the course of a historical review that highlights Israel's rejection of its divinely appointed leaders and its predilection for idolatry, Stephen attacks the temple of Solomon as an improper innovation in Israel's worship, on par with the worship of the golden calf. According to this conventional interpretation, the speech is thus driven by a tabernacle-temple dichotomy: God was content with the portable tent-shrine introduced in the wilderness period and did not desire a "house," that is, a permanent building that might identify God's presence with a single, specific location. Moreover, because this attitude toward the temple seems to be at odds with a more irenic view elsewhere in Luke-Acts, Stephen's speech has long tantalized scholars as a possible window into the theology of a radical Hellenist faction in the early church.[1]

---

[1] This line of interpretation goes back to F. C. Baur. For a comprehensive history, see Heinz-Werner Neudorfer, *Der Stephanuskreis in der Forschungsgeschichte seit F. C. Baur*, Monographien und Studienbücher 309 (Giessen: Brunnen, 1983); Craig C. Hill, *Hellenists and Hebrews: Reappraising Division within the Earliest Church* (Minneapolis: Fortress, 1992); and Todd C. Penner, *In Praise of Christian Origins: Stephen and the Hellenists in Lukan Apologetic Historiography*, Emory Studies in Early Christianity 10 (New York and London: T.&T. Clark, 2004). Penner concludes somewhat provocatively that "the importance attributed to the Hellenists in modern scholarship is a product of its own theological and historical commitments, and may have very little to do with the actual realities of life in the early church" (331). Notwithstanding this skepticism about the historical realities thought to lie behind the text, Penner's interpretation of the speech nevertheless embraces the conventional tabernacle-temple dichotomy (308-18).

The conventional interpretation sketched above is held together by three exegetical linchpins. One is the relationship between verse 47 and verse 48, where the statement that Solomon built a house (οἶκος) is immediately followed by the denial that God dwells in houses built by human hands (οὐχ ὁ ὕψιστος ἐν χειροποιήτοις κατοικεῖ). Here attention may be called to a possible word play between the noun οἶκος and the verb κατοικεῖ. A second exegetical linchpin is a perceived relationship between this rejection of humanly built edifices (χειροποιήτοις) and verse 41, which describes the worship of the golden calf as a "reveling in the works of their hands" (εὐφραίνοντο ἐν τοῖς ἔργοις τῶν χειρῶν αὐτῶν). This lexical resemblance is thought to place the golden calf and the Jerusalem temple on the same plane, as merely human and ultimately idolatrous constructions. The third and most significant linchpin is verse 44, which speaks positively of the tabernacle as having been constructed according to divine instructions (καθὼς διετάξατο ὁ λαλῶν τῷ Μωϋσῇ ποιῆσαι αὐτὴν κατὰ τὸν τύπον ὃν ἑωράκει). Collectively, these exegetical linchpins point to a fundamental distinction between the tent of testimony, viewed as acceptable in God's eyes, and the Solomonic temple, viewed as an improper and at least potentially idolatrous innovation.[2]

There have always been scholars who have resisted such a strong interpretation of the Stephen speech. As Dennis Sylva and others have pointed out, Stephen's apparent criticism of the temple can be read not as a denunciation of the temple's legitimacy, but merely as an affirmation of God's transcendence of it.[3] Such scholars have noted that Acts 7:48 echoes Solomon's prayer at the dedication of the temple (1 Kgs 8:22-53), which emphasizes that God's true abode is in heaven and therefore denies that God can be contained by the house that has been built. Although this "softer"

---

[2]L. W. Barnard saw in the Stephen speech an antitemple radicalism strong enough to be a direct influence on the later *Epistle of Barnabas*. "Saint Stephen and Early Alexandrian Christianity," *NTS* 7 (1960–1961): 31-45. Although few commentators on Acts have been willing to go quite so far, many have embraced a tabernacle-temple dichotomy as intrinsic to the logic of the speech.

[3]Recent advocates of the transcendence hypothesis include Dennis D. Sylva, "The Meaning and Function of Acts 7:46-50," *JBL* 106 (1987): 261-75; Hill, *Hellenists and Hebrews*, 74; and Marion L. Soards, *The Speeches in Acts: Their Content, Context, and Concerns* (Louisville: Westminster/John Knox, 1994) 68n.166. Sylva gives a list of earlier commentators who have favored this view (261-62n.4).

perspective on Stephen's temple critique seems to be gaining ground among scholars, it has yet to displace the older, conventional view of a more fundamental temple critique. Among commentaries published in the last dozen years, those of C. K. Barrett (1994), James Dunn (1996), and Charles Talbert (1997) endorse a more traditional view of Stephen's polemic.[4] It is my aim in the pages that follow to expose this view as resting on a set of inherently circular arguments. In so doing, I will ground the exegetical basis of the transcendence hypothesis in an alternative reading of Acts 7:44-50 and its relationship to the rest of the Stephen speech.

I. Exposing the Circularity of the Conventional View

Circular arguments are not always avoidable, nor are they necessarily wrong. It goes without saying that some exegetical decisions influence others, limiting the range of possible inferences or even our ability to see certain interpretive possibilities. The interrelatedness of our exegetical logic means that what often appears to be a convergence of data in reality rests on a few governing assumptions. This becomes problematic only if the governing assumptions are themselves flawed, but fail to be questioned because we have grown accustomed to seeing the inferences derived from them as independent corroboration.

It is my contention that the conventional interpretation of Acts 7:44-50 rests on just such a flawed governing assumption, the assumption that verse 44 functions as *an unqualified eulogy of the tabernacle, the intent of which is to show that the tabernacle sets a standard for the proper worship of Yahweh.*[5] When verse 44 is forced to carry so much freight, it is relatively easy to read the argument of verses 44-50 as serving a tabernacle-temple dichotomy. I suggest that this assumption is flawed not because it is a *misreading* of verse 44 as much as it is an *over-reading* of the verse that

---

[4]C. K. Barrett, *A Critical and Exegetical Commentary on the Acts of the Apostles*, 2 vols., ICC (Edinburgh: T.&T. Clark, 1994) 1:371-74; James D. G. Dunn, *The Acts of the Apostles*, Epworth Commentaries (Peterborough: Epworth, 1996) 90-91; and Charles H. Talbert, *Reading Acts: A Literary and Theological Commentary on the Acts of the Apostles* (New York: Crossroad, 1997) 77-78.

[5]So, e.g., Craig R. Koester, *The Dwelling of God: The Tabernacle in the Old Testament, Intertestamental Jewish Literature, and the New Testament*, CBQMS 22 (Washington DC: Catholic Biblical Association of America, 1989) 98: "[T]he tabernacle stands for worship that is in accordance with God's law and prophets."

invests the verse with greater significance within the speech than the context demands. Although it is beyond question that verse 44 praises the divine origin of the tabernacle, this assertion should not automatically be regarded as the fulcrum on which the entire argument of the speech turns. Below I will suggest an alternative reading that takes verse 44 at face value *without treating it as a thesis that drives the entire speech*. But first it is necessary to show how the tabernacle-temple dichotomy is sustained by several circular or inherently problematic arguments.

Perhaps the most obvious problem posed by the conventional reading is that it requires one to drive a highly dubious wedge between David and Solomon, the very David "who found favor with God" (7:46), but who the deuteronomist depicts as the first person who desired to build Yahweh's temple (2 Sam 7:1-3). According to the Chronicler, David even acquired the property for the temple site (1 Chr 21:18–22:1; 2 Chr 3:1; cf. 2 Sam 24:18-25) and began making material preparations for its construction (1 Chr 22:2-5, 14-16). Indeed, it would be possible for one who knows these scriptural traditions to find them not only acknowledged, but explicitly affirmed in verse 46.[6] This raises an obvious and much-discussed problem: How can the speech simultaneously praise the intention of David "to find a dwelling place for the [God? house?] of Jacob (εὑρεῖν σκήνωμα [τῷ θεῷ / τῷ οἴκῳ] Ἰακώβ)"[7] and to delegitimize the temple?

---

[6]Scholars who think that verse 46 refers to David's role in the inception of the Jerusalem temple include Sylva, "Meaning and Function," 265-67; Hill, *Hellenists and Hebrews*, 71-73; and Luke Timothy Johnson, *The Acts of the Apostles*, SP 5 (Collegeville MN: Michael Glazier, 1992) 132.

[7]The underlying textual problem is well known, some might say intractable. Several scholars have preferred the reading τῷ θεῷ as essential to an intelligible rendering of the text, despite acknowledging that τῷ οἴκῳ could be preferred on the grounds that it is the more difficult reading and that it has stronger external attestation. See, e.g., Earl Richard, *Acts 6:1—8:4: The Author's Method of Composition*, SBLDS 41 (Missoula MT: Scholars Press, 1978) 131-32; John J. Kilgallen, *The Stephen Speech: A Literary and Redactional Study of Acts 7,2-53*, AnBib 67 (Rome: Pontifical Biblical Institute, 1976) 29-30; Ernst Haenchen, *The Acts of the Apostles: A Commentary*, ed. and trans. Bernard Noble, Gerald Shinn, Hugh Anderson, and R. McL. Wilson (Oxford UK: Basil Blackwell; Philadelphia: Westminster, 1971) 285; Johnson, *Acts*, 132-33; and Soards, *Speeches*, 67n.164.

Some have tried to attenuate the force of this obvious difficulty by arguing that Acts 7:46 with its reference to "finding a dwelling place" (εὑρεῖν σκήνωμα) refers not to David's desire to build a temple, but only to his relocation of the ark to a tent shrine in Jerusalem (2 Sam 6:17). In theory such a reading permits David to be dissociated from the temple, the responsibility for which then falls entirely on Solomon. The highly tendentious nature of the resulting argument—that David had nothing to do with the building of the temple—is not usually thought to weigh against the plausibility of reading the text this way, primarily because it can be attributed to the polemical context of the speech.[8] Nevertheless, the internal logic of such a reading must still be held up to the bar of plausibility. If we presuppose a person familiar enough with the biblical tradition to write the speech we have in Acts 7:2-53—or a reader familiar enough to recognize the narratives the speech evokes—would such a person have found the resulting argument to be cogent or dubious on its very face?

In support of the claim that the speech's approbation of David is related only to David's relocation of the ark to a tent shrine in Jerusalem, several scholars have argued that Acts 7:46 is an allusion to Psalm 132(131):5.[9] Strong verbal resemblances make such a connection highly plausible,[10] and may possibly favor the transfer of the ark as the primary point of reference in Acts 7:46. Nevertheless, Craig Hill shows that an allusion to Psalm 132:5 effectively raises more problems than it solves. The ark itself is not mentioned until verse 8, and the psalm quickly goes on to exalt Yahweh's

---

[8]In other words, the argument might not be a very good one, but it is one that a sufficiently biased person might try to make! Cf. Penner, *In Praise of Christian Origins*, 314: "It must be stated that *it does not matter* that the Hebrew Bible text, viewed in its entirety, may negate such a picture. The function of the retelling is precisely to highlight the details that serve the function of the present narration" (emphasis added). I submit that "the function of the present narration" is precisely the point in question.

[9]E.g., Marcel Simon, "Saint Stephen and the Jerusalem Temple," *JEH* 2 (1951): 129-30.

[10]The combination of the verb εὑρίσκω and the noun σκήνωμα is itself significant, and the likelihood of an allusion is even stronger if one accepts the reading θεῷ Ἰακώβ in Acts 7:46 instead of οἴκῳ Ἰακώβ. On lexical grounds, the argument for at least a verbal echo—and perhaps a conscious allusion—to Ps 132:5 may be judged to be strong.

choice of Zion as the place where Yahweh rests, dwells, abides (vv. 7-8, 13-14). Such language, if pressed, leads to the very conclusion that the Stephen speech disputes in Acts 7:48-50. Moreover, given the relatively short period of time between the transfer of the ark and founding of the temple, one must assume that the actual recitation of Psalm 132 (whether in a pre- or post-exilic context) served to celebrate the Jerusalem cult and thus to legitimate the temple itself.[11] Thus, even in Psalm 132:5 the meaning of σκήνωμα is not beyond dispute and could point to the temple.[12] Given the full context, it seems likely that when Psalm 132:5 praises the intentions of David, this praise includes his desire to build Yahweh's temple. This, in fact, should be expected, for even though David is prevented from building the temple himself, both the Deuteronomist and the Chronicler praise his desire to do so (1 Kgs 8:17-19; 2 Chr 6:7-9).

Those who want to argue that the Stephen speech dissociates David from the temple are thus placed in an ironic position: by arguing that the act for which David receives praise is that of bringing the ark to Jerusalem, they nevertheless emphasize an event that anticipates the very transition from tabernacle to temple that the speech supposedly abhors. Moreover, the text invoked to show that verse 46 does *not* refer to the temple seems rather to illustrate *how inseparably linked David's actions were to the celebration of Zion as the locus of Yahweh's cultic presence.* I would therefore argue that regardless of the historical referent of the word σκήνωμα in Acts 7:46, the verse fails to effectively dissociate David from the temple. Moreover, *it cannot be expected to do so, since the text evokes what it wants to suppress.*[13] If the conventional interpretation is correct, one would have to concede that verse 46 does not advance the argument. It gets in the way, and the argument would be clearer if the verse were simply deleted.[14]

---

[11]Hill, *Hellenists and Hebrews*, 72-73.

[12]The word σκήνωμα refers to the temple in Pss 15[14]:1; 74[73]:7; 84:1 [83:2]. Cf. Pss 26[25]:8; 43[42]:3; 46[45]:4.

[13]Cf. also Sylva who argues that the story of the dedication of the first temple (1 Kgs 8:14-30; 2 Chr 6:3-21) underlies the sequence of assertions found in Acts 7:46-50 ("Meaning and Function," 266).

[14]Penner illustrates the problem of circularity when he states that "tabernacle" or "tent" is a more likely meaning for σκήνωμα in Acts 7:46 "given the argument, here, that David and Solomon are being distinguished in some way" (*In Praise of Christian Origins*, 313).

A second assumption undergirding the conventional interpretation is the view that the epithet χειροποίητος (and therefore the criticism contained in vv. 48-50) *necessarily applies only to the temple*. Since the literal meaning of χειροποίητος is "made by [human] hands," verse 48 might reasonably be interpreted as asserting simply that the Most High transcends all humanly constructed or material sanctuaries. If verse 48 is taken in this sense, one might ask how it is possible for the tabernacle to be exempted from its implications. One notes, for example, that the Exodus account speaks at great length of the material craftwork involved in the construction of the tabernacle (Exod 35–39). Philo (*Moses* 2.88) emphasizes precisely this point, calling the tabernacle a ἱερὸν χειροποίητον, though he does not intend thereby to disparage it. Similarly, Hebrews contrasts the essentially material or humanly constructed (χειροποίητος) quality of the tabernacle with the heavenly sanctuary into which Christ has entered (Heb 9, esp. vv. 11, 24). In principle, therefore, the criticism of verses 48-50 *ought* to be equally applicable to the prior sanctuary: the Most High transcends all material sanctuaries, however honorable their origins may be.

This interpretation, however, is not an option for those who are committed to a more robust reading of verse 44. If one has already concluded that the tabernacle *sets a standard for the proper worship of Yahweh*, it must be insulated from any possibility of criticism. It therefore follows that verses 48-50 apply only to the temple, and one may prove as much simply by pointing back to verse 44! Hans Conzelmann, for example, affirms, "[T]he tent is traced back to a heavenly prototype and thus is evaluated positively."[15] As unobjectionable as this assertion seems at first, one may justifiably ask whether the author would assume that the tabernacle's divine origin necessarily precludes its misuse or a false view of its significance. It is worth noting that the author of Hebrews is able to affirm the tabernacle's origin from a heavenly prototype while *simultaneously denying* that this gives it an ultimate and enduring significance (Heb 8:5).[16] By reframing the issue as a question of origins, an

---

[15]Hans Conzelmann, *Acts of the Apostles*, ed. Eldon Jay Epp and Christopher R. Matthews, trans. James Limberg, A. T. Kraabel, and Donald H. Juel, Hermeneia (Minneapolis: Fortress, 1987) 55. Cf. also Joseph A. Fitzmyer, *The Acts of the Apostles*, AB 31 (New York: Doubleday, 1998) 382-83, and Koester, *Dwelling of God*, 80.

[16]I do not wish to equate the intention of Acts 7:44-50 with Heb 8:5 but simply

inevitable circularity is introduced: if an honorable, divine origin removes the tabernacle beyond the reach of verses 48-50, one must simultaneously conclude that the temple lacks an honorable origin! But without this prior conclusion, the grammar of verses 46-47 scarcely suggests this by itself.[17]

There is, however, a further consideration relevant to the point under discussion. Advocates of the conventional interpretation frequently point out that throughout the LXX the word χειροποίητος is associated with graven images or other forms of idolatry.[18] If these connotations are attached to verse 48, the criticism becomes much sharper and means something like "the Most High does not dwell in idol-houses." Because such a statement would be difficult to reconcile even with a less strenuous interpretation of verse 44, this reading—if justified—would seem to make a tabernacle-temple dichotomy much more defensible.

Although this argument from the Septuagint's usage cannot simply be dismissed, the underlying evidence must be weighed carefully. In the first place, it should occasion no surprise that a word like χειροποίητος finds frequent use in Old Testament idol polemic. It is precisely because the Hebrew tradition understands Yahweh to *transcend all creation* that humanly constructed or material representations of the deity are forbidden (Deut 4:12-18). A temple or sanctuary is somewhat different in that its physical form is not intended to be a direct or visual representation of the deity; rather, it provides a locus where the deity may be approached according to the requirements of the cult. For this reason, the same cult of Yahweh that insisted on aniconic worship could tolerate (material) sanctuaries such as the tent of testimony or the Solomonic temple. The logic of Yahweh's transcendence still applied, but it applied in a different way (1 Kgs 8:27; 2 Chr 6:18; Isa 66:1-2; 2 Sam 7:5-7).[19] This perhaps explains why

---

to point out that the first issue (origin) does not necessarily decide the second (significance).

[17]Cf. Haenchen, *Acts*, 285: "The speaker sees in the building of the Temple an apostasy from the true service of God, though *in itself the text merely brings to a close the account of the tabernacle and the Temple*" (emphasis added).

[18]E.g., Koester, *Dwelling of God*, 80, and Dunn, *Acts*, 97. The commonly cited loci are Lev 26:1, 30; Isa 2:18; 10:11; 16:12; 19:1; 21:9; 31:7; 46:6; Dan 5:4, 23; 6:27[28]; Jdt 8:18; Wis 14:8; Bel 5 (Theod).

[19]2 Sam 7:5-7 is sometimes invoked in support of the tabernacle-temple distinction that scholars would see in Stephen's speech (e.g., Simon, "Saint

both Philo and other New Testament writers can apply the term χειροποιήτοις to the tabernacle and/or the temple without consciously implying that such sanctuaries are idolatrous by nature: their humanly constructed or material quality was not an issue as long as one did not lose sight of the divine transcendence.[20] Put more simply, all idols are χειροποίητα but not all χειροποίητα are idols. Because the examples of LXX usage customarily cited refer (with one possible exception) to cultic objects rather than temples, it is questionable whether they exert decisive import for the nuance of χειροποιήτοις at Acts 7:48.[21] All things considered, a more proximate source of influence is likely to be Mark 14:58. This passage, in which false witnesses accuse Jesus of threatening to personally destroy the temple, is strongly echoed in the charges against Stephen, which are also made by false witnesses (Acts 6:13-14). More importantly for the question at hand, it uses the word χειροποιήτοις in a purely denotative or "neutral" sense. That Acts 7:48 requires a harsher sense needs to be proven, not assumed.[22]

Stephen," 130). Nevertheless, in its canonical form, 2 Sam 7 cannot be read as an objection in principle to the idea of a temple, since verse 13 allows that Solomon will build Yahweh's house. Rather, verses 5-7 serve to affirm the divine transcendence by belittling David's "concern" (v. 2) that Yahweh lacks a proper temple: Yahweh cannot lack what Yahweh does not, in fact, need. Yahweh will allow a "house" to be built for Yahweh in Yahweh's time and on Yahweh's terms. In the meantime, Yahweh will build David a "house" (i.e., a dynasty, v. 11). Seen in larger perspective, the text permits the temple to redound to David's credit (a point noted in 1 Kgs 8:18 and amplified in preparations described by the Chronicler) by asserting that the only reason David himself did not build the temple was that Yahweh reserved the prerogative to decide who would build a house for whom (and when).

[20]Cf. Mark 14:58 (the temple); Heb 9:11, 24 (the tabernacle); Philo, *Moses* 2.88 (the tabernacle).

[21]The exception is Isa 16:12, where εἰς τὰ χειροποίητα αὐτῆς stands in for Heb. אל־מקדשו, but this appears to be a case where the LXX is trying to clarify the text. Instead of saying that Moab "enters his sanctuary" it is said that Moab "goes in to (see) her idols."

[22]Some might claim that the verbal similarity of Acts 17:24 to 7:48 argues in favor of just such a harsher sense. This is possible, but also potentially misleading. The context of the Areopagus speech presupposes a pagan audience in a city "brimming with idols" (κατείδωλον, 17:16) and thus prejudices the comparison.

An ancillary argument for the claim that Acts 7:48-50 refers only to the "house" is the presence of a verbal "echo" between the noun οἶκος in verse 47 and the verb κατοικέω in verse 48. Although this lexical resemblance is worth noting, it is relatively superficial unless one has *already* decided that there is a fundamental distinction in the speech between "tents" and "houses." If such a distinction is not already clear, the meaning of κατοικέω ("dwell," "reside") seems far too general to bring the argument home. Moreover, on purely lexical grounds, the case for such a distinction seems problematic: One finds an idolatrous "tent" (σκηνή) of Moloch as well as the divinely sanctioned "tent (σκηνή) of testimony;" the reference to David's σκήνωμα of verse 46 is not clear; that Solomon's "house" is a bad thing is precisely what waits to be proved. The logic of verses 44-50 cannot be reduced to σκηνή = good, οἶκος = bad.[23]

Finally, the conventional interpretation postulates that the conjunction δέ in verse 47 functions as a strong adversative.[24] David found favor with God for his desire to find a σκήνωμα *but* Solomon built a house. Although such a reading is *grammatically* possible, it is demanded only if one has already decided that the purpose of verses 44-50 is to praise the tabernacle and denigrate the temple. Moreover, it labors under all the difficulties noted above that result from trying to dissociate David from the temple. Hence, the argument is part of a hermeneutical circle and has no independent value.[25] The more clearly adversative ἀλλά does not appear until the next verse. As was also noted above, the prior assumption that the ensuing statement (vv. 48-50) applies *only* to the "house" (οἶκος) built by Solomon

---

Even granting the difference in context, it may be noted that Acts 17:24 is really a statement about divine transcendence, and shows that Luke understood how important Yahweh's transcendence was to a proper Jewish (or Christian) view of God. At the same time, Acts 17:24 illustrates how fundamental this emphasis can be to idol polemic: asserting the transcendence of the one true God implies that pagan deities are dependent upon material sanctuaries and human caretaking because they themselves have no existence beyond their material representation.

[23]Hill, *Hellenists and Hebrews*, 73.

[24]So Simon, "Saint Stephen," 128.

[25]Cf. Heikki Räisänen, *Jesus, Paul and Torah: Collected Essays*, JSNTSup 43 (Sheffield UK: JSOT Press, 1992) 178: "If Solomon did what David, God's favorite, could not yet do, this could not be a very bad thing; δέ can scarcely denote an emphatic contrast."

is the sole basis for regarding the temple as an idolatrous innovation—again creating a hermeneutical circle.[26]

From the standpoint of narrative logic, perhaps the strongest reason for questioning whether the point of verses 44-50 is to praise the tabernacle and denigrate the temple results from the fact that the speech in no way portrays the wilderness period as a golden age. When the author says, "*our ancestors had the tent of testimony in the wilderness*" (v. 44) this language harks back to verses 38-39, verses which highlight the theme of rebellion. It was the wilderness generation that "thrust aside" Moses, worshiped other gods, and ultimately came under divine judgment. The presence of the tabernacle—even if it be regarded as wholly positive—does not reverse *a decidedly negative judgment* of the wilderness period itself. Indeed, verses 39-43 imply that Israel's *entire history* down to the Babylonian exile is marred by idolatry! If so, it is difficult to see how verses 44-50 can be made to suggest that the nation's worship was properly ordered while the tabernacle was still in use but not after the temple was built.

My intention in the preceding paragraphs has not been to argue that the conventional interpretation is entirely without merit. It is one possible way of reading the speech that many scholars have considered persuasive. My intention, however, has been to show that what first appears to be a convergence of evidence pointing to a tabernacle-temple dichotomy largely rests on a single governing premise: that Acts 7:44 is an *unqualified* eulogy of the tabernacle, the intent of which is to show that *the tabernacle sets a standard for the proper worship of Yahweh*. Though possible, this is a much stronger reading of verse 44 than the verse itself requires, and predisposes one to the conclusion that the problem with the temple is that it is not the tabernacle! Without this assumption, there is no need to argue that the temple's very origins are flawed, that David had no part in its inception, that only the temple is χειροποίητος, or that δέ is a "strong adversative." Indeed, without this assumption, verses 46-47 may be read as a straightforward acknowledgement of the temple's own honorable origins: David found

---

[26]To translate v. 48 as "the Most High does not dwell in *houses* made with human hands" (NRSV) begs precisely this question, when one might translate more literally, "the Most High does not reside *in human handiwork*" (ἐν χειροποιήτοις) or more paraphrastically, "the Most High does not live in *material sanctuaries*." These translations reject the notion that God's presence is confined by any sanctuary of human construction.

favor with God, and what David began, Solomon brought to completion. The advantage of the transcendence hypothesis is that it facilitates a simpler reading of verses 48-50: The Most High transcends all material sanctuaries, however honorable their origins may be.[27] This (latter) reading has the added advantage of being more consistent with what a Jewish audience (or a biblically informed reader) could be expected to accept. It may be possible to read verses 46-47 against the grain of the biblical tradition, but this decision emerges from the governing premise rather than the language of the verses themselves. Of course, it is not enough simply to expose the circularity of the conventional reading; an alternative must be offered. To be viable, such an alternative must answer several questions. What is the nature of Stephen's critique? Why has Stephen been perceived as speaking against the temple itself? Why is the tabernacle mentioned at all, if it is not the focal point of comparison? How does God's transcendence of material sanctuaries—if that is all verse 48 really intends to affirm—manage to offend Stephen's audience in such a way that he is stoned as a result? In short, how do verses 44-50 relate to what precedes and what follows in a way that serves the unity of the speech and explains the outcome of the narrative?

II. The Rhetorical Unity of the Stephen Speech

The question of the unity of the speech and its relevance to the charges against Stephen is not new. Stephen stands accused of speaking "against this holy place and the law," saying that "Jesus of Nazareth will destroy this place" and change the customs handed down by Moses (6:13-14). Scholars have disagreed whether the Stephen speech addresses these charges directly, indirectly, partially, or not at all.[28] Martin Dibelius famously asserted that the speech's "most striking feature" was "the irrelevance of its main section."[29]

Verses 44-50 (or at least verses 48-50) are ultimately at the center of this issue, because it is only here that Stephen's remarks begin to show any

---

[27]Cf. Sylva notes that throughout the Stephen episode God is referred to as θεός except in verse 48, where the epithet "Most High" (ὕψιστος) is used, stressing the divine transcendence. Sylva, "Meaning and Function," 267.

[28]See the discussion in Kilgallen, *Stephen Speech*, 6-10.

[29]Martin Dibelius, *Studies in the Acts of the Apostles*, ed. Heinrich Greeven (Repr.: Mifflintown PA: Sigler, 1999; orig. 1951; ET 1956) 169.

relationship to the charge of speaking against the temple. In this sense, they are indispensable to the overall context of the narrative. At the same time these verses stand out from the rest of the speech for other reasons as well. Some scholars have felt the transitions before and after verses 44-50 to be difficult or abrupt. The difficulty is due, at least in part, to a chronological disjunction: while the end of verse 43 points forward all the way to the Babylonian exile, verse 44 brings the reader back, momentarily, to the wilderness period. Adding to the confusion is the abrupt transition from the idolatrous "tent (σκηνή) of Moloch" to the divinely sanctioned "tent (σκηνή) of testimony." Conzelmann argues that verses 43 and 44 "do not fit together" and finds the logical connection "difficult to follow."[30] Similarly, Haenchen speaks of "visible seams" after verses 43 and 47, and thinks Stephen's concluding denuniciation (vv. 51-53) evinces such an abrupt change in tone that the transition "can only be explained if the preceding verses form a radical denunciation of the Temple worship."[31] This is a problem to which we must return.

Prior to verses 44-50 the speech develops two related themes. The first of these is God's promises to the ancestors. Not surprisingly, this theme begins with a recitation of the call of Abraham (verse 2), extends to the time of the exodus (vv. 17-34), and focuses on the promise of land and progeny. Though Abraham himself would not live to see the full realization of God's promises (v. 5), these promises would be fulfilled for his posterity, who would come to dwell in the land Abraham had been shown and who would worship God in "this place" (v. 7). As this theme develops, a second begins to run alongside it, focusing on the threat to these promises posed by the disobedience of Israel's ancestors. Into this category fall the selling of Joseph into slavery (v. 9), the rejection of Moses' leadership (vv. 27, 35, 39) and the worship of the golden calf by the wilderness generation (v. 41).

The juxtaposition of these two themes creates an intrinsic tension between God's faithfulness in bringing about the fulfillment of the ancestral promises, and the actions of the ancestors themselves, which threaten to thwart this very fulfillment. This tension seems to reach something of a climax in verses 42-43, where the people are "handed over" and an oracle of judgment points forward to the Babylonian exile. Robert Tannehill has

---

[30]Conzelmann, *Acts*, 55.
[31]Haenchen, *Acts*, 289, 286.

called attention to the ironic reversal signified by the repetition of the verbs
λατρεύω and μετοικίζω: The promise that Abraham's posterity would
worship God in the promised land (v. 7) is thwarted by their worship of
idols (v. 42). The result is that Abraham's "relocation" toward the promised
land (v. 4) is reversed by the removal of his offspring (v. 43) from the
promised land back to Babylon (Ur of the Chaldees)![32]

Having reached something of a climax with this pronouncement of
judgment, it is worth noting how naturally Stephen's concluding denunciation (vv. 51-53) would fit immediately after verse 43. I suggest that this
observation is ultimately the key to the logic of the speech and to the
rhetorical function of the intervening verses (vv. 44-50).[33] After Stephen's
recitation of ancestral disobedience, the ground has been prepared for the
accusation that Stephen's opponents are just like their ancestors. Such an
accusation will imply that Stephen's interlocutors are courting divine
judgment, just as their ancestors did. Nevertheless, the moment of prophetic
accusation is suspended precisely so that Stephen can tie the question of the
temple to the argument he is building. Stephen says, in effect: *generations
past were not without their sanctuaries intended for the worship of Yahweh,
but these did not save them from the consequences of their disobedience.*
Since the wilderness generation had the benefit of the tabernacle but is
remembered for its idolatry, and since those who worshiped at Solomon's
temple ultimately went into exile, such sanctuaries are no guarantee of
God's saving presence. To assume otherwise treats Yahweh as a deity who
may be confined to a shrine and subjected to human manipulation. I would
thus argue that the rhetorical function of verses 44-50 is not to juxtapose the
tabernacle and temple one to the other, but to juxtapose the history of both
sanctuaries against the nation's history of rebellion. Although an insistence
on Yahweh's independence from material sanctuaries applies in principle
to the tabernacle, the brunt of verses 48-50 falls on the temple for no other
reason than it is the future of this sanctuary that now stands jeopardized by
the nation's disobedience.

---

[32]Robert C. Tannehill, *The Acts of the Apostles*, vol. 2 of *The Narrative Unity
of Luke-Acts: A Literary Interpretation* (Minneapolis: Fortress, 1990) 90.

[33]Cf. Penner, *In Praise of Christian Origins*, 98, who states: "Just when one
expects a resounding indictment of the people there arises this convoluted unit that
one must assume is advancing the argument even if in ambiguous ways."

It seems to me that such an interpretation facilitates a more integrated reading of Stephen's speech. Insofar as the remainder of the speech effectively juxtaposes God's faithfulness and Israel's disobedience (especially the rejection of Joseph, Moses, the prophets, and ultimately Jesus), the argument is reasonably linear and consistent.[34] Verses 51-53 offer a Deuteronomistic conclusion to an essentially Deuteronomistic argument. Yet the intervening verses (vv. 44-50) are indispensable if the speech is to have any relationship to the charges made against Stephen. The seemingly difficult transitions before and after verses 44-50 are eased if one allows that the section begins with a *concession* (vv. 44-47: ἡ σκηνὴ τοῦ μαρτυρίου ἦν τοῖς πατράσιν ἡμῶν ἐν τῇ ἐρήμῳ . . .) and ends with a *negation* (vv. 48-50: οὐχ ὁ ὕψιστος ἐν χειροποιήτοις κατοικεῖ . . .). With just a slight use of paraphrasis to break up the lengthy sentences, and the "strong adversative" delayed until verse 48, the passage might be rendered as follows.

> [Keep in mind that][35] the tent of testimony was with our ancestors in the wilderness—(the same tent) which the One who spoke to Moses directed him to make according to the pattern that he had seen.
>
> Our ancestors in turn brought it in with Joshua when they dispossessed the nations that God thrust out before our fathers.
>
> This lasted until the time of David, who found favor in the sight of God and asked permission to find a sanctuary for the house of Jacob; Solomon, then built them a house.
>
> Nevertheless, the Most High does not reside in material sanctuaries, as the prophet says, "Heaven is my throne, and the earth is my footstool. What kind of house will you build for me," says the Lord, "or what is the place of my rest? Did not my hand make all these things?"

With no need to fault the temple as an improper innovation, one may grant that both sanctuaries are seen as having honorable origins, namely the divine design of the tabernacle (v. 44) and the divinely approved intentions of David (v. 46). However honorable such origins may be, the Most High

---

[34]So, esp. H. Alan Brehm, "Vindicating the Rejected One: Stephen's Speech as a Critique of the Jewish Leaders," in *Early Christian Interpretation of the Scriptures of Israel: Investigations and Proposals*, ed. Craig A. Evans and James A. Sanders, JSNTSup 148 (Sheffield UK: Sheffield Academic Press, 1999) 266-99.

[35]I offer this introductory parenthesis as a way of making explicit how I think the reader is invited to view the material that follows.

transcends these (and all such) sanctuaries; the deity's cultic presence does not subject the deity to human manipulation. Since Stephen's audience knows what happened to previous generations and previous sanctuaries, it is implied that they should not think that the current temple is a guarantee of God's saving presence. Verses 44-47 are, in any event, a highly schematic account of the successive inception of tabernacle and temple. After the mention of exile (!) in verse 43, they do little more than divide the pre-exilic period between the two sanctuaries. Is there reason enough to think that these verses are intended as anything more than a summary of facts (vv. 44-47), introduced to show that in the end they made no difference (vv. 48-50)?

John Kilgallen rightly sees that the main point of the speech is to be found in verses 51-53: "You are just like your ancestors."[36] The real sting in such an indictment, however, comes from the awareness that such a comparison implies more than it says: Stephen's opponents know full well what happened to their rebellious ancestors; they, even now, are courting divine judgment as their ancestors did.[37] An insistence that the current temple does not guarantee God's saving presence any more than the prior sanctuaries is consistent with the Deuteronomistic tenor of the speech and casts Stephen in a Jeremianic mold (Jer 7:1-14; 26:1-6).[38] Moreover, the implication of impending judgment in 7:51-53 is strengthened when one compares these verses with Luke's use of the prophet-killing motif in the gospel (Luke 11:47-51; 13:34-35). These texts remind us that Luke knows full well that the temple itself will be destroyed. The Lukan Jesus has already declared Israel's "house" forsaken (Luke 13:35).[39] The Lukan Jesus laments that Jerusalem will ultimately be destroyed because of its failure to recognize the time of its visitation (Luke 19:41-44).[40] Perhaps most

---

[36]John J. Kilgallen, "The Function of Stephen's Speech (Acts 7,2-53)," *Bib* 70 (1989): 174-82.

[37]For the theme of the nation's sin equaling or exceeding the sins of its ancestors, cf. esp. Judg 2:18-21; 2 Kgs 17:13-18; 2 Chr 30:7-8; Ezra 9:7; Ps 78:8; Jer 7:25-26; 9:11-14; 16:9-13; Zech 1:4-6.

[38]Cf. Brehm, "Vindicating the Rejected One," 291.

[39]Suggesting perhaps that the divine presence has vacated the temple? Cf. *2 Bar.* 8:2; *4 Bar.* 4:2-3; Josephus *B.J.* 6.5.3 §300; Tacitus *Hist.* 5.13.1.

[40]Luke portrays the apostles summoning Israel to repentance for their sins, including the rejection of Jesus (Acts 2:38; 3:19; 5:31). It may be argued that a

importantly of all, the subsequent stoning of Stephen constitutes a narrative fulfillment of Luke 13:34 and thus confirms that Stephen's denunciation is correct: just like their ancestors, Stephen's opponents kill the prophets and stone those sent to them.

Echoing the earlier insights of Robert Tannehill, Nicholas Taylor has recently observed that Stephen's speech "is consistent with an implied affirmation that the Temple would be destroyed."[41] I would take this argument further: For the attentive reader of Luke-Acts, the future of the temple is never in doubt. Once the question of the destruction of the temple has been raised in 6:13-14, Luke expects his readers to recognize the narrative groundwork that he has previously laid. This means that even if the temple question seems initially to disappear from the response of Stephen, it does not recede from the larger narrative horizon. What seems at first to be an irrelevant response on the part of Stephen (vv. 2-43) is in reality part of a rhetorical strategy. By appealing to a shared heritage, Stephen evokes the assent of his accusers to certain judgments about the past, only to turn these very judgments back against his accusers. The temple therefore *must* recede from Stephen's reply long enough to draw his opponents into the trap. Seen in this way, Stephen's speech presupposes that the temple will be destroyed precisely because his opponents are so much like their ancestors. Luke may view the charges against Stephen as false, not because Stephen was innocent of making provocative assertions about the temple's future, but simply because these statements are misrepresented as blasphemy against God and the law. To equate an utterance against the temple with blasphemy against God would be to lose sight of the divine transcendence upon which verses 48-50 insist.[42]

---

summons to repentance presupposes the threat of judgment, even if this threat is not always explicit. (Note, however, that in Acts 3:22-23—the only other passage that speaks of the "prophet like Moses"—the threat of extirpation is explicit.) Whereas Peter's Pentecost sermon adopts an exculpatory tone, Stephen's speech is far more negative. In part, this may serve Luke's narrative intention to account for increasing Jewish rejection of the apostolic preaching, which leads to the preaching of the gospel beyond the confines of Jerusalem and Judea.

[41]Nicholas Taylor, "Luke-Acts and the Temple," in *The Unity of Luke-Acts*, ed. Joseph Verheyden, BETL 142 (Leuven: Peeters, 1999) 709-21, quotation 718. Cf. Tannehill, *Acts of the Apostles*, 93-95.

[42]It is also possible that Luke saw the charge as "false" for its assertion that

In sum, it is my claim that verses 44-50 play a different role in the Stephen speech than has usually been suggested. The significance of these verses is not to juxtapose the tabernacle and the temple against each other but to juxtapose the story of Israel with the history of its sanctuaries and *in this way* to relativize the latter. The rest of the speech, which emphasizes disobedience and implies judgment, would do so just as strongly in their absence, but verses 44-50 drive home the point that such disobedience has grave implications for the temple. The transcendence hypothesis is essentially correct, but the point is not that the (mobile) tabernacle preserved this insight and the temple does not.[43] The point is rather that the divine transcendence leaves God free to act—even against God's own house—as had happened before in the nation's past.[44]

One final observation may be made. The careful reader will have noticed that the translation of verses 44-50 given above presupposes the reading σκήνωμα τῷ οἴκῳ Ἰακώβ (rather than σκήνωμα τῷ θεῷ Ἰακώβ),

---

Jesus himself would destroy the temple rather than God. Although this sounds like a technicality, it must be understood from the standpoint of prophetic logic: The prophet announces God's intentions, not his own; God acts, vindicating God's prophetic spokesperson. Mark 14:57-58 (Luke's presumed source for the temple charge) requires similar resolution.

[43]To make mobility the issue is to read too much into the movements of the ancestors and to overlook the obvious fact that the tabernacle joins the wilderness generation "en route." In any event, the goal toward which such movement is directed is fulfillment of the promise that Abraham's progeny will worship God "in this place" (i.e., in the land of Canaan, v. 7). Although he still reads the speech on the basis of the tabernacle-temple dichotomy, Koester rightly states that "[t]he mobile character of the tabernacle was not central for Stephen" (*Dwelling of God*, 85).

[44]Joseph B. Tyson argues that Luke-Acts portrays a series of attempts on the part of Jesus and his followers to take possession of the temple and transform it from what it has become ("a den of robbers") to what God intended it to be ("a house of prayer for all nations"). Stephen's speech marks a turning point because it sends "a strong signal that the Jewish Temple will not finally be transformed, as Jesus had intended." Tyson's argument is more cogent if Stephen's speech is read (as here) in a way that emphasizes the implied threat hanging over the temple's future rather than as an assertion that "its very construction [w]as an act of disobedience to God." Tyson, *Images of Judaism in Luke-Acts* (Columbia: University of South Carolina Press, 1992) 115, 184.

which I have translated "a sanctuary for the house of Jacob." The interpretation of the Stephen speech that I have offered above neither stands nor falls on the basis of the variant chosen in verse 46. Nor does my present choice reflect an absolutely settled conviction on the matter. However, in working out the implications of my interpretive hypothesis I have begun to see the *lectio difficilior* as less problematic than I previously considered it to be. For if the speech simultaneously assumes that Israel's destiny was to worship God in its promised land ("in this place," v.7) and that God transcends all material sanctuaries, then the building of the temple was always for the benefit of Israel, not Israel's God.

Paul's Dream at Troas: Reconsidering the Interpretations of Characters and Commentators

John B. F. Miller

Dreams and visions abound in Luke's narrative,[1] and the present discussion explores some peculiarities in one of these dream-vision scenes: Paul's experience at Troas in Acts 16:9.[2] Although Luke does not hold as rigidly to the common form of the dream-vision report as do some ancient authors,[3]

---

[1]The roots of this study lie in a more comprehensive treatment of dream-visions in Luke-Acts. John B. F. Miller, *Convinced That God Had Called Us: Dreams, Visions, and the Perception of God's Will in Luke-Acts*, BINS 85 (Leiden: Brill, 2006). The discussion of the Troas episode in that larger examination has been revised and expanded in the present study.

Identifying dreams and visions in ancient literature is slightly more complicated than it may appear. See John Hanson, "Dreams and Visions in the Graeco-Roman World and Early Christianity," *ANRW* 23/2 (1980): 1395-1427, and Miller, *Convinced That God Had Called Us*, 8-14. But Luke employs explicit visionary terminology in Acts 16:9, describing Paul's experience as a ὅραμα ("dream" or "vision"). (Unless otherwise noted, translations in this essay are my own.)

[2]Use of the combined term "dream-vision" requires some explanation. In contemporary English usage, one is used to the distinction between dreams and visions as sleeping and waking experiences (respectively). As Hanson has observed, however, Greek terms for "dreams" and "visions" do not reflect a similar distinction. Instead, one finds a "a fairly loose application of a variety of terms that can mean 'dream' or 'vision' or both. . . . [indicating] the difficulty, if not impossibility, of distinguishing between a dream and a vision" based solely on terminology. Hanson, "Dreams and Visions," 1408. The ambiguity suggested by Hanson is supported by the evidence in Luke-Acts. In Acts 10:3, Cornelius sees a vision (ὅραμα) while praying (cf. Acts 10:30). In 16:9, a vision (ὅραμα) appears to Paul during the night (διὰ νυκτός)—presumably indicating a dream Paul had while sleeping. Given this lack of distinction in the Greek terms, Hanson suggests the hyphenated term "dream-vision," which is also employed here. "Dreams and Visions," 1408.

[3]Remarkable similarities in the form of dream-vision reports in antiquity have attracted significant scholarly attention. For example, questions of form criticism as they relate to dreams in Jewish Scripture are discussed by Ernst Ludwig Ehrlich (*Der Traum im Alten Testament*, BZAW 73 [Berlin: Alfred Töpelmann, 1953]), and

one element appears constant: whether dream-vision messages come from an angel, from a heavenly voice, from the Holy Spirit, or even from the risen Jesus, all of Luke's dream-vision scenes feature a message explicitly associated with a source somehow related to God. *All except one.* In Paul's dream-vision experience at Troas one finds a remarkable variation: here, it is not an otherworldly figure who appears to Paul, but a Macedonian man, asking Paul to come to Macedonia in order to help "us." Immediately, Paul and his companions interpret Paul's dream-vision as a call from God, and scholars commenting on this passage have agreed with the characters' interpretation. What makes this interpretation especially interesting is the narrative description of Paul's exploits in Macedonia—exploits that seem altogether anticlimactic in view of the narrative tension that builds in Acts 16:6-8, and is supposedly relieved in 16:9-10. The present study offers a narrative-critical treatment of the Troas passage, with emphasis on three elements of this story: (1) the lack of a divine agent in the dream itself, (2) the explicit act of interpretation (συμβιβάζω) that leads Paul and his companions to Macedonia, and (3) the limited success they have there. After examining this passage more closely and summarizing some of the scholarship on it, I will look at the Troas dream-vision within the broader narrative context of Acts 13-17, and conclude with some suggestions about the importance of this passage for understanding and appreciating the dream-visions in Luke-Acts.

Acts 15:36-16:5 describes the beginning of Paul's so-called "second missionary journey" and its initial success. Churches are strengthened

---

refined further by Wolfgang Richter ("Traum und Traumdeutung im AT: Ihre Form und Verwendung," *BZ* 7 [1963]: 202-20). Form criticism has also been important in scholarship on the related topic of theophany (e.g., J. Kenneth Kuntz, *The Self-Revelation of God* [Philadelphia: Westminster, 1967]). For a form-critical treatment of the Graeco-Roman material, see Hanson, "Dreams and Visions," as well as Hanson's earlier work, "The Dream-Vision Report and Acts 10:1-11:18: A Form-Critical Study" (Ph.D. diss., Harvard University, 1978). See also Michael Day, "The Function of Post-Pentecost Dream/Vision Reports in Acts" (Ph.D. diss., Southern Baptist Theological Seminary, 1994); Robert Karl Gnuse, *Dreams and Dream Reports in the Writings of Josephus: A Traditio-Historical Analysis*, AGJU 36 (Leiden: Brill, 1996); and David Handy, "The Gentile Pentecost: A Literary Study of the Story of Peter and Cornelius (Acts 10:1-11:18)" (Ph.D. diss., Union Theological Seminary [Richmond], 1998).

(15:40); Timothy, a new disciple/assistant, joins Paul (16:1-3); more churches are strengthened and their numbers grow (16:5). These summary successes are followed in 16:6-8 by even more abbreviated frustrations. Paul and his companions travel through Phrygia and Galatia, prevented by the Holy Spirit from speaking the word in Asia (16:6). Their frustration is heightened in 16:7 when they "attempt" to enter Bithynia, but the "Spirit of Jesus" will not permit them.

Prevented from entering Bithynia, they pass Mysia and come down to Troas. There, a dream-vision appears to Paul "during the night," in which "a certain Macedonian man" asks Paul "to come to Macedonia and help us." It is significant that this verse features both the adjective "Macedonian" and the noun "Macedonia." This repetition is furthered emphasized by the personal pronoun, ἡμῖν ("us"), which indirectly refers to Macedonia for the third time in this brief sentence. In the course of the next two chapters, Paul will travel to both Macedonia and Achaia.[4] The dream-vision, however, contains no reference of Achaia, but mentions Macedonia three times. This repetition deserves special notice, especially in light of the scholarly assessments (discussed below) that treat this passage as divine intervention guiding Paul to Macedonia *and* Greece. Far from a vague incentive to travel west, Luke's description of the dream-vision draws definite and specific attention to Macedonia. This emphasis raises a number of interesting questions, which will be taken up below.

Following the narrator's account of the vision in verse 9, one finds a striking transition in verse 10. The text simply states, "when *he* saw the vision, *we* immediately sought to go to Macedonia."[5] The participial phrase

---

[4]That Luke understands the distinction between Macedonia and Achaia is clear in Acts 18:12, 27, and 19:21.

[5]The ongoing debate over the nature and significance of the "we" passages in Acts is beyond the scope of this discussion. For summaries of the various opinions on this issue, see Ernst Haenchen, *The Acts of the Apostles: A Commentary*, ed. and trans. Bernard Noble, Gerald Shinn, Hugh Anderson, and R. McL. Wilson (Oxford UK: Blackwell; Philadelphia: Westminster, 1971) 489-91, and C. K. Barrett, *A Critical and Exegetical Commentary on The Acts of the Apostles*, 2 vols., ICC (Edinburgh: T.&T. Clark, 1994–1998) 2:772-73. See also James Blaisdell, "The Authorship of the 'We' Sections of the Book of Acts," *HTR* 13 (1920): 136-58; Henry J. Cadbury, "'We' and 'I' Passages in Luke/Acts," *NTS* 3 (1957): 128-32; Susan Marie Praeder, "The Problem of First-Person Narration in Acts," *NovT* 29

that follows in verse 10 is perhaps the most significant aspect of this vision for the topic at hand: συμβιβάζοντες ὅτι προσκέκληται ἡμᾶς ὁ θεός εὐαγγελίσασθαι αὐτούς ("convinced that God had called us to proclaim the good news to them"). The verb συμβιβάζω, when combined with ὅτι, can mean either "to demonstrate that" or "to conclude that."[6] This construction occurs nowhere else in the Old Testament or New Testament except in Acts, where it is found at 9:22 and the passage at hand. Acts 16:10 requires the latter meaning: the characters are drawing a conclusion based on Paul's visionary experience.

As noted above, all of the other dream-visions in Luke-Acts feature an otherworldly figure. One of the most intriguing anomalies in Paul's dream-vision at Troas, therefore, is the absence of any reference to a divine agent. Only in the characters' own conclusions about the meaning of the dream-vision is God mentioned at all.[7] Considering both the frequency of dream-visions in Luke-Acts, and the element of divine agency that pervades all of these *except* the Troas vision, puzzling questions arise: Why the change? Why here? For the purpose of the present examination, the absence of any reference to a divine agent in verse 9 is significant. With this absence in mind, it is interesting to find that commentaries and scholarly discussions of this passage seem to have one thing in common: they share, in some way, the characters' interpretation that Paul's dream-vision is a directive from

---

(1987): 193-218; Thomas E. Phillips, "Paul as Role Model in Acts 16 and Beyond," in *Acts and Ethics*, ed. Thomas E. Phillips (Sheffield UK: Sheffield Phoenix, 2005) 49-63; Stanley E. Porter, *The Paul of Acts: Essays in Literary Criticism, Rhetoric and Theology*, WUNT 115 (Tübingen: Mohr Siebeck, 1999) 1-66; and William S. Campbell, "Who Are We in Acts?: The First-Person Plural Character in the Acts of the Apostles" (Ph.D. diss., Princeton Theological Seminary, 2000). My interest here is not in the introduction of the first person, but in the way these "we" interpret Paul's dream-vision.

[6]Related to the verb συμβαίνω, συμβιβάζω has the literal meaning of "bring together" or "knit together." In metaphorical usage with ὅτι it comes to be used of drawing conclusions (LSJ, s.v. συμβιβάζω; cf. also BDAG, s.v. συμβιβάζω).

[7]The reference to "characters" here is a reflection of the first-person plural in the narrative. I am not using this term to advocate for any particular interpretation in the ongoing discussions of the "we" passages. In any case, the narrator has made clear that Paul is not alone, but is accompanied, at the very least, by Silas and Timothy.

God. In the interest of time, I will summarize a sampling of these opinions in categories that pertain to the present discussion.

Although it is a bit tangential to the question of divine guidance, the geographic significance of the Troas episode for a number of scholars is worthy of mention. Despite Luke's differentiation elsewhere between Macedonia and Achaia, several scholars have viewed the Troas passage as God's redirection of Paul's mission to *Greece*, or even somewhat anachronistically, as God's redirection of Paul's mission to Europe.[8] Likening Paul's dream-vision at Troas to the dream-visions that purportedly inspired Alexander's conquest of the East and Julius Caesar's usurpation of power in Rome, Alfred Wikenhauser's *religionsgeschichtliche* study equates Paul's foray to Macedonia with an expansion of his mission to Europe.[9] For Martin Dibelius, Paul's call to Macedonia is one and the same thing as a call to Greece, and it is this journey to Greece that Dibelius suggests is "an event affecting the entire world."[10] Henry J. Cadbury and Joseph A. Fitzmyer have offered similar views.[11]

---

[8]As Jacob Jervell has rightly pointed out, "Dass die Mission jetzt nach Europa kommt, wird bei Lukas gar nicht besonders vermerkt, denn es geht ja ohnehin um das römischen Imperium, und Kleinasien ist kaum weniger hellenistisch als Griechenland." *Die Apostelgeschichte*, KEK 17 (Göttingen: Vandenhoeck & Ruprecht, 1998) 417.

[9]Alfred Wikenhauser, "Religionsgeschichtliche Parallelen zu Apg 16, 9," *BZ* 23 (1935–1936): 186. Josephus describes the double dream-vision of Jaddus the high priest and Alexander the Great. Jaddus is told by God in a dream that he should present himself and the people to Alexander in white robes. When Alexander sees this spectacle, he kneels before Jaddus. Asked why he has done this, Alexander explains that he saw just such a spectacle in a dream at Dios—a dream that encouraged him to cross over to Asia without delay (*Ant.* 11.322-39).

Suetonius relates the story that Julius Caesar, wondering whether to cross the Rubicon, saw a vision of a fair figure playing music. When Caesar's soldiers begin to gather around this figure, the figure grabbed a trumpet from one of the soldiers, sounded a war blast, and went to the far bank of the river. Taking this as a sign from the gods, Caesar exhorted his troops to follow in the path of the visionary figure (*Jul.* 32).

[10]Martin Dibelius, *Studies in the Acts of the Apostles*, trans. Mary Ling and Paul Schubert (London: SCM, 1956; repr., Mifflintown PA: Sigler Press, 1999) 76.

[11]Henry J. Cadbury, *The Making of Luke-Acts*, 2nd ed. (London: MacMillan, 1958; repr., Peabody MA: Hendrickson, 1999) 305, and Joseph A. Fitzmyer, *Acts*

Also worth noting are the few studies that have drawn attention to what one might call the narrative tension between what the characters perceive as a breakthrough message from God and the actual results of their mission in Macedonia. An early evaluation of this nature was offered by John Calvin, who understood this scene as one in which the Lord "exercised the faith and patience" of Paul and his companions.[12] More recently, F. Scott Spencer and Beverly Roberts Gaventa have commented on this element in Luke's narrative.[13] Nevertheless, all three maintain that the dream-vision at Troas is an example of divine guidance.

As for ways of emphasizing this divine guidance, reactions have varied. On one extreme, Ernst Haenchen likened the Troas episode to Luke's story of Cornelius and Peter—a story that led Haenchen to denounce Lukan theology for its presentation of God "twitching . . . human puppets."[14] Without seeing such a stark depiction of divine compulsion, others have argued the Troas passage is evidence that God directs the mission of Paul in its entirety.[15] Others, like Robert Tannehill, insist that we also notice the human involvement in this scene.[16] Edmund Farahian, in a recent article-length study of Acts 16:9-10, even posits the idea of a *"sunergeia* between God and human beings."[17] Such emphasis on the human element is particularly compelling when one considers that Paul's second mission begins (Acts 15:36) without the formal, divine directive found in Acts 13:1-

of the Apostles: A New Translation with Introduction and Commentary, AB 31 (New York: Doubleday, 1998) 577.

[12]John Calvin, *The Acts of the Apostles, 14-28*, trans. John W. Fraser (London: Oliver & Boyd, 1966) 70.

[13]F. Scott Spencer, *Acts*, Readings: A New Biblical Commentary (Sheffield UK: Sheffield Academic Press, 1997) 164, and Beverly Roberts Gaventa, *Acts of the Apostles*, ANTC (Nashville: Abingdon, 2003) 236.

[14]Haenchen, *Acts of the Apostles*, 485, 362.

[15]E.g., Charles H. Talbert, *Reading Acts: A Literary and Theological Commentary on the Acts of the Apostles* (New York: Crossroad, 1997) 148, and Gaventa, *Acts*, 234-35.

[16]Robert Tannehill, *The Acts of the Apostles*, vol. 2 of *The Narrative Unity of Luke-Acts: A Literary Interpretation* (Minneapolis: Fortress, 1990) 195.

[17]Edmond Farahian, "Paul's Vision at Troas (Acts 16:9-10)," in *Luke and Acts*, ed. Gerald O'Collins and Gerald Marconi, trans. Matthew O'Connell (New York: Paulist, 1993), 207.

3.[18] These observations draw one back into the text and invite an examination of Paul's dream-vision at Troas within the broader narrative context of Acts 13-17.

Preceding Context (Acts 13:1-16:5)

Since a number of scholars have described Paul's dream-vision at Troas as a second commissioning scene that parallels the original commission of Barnabas and Saul in Acts 13:1-3,[19] it will be helpful to begin the present contextual examination with this first commission. Although a detailed examination of chapters 13-15 is beyond the scope of this discussion, a brief sketch of the events described in these chapters will prove illuminating.

In 13:1-2, the Holy Spirit spoke to the believers in Antioch "while they were worshiping the Lord and fasting," saying, "Set apart for me Barnabas and Saul for the work that I have called them to do."[20] Far from ambiguous, this "commissioning" is placed in the "mouth" of the Holy Spirit, whose role in directing Barnabas and Saul is further emphasized in 13:4 ("therefore, having been sent out by the Holy Spirit, they went down to Seleucia"). Although the exact course of their journey is not foreshadowed, the initiation and guidance of the Holy Spirit are clear.

Chapters 13-14 then describe a series of encounters in which Saul, now Paul, and Barnabas find themselves and their message sometimes received warmly and sometimes opposed. Although this opposition is often extreme, it is overshadowed by the success of their mission. Sergius Paulus, a Roman proconsul, is converted in 13:12. After a successful address in a synagogue of Psidian Antioch, Paul and Barnabas are invited back to speak again, and "many" Jews and proselytes follow them. When they return to speak on the

---

[18]Even with their emphasis on the human role in this narrative, it is important to note that both Tannehill and Farahian maintain the idea that God is behind Paul's dream-vision at Troas.

[19]E.g., Talbert, *Reading Acts*, 147, and Spencer, *Acts*, 161. On the problems with classifying this as *Paul's* missionary journey, see Gaventa, *Acts*, 190-91. The language of Acts 13:1-3 clearly designates this missionary journey as the work of the Spirit. My discussion generally focuses on the role of the human characters in this narrative unit, but this is not meant to deny those passages in which divine agency is clearly at work.

[20]On the inclusion of this and other manifestations of the Holy Spirit within the category of dream-visions, see Miller, *Convinced That God Had Called Us*, 13-14.

following Sabbath, "nearly the whole city" turns out to hear "the word of the Lord" (13:44). Even the Jewish opposition they face (13:45) is balanced by the receptivity of the Gentiles (13:48-49). In Iconium, a great crowd of Jews and Gentiles become believers (14:1). Again, the apostles face opposition in Iconium, but the narrative highlights instead the spread of the "good news" (14:7). When Paul heals a crippled man in Lystra, the response of the Gentiles is to receive him and Barnabas as gods, attempting to offer them sacrifice as incarnations of Hermes and Zeus (14:11-12). In 14:20, after Paul has been stoned and left for dead, he simply gets up and goes back into town. The very next day, he and Barnabas go to Derbe, where they make a large number of disciples (14:20-21). In each case, significant opposition—sometimes even catastrophic opposition—is overshadowed by more significant success.

Sometime after the Jerusalem Council,[21] Paul suggests to Barnabas a return tour: "Let us visit the brethren in every city in which we proclaimed the word of the Lord [to see] how they are doing" (15:36). This is an interesting and peculiar transition in the narrative. The commission for the first journey comes directly from the Holy Spirit (13:2). The narrator offers no indication whatsoever of divine guidance for this second journey. That Luke is drawing a parallel between the two scenes, however, is made clear by his use of the particle δή, a particle which he uses only twice in Acts—in 13:2 and 15:36.[22]

---

[21]I use this title to refer to the meeting between representatives of the Antiochene church and those of the church at Jerusalem described in Acts 15:4-29. The primary issue is whether Gentile believers must be circumcised, but other questions of observance seem to arise as well (Acts 15:1; cf. 15:29). For a summary of various interpretations of this passage, see Haenchen, *Acts of the Apostles*, 455-72. On the problem of calling it a "Council," see Fitzmyer, *Acts*, 543-45.

[22]So also Haenchen, *Acts of the Apostles*, 473. The parallel use of this particle in 13:2 and 15:36 underscores the absence of the Holy Spirit in the latter passage. Indeed, the surrounding context complicates this question of the Holy Spirit's role in these events. Describing the letter representing the culmination of the Jerusalem Council, Acts 15:28 begins "for it seemed good to the Holy Spirit and to us." James's inclusion of the Holy Spirit in his decision is peculiar, especially since there has been no appeal to the Spirit in the deliberations of the council. Some scholars have interpreted 15:28 very positively. William Shepherd argues: "Here Luke presents both the Spirit and the church jointly as actors; the Spirit is directly involved in this conflict, and takes a side." *The Narrative Function of the Holy*

Further complications of this "second" journey arise in the next verse. The stated purpose of the return tour in 15:36 is to "visit the brethren in every city in which we proclaimed the word of the Lord." In 15:41, however, the narrator says, "[Paul] went through Syria and Cilicia, strengthening the churches." In the description of the first mission, there is no mention of *any* activity in Syria (outside of Antioch), and "Cilicia" as a region is not mentioned at all. Instead, these would appear to refer back to the addressees of the letter mentioned in 15:23.[23] In the first journey, the sea routes traveled by the apostles obviated the need to travel through Syria. Even with the understanding that Paul would not follow Barnabas to Cyprus, the emphasis on a *return* trip to Syria and Cilicia is strange.

After the acquisition of Timothy in Lystra (16:1-3), Paul takes another subtle turn, this time to the north and west—a turn for which the narrative gives no explanation, certainly no "divine" explanation. Recalling again the purpose of this trip—to return to those places where Paul and Barnabas had proclaimed the word—it seems all the more odd that the narrative provides no explicit impetus for the northwesterly expansion of Paul's mission.[24] In

---

Spirit as a Character in Luke-Acts, SBLDS 147 (Atlanta: Scholars Press, 1994) 218. Luke Johnson goes even further, comparing 15:28 to the commissioning scene in Acts 13: "The invocation of the Holy Spirit as a partner to the decision has an odd sound to contemporary ears, but it nicely captures the dynamics of the process as portrayed by Luke. For similar language establishing an interplay between the activity of humans and of the Holy Spirit, see Acts 13:1-3." *The Acts of the Apostles*, SP 5 (Collegeville MN: Liturgical Press, 1992) 277.

The problem with such interpretations is that the narrative does *not* establish such "interplay." Luke goes on at length about the deliberations of those gathered in Jerusalem. God and the Holy Spirit are mentioned by the characters in this scene. The narrator never depicts God or the Holy Spirit interacting with the characters, however, nor do the characters themselves attempt to seek God's guidance (e.g., through prayer).

[23]So also Haenchen, *Acts of the Apostles*, 475, and Barrett, *Acts*, 758. This letter, which confirms that Gentile believers need not be circumcised, is sent by the "apostles" and "elders" of the church at Jerusalem to the "Gentile brothers and sisters" in Antioch, Syria, and Cilicia (Acts 15:23).

[24]Tannehill offers an interesting discussion of this point: "developments do not follow Paul's plan. . . . Paul's attempts to expand his previous mission into neighboring areas are frustrated. . . . Paul's plan and God's plan do not coincide at this point. Paul must endure frustrating experiences until the moment of discovery

this context, however, the Spirit(s)'s hindrance of Paul and his companions is quite striking.[25] Nowhere from 15:36 to 16:5 does Luke give any indication that God (or the Spirit) is pressing Paul into new missionary territory.

After running into several "spiritual" roadblocks in 16:6-7, the characters treat Paul's ὅραμα at Troas as a breakthrough, interpreting this event as divine guidance for the course of their mission. They seek "immediately" (εὐθέως) to go to Macedonia, because they have concluded (συμβιβάζω) that God has called them to do so. Expectations are heightened by the language in 16:11-12. Paul and his companions make rapid progress across the Aegean Sea, which Hans Conzelmann takes as implicit evidence of the divine sanction for their journey.[26] In verse 12, they arrive at Philippi, a city to which Luke ascribes unique importance: it is "a prominent city of the region of Macedonia" and a "colony."[27] Given the tension involved in this plot transition—the hindrance of the Spirit(s) in Acts 16:6-7, the dream-vision in verse 9, the interpretation of this dream-vision as a call from God in verse 10, and the description of their successful arrival in the important city of Philippi in verse 12—the reader might reasonably expect that great success will soon follow. Such expectations, however, are not fulfilled.

---

of the new opportunity for mission. This discovery expands Paul's horizons beyond his original plans" (*Acts of the Apostles*, 194). Unfortunately, "Paul's plan" is something into which the narrative gives little insight.

[25]The reference to "Spirit(s)" here is meant to emphasize the references to the "Holy Spirit" in Acts 16:6 and the "Spirit of Jesus" in Acts 16:7. Some scholars simply gloss over this variation, claiming that the "Spirit of Jesus" is the same as the "Holy Spirit." See, e.g., Haenchen, *Acts of the Apostles*, 484. Fitzmyer regards this as a "parallelism with the 'Holy Spirit'" in v. 6 (*Acts*, 578). Noting that some manuscript traditions have attempted to fix this problem by changing it to πνεῦμα κυρίου, Johnson asserts that "Spirit of Jesus" is probably correct and fits with Jesus' continuing activity in the narrative of Acts (*Acts*, 285). Spencer concurs that this phrase conveys "the abiding sense of Jesus' involvement with his emissaries" (*Acts*, 162).

[26]Hans Conzelmann, *Acts of the Apostles*, trans. James Limburg, A. Thomas Kraabel, and Donald H. Juel, Hermeneia (Philadelphia: Fortress, 1987) 129.

[27]As Gaventa and others have noted, this unique ascription is strange, especially given that Paul has proclaimed his message in a number of "colonies" like Psidian Antioch and Lystra previously in the narrative (*Acts*, 236).

Unlike other areas, in which Paul and his companions typically find a synagogue,[28] they must go *outside* the gates of Philippi to a location where they "think" (νομίζω) there might be a place of prayer. Here, they encounter a group of women who have gathered. Among them is a "dealer of purple cloth"[29] and "worshiper of God" named Lydia, from the city of Thyatira.[30] Lydia becomes significant as one of only two people described as accepting Paul's message in Philippi. If Paul's mission in Macedonia is unremarkable up to this point, things take a turn for the worse in verses 16 through 40. In 16:16-18, the characters are confronted repeatedly by a female slave possessed of a "Pythian" spirit. This scene contrasts nicely with Paul's earlier encounter with the false prophet, Bar-Jesus (13:6-12). In the earlier story, Paul is filled with the Holy Spirit and "defeats" his religious opponent. As a result, the Roman proconsul, Sergius Paulus, believes in the apostles' message. No such filling of the Spirit is mentioned in Acts 16:11-17:15. In fact, the only spirit mentioned in this part of Acts is the slave's πνεῦμα πύθων (16:16). Despite Paul's ability to cast out the "Pythian" spirit in the name of Jesus, his encounter with the Philippian authorities leads only to opposition and imprisonment.

Whereas Acts 13-14 present the apostles encountering large groups of people, the initial stories of the Macedonian experience deal with

---

[28]E.g., Salamis (Acts 13:5), Psidian Antioch (Acts 13:14), Iconium (Acts 14:1), Thessalonica (Acts 17:1), and Beroea (Acts 17:10).

[29]Commentators tend to emphasize various interpretive possibilities with regard to the conversion of Lydia. On the one hand, she is a woman of means who heads a household (16:15). On the other, however, she is a πορφυρόπωλις (purple-cloth merchant). If this means she is involved in the production of purple cloth, Spencer's comments shed an interesting light on this passage: "While suggesting a degree of wealth and independence . . . Purple-dyeing was particularly stigmatized as a smelly, 'dirty' process involving the use of animal urine" (*Acts*, 165). Ivoni Richter Reimer's extensive research into evidence for the dye trade in Thyatira indicates that "purple" dyeing did not necessarily imply luxury items, nor would this profession have implied any particular wealth or high status. *Women in the Acts of the Apostles: A Feminist Liberation Perspective*, trans. Linda M. Maloney (Minneapolis: Fortress, 1995) 98-105. It is difficult to know how Luke's original audience might have responded to Paul's only "success" in this early stage of the Macedonian mission.

[30]Ironically, Lydia is from a city in a region where Paul and his companions were prevented from proclaiming their message (16:6).

individuals: Lydia in 16:13-15, and now the Philippian jailer. After an earthquake shakes the foundations of the prison, leaving the prisoners free of their bonds, the jailer finds that no one has left (16:26-29). Rather than believing as a result of an astonishing sign like Sergius Paulus (13:12), the jailer's belief is somehow motivated by the refusal of Paul and the other inmates to escape. In contrast to earlier stories in which an angel rescues the characters from prison (Acts 5:19-20; 12:7-10), it is interesting to note that this passage features neither an angelic rescuer, nor an escape.[31] Rulers somehow opposing God's purpose earlier in Acts have met with divine catastrophe (see, for example, Herod's demise in Acts 12:23). In Acts 16, however, the leaders become afraid only when they hear that Paul and Silas, prisoners whom they have had beaten, are Roman citizens (16:38). The contrast between this portion of Acts and the description of Paul's previous journey is remarkable. Indeed, given the assumptions of divine agency in Paul's dream-vision at Troas, it is interesting to notice the *continuing absence* of divine agency in this part of Acts. References to the divine (that is, references to "God," "Jesus," and "Lord") occur frequently in Acts 16:11-17:15, but with the sole exception of 16:14, each reference depicts God as the object of an action, rather than the subject of an action.[32]

Although still not approaching the success found in Acts 13-14, Paul and his companions are received more favorably in Thessalonica (17:1-4). Paul and Silas spend several Sabbaths in the synagogue there, and "some of the Jews, a significant number of worshiping Greeks, and not a few of the leading women" are persuaded by Paul's message. Although this marks the greatest success since "we" left Troas, it still does not compare to descriptions like "nearly the whole city" turning out in 13:32-34. Paul and Silas find greater receptivity among the Jews in Beroea (17:11).[33] As in

---

[31]The Greek noun σεισμός ("earthquake") is associated with the work of the Lord in a number of biblical passages (e.g., Isa 29:6; Jer 23:19; Matt 28:2). In such contexts, however, the divine connection is made explicit. This passage may also recall Luke 21:11-12, in which persecution precedes earthquakes and famine.

[32]More specifically, note the following: "God" in 16:14, 17, 25, 34; 17:13; "Jesus" in 16:18, 31; 17:3, 7; and "Lord" in 16:31-32. I am not including here the uses of κύριος in 16:14, 15, 16, 19, and 30, since these refer neither to God nor Jesus.

[33]It is interesting that Paul finds his most receptive audience just before leaving Macedonia.

14:19, however, the opponents of Paul's message will travel to other towns to stop the spread of the word; so, in 17:14, Paul is whisked away to the coast, from which he will sail to Athens in the province of Achaia. Paul's departure from Macedonia is not telegraphed in the narrative. There is no deliberation about where to go next. A journey that began "immediately" (εὐθέως, 16:10) after the characters interpreted Paul's dream-vision as God's directive to proclaim the good news in Macedonia ends immediately (εὐθέως, 17:14) with Paul's departure for Achaia—a quiet, anticlimactic end to a journey with anything but a quiet beginning.

Interpretation and Implications of the Troas Episode

It would be easy to misunderstand this discussion, if one were to think that its purpose is to argue that both the characters and commentators are "wrong" in their interpretation of Paul's dream-vision as a directive from God. God is mentioned in this part of the narrative only in the characters' interpretation of the event. To ask whether the author *intended* the reader to share the characters' conclusion is, of course, unanswerable. Because it is unanswerable, it may not be the most helpful question. Instead, I would suggest there are other questions invited by this passage. For instance: How are we to understand the significance of Paul's dream-vision *in the context of Luke's narrative*? What is the significance of Luke's presentation of the Troas dream-vision as one that is interpreted by the characters in the story? What is the significance of the fact that the subsequent events in the story do *not* necessarily bear up the interpretation given by these characters?

Answers to these questions should be sought organically, within the narrative itself. In Acts 16:9-10, Luke describes a dream-vision appearing to Paul in Troas in the wake of several frustrating missionary experiences. Luke's unique language of the Spirit(s) hindering Paul and his companions underscores the *lack* of any divine agent in Paul's dream-vision. Despite this lack of divine agency, the characters interpret Paul's experience as a call from God to proclaim the good news to the Macedonians in 16:10. The characters draw their own conclusion (συμβιβάζω) about Paul's experience. In a text like Luke-Acts that focuses so often on divine action,[34] it is

---

[34]Numerous studies have underscored the importance of God's direction in Luke-Acts. E.g., S. Schulz, "Gottes Vorsehung bei Lukas," *ZNW* 54 (1963): 104-16; Charles Cosgrove, "The Divine DEI in Luke-Acts," *NovT* 26 (1984): 168-90; and John T. Squires, *The Plan of God in Luke-Acts*, SNTSMS 76 (Cambridge UK:

important to be sensitive to those passages that do not. This section of Acts begins with a human decision (15:36), describes a transition based on human interpretation (16:10), and continues in a rather anticlimactic way until Paul quietly leaves Macedonia altogether (17:15). Although Luke certainly wants to show God's role in the shaping of the early church and the dramatic impact of early evangelism, he also shows human decisions and interpretations—even when these decisions and interpretations lead to lackluster success. When one focuses too much on the divine action in Luke's story, one misses the fullness of Luke's message. Part of appreciating that fullness includes understanding the relationship between dream-vision experiences and the characters' perception of God's will throughout Luke-Acts.

At the heart of this discussion are the relationship between the human and the divine in Luke's narrative and the way one reads Acts 16:10 in light of one's understanding of that relationship. If the Spirit's command in Acts 13:1-3 highlights the divine guidance for Paul's first journey, then Paul's personal decision to make another trip (15:36) must be emphasized as well. Those who would assume, along with the characters, that Paul's dream-vision at Troas is evidence of divine guidance must also account for the lackluster success experienced on the Macedonian mission field. More broadly, the tendency to view God as the prime mover within the plot of Luke-Acts must be balanced by an understanding of those passages in which the human characters are forced to *interpret* God's will.

As noted above, Tannehill and others have argued that we should appreciate the role of human decision and human action in Luke's story. I would agree with that argument and would suggest that this part of Acts implores us to do just that. Precisely at the moment of a supposed visionary breakthrough, we find Luke's characters compelled to *interpret* Paul's experience. What if the lack of a divine agent in this dream-vision is *not* a coincidence? How significant would it be that precisely here—in a passage Haenchen likened to the Cornelius-Peter episode, with the full connotation of Luke depicting God twitching human puppets[35]—if the characters interpreted Paul's dream-vision as a divine directive a bit too hastily? This comment is not meant to denigrate Haenchen. Indeed, he poignantly describes what many find in Luke's story: an irruptive presence of God that

---

Cambridge University Press, 1993).

[35]Haenchen, *Acts of the Apostles*, 485, 362.

somehow seems to obviate human deliberation and struggle. Or, as Haenchen put it: an irruptive presence of God in the face of which "faith loses its true character of decision."[36]

What if, instead, Luke is depicting a *balance* between irruptive divine guidance and the necessity of human interpretation? What difference would it make for our understanding of Lukan theology if that depicted human interpretation is sometimes . . . well, if not wrong, then not exactly right? These sorts of questions invite a closer examination of Luke's dream-vision scenes, particularly those in which we find Luke's characters interpreting their visionary experience.

There can be no question that Luke often presents dream-visions in ways that emphasize God's role in the story. In some of these passages, characters respond automatically to the message of their dream-vision, with no suggestion of interpretation.[37] It would be a mistake, however, to conclude that all dream-vision scenes in the story function in such a unilateral manner. In response to other dream-visions, Luke's characters offer their own understanding of their experience. In these character-filtered[38] accounts, the reader sometimes finds a complex relationship between the narrator's description of the event and the significance a character ascribes to it.[39]

---

[36]Haenchen, *Acts of the Apostles*, 362.

[37]Following the angelic announcement of Jesus' birth, Luke 2:15 depicts the shepherds saying to one another, "Let's go to Bethlehem and *see this thing that has happened*" (NIV). The use of the perfect participle in the latter half of the phrase (ἴδωμεν τὸ ῥῆμα τοῦτο τὸ γεγονός) is telling; they regard the event of the angel's proclamation as something that has already taken place. In Acts 8:26, an angel tells Philip to "arise and go"; without any description of Philip's reaction to this experience, the next verse indicates that he "arose and went."

[38]"Character filter" is a term coined by Seymour Chatman. It refers to those points in a narrative when the point of view shifts from the narrator to a character in the story. *Coming to Terms: The Rhetoric of Narrative in Fiction and Film* (Ithaca NY: Cornell University Press, 1990) 144.

[39]Elsewhere, e.g., I have argued that this idea of character-filtered, or character-interpreted, dream-vision reports provides a helpful lens for reading the visionary experiences of Zechariah and Mary in Luke's infancy narrative. *Convinced That God Had Called Us*, 110-46.

The purpose of this discussion, therefore, is *not* simply to argue that the characters are wrong about Paul's dream-vision at Troas. Instead, I am suggesting that Luke's dream-visions are helpful for understanding not only the role of God in this narrative, but also for understanding the role of God's people in the narrative. It is in these scenes, at least as dramatically as in any others, that one finds the intersection of the human and the divine in Luke-Acts.

Embedded Letters and Rhetorical αὔξησις in Sallust, Chariton, and Luke[1]

Justin R. Howell

The difficulty of interpreting the historical and literary roles played by letters in ancient texts has long been a reality in the academy. A survey of scholarly positions on letters contained in Sallust's *Bellum Catilinae*, the book of Acts, and Chariton's *Callirhoe* shows the interpretive complexities that arise and that, especially in the case of letters in the former two texts, scholars have yet to reach a consensus. The previous scholarship on the letter of Lysias in Acts 23:26-30 contextualizes some of the major issues scholars have addressed regarding letters that appear in narratives—issues that often relate to whether a given letter is genuine or spurious. These concerns appear as early as 1914 with Julius Wellhausen claiming the Lukan composition of the letter of Lysias[2] and as recently as the 1990s with the appearance of the multi-volume *The Book of Acts in its First Century Setting*, which contains numerous voices either presupposing or arguing for the authenticity of the letter.[3]

---

[1]I wish to thank participants in the Book of Acts Section at the annual meeting of the Society of Biblical Literature, November 2006, those in the Early Christian Studies Workshop at the University of Chicago, and especially Professors Hans-Josef Klauck and Margaret M. Mitchell for their comments on earlier versions of this paper.
[2]Julius Wellhausen, *Kritische Analyse der Apostelgeschichte*, Abhandlungen der königlichen Gesellschaft der Wissenschaften zu Göttingen: Philologisch-historische Klasse 15/2 (Berlin: Weidmanns, 1914) 48. Wellhausen states that "Der Wortlaut des Briefes an Felix, den ersten Prokurator der in der AG vorkommt, konnte dem Berichterstatter nicht bekannt sein. Er hat ihn selber verfaßt und dabei auf die Synedrialsitzung von 22,30-23,10 Rücksicht genommen, die in Wahrheit schwerlich stattgefunden hat."
[3]See Darryl W. Palmer, "Acts and the Ancient Historical Monograph," in *The Book of Acts in Its Ancient Literary Setting*, ed. Bruce W. Winter and Andrew D. Clarke, BAFCS 1 (Grand Rapids MI: Eerdmans, 1993) 28; Loveday C. A. Alexander, "Acts and Ancient Intellectual Biography," in *The Book of Acts in its Ancient Literary Setting*, 47; Bruce W. Winter, "Official Proceedings and the Forensic Speeches in Acts 24-26," in *The Book of Acts in its Ancient Literary Setting*, 335; Brian Rapske, *The Book of Acts and Paul in Roman Custody*, BAFCS 3 (Grand Rapids MI: Eerdmans, 1994) 85n.83, 152-53. See also Jacob Jervell, "The

Joel Cadbury agreed with Wellhausen when he claimed that the letters in Acts "are so characteristic of the author's style as to support the presumption that he is responsible for them."[4] In this line of argument, the place of the letters has often been likened to that of the speeches in Acts— i.e., as accounts of what Luke thinks the various characters of Acts *should* have stated in their delivery of speeches and in their composition of letters (cf. Thucydides 1.22).[5] More recently, Richard Pervo has claimed that the letters in Acts "create a warm and personal atmosphere, and they serve as a kind of documentation lending verisimilitude to the situation." Pervo maintains that the letter of Lysias, for example, is "an invention, based upon neither data nor probability but wish."[6]

Arguments for the authenticity of the letters in Acts are also quite common in previous scholarship. Foakes-Jackson is one early representative of this position. He claims that the letter of Lysias "bears every trace of

---

Future of the Past: Luke's Vision of Salvation History and its Bearing on his Writing of History," in *History, Literature, and Society in the Book of Acts*, ed. Ben Witherington III (Cambridge UK: Cambridge University Press, 1996) 118.

[4]Henry J. Cadbury, *The Making of Luke-Acts* (New York: Macmillan, 1927) 191.

[5]See, e.g., Cadbury, *Making of Luke-Acts*, 190; Cadbury, "The Speeches in Acts," in *The Beginnings of Christianity*, 5 vols., ed. F. J. Foakes-Jackson and Kirsopp Lake (London: Macmillan, 1920–1933) 5:402; Henry J. Cadbury, F. J. Foakes-Jackson, and Kirsopp Lake, "The Greek and Jewish Traditions of Writing History," in *The Beginnings of Christianity* 2:13; C. K. Barrett, "Quomodo Historia Conscribenda Sit," *NTS* 28 (1982): 305; George A. Kennedy, *New Testament Interpretation through Rhetorical Criticism* (Chapel Hill: University of North Carolina Press, 1984) 114-40; Gerhard A. Krodel, *Acts*, ACNT (Minneapolis: Augsburg, 1986) 432; David E. Aune, *The New Testament in Its Literary Environment* (Cambridge UK: James Clarke & Co., 1987) 128, 169; and Richard I. Pervo, *Profit with Delight: The Literary Genre of the Acts of the Apostles* (Philadelphia: Fortress, 1987) 77. For a discussion of the history of scholarship on the speeches, see Marion L. Soards, *The Speeches in Acts: Their Content, Context, and Concerns* (Louisville: Westminster/John Knox, 1994) 1-17.

[6]Pervo, *Profit with Delight*, 77. See also C. K. Barrett, who states: "It is hard to imagine how Luke could have obtained access to Roman archives whether in Jerusalem or in Caesarea." *A Critical and Exegetical Commentary of the Acts of the Apostles*, 2 vols., ICC (Edinburgh: T.&T. Clark, 1998) 2:1071.

being genuine."[7] More recent, and quite influential, is the argument of E. A. Judge.[8] Commenting upon the double occurrence of τύπος (cf. Acts 23:25-30) in P.Oxy. XLVII 3366, Judge argues that one must consider "whether the author of Acts did not mean his readers to take them [i.e., the letters in Acts 15:23-29 and 23:26-30] as the direct citation of transcripts available to him."[9] The value of Judge's argument, however, is limited because on the one hand τύπος does not occur in Luke's description of the letter in Acts 15:23-29, and on the other hand his argument proposes only two possibilities for the status of the letter in Acts 23:26-30: (1) that it is a "rhetorical approximation" of an actual letter written by Lysias or (2) that it is a copy of a letter "made verbatim" from a letter written by Lysias.[10] The problem with Judge's assessment is that both of his possibilities presuppose the existence of an actual letter written by Lysias.[11]

---

[7]F. J. Foakes-Jackson, *The Acts of the Apostles*, MNTC (London: Hodder & Stoughton, 1931) 211. See also Kirsopp Lake and Henry J. Cadbury, *The Beginnings of Christianity* 4:294. Noting the occurrences of τύπος (cf. Acts 23:25) in reference to documents in ancient literature, Lake and Cadbury suggest: "In all these cases the context gives not only the tenor of the document referred to, but, after the manner of ancient writers, what might be regarded as the actual wording and form of the letter, an *exemplum* of the verbal contents." There is a discrepancy, however, in *The Beginnings of Christianity* for, in another context, Cadbury, Foakes-Jackson, and Lake state: "Verbatim copying of sources was not tolerated, for no matter how slavishly one followed the substance of his predecessor's narrative one must recast his style." "The Greek and Jewish Traditions," in *The Beginnings of Christianity* 2:13.

[8]For those who follow Judge, see, e.g., Raymond Samuel Coleman, Jr., "Embedded Letters in Acts and in Jewish and Hellenistic Literature" (Ph.D. diss., Southern Baptist Theological Seminary, 1994) 212-13, and Ben Witherington III, *The Acts of the Apostles: A Sociorhetorical Commentary* (Grand Rapids MI: Eerdmans, 1998) 698-99.

[9]E. A. Judge, "A State Teacher Makes a Salary Bid," in *A Review of the Greek Inscriptions and Papyri Published in 1976*, New Documents Illustrating Early Christianity 1, ed. G. H. R. Horsley (North Ryde NSW: The Ancient History Documentary Research Centre, Macquarie University, 1981) 77-78.

[10]Judge, "A State Teacher Makes a Salary Bid," 77.

[11]By assuming the existence of a letter of Lysias, Judge repeats the mistake of F. F. Bruce, who writes: "It is idle to speculate how Luke knew the terms of the letter which the tribune wrote to Felix to explain why he was sending Paul to

One must not, however, single out for critique Judge's argument or any other argument claiming the authenticity of the letters in Acts. Offhand comments suggesting that Luke himself composed the letters in Acts are also not without problems. A claim that likewise leaves one longing for more evidence is Pervo's "warm and personal atmosphere" (even though this is arguably true in describing the letter's effect and therefore a reasonable assertion for the goal of Pervo's project).

While various answers to the question regarding *whether* an ancient author composed a letter contained in his or her respective text are frequently offered, the question of *why* an author might have composed a letter is all too often overlooked. Therefore, I propose that answering the latter question is logically prior to providing an answer to the former. More specifically, as I shall address in this essay, reading an embedded letter as a rhetorical and literary carrier of a narrative must precede the issue regarding the letter's "authenticity." Rather than extracting an embedded letter from its context, a first step should seek to take the appearance of an embedded letter at face value (i.e., that it is a part of a narrative proper) while avoiding the initial assumption that the letter had a previous life before it came to occupy its present position. Patricia A. Rosenmeyer's recent work entitled *Ancient Epistolary Fictions*—which should now accompany Adolf Deissmann's classic and standard work[12]—is particularly helpful as it

---

Caesarea. In any case, he does not profess to reproduce it *verbatim*; the phrase 'after this form' may imply that only the general purport of the letter is given." *Commentary on the Book of the Acts*, NICNT, rev. ed. with new preface and introduction (Grand Rapids MI: Eerdmans, 1977; 1st ed., 1954) 459.

[12]Adolf Deissmann, *Light From the Ancient East: The New Testament Illustrated by Recently Discovered Texts of the Graeco-Roman World*, trans. Lionel R. M. Strachan (New York: Harper & Brothers, 1927) and Patricia A. Rosenmeyer, *Ancient Epistolary Fictions: The Letter in Greek Literature* (Cambridge UK: Cambridge University Press, 2001).

contributes to the role of embedded letters in narrative discourse.[13] After briefly considering Rosenmeyer's contribution below, I shall analyze the narrative roles of select letters in Sallust's *Bellum Catilinae*, the book of Acts, and Chariton's *Callirhoe*. Following this analysis, I shall take the letter of Lysias in Acts 23:26-30 as a test case and investigate the use of documentary evidence, including letters, in Greco-Roman rhetoric—and more specifically the invention (εὕρεσις) and arrangement (τάξις) of such documents—and show that the letter of Lysias functions as Luke's proof (πίστις) for the innocence of Paul as declared by the Roman authorities in Acts 23:11-26:32. The statement of such a proof and its recapitulation in this context of Acts, I shall argue, is best understood through rhetorical αὔξησις.

The Narrative Role of Embedded Letters

Rosenmeyer's work offers the most recent and extensive treatment of embedded letters as they appear in ancient narrative discourse. Through her analysis of both autonomous letters and those contained in a larger context such as a play or novel, she offers an important resource for scholars attempting to understand better the workings of Greek epistolography in the ancient world. She has convincingly shown that embedded letters often—in the Greek novels at least—are a part of the novel proper and not sources that the author had at his or her disposal when writing. Such letters are therefore properly termed "epistolary fictions" because they "are crucial to the workings of the plot."[14] She begins her study of the embedded letters by

---

[13]On embedded letters, see also Aune, *New Testament in Its Literary Environment*, 169; Michael Trapp, ed., *Greek and Latin Letters: An Anthology, with Translation* (Cambridge UK: Cambridge University Press, 2003) 33-34; and Hans-Josef Klauck, *Ancient Letters and the New Testament: A Guide to Context and Exegesis*, trans. Daniel P. Bailey (Waco TX: Baylor University Press, 2006) 133-39, 420. See also Coleman's extensive catalogue of embedded letters that appear in both Hellenistic and Jewish narratives ("Embedded Letters").

[14]Rosenmeyer, *Ancient Epistolary Fictions*, 135. As Rosenmeyer shows, "letters in the novel often provide a central impetus for movement in the narrative, in a genre that is characterized above all by action, movement, and revelation" (137). Rosenmeyer's observations from a literary perspective are quite similar to the comments of Demetrius on προσωποποιΐα, namely, that through its usage a passage "appears far more vigorous and powerful, and becomes much more dramatic inartis-

showing that as early as the fifth century BCE such letters in the plays of Euripides "were introduced presumably to liven up a scene, to support an argument with a visual aid, or to impart critical information that could not, according to dramatic conventions, otherwise be revealed."[15] As she shows, there is an almost seamless transition from the appearance of letters in plays to that in the Greek novels of the Second Sophistic. In addition to the use of letters in plays, she also argues that "fictive prose letters" were included in historical prose, taking Herodotus and Thucydides as examples.[16] Because she does not include later historians in her treatment, it is especially important that a work of historical prose that appeared near the time of the composition of Acts receive analysis in the present study in addition to an ancient novel.

In the paragraphs that follow, therefore, I shall examine embedded letters in three narratives, including Acts, that were written within an approximate time span of one hundred twenty-five years (25 BCE–100 CE), with a particular focus on the letter of Lysias in Acts 23:26-30. The selection of Sallust's *Bellum Catilinae* and Chariton's *Callirhoe* as comparative material for contextualizing Acts is deliberate since both of these narratives overlap significantly with the hybrid nature of Acts. While Chariton has been an informative conversation partner in past scholarship on Acts, I propose that adding Sallust's *Bellum Catilinae* to the dialogue provides a more complete colloquium. If scholarship on Acts in the recent past has shown anything,

---

tically (ἀτεχνῶς)" (*Eloc.* 5.266). (All translations of ancient sources are mine.)

[15]Rosenmeyer, *Ancient Epistolary Fictions*, 63. See also Aristotle *Poet.* 4.20. In the context of a play, Rosenmeyer explains, one may compare letters to props such as "rings, swaddling clothes, and locks of hair." In these plays, she observes, "letters become more than just a means of passing on information: they become actors in their own right, personified as speaking voices. . . . Letters serve to further the plot by misdirection and misinformation, as well as by providing crucial information hitherto unknown. They are never mere devices in the hands of Euripides, but rather objects on stage with all the power and authority of a main character, agents of change, and a reminder that written text, not performed speech, often has the last word" (*Ancient Epistolary Fictions*, 95-96).

[16]Rosenmeyer, *Ancient Epistolary Fictions*, 11. Her discussion includes Euripides' plays (*Hippolytus*, *Iphigenia in Tauris*, and *Iphigenia in Aulis*) and the following novels: Chariton's *Callirhoe*, Achilles Tatius's *Leucippe and Clitophon*, and Heliodorus's *Ethiopian Story*.

it has shown that its genre is complex in that it incorporates elements from multiple genres, including biography, the novel, and history.[17] Not only does *Bellum Catilinae* represent the historical genre and *Callirhoe* the novel, but both narratives overlap significantly with biography and therefore provide a fitting pair for engaging interpretive issues in Acts.

A. Bellum Catilinae 35.1-6. Sallust's *Bellum Catilinae*, which contains two embedded letters (35.1-6; 44.5), provides a context in which the role played by embedded letters in historical prose may receive analysis.[18] Taking the letter of Catiline in *Bell. Cat.* 35.1-6 as an example, one notices that the letter contains themes consistent with the narrative in which it is couched. At least one explanation for this consistency is that the letter is a genuine document that serves as the basis for the emergence and employment of other themes throughout the narrative.[19] This view is problematic, however, because it assumes the existence of an actual letter from which these themes stem, when it is also possible that the letter is simply one aspect of Sallust's broader literary and rhetorical agenda and therefore an aspect of which Sallust himself is also in complete control.

Though there is a consistency between the personality of Catiline as seen in the letter and its narrative context, such consistency could as easily indicate the Sallustian composition of the letter as it could the Catilinian. That a letter reveals the personality of its author, as attested by the ancient rhetorical and epistolary theorists,[20] finds particular expression when the

---

[17]This complex issue has been summarized most recently by Thomas E. Phillips, "The Genre of Acts: Moving toward a Consensus?" *CBR* 4 (2006): 365-96.

[18]Some identify a third letter in *Bell. Cat.* 33.1-5, e.g., P. McGushin, *C. Sallustius Crispus, Bellum Catilinae: A Commentary*, MBCBS 45 (Leiden: E. J. Brill, 1977) 189, and Richard Patrick Geckle, "The Rhetoric of Morality in Sallust's Speeches and Letters" (Ph.D. diss., Columbia University, 1995) 87-89. See, however, Kathryn F. Williams, "Manlius' *Mandata*: Sallust *Bellum Catilinae* 33," *CP* 95 (2000): 160-71.

[19]See, e.g., Williams, "Manlius' *Mandata*," 170. Williams states, "Catiline's genuine letter prompted the cause of the *miseri* as a topic for both quotations."

[20]Cicero's brother Quintus writes to him in a letter: "I have seen all that is you in your letters [*litterae*]." Cicero *Fam.* 44.2 (16.16.2). Noting the emperor Marcus Arelius as being one who used epistolary style well, Philostratus explains that "in addition to his judicious speech, his steadfast character has also been carved into his letters (γράμματα)" (*Ep.* 2.1.6-7).

letter is embedded in a narrative in which the narrator is able to relate third-person accounts that supplement the first-person dialogue contained in the letter. The comments of Demetrius are particularly insightful on this issue:

> The letter, just as the dialogue, should have a strong use of characterization. For everyone, more or less, writes a letter as an image of his or her own soul. It is also possible to see the character of the writer in every other form of written-communication, but in none so clearly as in the letter. (*Eloc.* 4.227; cf. Cicero *Quint. fratr.* 1.45)

Accordingly, a letter provides a medium through which an audience is able to see the character (i.e., the letter writer) most clearly—whether the letter is autonomous or embedded in a narrative.

In *Bellum Catilinae*, the narrator's portrayal of Catiline is authenticated through first-person accounts that appear in two forms: two speeches of Catiline to his fellow conspirators (20.2-17; 58.1-21) and the letter of Catiline that is written to Quintus Catulus (35.1-6).[21] Catiline, who prior to the letter is characterized at length as one who had "an evil and perverse nature" (5.1-8) and who identified with those afflicted with shame (*flagitium*), poverty, and a corrupt conscience (14.3; 18.4), is now vividly confirmed through the letter as possessing the characteristics that the narrator has previously attributed to him. In the letter Catiline appears as a crafty and seditious figure who now neither admits to his charges nor offers a self-defense. The narrator's portrayal of Catiline as having rallied a group of impoverished and prosecuted individuals (20.8-17)[22] is corroborated by Catiline's statements in the letter. Catiline's support of "the common cause of the unfortunate," his witness of "the unworthy dignified with honor" (*non dignos homines honore honestatos*), and his realization that he himself "had become alienated because of false suspicion" (35.3) are key aspects of

---

[21]On the issue of Catiline's characterization in general, see, Francesca Santoro L'Hoir, *The Rhetoric of Gender Terms: "Man," "Woman," and the Portrayal of Character in Latin Prose*, MBCBS 120 (Leiden: E. J. Brill, 1992) 56-59, and Ann Thomas Wilkins, *Villain or Hero: Sallust's Portrayal of Catiline*, AUS 17/15 (New York: Peter Lang, 1994) 29-70.

[22]In Catiline's speech to his prospective compatriots, he reminds his hearers of the "popularity, power, honor, and wealth" of their oppressors, which is contrasted with the "dangers, rejections, judgments, and poverty" of Catiline and his hearers. *Bell. Cat.* 20.8-17.

his character in the overall narrative. These aspects, as they appear in the letter, carry forward Catiline's motives for rallying the people with whom he identifies and point forward to his continued pursuits in waging war with Rome.[23]

Also notable is Catiline's refusal to offer a self-defense in spite of his alleged innocence (35.2)—a major point emphasized by the narrator in Catiline's portrayal as one who inculpably and willingly goes into exile in order to prevent political unrest.[24] Furthermore, the employment of the epistolary *topos* in the closing of the letter—namely, that of stating that there is more to say but now is not the most expedient time to do so—provides an appropriate transition to the account that immediately follows. Explaining that the letter comes to a close because he receives news that he is "about to be attacked" (35.5), the subsequent narrative qualifies this imminent threat as a plan for Antonius to pursue Catiline with an army (36.1-3). One of the letter's primary functions in the narrative, therefore, is to substantiate through a first-person account what the narrator has already claimed and will claim through third-person reports concerning Catiline and his pursuits.

B. Acts 23:26-30. As I have shown that the letter in *Bellum Catilinae* plays a crucial role in its narrative, the embedded letter in Acts 23:26-30 should thus undergo examination as part of the narrative proper in order to detect consistent literary themes throughout Luke-Acts. Analyzing the parallel characterizations of Jesus and Paul in Luke-Acts[25]—specifically that of their trials before the ruling authorities—is essential for the contextualization of the letter of Lysias.[26] Scholars have long noted the legal terminology contained in the letter,[27] which is reminiscent of and meant to evoke

---

[23]In the second letter of *Bellum Catilinae*, which is sent from Lentulus to Catiline, Catiline is reminded of his danger and limits and is urged to "seek help from all, even from the lowest." *Bell. Cat.* 44.5.

[24]The narrator shows how Catiline ardently denies the charges brought against him as he faces the senate. *Bell. Cat.* 31.7.

[25]On this issue in general, see David P. Moessner, " 'The Christ Must Suffer': New Light on the Jesus—Peter, Stephen, Paul Parallels in Luke-Acts," *NovT* 28 (1986): 220-56.

[26]Charles H. Talbert, *Literary Patterns, Theological Themes, and the Genre of Luke-Acts*, SBLMS 20 (Missoula MT: Scholars Press, 1974) 17, 22.

[27]See, e.g., Hans Conzelmann, *Acts of the Apostles*, trans. James Limburg,

the questioning and examination of Jesus (Luke 22:16-23:16). Lysias's report that Paul was "arrested (συλλαμβάνω) by the Jews" (23:27) also echoes Jesus' arrest (συλλαμβάνω)—presumably by the Jews in this context as well since he is taken "to the home of the high priest" (Luke 22:54; cf. Acts 1:16; 12:3; 26:21). Similarly, the issue of the "plot" (ἐπιβουλή) "to kill" (ἀναιρέω) Paul reported in the letter (23:27, 30) reverberates the ongoing theme of the plots of the Jews to put Jesus to death (Luke 22:2; 23:32; Acts 2:23; 10:39; 13:28) and continues the theme of the plots of the Jews to execute Paul that are delineated earlier in the narrative of Acts (9:23-24, 29; 20:3, 19; 23:15, 21).[28] The accusation noted in the letter, which concerns "questions of their law" (23:29), likewise brings forward the charges against Stephen (who is also paralleled with the Lukan Jesus [Luke 23:34, 46; Acts 7:59-60] and who is noted as one who did not cease speaking against the law [6:13]) and the earlier charges against Paul (18:13; 21:28; cf. 25:8).[29] As the letter comes to a close, it appropriately introduces Paul's "accusers" (κατήγοροί), and not only shows Paul encountering accusations from the Jews as did the Lukan Jesus (Luke 6:2; 23:1-16), but it also provides a segue into the subsequent (and immediate) narrative containing the accusations (κατηγορέω) of the ῥήτωρ Tertullus and the Jews (24:1-9) and the ultimate failure of Paul's opponents to "accuse"

A. Thomas Kraabel, and Donald H. Juel, Hermeneia (Philadelphia: Fortress, 1987) 195; Allison A. Trites, "The Importance of Legal Scenes and Language in the Book of Acts," *NovT* 16 (1974): 278-84; H. W. Tajra, *The Trial of St. Paul: A Juridical Exegesis of the Second Half of the Acts of the Apostles*, WUNT (Tübingen: Mohr Siebeck, 1989) 106-108; Barrett, *Acts of the Apostles* 2:1083-84; and Joseph A. Fitzmyer, *The Acts of the Apostles: A New Translation and Commentary*, AB 31 (New York: Doubleday, 1998) 727-28.

[28]On the troubling portrayal of Jews and Judaism in Luke-Acts and among Lukan scholars, see Joseph B. Tyson, *Images of Judaism in Luke-Acts* (Columbia: University of South Carolina Press, 1992) and *Luke, Judaism, and the Scholars* (Columbia: University of South Carolina Press, 1999).

[29]Cf. the accusations concerning the law against Stephen and Paul in Acts 6:13 (Ὁ ἄνθρωπος οὗτος οὐ παύεται λαλῶν ῥήματα κατὰ τοῦ τόπου τοῦ ἁγίου [τούτου] καὶ τοῦ νόμου·) and Acts 21.28 (οὗτός ἐστιν ὁ ἄνθρωπος ὁ κατὰ τοῦ λαοῦ καὶ τοῦ νόμου καὶ τοῦ τόπου τούτου πάντας πανταχῇ διδάσκων, ἔτι τε καὶ Ἕλληνας εἰσήγαγεν εἰς τὸ ἱερὸν καὶ κεκοίνωκεν τὸν ἅγιον τόπον τοῦτον).

(κατηγορέω) him of wrong on legitimate grounds (24:10-21; 25:5, 11, 14b-21).[30]

Within the context of a major section containing the declaration of Paul's innocence by the Roman authorities (Acts 23:11-26:32),[31] perhaps most notable in the letter is Lysias's statement that he finds Paul "having done nothing worthy of death or imprisonment (μηδὲν ἄξιον θανάτου ἢ δεσμῶν)" (23:29). Because such a statement is presented as a first-person account of a Roman authority, it provides an official utterance concerning Paul's innocence and simultaneously presents Paul as being acquitted by Lysias like the Lukan Jesus who was acquitted by Pilate (23:4, 13-16, 22; cf. Luke 23:41, 47; Acts 13:28).[32] Lysias's statement of Paul's innocence will receive confirmation also by Festus's declaration—"I find him to have done nothing worthy of death (μηδὲν ἄξιον θανάτου)"—in the later speech (25:24-27)[33] and by the agreement among Agrippa, Bernice, and their associates that Paul is doing "nothing worthy of death or imprisonment" (Οὐδὲν θανάτου ἢ δεσμῶν ἄξιον) (26:30-32).

C. Callirhoe 4.4.7-10; 8.4.5-6. Given that embedded letters, such as the one in *Bellum Catilinae*, play an important role in ancient historiography, it comes as no surprise to find the same phenomenon in the ancient novel—since the latter tends to imitate and develop the historical genre. Chariton's

---

[30]Rudolf Pesch states: "Falls Lukas den Brief verfaßte, gab er dem Leser schon einen Vorblick auf das weitere Geschehen (vgl. 24,1-23)." *Die Apostelgeschichte*, 2 vols., EKKNT 5 (Zürich: Benziger; Neukirchen-Vluyn: Neukirchener Verlag, 1986) 2:251.

[31]See Charles H. Talbert, *Reading Acts: A Literary and Theological Commentary on the Acts of the Apostles* (New York: Crossroad, 1997) 203-25. See also Philip Francis Esler, *Community and Gospel in Luke-Acts: The Social and Political Motivations of Lucan Theology*, SNTSMS 57 (Cambridge UK: Cambridge University Press, 1987) 204, and Charles H. Talbert, *Reading Luke-Acts in Its Mediterranean Milieu*, NovTSup 107 (Leiden: E. J. Brill, 2003) 185.

[32]The letter also provides the greatest window into the soul of Lysias, as he speaks more here than in any other part of the narrative. As such Lysias is characterized as a crafty figure who, as Klauck states, "not only presents the past course of events in abbreviated form; he also reveals a pronounced tendency to color the picture positively when it comes to his own behavior." *Ancient Letters*, 433.

[33]See Soards, *Speeches in Acts*, 120-22.

Callirhoe—which contains a total of five embedded letters, with three occurring about midway through the narrative (*Chaer.* 4.4.7-10; 4.5.8; 4.6.3-4) and two toward the end (*Chaer.* 8.4.2-3; 8.4.5-6)—serves as only one example. That the letters in *Callirhoe* are vehicles that Chariton uses to give a first-person point of view of the characters while simultaneously recapitulating the major themes of the narrative was recognized years ago by Tomas Hägg.[34] Though Hägg deemed the letters genuine, Rosenmeyer's work on "epistolary fictions," and the letters in *Callirhoe* in particular, poses serious doubt concerning the letters' authenticity.[35] The first and final letters of the novel, because they reciprocate aspects of plot by pointing to each other, are particularly noteworthy.[36]

The first letter appears as Chaereas, in the attempt to reunite himself with Callirhoe, writes to inform her that he is alive and to remind her of their previous love (*Chaer.* 4.4.7-10). The letter, however, falls into the hands of Dionysius, who is now married to Callirhoe. As Rosenmeyer ob-

---

[34]Tomas Hägg, *Narrative Technique in Ancient Greek Romances: Studies of Chariton, Xenophon Ephesius, and Achilles Tatius*, SUSIA 2/8 (Stockholm: Svenska Institutet i Athen, 1971) 175, 255-67.

[35]See, e.g., Rosenmeyer, *Ancient Epistolary Fictions*, 133-68, esp. 137-47.

[36]Chariton's rhetorical savvy is undisputed. See, e.g., Gareth L. Schmeling, *Chariton*, TWAS 295 (New York: Twayne, 1974) 116-18, 156-59; Tomas Hägg, *The Novel in Antiquity* (Los Angeles: University of California Press, 1983) 13, 16; Carlos Hernandez Lara, "Rhetorical Aspects of Chariton of Aphrodisias," *GIF* 42 (1990): 267-74; B. P. Reardon, "Chariton," in *The Novel in the Ancient World*, ed. Gareth Schmeling, MBCBS 159 (Leiden: E. J. Brill, 1996) 325, 331-32; Marie Marcelle Jeanine Laplace, "Le Roman de Chariton et la Tradition de l'Éloquence et de la Rhétorique: Constitution d'un Discourse Panégyrique," *RMP* 140 (1997): 38-71; Ronald F. Hock, "The Rhetoric of Romance," in *Handbook of Classical Rhetoric in the Hellenistic Period: 330 B.C.–A.D. 400*, ed. Stanley E. Porter (Leiden: E. J. Brill, 1997) 445-65; and Hock, "The Educational Curriculum in Chariton's *Callirhoe*," in *Ancient Fiction: The Matrix of Early Christian and Jewish Narrative*, SBLSymS 32, ed. Jo-Ann A. Brant, Charles W. Hedrick, and Chris Shea (Atlanta: Society of Biblical Literature, 2005) 15-36. Chariton's claim in the opening line of the novel to have been the secretary of a ῥήτωρ combined with his inclusion of multiple rhetorically arranged speeches, some of which are delivered in the courtroom, are among the most obvious indicators of his rhetorical abilities. His inclusion of the letters, the first of which is used in a courtroom scene (5.6.10), is equally suggestive.

serves, the letter of Chaereas to Callirhoe marks a turning point in the narrative. Because Dionysius obtains the letter before it reaches Callirhoe, she never actually learns of the letter's content until it is read in a courtroom scene (*Chaer.* 5.5.9-6.11). "Precisely because the letter is read by almost all the novel's main characters *except* its intended addressee, it functions as the central engine of the second half of the novel, the impetus for all the action that follows."[37] Although Dionysius uses the letter as documentary evidence in his case against Mithridates—claiming that Mithridates forged the letter in the name of Chaereas, who is supposedly dead—the audience of the novel knows that Chaereas is in fact the real author and that he is alive. The use of the letter in Dionysius's courtroom speech, then, serves—at least in his mind—as evidence for his case. In the mind of the audience, however, his use of the letter further demonstrates his chicanery in his attempts to remain the husband of Callirhoe by attempting to conceal the fact that Chaereas is alive.

Just as the first letter of the novel provides a significant shift in the narrative, the final letter of the novel—that of Callirhoe to Dionysius informing him of their now dissolved marriage (*Chaer.* 8.4.5-6)—brings closure to the competition between Dionysius and Chaereas, who are both vying for Callirhoe.[38] With the appearance of this final letter, an important point of irony is disclosed in the narrative, namely that Dionysius himself—the one who earlier in the narrative conceals the initial letter in order to prevent the reunion of Callirhoe and Chaereas (*Chaer.* 4.5.9-6.2)—receives a letter written by Callirhoe as a result of the reunion between Callirhoe and Chaereas, marking the termination of Dionysius's marriage to Callirhoe.

The letter of Callirhoe to Dionysius also brings closure to Dionysius's character in the novel and shows the audience the final encounter between Callirhoe and Dionysius. After receiving the letter from Statira, the letter carrier, the narrator explains that Dionysius

> returned home and shut himself up. When recognizing Callirhoe's handwriting, he first kissed the letter. Then opening it, he clasped it to his heart as though she were present [πάρειμι] and held it there for a long

---

[37]Rosenmeyer, *Ancient Epistolary Fictions*, 139.

[38]The dissolution of the marriage between Callirhoe and Dionysius is realized by Dionysius when he reads that it is addressed to "Dionysius, my benefactor" as opposed to "Dionysius, my husband." *Call.* 8.5.13.

time, unable to read it because of his tears. Although his tears had hardly ceased, he began to read it, and his first reaction was to kiss Callirhoe's name (*Chaer.* 8.5.13).[39]

This detailed expression of the Parousia motif[40]—showing the final personal interaction between Callirhoe and Dionysius—illustrates the significant role that the letter plays as the narrative comes to a close. The letter is indeed a replication of Callirhoe herself and as such provides a first-person account that allows both the character and the audience of the novel to interact with the mind of Callirhoe at this juncture in the story. Chariton's *Callirhoe*, then, shows that letters were used in what is appropriately deemed ancient fiction (πλάσμα), and as such uses fictitious correspondence to simulate a vivid and "real" exchange among the characters of the narrative.

The Rhetorical Function of Documentary Evidence

While Rosenmeyer has shown that the theater of ancient Greece is one apparent source from which the phenomenon of embedded, fictitious letters surfaced, an equally important stream that feeds this literary technique is the use of documentary evidence in the courtroom as discussed in the Greek

---

[39]Kissing and admiring the sender of the letter through the document itself is not an uncommon motif in ancient letter writing. See, e.g., the letter of Apion (BGU II 423), who asks that his father write to him so that he may "make obeisance," or perhaps "kiss," (προσκυνέω) his handwriting. Deissmann, *Light from the Ancient East*, 179-83. See Klauck, *Ancient Letters*, 12.

[40]See also Heikki Koskenniemi, *Studien zur Idee und Phraseologie des griechischen Briefes bis 400 n. Chr.*, Suomalaisen Tiedeakatemian Toimituksia/ Annales Academiae Scientiarum Fennicae B, 102/2 (Helsinki: Akateeminen Kirjakauppa, 1956) 183-84; Rosenmeyer, *Ancient Epistolary Fictions*, 155; and Klauck, *Ancient Letters*, 188-93. Seneca states: "I give thanks that you frequently write to me. For in the only way that you can, you are revealing yourself to me. For I never receive a letter [*epistula*] from you without us immediately being in communion. If pictures of our absent friends are pleasing to us, which refresh the memory and ease our longing by a feigned and unsubstantial consolation [*falsum atque inane solacium*], how much more pleasing are letters [*litterae*], which bring real traces [*uera uestigia*] of an absent friend, real indications [*uerae notae*]? For that which is sweetest about presence [*conspectus*]—that is, being recognized—is maintained by the impress of a friend's hand upon a letter [*epistula*]." *Ep.* 40.1.

and Latin rhetorical handbooks. The integral relationship between argumentation in the courtroom to that in a narrative is undeniable.[41] That rhetorical theory of antiquity was equally useful in both the courtroom and in the composition of narrative is illustrated by Quintilian's discussion of the value of writing narratives, especially historical ones, as training for students of rhetoric (*Inst.* 2.4.2).[42]

Long before Quintilian, the *Rhetorica ad Alexandrum* had argued that a proper use of rhetorical techniques such as amplifications (αὐξήσεις), minimizations (ταπεινώσεις), and recapitulations (παλιλλογίαι), allow one to acquire a "great facility both in speaking and writing" (*Rhet. Alex.* 28.2-4) and concluded that "both in speaking and writing" the reader should adhere to and practice the principles set forth (*Rhet. Alex.* 38.1). Because rhetoric served as a kind of literary theory in antiquity,[43] the need to consider a letter's rhetorical function within its broader rhetorical agenda is evident. Using the letter of Lysias in Acts 23:26-30 as a test case—a letter that is clearly a Lukan composition based upon the common themes, vocabulary, and phraseology shared by the letter and larger narrative of Luke-Acts—I shall now explore the εὕρεσις and τάξις of fictitious docu-

---

[41]As H. I. Marrou observed, because reading was done aloud in antiquity "there was no borderline between the written and the spoken word; the result was that the categories of eloquence were imposed on every form of mental activity," including literary works. *A History of Education in Antiquity*, trans. George Lamb (New York: Sheed and Ward, 1956) 195. See also Laurent Pernot, *Rhetoric in Antiquity*, trans. W. E. Higgins (Washington DC: Catholic University of America Press, 2005) 135-36, 196-201.

[42]See also Quintilian, *Inst.* 2.5.18-20; 2.18.5; Theon, *Prog.* 60.3-8; Men.Rh. 1.333-34; 1.335.23-30; 1.338.28-339.2; and Raffaella Cribiore, *Gymnastics of the Mind: Greek Education in Hellenistic and Roman Egypt* (Princeton NJ: Princeton University Press, 2001) 234-35, 238. Malcolm Heath explains that the analysis of narrative was "an important skill in the handling of judicial cases, in which it is often necessary to cast doubt on the opponent's account of events." "Invention," in *Handbook of Classical Rhetoric*, 94. See also Margaret M. Mitchell, "Rhetorical and New Literary Criticism," in *The Oxford Handbook of Biblical Studies*, ed. J. W. Rogerson and Judith M. Lieu (New York: Oxford University Press, 2006) 615-33, esp. 622-23.

[43]George A. Kennedy, *A New History of Classical Rhetoric* (Princeton NJ: Princeton University Press, 1994) 165-66 and Wilhelm Wuellner, "Arrangement," in *Handbook of Classical Rhetoric*, 52, 74.

ments, including letters, as discussed by the ancient rhetorical theorists. Because the theorists often discuss εὕρεσις and τάξις together, I will do the same in the present context. Moreover, a discussion of documentary evidence within the framework of a document's invention and placement within an argument is a discussion of how such a document embellishes and, more specifically, amplifies an argument. As Cicero summarizes, "An orator must consider three things: what to say, how to arrange it, and by what means" (*Or. Brut.* 14.43).[44]

A. Documentary Evidence and εὕρεσις. That ancient forensic speeches often included the reading of documents, followed by meticulous interpretations of those documents, is well-attested in the rhetorical handbooks.[45] Cicero, for example, shows the important role of the orator as interpreter of written documents and notes that students of rhetoric were taught that "the written text" (*scriptum*) should hold chief importance in trials.[46] While the interpretation of documents often centered on the letter and spirit of laws, other documents such as contracts, wills, receipts, and letters also served as proofs and were given equal status to laws as evidence for analysis.[47] As Quintilian acknowledges, the use of documentary evidence in constructing persuasive speech had long ago been explicated by Aristotle when he distinguished non-artistic proofs from artistic ones—explaining that the former included "witnesses, tortures, written documents (συγγραφαί), and

---

[44]Cf. Aristides's comments: "For to do the work of a rhetor is doubtless to invent (ἐχευρίσκω) what is necessary and to arrange (τάσσω) and present what is fitting with embellishment (κόσμος) and force." *Rh.* 2.382. See also Cicero, *Inv.* 1.30.50-37.67; *De or.* 1.31.142; *Part. or.* 3.9; Kennedy, *New History*, 5, 45; and Heath, "Invention," 91.

[45]See, e.g., *Rhet. Her.* 2.9.13-11.16; Cicero, *Inv.* 1.12.17-13.18; 1.30.49; *De or.* 1.31.140; 2.26.110-13; *Part. or.* 4.14; 31.107-08; 38.132-39.138; *Top.* 25.95-26.96; and Quintilian, *Inst.* 2.13.8; 3.5.4; 7.5.5-6.12; 12.1.45; 12.8.14. See also Pseudo-Quintilian, *Decl. min.* 308; 332.2; 339; and Heath, "Invention," 100.

[46]Cicero, *Inv.* 2.40.116–51.154, esp. 2.48.142-43; and *De or.* 1.57.244; 2.24.100.

[47]Quintilian, *Inst.* 5.10.106-07; 7.5.6. See Quintilian's discussion of Alexander's discovery of documents showing that the Thebans had lent a hundred talents to the Thessalians. The documents initiate a case and serve as evidence for the Thessalians' need to repay the money to the Thebans. *Inst.* 5.10.111-18. See also Hermogenes, *Stat.* 2.72–3.25; 7.1-21; 8.1-49.

the like" (Aristotle *Rhet.* 1.2.2; Quintilian *Inst.* 5.1.1-2.).[48] Quintilian provides an example of such documentary evidence when he notes that letters (*codicilli*) found (*inuenio*) in the house of a particular person serve as evidence in forensic arguments in which that person is being charged with adultery (*Inst.* 7.2.52.).[49]

The letter interpreted by Cicero in the prosecution of Verres provides an actual example of a letter used in a forensic speech (*Verr.* 2.3.66-67). Cicero had intended to read the letter at the end of his speech, interspersed with running commentary that argued for the corruption of Verres's administration. Although he never actually read the letter in making his case—since the accused party had accepted defeat prior to the letter's appearance in court[50]—its written form illustrates how letters embedded in speeches provided evidence for the case, which in this context presents the accused as corrupt and therefore guilty.[51]

Letters and documents in the courtroom, however, were not only used to incriminate opponents. A document was also used when the author of such could not make a personal appearance in court, even though this, as Quintilian explains, would often excite suspicion among the jury on the grounds that the author of the document lacked the confidence to appear as a witness. Consequently, it was easier to dispense with a document or at least question its authenticity (*Inst.* 5.7.1-2).[52] Quintilian's discussion of how documents (*tabulae*) were often attacked as forgeries and his practical advice of how performing even a simple inspection of such in order to

---

[48]See also *Rhet. Alex.* 6.1-7.3; 15.1-8; 32.1-9; *Rhet. Her.* 4.41.53; Cicero, *De or.* 2.27.115-20; 2.40.173; 2.79.331; *Anonymous Seguerianus* 1.1-7; 145.1-11; and Apsines, *Rh.* 4.260.5-6; 5.269.16-22; 9.296.22-23. Cf. also Demetrius's brief discussion on Aristotle's use of proofs that are suitable for letters (*Eloc.* 4.233).

[49]Cicero includes "a writing [*scriptum*] or a sealed document [*obsignatum*]" among the most powerful evidence used to render the accused as guilty of the charges set forth. *Part. or.* 33.114.

[50]See Trapp, *Greek and Latin Letters*, 314-16.

[51]Ending his discussion of the letter, Cicero states: "Now, judges, I have only read the letter of this convict to you so that from it you might learn the rules, practices, and habits of the entire group." *Verr.* 2.3.68.157.

[52]Cf. Quintilian, *Inst.* 5.7.25; 5.7.32-33. Quintilian's evaluation of the use of documentary evidence, of course, assumes the orator's reliance upon such evidence.

detect forgeries implies that the practice of constructing fictitious documents was not uncommon (*Inst.* 5.5.1-2.).[53]

The *Rhetorica ad Herennium* is more explicit in discussing this practice as the author offers advice on how to give fictitious documents verisimilitude. Discussing the importance of constructing a plausible *narratio*, the author acknowledges two situations in which one makes an argument: (1) a situation in which the matter is actually true (2) and one in which it is fictitious. After outlining the precautions about how to demonstrate the credibility of a matter that is true, the author explains that in fictitious matters, the prescribed precautions "will have to be observed even more. Fabricating must be done with care in those matters in which documents [*tabulae*] or a reliable invention [*firma auctoritas*] of someone will be seen to have played a role" (*Rhet. Her.* 1.9.16.).[54]

This openly acknowledged practice of fabricating documents, and more specifically letters, was carried out in exercises of Greco-Roman *paideia*. It has long been recognized that fictitious letter-writing was a form of exercise in the schools by the end of the second century BCE.[55] Elementary students, in developing and practicing compositional skills, studied and copied sample letters. Then at a more advanced level, students honed their letter-writing skills by appropriating the personal traits of a particular figure in order to write a letter in a fictive context.[56] This exercise, προσωποποΐα,

---

[53]See also Quintilian's discussion of the use of humor in speeches. Here he tells of Fulvius Propinquus, who "when asked by the ambassador whether there was an autograph in the documents [*tabulae*] that he brought forth, he replied, 'even a real one [*verus*], sir.' " *Inst.* 6.3.100. Cf. Pseudo-Quintilian, *Decl. min.* 332.10.

[54]As Cicero explains, one will have a plausible *narratio* if it contains "details that are accustomed to appear in real life [*ueritas*]; if the proper qualities of the characters [*personarum dignitates*] are preserved . . . if the account is suited to the nature of the actors and to the habits of ordinary people and the beliefs of the audience." *Inv.* 1.21.29. See also Quintilian's comments on the use of fictitious statements for the purpose of arousing the emotions of the judges. *Inst.* 4.2.19.

[55]See M. Luther Stirewalt, Jr., *Studies in Ancient Greek Epistolography*, SBLRBS 27 (Atlanta: Scholars Press, 1993) 35; Kennedy, *New History*, 208; Teresa Morgan, *Literate Education in the Hellenistic and Roman Worlds*, CCS (Cambridge UK: Cambridge University Press, 1998) 60; and Cribiore, *Gymnastics of the Mind*, 215-19.

[56]See Stirewalt, *Ancient Greek Epistolography*, 20-21. One example that illustrates how the phenomenon of composing fictitious letters moved beyond the

is defined by Aelius Theon, for instance, as "the introduction of a person who recites words that are indisputably suitable to both the speaker and the matters discussed" (*Prog.* 115.11-14).[57]

Though modern scholars rightfully acknowledge the use of προσωποποιία in discussions of fictitious speeches composed by ancient historians and other writers,[58] the use of the figure in the composition of letters is often overlooked. Theon includes letter writing in his list of contexts in which προσωποποιία is used. Describing the way that students of rhetoric would personify the words spoken by a particular character, Theon illustrates his point by explaining that a speaker might portray, for instance, "what words a man would say to his wife as he is about to go on a journey

---

elementary stage is the letters of Epicurus, which appear to have been composed in order "to preserve or propagate" the teachings of Epicurus and those of a later Epicurean school. Stirewalt, *Ancient Greek Epistolography*, 22. The practice of writing fictitious letters in school exercises, as Stirewalt (*Ancient Greek Epistolography*, 22, 43-64) hypothesizes, may also be represented by the letters attributed to Diogenes and Crates, which appear "to recount the words and deeds of the philosopher and his student, to preserve his image, and to defend the school's tradition." See these letters in Abraham J. Malherbe, *The Cynic Epistles: A Study Edition*, SBLSBS 12 (Missoula MT: Scholars Press, 1977).

[57]The edition of Theon's *Progymnasmata* that I have consulted is that of Michel Patillon, ed., *Aelius Théon: Progymnasmata*, Collection des Universités de France (Paris: Les Belles Lettres, 1997). The page and line citations are those of the Spengel edition.

[58]In his discussion of προσωποποιία Quintilian notes examples of fictitious speeches (*ficta oratione*) of persons, namely, those produced by Cicero as he adopts the personae of Appius Caecus and her brother Clodius in their speeches to Clodia. *Inst.* 3.8.54. As explained by Quintilian, when ghostwriting speeches, the words are "adapted to the situation and life" of the ones who will deliver the speeches. *Inst.* 3.8.50. In imitating individuals, the ability to appropriate the specific characteristics of the individuals being imitated was crucial. Noting Cicero's ability to portray uniquely each character whom he personified (i.e., his avoidance of assuming the same character when portraying different individuals) in certain speeches, Quintilian commends him for his ability to take into account the particular characteristics of the imitated speaker and therefore to create a situation in which the imitated speaker himself or herself appeared to speak. *Inst.* 3.8.50. Cf. *Rhet. Her.* 1.2.3; 4.2.2-3.

or a general to his soldiers in dangerous situations" (*Prog.* 115.14-17).[59] According to the evidence of Theon, it is in such hypothetical situations that students would personify characters, whether real or imagined, in order to capture the essence of the personalities being personified.[60] Theon explains that of all the exercises, προσωποποιΐα is "the most receptive of characters and emotions" (*Prog.* 117.33-34). Importance, therefore, was placed upon creating the context in which the personified character would most appropriately appear. The speaker's personality, audience, age, social status, and the occasion and place of the speech are among the details that students would need to consider in performing the exercise (*Prog.* 115.23-26).[61]

Quintilian's discussion of προσωποποιΐα as a rhetorical figure is perhaps even more helpful for gaining a sense of the construction of fictitious documents. He describes προσωποποιΐα in general as giving "wonderful variety and animation to a speech" (*Inst.* 9.2.29). With it, he explains,

> we credibly introduce our conversations with others and those of others among themselves and portray the appropriate characters [*personas idoneas damus*] by advising, rebuking, complaining, praising, and lamenting. Indeed, in this form of speaking, we are even allowed to bring down the gods and to raise the dead; even cities and peoples receive a voice. (*Inst.* 9.2.30-31)[62]

---

[59]On προσωποποιΐα, see also Marrou, *History of Education*, 203, 286; George Kennedy, *The Art of Rhetoric in the Roman World: 300 B.C.–A.D. 300* (Princeton NJ: Princeton University Press, 1972) 316-17; and Stanley F. Bonner, *Education in Ancient Rome: From the Elder Cato to the Younger Pliny* (Los Angeles: University of California Press, 1977) 267-69.

[60]Although later teachers of rhetoric (e.g., Apsines, *Rh.* 10.301.14-18; 10.317.19-318.6; Nicolaus, *Prog.* 64.20-65.10) would make a clear distinction between προσωποποιΐα and ἠθοποιΐα—reserving the former for fictional characters and the later for real individuals—Theon makes no such distinction in his description of προσωποποιΐα, as shown by his further examples of its use: "What words Cyrus would say as he marches against the Massagetae, or Datis as he meets the king after the battle of Marathon." *Prog.* 115.18-20.

[61]Writing on ἠθοποιΐα, Nicolaus the Sophist would later reflect on the practice of writing fictive letters: "[ἠθοποιΐα] also seems to me to exercise us in the style of letter writing, since in such it is necessary to foresee the character of the ones sending the letter as well as the ones to whom the letter is sent." *Prog.* 67.2-5.

[62]Cf. Cicero's comments on representing the state as speaking and calling up the dead. *Or. Brut.* 25.85. Here Cicero advises against using such figures of

After noting the use of προσωποποιΐα in creating fictitious sayings (*dicta*), Quintilian shows that one may also use the figure in the construction of fictitious writings (*scripta*). The brief example that he gives, which is an imitation of an opponent's writing (*Inst.* 9.2.34.), illustrates the speaker's freedom to present evidence that appears to the audience as both tangible and "real."

As Quintilian explains, though προσωποποιΐα are "most difficult" to perform, they are "most useful" and "of the greatest use to poets and future writers of history [*historiarum futuri scriptores*]" (*Inst.* 3.8.49). This figure, he notes, is sometimes used "with controversies that have been composed from histories and include proceedings with actual historical people" (*Inst.* 3.8.52).[63] This acknowledged usefulness of προσωποποιΐα to historians of antiquity deserves more attention when reading the two embedded letters of Sallust's *Bellum Catilinae*—letters that most scholars consider as either verbatim copies or close approximations of actual documents.[64] It is arguable that such claims are too confidently made given that Quintilian acknowledges that Sallust in particular is in control of the words uttered by Catiline's character in *Bellum Catilinae* (*Inst.* 3.8.45).[65] Though this

---

thought. His criticism of this practice, of course, assumes their employment.

[63] Although προσωποποιΐα was important for writers of history, in προσωποποιΐα itself, as Kennedy notes, "Historicity was not important" (*New History*, 169). Cicero, in comparing styles of historiography, commends Antipater's method because "he had exalted himself somewhat, and had imparted to history a greater style." In contrast, he notes, "other writers were not embellishers [*exornates*] of subjects, but simply narrators [*narratores*]." *De or.* 2.12.54. On rhetoric and historiography see, e.g., A. J. Woodman, *Rhetoric in Classical Historiography* (Portland OR: Areopagitica Press, 1988) and Clare K. Rothschild, *Luke-Acts and the Rhetoric of History: An Investigation of Early Christian Historiography*, WUNT 175 (Tübingen: Mohr Siebeck, 2004).

[64] See, e.g., McGushin, *Bellum Catilinae*, 195-99, and J. T. Ramsey, *Sallust's Bellum Catilinae: Edited with Introduction and Commentary*, APATS 9, ed. Gilbert W. Lawall (Chico CA: Scholars Press, 1984) 159. Geckle argues that the letter of Catiline is likely a "paraphrase of a genuine letter." He offers this suggestion while also concluding "that almost all the speeches and letters are essentially Sallustian creations." "Rhetoric of Morality," 58, 79.

[65] See also Stefan Rebenich, "Historical Prose," in *Handbook of Classical Rhetoric*, 317n.251.

acknowledgement refers to one of the speeches given by Catiline (*Bell. Cat.* 20), Quintilian's statement on fictitious writings (*scripta*) in his discussion of προσωποποιΐα (*Inst.* 9.2.34)—not to mention Theon's inclusion of letter writing in his description of προσωποποιΐα in addition to his concern for writing historical narratives well (*Prog.* 60.3-8; 115.22)—should receive more attention than it has thus far.[66]

Quintilian's description of προσωποποιΐα appears within his treatment of figures of thought.[67] Following those before him, he discusses two main types of rhetorical figures: figures of speech and figures of thought, both of which fall under a broader rhetorical feature that is expressed in a variety of ways, including: among the Greek-speaking theorists, καλλωπισμός and κόσμος, and among the Latin, *exornatio, lumen orationis*, and *ornamentum.* Because variety of expression in repetition is one of the chief tenets of this feature—often rendered in English as "embellishment"[68]—it is only appropriate that the descriptive terms used to describe such a phenomenon are themselves subject to an assortment of labels.[69]

The *Rhetorica ad Herennium* includes *exornatio* in a list of the five ingredients that culminate in the most complete and perfect argument (2.18.28). One primary goal of embellishment is to supply the argument with ornamentation so as to lend it verisimilitude. Cicero notes that "common topics are discussed with greater emphasis and embellishment [*ornatius*], and with lofty words and then with lofty thoughts. For in the arguments this is the goal, so that what is said may appear to be true" (*Inv.*

---

[66]At least one scholar who touches on these issues is Rebenich ("Historical Prose," 265-337).

[67]See also the discussion in Donald Lemen Clark, *Rhetoric in Greco-Roman Education* (New York: Columbia University Press, 1957) 90-91.

[68]Figures, according to Quintilian, are the tools of embellishment. *Inst.* 11.1.2; cf. 10.5.3. See also *Rhet. Her.* 4.13.18; and Demetrius, *Eloc.* 59.263-66.

[69]Note Quintilian's discussion of repetition, in which he employs the very phenomenon he is describing by reiterating the same thought in a number of ways: "What satisfaction can a person have or what evidence is there of even moderate learning, unless one knows how to establish some points by repetition and others by dwelling on them, how to digress from a subject and to return to one's main point, to remove the blame from oneself and transfer it to another, to decide what points to leave out and what points may be considered insignificant?" *Inst.* 9.2.4. See also Cicero, *Or. Brut.* 39.137.

2.16.51).[70] As Menander Rhetor shows, one embellishes a speech by inserting examples for clarification or stories that sound pleasing to the hearers. He adds that "it is also necessary to fabricate (πλάσσω) dreams or to pretend (προσποιέω) to have heard some report (ἀκοή)" (2.390.4-5).[71]

According to Quintilian, proofs—which he qualifies as witnesses, documents (*tabulae*), arguments, and the like—also require embellishment lest the evidence remain weak and lifeless (*Inst.* 5.13.56-57). Although Aristotle and other theorists had classified documents as non-artistic proofs—and therefore ones that are not invented but discovered—the figure of προσωποποιΐα and the practice of fabricating documents show that the εὕρεσις of documentary evidence could, at times, move into the realm of the artistic while the usage of such evidence would maintain its classification of nonartistic.

B. Documentary Evidence and τάξις. According to Cicero, it is the embellishment (*exorno*) of what has been invented (*invenio*) and the arrangement (*distinguo*) of it into definite divisions that is most pleasing to an audience (*Inv.* 1.30.50). Amplification (αὔξησις/*amplificatio*)—which the *Rhetorica ad Herennium* includes as one of several kinds of embellishment that "results in the expansion and enrichment of an argument" (2.29.46)— helps to explain how a document often functions in a given argument.[72] The author of *De sublimitate* defines amplification (αὔξησις) as "an aggregation of pieces and common-places that pertain to the subject, thus strengthening what has been proposed by dwelling upon it" (12.2). The rhetorical theorists generally agree that the strongest argument in a speech should appear first and that the speaker should reiterate and amplify such an argument throughout the subsequent parts of the speech.[73] The *Rhetorica ad*

---

[70]Cicero then clarifies that in the common topics, although giving the argument verisimilitude is necessary, "still the goal is amplification [*amplitudo*]." *Inv.* 2.16.51.

[71]Cf. Menander Rhetor's discussion on giving a speech when taking leave of a city in which he states: "You should embellish (καλλωπίζω) the speech with images, historical examples (ἱστορίαι), comparisons, and other sweet elements" (2.433.13-14). On the invention and discovery of other elements that give the speech relevance, see also Men.Rh. 2.390; 2.443-44.

[72]On amplification as embellishment, see also Cicero, *Inv.* 2.16.51; *De or.* 1.21.94; and *Or. Brut.* 21.82.

[73]That the strongest arguments come first is especially the case for a defense.

Herennium shows that in some cases—only when the situation calls for it—the reading of a document might serve as this strongest argument and therefore appear first in the arrangement (3.9.16-17). The author also stresses the importance of dwelling on the same thought or topic—which is often the strongest and most important topic—yet stating it in a variety of ways by means of both figures (*exornationes*) of speech and thought.[74] Theon observes Demosthenes practice of repeating the same idea in various ways not only from one speech to another, but also within the same speech, where the same issues "often appear stated in a number of ways" (*Prog.* 64.1-3).[75] Cicero expounds upon the need to cast the same idea in a number of ways when he discusses the importance of figures of thought, emphasizing the necessity "to embellish (*illumino*) in some way either all or at least most thoughts." An orator, he explains, "will often whirl around the same subject in many ways, sticking to the same idea, and lingering on the same thought" (*Or. Brut.* 39.137).[76] That a proof such as a document receives amplification in the subsequent parts of the speech is demonstrated by the *Rhetorica ad Alexandrum* when it discusses the use of proofs in

---

Quintilian, *Inst.* 7.1.10-12; 7.10.12. See also *Rhet. Her.* 3.10.18; Cicero, *De or.* 2.73.296; Quintilian, *Inst.* 5.12.14; 6.4.22; and Heath, "Invention," 100. Cf., however, Apsines: "It is necessary to place the weaker refutations first, and the stronger second; for if the stronger ones are placed first, the weaker ones will no longer have a place." *Rh.* 5.277.26–278.3.

[74]*Rhet. Her.* 4.42.54; 4.43.56; 4.44.58-45.58. As Cicero comments: "[B]ut my approach in speaking allows me to take the good points and be circumlocutory, embellishing [*exorno*] and magnifying [*exaggero*] and lingering and dwelling on and sticking to them, but any bad part or imperfection of the case, I thus abandon, not so that I seem to flee from it, but to disguise it so that it may be covered completely by embellishing [*orno*] and amplifying [*augeo*] that good point." *De or.* 2.72.292.

[75]See Vernon K. Robbins's discussion on this practice as illustrated through the writings of Plutarch and the canonical gospels. "Writing as a Rhetorical Act in Plutarch and the Gospels," in *Persuasive Artistry: Studies in New Testament Rhetoric in Honor of George A. Kennedy*, ed. Duane F. Watson, JSNTSup 50 (Sheffield UK: JSOT Press, 1991) 142-68.

[76]Cicero shows the necessity (*oportet*) of variety in amplification when he notes that this often separates "the greatest orators" from "the ordinary ones." *Inv.* 1.41.75-76. See also Cicero, *De or.* 3.53.202; *Or. Brut.* 15.49; Quintilian, *Inst.* 9.2.4; and Pseudo-Hermogenes, *Inv.* 3.5.183-91; 3.15.60-89.

making a defense: "If they deny the deed, we must amplify (αὐξητέον) the proofs (πίστεις) that we have already stated, and criticize and minimize the ones that they are preparing to bring forth" (36.19).[77]

Concerning the use of amplified proofs in an argument, it is also important to note that amplification was often accomplished by means of προσωποποιΐα. In the "amplification (*amplificatio*) of things," Cicero explains, "fictitious persons and even mute objects" are given a voice (*Part. or.* 16.55). He comments that "in explaining (*illustro*) and amplifying (*amplifico*) what is set forth" and with the goal of "making what we amplify (*augeo*) appear to the audience as important as eloquence is able to make it," the speaker might employ, among many other techniques, "imitation of manners and life (*morum ac vitae imitatio*) that are either given in character or not" and "the introduction of a fictitious person" (*personarum ficta inductio*), the later of which he qualifies as being "certainly the most emphatic way of amplifying (*lumen augendi*)" (*De or.* 3.53.202-54.206).[78] When a letter appears within a narrative, the relationship between προσωποποιΐα and αὔξησις often finds clear expression. Through the letter the author is able to reveal a personal portrait of the character, thus amplifying his character portrayal, while simultaneously giving the narrative verisimilitude.

C. The Letter of Lysias as Documentary Evidence. The letter of Lysias in Acts 23:26-30 provides one piece of substantial evidence that confirms Paul's innocence, which is best understood by noting the rhetorical function of the letter within the broader context of the section that declares Paul's innocence by the Roman authorities (Acts 23:11-26:32). That the letter appears near the beginning of this section reflects a careful arrangement of material on Luke's part. Granted, Cicero explains that when embellishing a point the speaker may arrange the material in a variety of ways (*Part. or.* 3.10-4.12).[79] But because it is often the strongest points that appear first, and that sometimes documents function as these strongest and initial points, the τάξις of this section is telling of Luke's rhetorical goal. More specifically, Luke uses the letter as a proof (i.e., a piece of documentary evidence that supports his case for Paul's acquittal) and then, through

---

[77]See also Aristotle, *Rhet.* 3.17.

[78]Quintilian quotes this passage from Cicero as the former is discussing "figures of thought." *Inst.* 9.1.30-31.

[79]Cf. Cicero, *De or.* 2.85.350; 3.38.152.

προσωποποιΐα, amplifies this statement of Paul's innocence by having other Roman authorities draw the same conclusions as those of Lysias. Paul's innocence as declared by the Roman authorities, then, is repeated multiple times in Acts 23:11-26:32[80] as with Jesus in Luke 23:1-49, yet Luke adheres to rhetorical precedents and expresses Paul's innocence in a variety of ways: (1) a letter from the tribune, Lysias, to the governor, Felix (23:26-30); (2) a speech delivered by Felix's successor, Festus, to Agrippa and others (25:24-27); and (3) an indirect statement reflecting the agreement made by King Agrippa, Bernice, and their cohorts (26:30-32).

Conclusion

Based on the analysis of letters in *Bellum Catilinae*, Acts, and *Callirhoe*, authors use embedded letters to perform at least three functions: (1) A letter supplements the narrative by recapitulating the themes of the context in which it appears by means of the content of the letter itself—thereby reinforcing the narrative in which it is embedded. Catiline's letter to Quintus Catulus (*Bell. Cat.* 35.1-6) provides one example. In a fictive sense, Catiline's character is displayed through his own words in the letter—providing the audience with a piece of evidence that substantiates the credibility of the narrator's characterization of Catiline. (2) The use of the Parousia motif in a letter provides an image, as it were, of the character in the story. One notices such a role in the letters of *Callirhoe*—particularly the letter of Callirhoe to Dionysius (*Call.* 8.4.5-6). The narrator's detailed description of Dionysius reading the letter has this function (*Call.* 8.5.13). (3) A letter—like other documents that are used in forensic rhetoric—serves as authoritative evidence in acquitting or convicting a character in the narrative who is on trial, whether in the fictive context of the narrative's audience or in the narrative itself. The letter of Lysias (Acts 23:26-30) embodies this role by appearing as the first and official utterance of Paul's acquittal as given by the Roman authorities in Acts 23:11-26:32. There are elements, of course, of all three of these functions in all three of the narratives that have been discussed.

---

[80]On the issue of repetition and the letter of Lysias, see also Beverly R. Gaventa, *The Acts of the Apostles*, ANTC (Nashville: Abingdon, 2003) 318, and Rothschild, *Luke-Acts and the Rhetoric of History*, 138-39.

Using the embedded letter in Acts 23:26-30 as a test case, the burden of proof concerning the question of the letter's authenticity lies not on the fact that many ancient authors possessed the capacity to compose fictitious letters for use in argumentation, but rather on the fact that the letter (with its Lukan vocabulary and phraseology) fits within Luke's broader rhetorical goal of showing the innocence of the early Christian movement, which is demonstrated most clearly through the innocence of his two main characters, Jesus and Paul. Therefore, taking the letter of Lysias at face value (i.e., as part of the narrative) and asking *why* Luke would have composed it provides the most important evidence as to *whether* he composed it. That ancient orators and authors fabricated and included letters in their argumentation simply shows the nuts and bolts and therefore answers *how* an argument, with its letter(s), was composed and put together by an ancient author such as Luke.

As Rosenmeyer has shown, the literary phenomenon of embedded "epistolary fictions" was common in the Second Sophistic. This phenomenon would develop to such an extent that, as Hägg observes, in the *Alexander Romance* (ca. 200–300 CE), the "main lines of the historical course of events are mirrored in fictitious letters exchanged between persons involved."[81] In light of these observations, and as I have demonstrated, the letter of Lysias in Acts 23:26-30 appears situated in an earlier developmental stage of this literary phenomenon. While the confines of the present essay have not allowed me to explore all the letters contained in the three narratives considered, perhaps the essay has provided at least a starting point for carrying out such explorations. What the essay has hopefully demonstrated, however, is that in addition to the literary and rhetorical abilities of all three authors considered—abilities that are widely acknowledged by the academy—the capacity of composing fictitious letters for the goals of constructing a plausible argument and developing the plot should also have a place in the discussion.

---

[81]Hägg, *Novel in Antiquity*, 126.

"Friendly" Pharisees and Social Identity in Acts

Raimo Hakola

The portrayal of the Pharisees in Luke-Acts has produced conflicting inter-pretations concerning their characterization. Some scholars say that Luke is, in both parts of his double work, sympathetic to the Pharisees, some claim that the Pharisees are presented consistently in a negative light, and still others say that the Pharisees in Acts are presented as friendlier than the Pharisees in the Gospel of Luke. In this essay, I approach the portrayal of the Pharisees in Acts from a social-identity perspective. I focus especially on the surprising appearance of some "friendly" Pharisees in Acts (Acts 5 and 23) and claim that they make an important contribution to the validation of the social identity of early Christians. The social-identity perspective explains how Luke can present these non-Christian Pharisees as fairly sympathetic to early Christians whereas Christian Pharisees (Acts 15) repre-sent convictions that are misguided from Luke's perspective. Furthermore, the role of these "friendly" Pharisees is not necessarily in conflict with critical attacks on the Pharisees in the Gospel of Luke; both the criticism of the Christian Pharisees and the appearance of "friendly" non-Christian Pharisees serve the need to categorize early Christians as a group distinct from Judaism.

I. Luke-Acts and the Pharisees in Recent Studies: Overview and Criticisms

A. Luke-Acts and the Jews. The confusion concerning the characteriza-tion of the Pharisees mirrors the confusion concerning Luke's assessment of Jews and Judaism in general. There is no consensus on this question to date, even though in recent decades scholars have been more willing than they were earlier to admit that there are important positive images of Jewish people and Jewish religion in Luke-Acts alongside more or less overt criticism. Joseph B. Tyson has traced this change in scholarly attitudes to the historical developments in the twentieth century and especially to the aftermath of the Holocaust.[1] This catastrophic event in the heart of Christian Europe challenged previous ways of understanding relations between Jews

---

[1]Joseph B. Tyson, *Luke, Judaism, and the Scholars: Critical Approaches to Luke-Acts* (Columbia: University of South Carolina Press, 1999).

and Christians and prevailing views concerning early Christian origins. According to Tyson, "the major shift . . . in the understanding of Luke's treatment of Judaism was, to a significant degree, influenced by a recognition of the connections between NT scholarship, Christian anti-Judaism, and the anti-Semitism that prevailed in the late nineteenth and early twentieth centuries."[2] Before this shift, such scholars as Adolf von Harnack or Adolf Schlatter, despite great differences in their theological outlook, pointed to the negative images of Jews and Judaism in Luke-Acts "without recognising that there might be social problems."[3] Ernst Haenchen and Hans Conzelmann continued this tradition even in the post-Holocaust situation, even though they both "questioned the anti-Jewish tradition of critical scholarship at a number of points."[4] For Tyson, the work of Jacob Jervell represents a major shift in the studies on Luke-Acts and Judaism.[5] In a series of publications, Jervell has quite deliberately challenged earlier scholarship and has claimed that Luke does not present the Jewish people as totally rejecting the Christian proclamation and the church as the replacement of Israel. While many scholars have seen the failure of the Jews to receive Jesus as a part of Luke's schematic view of history and as the necessary condition for the Gentile mission, Jervell emphasizes the division of the Jews into the repentant and the obdurate in Luke-Acts.[6] Jervell has even stated that "Luke knows that *extra Israel nulla salus est*, that Israel is the one and only people of God destined for salvation."[7]

---

[2]Tyson, *Luke*, 147-46.

[3]Tyson, *Luke*, 136. For a detailed presentation of von Harnack's and Schlatter's work on Luke-Acts, see 30-65.

[4]Tyson, *Luke*, 135, in detail 66-90.

[5]Tyson, *Luke*, 91-109.

[6]Jacob Jervell, *Luke and the People of God: A New Look at Luke-Acts* (Minneapolis: Augsburg, 1972). The programmatic essay in this collection, "The Divided People of God: The Restoration of Israel and Salvation for the Gentiles," first appeared as "Das gespaltene Israel und die Heidenvölker: Zur Motivierung der Heidenmission in der Apostelgeschichte," *ST* 19 (1965): 68-96. Jervell later developed these views in his *The Theology of the Acts of the Apostles*, New Testament Theology (Cambridge UK: Cambridge University Press, 1996) and *Die Apostelgeschichte*, KEK 3 (Göttingen: Vandenhoeck & Ruprecht, 1998).

[7]Jacob Jervell, "The Future of the Past: Luke's Vision of Salvation History and Its Bearing on His Writing of History," in *History, Literature, and Society in the Book of Acts*, ed. Ben E. Witherington III (Cambridge UK: Cambridge University

Jervell's interpretation has opened the way to accentuate Luke's positive attitudes toward Judaism and to challenge, in the post-Holocaust climate, the claims that Luke-Acts represents Christian anti-Judaism.[8] However, not all scholars have been satisfied with this development. Jack T. Sanders has represented a position quite opposite to that of Jervell and his sympathizers.[9] Sanders has noted that pre-Holocaust New Testament scholars "had no difficulty seeing Luke's portrayal of the Jews for what it is, a condemnation of them for rejecting the offer of salvation in Christ (for which God has rejected them) and for being Christ-killers." According to Sanders, New Testament scholars in our time are divided into two camps: those who see Luke's anti-Jewish intent accurately and condemn it–like Sanders himself–and those who refuse to see anything condemnable in the New Testament and, therefore, "grasp at straws to explain it away."[10]

B. Luke-Acts as Favorable to the Pharisees. Joseph Tyson has summarized his review of scholarship on Luke-Acts and Jews by saying that there is—and was even in much pre-Holocaust scholarship—"an impressive if generally unacknowledged agreement" that "there are both pro-Jewish and

---

Press, 1996) 104-26, quotation 123. Tyson notes that Jervell is the first to attribute this motto to Luke, a motto which embraces the main contention of Luke-Acts for Jervell (*Luke*, 103).

[8]Robert L. Brawley, *Luke-Acts and the Jews: Conflict, Apology, and Conciliation*, SBLMS 33 (Atlanta: Scholars Press, 1987) and "The God of Promises and the Jews in Luke-Acts," in *Literary Studies in Luke-Acts: Essays in Honor of Joseph B. Tyson*, ed. Richard P. Thompson and Thomas E. Phillips (Macon GA: Mercer University Press, 1998) 279-96.

[9]Jack. T. Sanders, *The Jews in Luke-Acts* (Philadelphia: Fortress Press, 1987). Various positions in the debate on Luke's portrait of Jews and Judaism—including articles both from Jervell and Sanders—are presented in Joseph B. Tyson, ed., *Luke-Acts and the Jewish People: Eight Critical Perspectives* (Minneapolis: Augsburg, 1988). For more literature, see Thomas E. Phillips, "Subtlety as a Literary Technique in Luke's Characterization of Jews and Judaism," in *Literary Studies in Luke-Acts*, 313-26, esp. 313-15. For a critical review of some recent discussion on the topic, see also Martin Rese, "The Jews and Luke-Acts: Some Second Thoughts," in *The Unity of Luke-Acts*, ed. Joseph Verheyden, BETL 142 (Leuven: Leuven University Press, 1999) 185-201.

[10]Jack T. Sanders, "Can Anything Bad Come out of Nazareth, or Did Luke Think That History Moved in a Line or in a Circle?" in *Literary Studies in Luke-Acts*, 297-312, quotation 311.

anti-Jewish materials in Luke-Acts."[11] The same kind of ambivalence characterizes Luke's presentation of the Pharisees which has made it difficult to find consensus concerning their function and role in Luke's two volumes. Those who hold that Luke is favorable in his overall presentation of the Pharisees find support for their case especially in Acts. In Acts 5, Luke tells how the apostles were brought before the members of the council who, after listening to Peter and other apostles, "were enraged and wanted to kill them" (Acts 5:33). In this context, Luke tells how Gamaliel, a Pharisee, stands up to put a stop to the execution of the apostles. Gamaliel's intervention for the apostles is successful, inasmuch as they are released after being flogged and ordered not to speak in the name of Jesus (v. 40). After this, there appear in the apostolic meeting in Jerusalem "some believers who belonged to the sect of the Pharisees" (Acts 15:5). The Pharisees as a group appear for the last time in Acts 23 where Paul defends himself in front of the Jerusalem council (Acts 22:30-23:10). The high priest and his allies are eager to convict Paul, whereas "certain scribes of the Pharisees' group" defend Paul by saying, "We find nothing wrong with this man. What if a spirit or an angel has spoken to him?" In this context, Paul himself testifies that he once was a Pharisee, a theme that is developed further when Paul defends himself in front of the king Agrippa (Acts 26:5).

Many scholars have proposed that the fairly positive roles assigned to the Pharisees in Acts are suggestive of Luke's intent in the gospel as well. Redaction-critical comparisons of Luke to Mark and Matthew have provided reasons to describe Luke's portrayal of the Pharisees as more positive than other early Christian portrayals. John Ziesler has concluded that, although Luke does not minimize the theological distance between Jesus and the Pharisees and does not shrink on occasion from accusing the Pharisees of hypocrisy, his overall tendency is to soften the opposition found in Mark.[12] This tendency found in the gospel is in line with Acts where the Pharisees are throughout "shown in a favourable light as the 'political,' if not always as the theological, friends of the Church."[13] In a similar vein, Robert Brawley maintains that the third gospel already "tends to present the Pharisees in comparatively favorable light" and thus antici-

---

[11]Tyson, *Luke*, 140.
[12]John A. Ziesler, "Luke and the Pharisees," *NTS* 25 (1978): 146-57.
[13]Ziesler, "Luke and the Pharisees," 148.

pates their presentation in Acts. In the two volumes, Luke describes the Pharisees "as respected and authoritative representatives of Judaism who can hover close to the edge of Christianity."[14] In Acts, the Pharisees legitimate the apostles, Paul, and Christianity. In Luke, they legitimate even Jesus. The Pharisees can fulfill this role because Luke writes from a post-70 perspective and "takes over the Pharisees in a historical, cultural, and religious context in which they demand admiration and assigns them a commensurate role."[15]

Peter Tomson follows Ziesler and Brawley in describing the Pharisees in Luke-Acts in quite positive terms. He knowingly rejects all attempts to understand Luke's work as anti-Pharisaic and concludes that, "while the gospel is clear about the differences between Jesus and the Pharisees and candid in its criticism of the latter, the Lukan author on the whole displays a remarkable sympathy for them."[16] Tomson focuses on Gamaliel's intervention and says that "the well-respected and popular Pharisee does not in fact choose position: he leaves the discussion undetermined. This implies no irony, at least no sarcasm." According to Tomson, Luke "puts Gamaliel and other Pharisees in a role of permissive tolerance towards Christianity."[17] Tomson compares this attitude to rabbinic traditions connected to the house of Hillel.[18] These traditions suggest that Luke "puts a saying of apparent

---

[14]Brawley, *Luke-Acts*, 84.

[15]Brawley, *Luke-Acts*, 105. According to Brawley, Luke writes in an environment where "the Pharisees continue to win respect" and their prestige "stands out" (97). However, there have been dramatic changes in the estimation of the power and influence of the early rabbinic movement which, in one way or another, carried on the heritage of Pharisaism in the post-70 situation. The early rabbinic movement has been repeatedly described as a relatively powerless group that did not have much influence on non-rabbinic Jews. For a discussion, with full references to recent rabbinic studies, see Raimo Hakola, *Identity Matters: John, the Jews and Jewishness*, NovTSup 118 (Leiden: Brill, 2005) 55-74.

[16]Peter J. Tomson, "Gamaliel's Counsel and the Apologetic Strategy of Luke-Acts," in *The Unity of Luke-Acts*, 585-604, quotation 592.

[17]Tomson, "Gamaliel's Counsel," 596.

[18]Tomson, "Gamaliel's Counsel," 601, refers especially to *Avot de Rabbi Nathan* 46 (parallels in *m. Avot* 4:11 and 5:17): "Every gathering in the name of Heaven will keep existing in the end, but every gathering (that is) not in the name of Heaven will not keep existing in the end. What is the gathering in the name of Heaven? You should say: That is the gathering of Israel before Mount Sinai. Every

Hillelite vintage in the mouth of Gamaliel, to the effect that Jewish leaders must leave the ultimate truth about the new movement for Heaven to decide."[19]

It is problematic to describe Luke's attitude to the Pharisees on the whole as sympathetic, even though the Pharisees, including Gamaliel, appear in Acts in fairly positive roles. To be sure, Luke sometimes seems to soften the harsh tone of his sources in the gospel (e.g., in 6:11, cf. Mk 3:6), but these cases are counterbalanced by instances of Pharisaic opposition that are not found in other sources.[20] For example, Luke attaches a fitting conclusion to Jesus' attack on the Pharisees and the lawyers (Luke 11; cf. Matt 23) by stating that "the scribes and the Pharisees began to be very hostile toward him and to cross-examine him about many things, lying in wait for him, to catch him in something he might say" (11:53-54). Luke also adds a scene where the Pharisees and the scribes grumble about Jesus welcoming sinners and eating with them (15:2) and has Jesus describe the Pharisees as lovers of money and as those who justify themselves in the sight of others (16:14-15). The self-righteousness of the Pharisees is further illustrated in the parable of a Pharisee and a tax collector, a parable peculiar to Luke (18:9-14).

Furthermore, the narrative of the gospel—if read in its own right and not in comparison to other Synoptics—does not give any inkling of the narrator approving of the Pharisees. The narrator introduces the Pharisees in a series of conflict stories where Jesus disputes with them over forgiveness of sins (5:17-26), eating with the sinners (5:27-32), fasting

---

dissent in the name of Heaven will keep existing in the end, but every dissent (that is) not in the name of Heaven will not keep existing in the end. What is a dissent in the name of Heaven? You should say: That is the dissent of Shammai and Hillel." Tomson recognizes that he is not the first to refer to these passages. E.g., C. K. Barrett, *The Acts of the Apostles*, ICC (London: T.&T. Clark, 1994) 1:297: "It is probably true that some Jews, including some influential Jews, took this line [as evidenced in *m. Avot* 4:11 and 5:17] with regard to the Christians, and it may be correct to infer that their tolerant attitude made possible the emergence of Christianity."

[19]Tomson, "Gamaliel's Counsel," 602-603.

[20]Cf. Jack T. Sanders, "The Pharisees in Luke-Acts," in *The Living Text: Essays in Honor of Ernest W. Saunders*, ed. D. E. Groh and Robert Jewett (Lanham MD: University Press of America, 1985) 141-88, esp. 150-51.

(5:33-39) and the Sabbath (6:1-11). After these conflicts, the narrator comments that the Pharisees "were filled with fury and discussed with one another what they might do to Jesus" (6:11). The narrator later makes this disapproving stance on the Pharisees unmistakable in a narrative aside where he says "by refusing to be baptized by him [John the Baptist], the Pharisees and the lawyers rejected God's purpose for themselves" (7:30).[21] After this sweeping statement, however, several individual Pharisees still invite Jesus to dine with them in their homes. These repeated meals (7:36-50; 11:37-12:1; 14:1-6) picture the Pharisees as open to Jesus and, therefore, seem to soften their characterization. Time and time again, however, these meal scenes develop into more or less open conflicts. During one of these meals, Jesus scorns the religious practice of the Pharisees by saying that they are "full of greed and wickedness" and "neglect justice and the love of God" (11:39, 42). After this, the sudden appearance of Pharisees who warn Jesus that Herod is trying to kill him (13:31) is not developed further in the gospel. The Pharisees appear for the last time when "some of the Pharisees in the crowd" ask Jesus to rebuke his disciples who acclaim Jesus as Messiah (19:39).

Because the Pharisees disappear from the story before Jesus has even entered Jerusalem and are not mentioned in the Passion Narrative, several scholars have concluded that Luke quite deliberately exonerates them from any responsibility for the death of Jesus.[22] This is not at all clear, however, because the Pharisees are closely associated in many passages with the scribes (5:21, 30; 6:7; 11:53; 15:2) who frequently appear in the Passion Narrative together with the chief priests (19:47; 20:1, 19; 22:2, 66; 23:10). The Pharisees and the scribes discuss what they might do to Jesus (6:11) and cross-examine him about many things to catch him in something he might say (11:54), which speaks for their shared willingness to act against Jesus.[23] All in all, despite some ambiguous and undeveloped signs that they

---

[21]Again, this narrative comment is not found in Matthew's parallel version of the scene, Matt 11:11-19; see, however, Matt 21:31-32.

[22]Ziesler, "Luke and the Pharisees," 154-55 and Sanders, "The Pharisees in Luke-Acts," 146-49. The force of this argument is not great because the Pharisees do not appear in Mark's Passion Narrative either; in Matthew and John they appear only in passing (Matt 27:62; John 18:3; cf. also John 11:43-52).

[23]For detailed criticisms of the view that Luke absolves the Pharisees of guilt for Jesus' death, see Jack Dean Kingsbury, "The Pharisees in Luke-Acts," in *The

could be open to Jesus' message, the Pharisees in the gospel repeatedly misunderstand Jesus and oppose him, are disbelieving at the best, corrupt and wicked at the worst.

   C. Luke-Acts as Critical of the Pharisees. Some scholars have claimed that Luke's critical stance on the Pharisees evident in the gospel continues in Acts, where the Pharisees appear only in seemingly positive roles. Jack Dean Kingsbury asserts that the portrayal of the Pharisees in Acts is neither positive nor serves to legitimate Christianity. Gamaliel's evaluative point of view is clearly different from Luke's own point of view. Gamaliel connects the Jesus movement to the previous Theudas and Judas movements and thus betrays that he anticipates that this new movement will also fail (Acts 5:36-38). Gamaliel's advice that if this movement is of God, "you may even be found fighting against God," is, of course, true from Luke's own point of view (5:39). Gamaliel, however, speaks these words unwittingly which makes him an "ironic character," who "is not knowingly either a friend of Christianity or an ally of the apostles."[24] In a similar vein, John Darr contends that Luke's reader knows that Gamaliel's words are of God but identifies Gamaliel's response as ironic, as "sadly misguided, presumptuous, even ludicrous."[25] Darr has no difficulty in reading the Gamaliel episode or the remaining appearances of the Pharisees in Acts as a continuation of the Gospel of Luke. For Darr, "what one reads in Acts merely nuances and intensifies some of the negative traits that have already been attributed to Pharisees in the Gospel."[26] Gamaliel is not to be seen as "a prototype for Jewish appreciation of Christianity, a figure to help bridge the hurtful gap between sibling faiths."[27]

Four Gospels: Festschrift Frans Neirynck, ed. F. Van Segbroeck et al., BETL 100 (Leuven: Leuven University Press, 1992) 2:1497-1512, esp. 1502-1503 and William John Lyons, "The Words of Gamaliel (Acts 5.38-39) and the Irony of Indeterminacy," *JSNT* 68 (1997): 23-49, esp. 32-33n.29.

   [24]Kingsbury, "The Pharisees in Luke-Acts," 1506.

   [25]John A. Darr, *On Character Building: The Reader and the Rhetoric of Characterization in Luke-Acts*, Literary Currents in Biblical Interpretation (Louisville: Westminster/John Knox, 1992) 119. See also John A. Darr, "Irenic or Ironic? Another Look at Gamaliel before the Sanhedrin (Acts 5:33-42)," in *Literary Studies in Luke-Acts*, 121-39.

   [26]Darr, *Character Building*, 116.

   [27]Darr, "Irenic or Ironic?" 139.

The question remains, however, whether those who see the Pharisees in Luke-Acts consistently in a negative light underplay some notable shifts between Luke's two volumes. Even though Gamaliel may not be "an ally of the apostles," or "a prototype for Jewish appreciation of Christianity," there are sufficient signs in the narrative which make him unlike his openly hostile and plotting fellows in the gospel or other members of the council in Acts. For example, Luke introduces Gamaliel with the words "But a Pharisee in the council stood up (ἀναστὰς δέ τις ἐν τῷ συνεδρίῳ φαρισαῖος)" (Acts 5:34). The use of the participle ἀναστάς "often introduces fresh action in Acts."[28] By using this introduction Luke clearly separates Gamaliel from his associates in the council and presents his action as a counterforce to their openly murderous intentions.[29] Steve Mason has rightly noted that Gamaliel "is the only councillor we have met [in Luke-Acts] who has the slightest interest in discussing the Christians' claims, and this alone sets him apart from the chief-priestly councillors."[30] Furthermore, Luke says that Gamaliel was "a teacher of the law, respected by all the people," which reminds us of his earlier remark that the people held the apostles in high esteem (5:13, cf. also 2:47, 4:21). As Jack Dean Kingsbury details, this remark serves to portray Gamaliel "as an exemplary Jew and man of authority" who is "right in character when he suddenly stands up;" furthermore, this remark helps Paul, at a later point in Acts, to show that "his pedigree is that of the exemplary Jew" because the respected Gamaliel was his teacher (Acts 22:3).[31]

---

[28]Barrett, *Acts*, 282.

[29]Darr does not appreciate this as he says that "neither the narrator nor any other authoritative textual evidence serves to dissociate Gamaliel from the Sanhedrin and its decisions concerning Jesus and his followers." "Irenic or Ironic?" 126.

[30]Steve Mason, "Chief Priests, Sadducees, Pharisees, and Sanhedrin in Acts," in *The Book of Acts in Its Palestinian Setting*, ed. Richard Bauckham, BAFCS 4 (Grand Rapids MI: Eerdmans, 1995) 115-77, quotation 150.

[31]Kingsbury, "The Pharisees in Luke-Acts," 1504. Darr says that the attribution of honor is far from a good thing in Luke-Acts but just about "a backhanded compliment" because, "as virtual paradigms of unreliability, the people can by no means establish any other character's reliability." "Irenic or Ironic?" 135. However, in Acts 5 both the apostles and Gamaliel are described as honored by the people, which creates a common bond—however vague it may be—between them and adds a new and at least somewhat positive dimension to Gamaliel's portrait.

There is no reason to play down the fairly positive implications that the Gamaliel scene and the later scene where some Pharisees defend Paul (Acts 23) have for the overall presentation of the Pharisees in Luke-Acts. John Darr claims that the harsh and consistent censure of the Pharisees in the gospel also colors later incidents in Acts "which, if isolated from the narrative flow, would seem to reflect well on the Pharisees," but now "actually assume a dark and ironic aspect."[32] Darr emphasizes the significance of the "'primacy effect,' which holds that what comes first in a narrative conditions the reader's understanding of what comes later, and therefore, that the critic is to weigh earlier data more heavily than later information."[33] This methodological point of departure, however, if taken to its logical conclusion, becomes "a formula for producing stereotypes in reading" because it implies that "the same characters will always do the same thing," as Robert Tannehill notes in his criticism of Darr's reading of the Lukan Pharisees.[34] Tannehill also points out how many literary critics and biblical scholars have both argued that characters in ancient literature, including the Hebrew Bible and the New Testament, are not unavoidably simple, static types.[35] Literary critic Meir Sternberg, whom Darr cites as giving support for the "primacy effect," has traced in the Hebrew Bible "the procedure whereby the narrative lures us into a false impression about a character or event and then springs the truth at the least expected moment."[36] Sternberg remarks that "even the most static characters . . . change or crystallize;" sometimes new features "even fall out of character, that is, out of the particular image given or formed earlier. . . . It is by trial

---

[32]Darr, "Irenic or Ironic?" 133.

[33]Darr, "Irenic or Ironic?" 133n.33.

[34]Robert C. Tannehill, "Should We Love Simon the Pharisee? Hermeneutical Reflections on the Pharisees in Luke," *CurTM* 21 (1994): 424-33, quotation 427. In his reply to Tannehill, Darr rejects (with some good arguments) Tannehill's interpretation of the Simon episode in Luke 7:39-47 but does not comment on Tannehill's methodological remarks in any way. "Irenic or Ironic?" 132n.32.

[35]Tannehill, "Should We Love Simon?" 428-29. Tannehill refers to several articles in *Semeia* 63 (1993) titled *Characterization in Biblical Literature*.

[36]Meir Stenberg, *The Poetics of Biblical Narrative: Ideological Literature and the Drama of Reading* (Bloomington: Indiana University Press, 1985) 56.

and error, as always, that the reader learns the lessons of complex character and difficult coherence."[37]

The Pharisees in Luke-Acts may not pass for a truly complex and profound group of characters, but there should be no methodological or other reason for crossing out some key signs of indeterminacy from their portrait.[38] Although Gamaliel and his fellow Pharisees in Acts are not on their way to faith in Jesus, even Darr admits that Gamaliel "courageously resists the momentum of mob violence that grips his fellow council members. His discourse encouraging a patient, wait-and-see attitude is a model of practical wisdom for all religious and political leaders who must deal with upstart sects."[39] It remains to be asked what the special function of this kind of a *relatively* positive Pharisee is for Luke and his readers.

D. Luke's Portrait of the Pharisees Is Ambiguous. Many scholars have concluded that Luke uses the Pharisees in Acts to legitimate Christianity, even though they have not been convinced that Luke presents the Pharisees consistently in a positive light. According to Jack T. Sanders, the friendly, non-Christian Pharisees in Acts are presented in positive terms and they demonstrate the continuity between ancient Judaism and Christianity and underscore that Christianity is the true and authentic Judaism.[40] The Christian Pharisees in Acts and the Pharisees in the gospel, however, are negative characters who stand for Jewish Christians of Luke's own day who

---

[37]Stenberg, *Poetics*, 346-48.

[38]Darr's reading is a case in point of how literary critics quite often prefer interpretations advancing the unity of a literary work. Cf. Malcolm Heath, *Unity in Greek Poetics* (Oxford UK: Clarendon Press, 1989) 1-2: "Techniques of literary criticism provide us [professional critics] with a range of devices for eliciting unified interpretations from apparent inconsequentiality; we are familiar with concepts of ambiguity, irony, symbolism, and other kinds of literary indirectness that help us bring *prima facie* ill-formed texts under proper control." For the question of how to assess the narrative unity of the gospels, see Petri Merenlahti and Raimo Hakola, "Reconceiving Narrative Criticism," in *Characterization in the Gospels*, ed. David Rhoads and Kari Syreeni, JSNTSup 184 (Sheffield UK: Sheffield Academic Press, 1999) 13-48. For a more complete discussion, see Petri Merenlahti, *Poetics for the Gospels? Rethinking Narrative Criticism*, Studies of the New Testament and Its World (London: T.&T. Clark, 2002).

[39]Darr, "Irenic or Ironic?" 123.

[40]Sanders, "The Pharisees in Luke-Acts," 161, 166.

opposed accepting uncircumcised Gentiles into the church and insisted on maintaining Pharisaic *halakha*.[41] John Carroll also allows that the Pharisees in the gospel "in the end refuse participation in the kingdom defined by Jesus."[42] Carroll understands that this raises the question of how the positive role of the Pharisees in Acts is to be explained. Carroll solves this problem by taking the Pharisees in Acts as legitimators of Christian faith. For example, Luke uses the figure of Gamaliel "to make a statement not about the Pharisees but about Christian faith and its preachers. They are legitimate, directed by the God of Israel."[43]

David Gowler has perhaps most strongly represented the position that the presentation of the Pharisees in the Gospel of Luke is at odds with their presentation in Acts. Gowler rejects the attempts to describe the Pharisees in the gospel in positive terms and concludes that "the portrait of the Pharisees in Luke is primarily negative, whereas the portrait of the Pharisees in Acts is primarily positive." Like Sanders and Carroll, Gowler sees that the Pharisees in Acts serve as "positive legitimation of Christianity."[44] But Gowler also advises scholars to acknowledge the discontinuity in Luke's portrayal because, as a matter of fact, "the portrait of the Pharisees in Acts deconstructs the portrait found in Luke."[45] Gowler does not connect this conclusion to the ongoing discussion about the literary unity of Luke-Acts, but William John Lyons has claimed that it is this question that is at stake here. For Lyons, Gowler's conclusion is understandable only as "*resulting from the prior assertion that the two texts* [Luke and Acts] *are separate*," a suggestion made especially by Mikeal Parsons and Richard Pervo.[46] For Lyons, however, John Darr's position that takes the Pharisees in Acts

---

[41]Sanders, "The Pharisees in Luke-Acts," 159-60.

[42]John T. Carroll, "Luke's Portrayal of the Pharisees," *CBQ* 50 (1988): 604-21, quotation 616.

[43]Carroll, "Luke's Portrayal," 617.

[44]David B. Gowler, *Host, Guest, Enemy, and Friend: Portraits of the Pharisees in Luke and Acts*, Emory Studies in Early Christianity 2 (New York: Peter Lang, 1991) 301.

[45]Gowler, *Host*, 315.

[46]Lyons, "Words," 35; italics in original. For the view that Luke and Acts are separate literary works, see Mikeal C. Parsons and Richard I. Pervo, *Rethinking the Unity of Luke and Acts* (Minneapolis: Fortress Press, 1993).

simply as another variation of the negative appraisals made in the gospel is quite logical and unavoidable if Luke-Acts is read as a unified narrative.

Like Gowler, Steve Mason emphasizes that scholars should put aside their desire to make the Pharisees "a static symbol of some kind" because "Luke's whole narrative seems to resist static identifications." According to Mason, "to make sense of all the narrative indicators, one must respect Luke's avowed *historical* interest . . . and shed the old form-critical bugbear that requires each item in the story to correspond to some aspect of the reading community's life."[47] Luke uses the Pharisees or other Jewish leaders in his gospel simply because "he thinks that they were important in Jesus' career."[48] Likewise, the portrait of Gamaliel is an example of "a historian's concern for verisimilitude."[49]

In the following, I agree with those who think that Luke's portrait of the Pharisees is ambiguous and claim that the differences between Luke and Acts should not be denied.[50] I draw on social-identity approach which makes it possible to take seriously both the criticism of the Pharisees in the gospel and the, at least comparatively, positive roles of the Pharisees in Acts. I suggest that, while a purely text-centered approach goes only half-way toward explaining Luke's conflicting images, a wider perspective clarifies that these seemingly conflicting pictures do not really deconstruct each other, but, rather, both negative and positive appraisals of the Pharisees contribute to an early Christian identity. While differing portraits may clash in the *text* world, they may well have a parallel function as different components of the *symbolic* world that validates the social identity of the writer and his audience.[51] For this reason, it is not merely Luke's interest in

---

[47]Mason, "Chief Priests," 158; italics in original.

[48]Mason, "Chief Priests," 130.

[49]Mason, "Chief Priests," 151.

[50]In addition to the above-mentioned scholars, see also Tyson, *Luke*, 126: "The role of Pharisees in Luke-Acts is complicated."

[51]My larger hermeneutical background here is the so-called three-world model that is based on a distinction among a literary work's *text world*, *symbolic world* and the *real world* behind the text. See Kari Syreeni, "Wonderlands: A Beginner's Guide to Three Worlds," *SEÅ* 64 (1999): 33-46, and "Peter as Character and Symbol in the Gospel of Matthew," in *Characterization in the Gospels*, 106-152. For an evaluation of the model, see Merenlahti, *Poetics*, 119-24. I have applied the model to John's views on Jews in my *Identity Matters*, 33-40.

historical verisimilitude that accounts for his representation of the Pharisees, but his portrait complies with the need to construct and maintain the identity of early Christians as a group distinct from other Jews.

II. The Social-Identity Approach

The social-identity theory was first developed by social psychologist Henri Tajfel and his colleagues in the late 1960s and early 1970s.[52] This approach has also increasingly been applied to early Jewish and Christian sources.[53] One of the key ideas behind the theory was formulated by Tajfel as the

---

[52]For general introductions to the theory, see Michael A. Hogg and Dominic Abrams, *Social Identifications: A Social Psychology of Intergroup Relations and Group Processes* (New York: Routledge, 1988) 6-29; John C. Turner, "Some Current Issues in Research on Social-Identity and Self-Categorization Theories" in *Social Identity: Context, Commitment, Content*, ed. Naomi Ellemers, Russell Spears, and Bertjan Doosje (Oxford UK: Blackwell, 1999) 6-34; Rupert Brown, "Social-Identity Theory: Past Achievements, Current Problems and Future Challenges," *European Journal of Social Psychology* 30 (2000): 745-78; and S. Alexander Haslam, *Psychology in Organizations: The Social-Identity Approach* (London: Sage Publications, 2001) 26-57.

[53]Philip Esler, *Galatians* (London and New York: Routledge, 1998) 40-57; *Conflict and Identity in Romans: The Social Setting of Paul's Letter* (Minneapolis: Fortress Press, 2003) 19-39; Jutta Jokiranta, "Social-Identity Approach: Identity-Constructing Elements in the Psalms Pesher," in *Defining Identities: We, You, and the Other in the Dead Sea Scrolls. Proceedings of the Fifth Meeting of the IOQS in Gröningen*, ed. Florentino G. Martínez and Maden Popovic (Leiden: Brill, 2008); Robert L. Brawley, "Social Identity and the Aim of Acomplished Life in Acts 2," in *Acts and Ethics*, ed. Thomas E. Phillips (Sheffield UK: Sheffield Phoenix Press, 2005) 16-33; and Raimo Hakola, "Social Identities and Group Phenomena in Second Temple Judaism," in *Explaining Christian Origins and Early Judaism: Contributions from Cognitive and Social Science*, Biblical Interpretation Series 89, ed. Petri Luomanen, Ilkka Pyysiäinen, and Risto Uro (Leiden: Brill Academic Publishers, 2007).

"minimal group paradigm."[54] In a series of experiments Tajfel and his colleagues found out that, even in minimal groups where there is neither conflict of interest nor previously existing hostility, people tend to favor ingroup members over outgroup members. This means that "the mere perception of belonging to two distinct groups—that is, social categorization *per se*—is sufficient to trigger intergroup discrimination favoring the ingroup."[55] The need for social differentiation between groups "is fulfilled through the creation of intergroup differences when such differences do not in fact exist, or the attribution of value to, and the enhancement of, whatever differences that do exist."[56]

The findings connected to minimal group studies resulted in the formulation of the concept of social identity which can be understood as "that part of an individual's self-concept which derives from his knowledge of his membership of a social group (or groups) together with the value and emotional significance attached to that membership."[57] The concept of social identity was later developed into a more general explanation of all cognitive processes connected to group formation in self-categorization theory. According to John Turner and other social psychologists, "the central hypothesis for group behaviour is that, as shared social identity becomes salient, individual self-perception tends to become depersonalized."[58] This means that when we experience ourselves as identical with a certain class of people and in contrast to some other classes, we tend to stereotype not only the members of outgroups, but also ourselves as a member of our own ingroup. Therefore, the process of categorization concerns both the self-conception of an individual in relation to his or her ingroup and people who are experienced as different from the ingroup. Social categorization helps individual group members to orientate

---

[54]For minimal groups, see Henri Tajfel, *Human Groups and Social Categories: Studies in Social Psychology* (Cambridge UK: Cambridge University Press, 1981) 233-38 and 268-76; and Henri Tajfel and John Turner, "An Integrative Theory of Intergroup Conflict," in *The Social Psychology of Intergroup Relations*, ed. William G. Austin and Stephen Worchel (Monterey CA: Brooks/Cole, 1979) 33-47, esp. 38-40.

[55]Tajfel and Turner, "Integrative Theory," 38.

[56]Tajfel, *Human Groups*, 276.

[57]Tajfel, *Human Groups*, 255.

[58]Turner, "Some Current Issues," 12.

themselves in variable social environments by making those environments more predictable and meaningful. Self-categorization theory emphasizes that categorization is always a dynamic, context-bound process, which results in maximizing the clarity of intergroup boundaries in a given social context. Social categories are not inflexible but always dependent on the specific social environment and those comparative relations that are present in that environment. It can even be claimed that "people who are categorized and perceived as different in one context . . . can be recategorized and perceived as similar in another context."[59]

The social-identity theory was originally developed to explain intergroup discrimination and it addressed such questions as, "Why do people in groups discriminate against each other?" From a social-identity perspective, a simple answer would be that, because of social categorization, people commonly tend to favor ingroup members and discriminate against outgroup members. Some recent studies, however, have revealed that it is problematic to think that ingroup members are universally regarded as more attractive than outgroup members. As a matter of fact, we who deal with religious sources and religious groups know very well that those members of a group who deviate from ingroup norms quite often receive much harder criticism than obvious outgroup members. Deviant group members have recently received much attention among social-identity theorists, especially José Marques and his colleagues who have tried to explain the function of deviant group members for social identity.[60] In a series of experiments, they

---

[59]Penelope J. Oakes, S. Alexander Haslam and John C. Turner, *Stereotyping and Social Reality* (Oxford UK: Blackwell, 1994) 98.

[60]José M. Marques, V. Y. Yzerbryt and J.-P. Leyens, "The 'Black-Sheep Effect': Extremity of Judgments towards Ingroup Members as a Function of Group Identification," *European Journal of Social Psychology* 18 (1988): 1-16; José M. Marques and V. Y. Yzerbryt, "The Black-Sheep Effect: Judgmental Extremity towards Ingroup Members in Inter- and Intra-Group Situations," *European Journal of Social Psychology* 18 (1988): 287-92; José M. Marques, "The 'Black-Sheep Effect:' Outgroup Homogeneity in Social Comparison Settings," in *Social-Identity Theory: Constructive and Critical Advances*, ed. Dominic Abrams and Michael A. Hogg (London: Harvester Wheatsheaf, 1990) 131-51; José M. Marques, E. M. Robalo, and S. A. Rocha, "Ingroup Bias and the 'Black Sheep' Effect: Assessing the Impact of Social Identification and Perceived Variability on Group Judgments," *European Journal of Social Psychology* 22 (1992): 331-52; José M. Marques,

found evidence for what they called the "black-sheep effect." This term conceptualizes a common sense observation that a person who behaves against the norms of an ingroup is even more strongly rejected than the members of outgroups. "Black-sheep effect" means that ingroup members are judged more harshly than outgroup members who have similar attitudes and values. This phenomenon has nothing to do with the personal qualities of members in question but is dependent on the significance of the ingroup norms for social identity. Antinorm behavior of an ingroup member is something unexpected that forms a threat to social identity because such behavior challenges the authority of ingroup norms and reduces social differentiation between groups. However, an outgoup member, by definition, is supposed to act against ingroup norms and, therefore, similar behavior is tolerable for the outsiders.

An interesting observation made in the research on the "black-sheep effect" is that an outgroup member who behaves against the norms of the outgroup in a way that is in line with ingroup norms is quite often evaluated more positively than an ingroup member who acts against the ingroup norms. The relative approval of the "friendly" outgroup members is explained by the fact that, from the perspective of an ingroup, outgroup deviants help to undermine the legitimacy of the outgroup and, at the same time, help to verify the social reality implied by the ingroup norms.[61]

By primarily focusing on social rather than personal identity, the social identity approach maintains that under certain conditions social identity is more relevant than personal identity in the self-conception of human beings. Two things suggest that this may well have been the case with early Christian groups. First, many cultural anthropologists have made a distinction

---

Dominic Abrams, D. Páez, and C. Martinez-Taboada, "The Role of Categorization and In-Group Norms in Judgments of Groups and Their Members," *Journal of Personality and Social Psychology* 75 (1998): 976-88; and José M. Marques, Dominic Abrams, D. Páez, and Michael A. Hogg, "Social Categorization, Social Identification, and Rejection of Deviant Groups Members," in *Blackwell Handbook of Social Psychology: Group Processes*, ed. Michael A. Hogg and R. Scott Tindale (Oxford UK: Blackwell, 2001) 400-24.

[61]Marques et al., "The Role of Categorization," 986-87; Dominic Abrams, J. M. Marques, N. Brown and M. Henson, "Pro-Norm and Anti-Norm Deviance within and between Groups," *Journal of Personality and Social Psychology* 78 (2000): 906-12, esp. 911; and Marques et al., "Social Categorization," 418.

between individualistic and collectivist cultures; ancient Mediterranean culture is mostly described as a collectivist culture where people "depend on ingroup others to provide them with a sense of who they are."[62] Individuals did not act or think of themselves as persons independent of these groups. Second, many studies on the Dead Sea Scrolls and early Christian writings, especially the gospels, have emphasized communal aspects in these writings; while written by different individuals, these writings give voice to different groups by expressing their collective convictions and shared view of the world. From this perspective, the first readers may not have approached the characters in early Christian writings simply as literary constructs with recognizable individual features but as symbols of groups that had a crucial function for how they understood their position in the world. It is fully legitimate, therefore, to ask what function the literary portrait of the Pharisees has for the social identity of Luke's readers.

III. Conclusions:
Social Identity and "Friendly" Pharisees in Acts

The above overview enables us to see what possibilities the social identity perspective has for explaining Luke's portrait of the Pharisees. I think that this perspective increases our understanding in at least four ways.

First, the social identity approach proposes that social categories are not fixed but may vary if there are changes in the social context that provides the nearby points of comparison. According to social identity theory, "individuals' social identities have a multitude of facets" which "may gain different weights in different situations." Also, the findings connected to the "black-sheep effect" speak for "the subjects' flexibility with regard to which aspect of their social identity is actually used."[63] This means that, although the members of a group like the Pharisees are on one occasion defined clearly as outsiders, this categorization need not be absolute but may be adjusted to any given social environment. It is obvious that the contexts where the Pharisees appear in the Gospel of Luke and in the book of Acts are very different. In the gospel, the Pharisees are compared to Jesus or to his followers, or, in a more unspecified way to the poor, the hungry or

---

[62]Bruce J. Malina and Richard L. Rohrbaugh, *Social-Science Commentary on the Gospel of John* (Minneapolis: Fortress Press, 1998) 163. See also Esler, *Galatians*, 45-49.

[63]Marques, Yzerbryt, and Leyens, "Black-Sheep Effect," 12.

the humble. It is clear that the Pharisees do not fare well in comparison with these groups. Things change, however, in Acts where the nearest points of comparison for the Pharisees are the overwhelmingly hostile priestly circles and the Sadducees. There appear new shades of meaning in Luke's portrayal of Pharisees, because Gamaliel and later unnamed Pharisees in the council are contrasted with some more fundamentally distinct other. While the Pharisees are used mostly as a negative foil in the gospel, now they appear in a comparatively positive light, thanks to the fully wicked and hostile Sadducees.

Second, from a social identity perspective, the role of outsiders who endorse ingroup norms can be described as *relatively* positive. This means their role is closely related to their being outsiders. Therefore, the function of the somewhat friendly Pharisees for a Christian identity does mean that they are presented as the group closest to Christianity. Their role does not mean that they are described as turning into insiders. It is not correct, either, to maintain that Luke uses Gamaliel and other sympathetic Pharisees to underline the Jewishness of Christianity and to show that early Christians represent a movement inside Israel.[64] Rather, it is especially in their role as outsiders in relation to Christians that these Pharisees can give a boost to an early Christian social identity. The mere presence of the Pharisees who do not consistently sustain the rejection of the Christian gospel serves to contest the principles they represent for Luke and his readers.[65] It can be even argued that, because the Pharisees as a whole are presented as outsiders in the Gospel of Luke, they can support early Christians and legitimate their identity in Acts.

Third, from a social identity perspective, the Christian Pharisees are to be separated from non-Christian, friendly Pharisees. These believing Pharisees represent convictions that are, in the end, misguided from Luke's perspective. Christian Pharisees can be seen as ingroup deviants whose appear-

---

[64]This is claimed by Jacob Jervell, *Die Apostelgeschichte*, KEK 3 (Göttingen: Vandenhoeck & Ruprecht, 1998) 212.

[65]Cf. Hans Conzelmann, *The Acts of the Apostles*, trans. J. Limburg, A. T. Kraabel, and D. H. Juel, Hermeneia (Philadelphia: Fortress Press, 1989) 192. Conzelmann comments on the confusion stirred up by the Pharisees who defend Paul in the council (Acts 23:9): "The desired result occurs immediately, and the reader sees that the Jews are not clear about their own religion." Thus also Jervell, *Die Apostelgeschichte*, 557.

ance poses a threat to the social identity of the ingroup which results in their rejection. It is often noted that Luke's way of presenting these Pharisees in Acts (15:5) is reminiscent of the negative portrayal of the Pharisees in the gospel, where the Pharisees repeatedly take care that the law is not broken.[66] Luke joins these Christians who support the keeping of the law to clearly disbelieving Pharisees in the gospel and thus discredits their position. Luke's critical stance on the believing Pharisees is not necessarily contrary to a qualified approval of those non-Christian Pharisees who support Christians. Both of these groups undermine the integrity of their respective groups, which is a bad thing in the case of ingroup deviants, Christian Pharisees, and a good thing in the case of outgroup deviants, non-Christian Pharisees.[67]

Fourth, from a social identity perspective, the criticism against the Pharisees in the gospel is not in conflict with the appearance of the relatively friendly Pharisees in Acts. The completely negative portrayal in the gospel is not deconstructed but is adjusted to a new comparative context in Acts. Both the criticism of the Pharisees and the "friendly" Pharisees promote the social identity of early Christians by clarifying the intergroup boundaries between emergent early Christianity and the Pharisees. Rather than affirming the theological continuity between Judaism and Christianity, the Lukan portrayal of Pharisees serves the need to categorize early Christians as a group that is distinct from the kind of Judaism typified by the Pharisees. At the same time, Luke presents early Christians as a group that had to be legitimated even by the best among those who represented "the strictest sect of our religion," as the Lukan Paul has it (Acts 26:5).

---

[66]Cf. Gowler, *Host*, 282.
[67]Cf. Marques et al., "Social Categorization," 418.

The Downfall of Eutychus:
How Ancient Understandings of Sleep Illuminate Acts 20:7-12

Andrew Arterbury

In Acts 20:7-12, Luke narrates Paul's final visit to Troas. Paul and a young boy, Eutychus,[1] are among those gathered for worship in an upper room. After Paul's sermon lasts half of the night,[2] Eutychus falls asleep, and then falls out of the window and dies. Thankfully, however, Paul is not asleep. Instead, he goes down and raises Eutychus from the dead. Afterward Paul simply returns to the upper room and resumes his sermon while the church eats its long-awaited meal.

In his commentary on the book of Acts, which is commonly dated between 709 and 716 CE,[3] the Venerable Bede contrasts this pericope with Acts 9:36-42, which features Peter raising Tabitha from the dead. Bede writes, "It is harder work to revive those who sin through negligence than it is to revive those who do so through weakness. The former is represented by Eutychus, the latter by Tabitha."[4] While it is not surprising that Bede provides an allegorical interpretation of Acts 20:7-12, it is somewhat surprising that he attributes Eutychus's death to "sin through negligence" even though Luke himself only tells us that Eutychus fell asleep.

In this article, I would like to suggest that if we work with ancient understandings of sleep, we too may come to a conclusion that is similar to Bede's. To set up this conversation I will first contend that the structural

---

[1]On the man's youth as a factor in his characterization, see F. Scott Spencer, "Wise Up, Young Man: The Moral Vision of Saul and Other νεανίοκοι in Acts," in *Acts and Ethics*, ed. Thomas E. Phillips (Sheffield UK: Sheffield Phoenix, 2005) 34-48.

[2]Ernst Haenchen, *The Acts of the Apostles: A Commentary*, ed. and trans. Bernard Noble et al. (Oxford UK: Basil Blackwell; Philadelpha: Westminster, 1971) 584. In this instance, Haenchen translates διαλέγομαι as "preach." For a similar rendering see, Barclay M. Newman and Eugene A. Nida, *A Translator's Handbook on The Acts of the Apostles*, Helps for Translators 12 (London: United Bible Societies, 1972) 384.

[3]*Commentary on the Acts of the Apostles*, trans. Lawrence T. Martin (Kalamazoo MI: Cistercian, 1989) xviii.

[4]Venerable Bede, on Acts 20:10 (Martin).

emphasis of Acts 20:7-12 is placed upon Eutychus's sleep. Second, because of the important role that sleep plays in Acts 20:7-12, I will widen the conversation beyond the Lukan corpus and examine the role of sleep in a variety of ancient Near Eastern and Mediterranean texts. As a result, I will demonstrate that long before Bede, it would have been both historically and literarily appropriate for Luke's first audience to interpret Eutychus's sleep metaphorically.[5]

Yet, even if we interpret Eutychus's sleep in Acts 20:7-12 metaphorically, we must still ask what meaning Luke's first audience would have derived from the metaphor. For instance, I will show that in ancient literature, sleep often functioned metaphorically in at least four different ways. Sleep was closely associated with death, human mortality, the gods, and human irresponsibility. As a result, we must ultimately ask whether Luke's first audience would have seen Eutychus as an innocent victim or a negligent sinner. Both interpretations would be consistent with ideas present in Luke's Mediterranean milieu. Yet, in my opinion, the latter option, the portrayal of Eutychus as a negligent sinner who is spiritually distracted, provides the most plausible answer.

I. The Structure and Emphasis of Acts 20:7-12

A close analysis of the structure of Acts 20:7-12 should help us see how Luke's first readers worked their way through the story. Importantly, Luke narrated the story in a chiastic fashion.[6] For instance, A (vv. 7-8) and A' (v. 11) address the congregational setting in Troas along with Paul's interaction with the Christians who had gathered for worship. In both the beginning and ending sections, we see references to the upper room, the breaking of bread, Paul's sermon, and Paul's departure. Alternatively, B (v. 9a) and B' (v. 10) primarily deal with Eutychus, both before and after he falls asleep.

---

[5]For a similar methodological approach, see Charles H. Talbert, *Reading Acts: A Literary and Theological Commentary on the Acts of the Apostles*, Reading the New Testament (New York: Crossroad, 1997) ix, and *Reading Luke-Acts in Its Mediterranean Milieu*, NovTSup 107 (Leiden: Brill, 2003) 14-18.

[6]Contra Bernard Trémel, "À propos d'Actes 20,7-12: Puissance du Thaumaturge ou du témoin?" *RTP* 112 (1980): 361-62. In this helpful article, Trémel comments on the structure of Acts 20:7-12. In particular, Trémel points out an inclusion, which is constituted by vv. 7 and 11 and which frames the entire episode. Yet, he fails to notice the overarching chiastic pattern in this pericope.

In these verses we see Eutychus sitting in the window, falling out of the window, and being resuscitated by Paul. Finally, C and C' constitute the center of this chiastic structure in verse 9b and c, where twice Luke tells us that Eutychus is overcome by sleep. Twice in the center of this passage, Luke uses the same noun (ὕπνος, sleep) and the same verb (καταφέρω, to be overcome). Thus, the chiastic structure of Acts 20:7-11 is

A – vv. 7-8   The Christians in Troas gathered to break bread (κλάσαι ἄρτον). Paul spoke (διελέγετο) until midnight because he was about to depart the next day. They were in an upper room (ὑπερῴῳ).

    B – v. 9   Eutychus was sitting in a window.

        C – v. 9   Being overcome (καταφέρω) by a deep sleep (ὕπνος)

        C' – v. 9   Being overcome (καταφέρω) by sleep (ὕπνος)

    B' – vv. 9-10   Eutychus fell down and was taken up dead. Paul went down, fell upon him, and raised him from the dead.

A' – v. 11   After returning to the upper room, breaking bread (κλάσας τὸν ἄρτον), and eating, Paul conversed with them until his departure at dawn.

Verse 12 then functions as an epilogue.[7] After Paul has already departed from the scene, verse 12 then turns the readers' attention away from Paul and back to Eutychus thereby assuring that the audience's final thoughts will be focused upon Eutychus and the congregation.

Given the structure of Acts 20:7-12 as explained above, we can see that ancient readers would have readily noticed the beginning and the end of the chiasm. This tandem highlights the congregation as an entity.[8] The passage

---

[7]While discussing fables in his *Exercises*, Theon indicates that it was perfectly acceptable for ancient authors to provide "several conclusions (*epilogoi*) for one fable when we take a start from the contents of the fable" (75). See George A. Kennedy, *Progymnasmata: Greek Textbooks of Prose Composition and Rhetoric*, Writings from the Greco-Roman World 10 (Atlanta: Society of Biblical Literature, 2003) 26. I assert that in this case, Luke has provided two epilogues for the same narrative. Both v. 11 and v. 12 function as important conclusions to the narrative.

[8]Beverly Roberts Gaventa, "Theology and Ecclesiology in the Miletus Speech: Reflections on Content and Context," *NTS* 50 (2004): 37-43. Gaventa argues that all of the narrative units between Acts 20:1 and Acts 21:17—depictions of the believing communities in Troas (Acts 20:7-12), Miletus, and Caesarea along with four travel reports—collectively create an "extended portrait" of the church's "community life" (43).

begins by showing us that this congregation is aligned with the true Christian movement. They are breaking bread in an upper room as they gather for worship on the first day of the week (20:7-8). Likewise at the end of the passage, despite the frightening events of the night, we once again see that this congregation has the marks of a true and faithful Christian fellowship.[9] The people are once again present in the upper room, where they break bread and converse with Paul until morning (20:11).

Yet, since we know the strongest structural emphasis is generally found in the center of a chiasm,[10] I assert that verse 9 would have held the key to interpreting Acts 20:7-12 for Luke's first readers. While the plot of the second half of Acts clearly revolves around Paul, the chiastic structure of Acts 20:7-11 and the epilogue in 20:12 suggest that most ancient readers would have focused upon Eutychus and the sleep that overtakes him.

II. Metaphorical Sleep
in Ancient Near Eastern and Mediterranean Texts

Since Eutychus's sleep is highlighted in Acts 20:7-12 by appearing twice in the middle of this pericope, we would do well to read other texts from the ancient world to see how other authors spoke about ill-timed sleep and its tragic consequences. Importantly, beyond simply referring to literal sleep or the sleep of death (e.g., 1 Thess 4:13-14 and 5:10), ancient authors often spoke of sleep in metaphorical terms. Hence, below I will examine ancient Sumerian, Hebraic, Greek, and Roman texts as a way of mapping some of the Near Eastern and Mediterranean perspectives on sleep that contributed to the cultural heritage of Luke's earliest readers.

---

[9]Gaventa, "Theology and Ecclesiology in the Miletus Speech," 43. Gaventa points out that in Acts the church is characterized by instruction, fellowship, the breaking of bread, prayer, the sharing of possessions, and the anticipation of resistance.

[10]Ronald E. Man, "The Value of Chiasm for New Testament Interpretation," *BSac* 141 (1984): 147-51. Also see Donald R. Miesner, "Chiasm and the Composition and Message of Paul's Missionary Sermons" (S.T.D. thesis, Lutheran School of Theology at Chicago, 1974) 34. Miesner writes, "The position of members in a chiastic structure indicates points of emphasis. . . . In respect to both form and sense, the rest of the structure pivots around the center, which may be either a single or a double unit. Thus, the exegete must attach special importance to the center of a chiastic structure."

A. *The Epic of Gilgamesh*. An ancient Sumerian tale that most likely dates from "around 1700 BCE,"[11] *The Epic of Gilgamesh* provides us with a helpful example of how ancient Near Eastern people envisaged sleep. When the central character, Gilgamesh, hopes to obtain immortality, his instructor, Utanapishtim directs Gilgamesh to "try not to sleep for six days and seven nights"(11.212). Yet, when Gilgamesh falls asleep, it simply proves that Gilgamesh is and will always be mortal. In fact, the author emphasizes this point by noting the speed with which Gilgamesh succumbs to sleep.[12] The narrator observes, "As he sat there on his haunches, Sleep was swirling over him like a mist" (11.213-14). Furthermore, Gilgamesh does not merely sleep for one night. Instead, he sleeps continuously for seven days until Utanapishtim finally wakes him (11.218-44). Thus, by sleeping, Gilgamesh completely fails the test of immortality.

Conversely, the ability to resist sleep is also associated with meritorious, superior, or divine-like behavior at points in *The Epic of Gilgamesh* (e.g., 1.232).[13] For instance, in 1.235-39, Gilgamesh is praised for being superior to most mortals. In doing so, the author writes, "Look at him, gaze upon his face, He is radiant with virility, manly vigor is his, The

---

[11]Benjamin R. Foster, *The Epic of Gilgamesh: A New Translation, Analogues, Criticism*, Norton Critical Edition (New York: W. W. Norton, 2001) xiii. Also see E. A. Speiser, "The Epic of Gilgamesh," in *Ancient Near Eastern Texts Relating to the Old Testament*, 3rd ed. with supplement, ed. James B. Pritchard (Princeton NJ: Princeton University Press, 1969) 73; Andrew George, *The Epic of Gilgamesh: The Babylonian Epic Poem and Other Texts in Akkadian and Sumerian*, trans. Andrew George; (London: Penguin, 1999) xvi; and Jeffrey H. Tigay, *The Evolution of the Gilgamesh Epic* (Philadelphia: University of Pennsylvania Press, 1982) 241-44. All citations of *Gilgamesh* in this article will be taken from the Foster translation.

[12]Foster, *The Epic of Gilgamesh*, 91. Foster's commentary on 11.212-14 reads as follows: "Utanapishtim has challenged Gilgamesh to go without sleep for a week; if he fails this test, how could he expect to live forever? Even as he speaks, Gilgamesh drifts off to sleep." Also see A. R. George, *The Babylonian Gilgamesh Epic: Introduction, Critical Edition and Cuneiform Texts*, 2 vols (Oxford UK: Oxford University Press, 2003) 1:210-11. George writes: "The hero did without sleep in quest of his goal but now, at last, he cannot keep his eyes open a moment longer and falls immediately into a deep slumber that lasts the whole week of the test."

[13]It should be noted that at other points in *The Epic of Gilgamesh*, sleep refers to either biological sleep or bodily death (e.g., 8.54).

whole of his body is seductively gorgeous. Mightier strength has he than you, Never resting by day or night." Similarly, in 2.45-49, Enkidu is portrayed more positively than the other shepherds. The author indicates that the chief shepherds would sleep at night, whereas Endiku would slay wolves and lions while serving as the wakeful watchman. These references certainly do not have to be interpreted metaphorically, but sleep nonetheless functions as the distinguishing factor between responsible and irresponsible human behavior. Finally, it should be noted that at numerous points the author appears to describe sleep as an active force. For instance, when Gilgamesh begins to have multiple dreams in Tablet 4, the author repeatedly refers to sleep's movements. In particular, the author uses the following refrain five times: "Gilgamesh sat there, chin on his knee. Sleep, which usually steals over people, fell upon him" (cf. 4.15-16, 49-50, 89-90, 127-28, 165-66).

In short, it is clear that from a very early date, at least some people groups in the Fertile Crescent referred to sleep in metaphorical terms.[14] In addition to physical rest and death, the author of *The Epic of Gilgamesh* uses Gilgamesh's seven day sleep metaphorically to distinguish him from the immortal gods. Furthermore, the author provides a negative evaluation of sleeping shepherds who neglect their duties.

B. Greek Literature. The authors of ancient Greece often place great emphasis upon sleep and its role within human affairs. In addition to simple references to biological rest or euphemisms for death, the ancient Greeks frequently refer to sleep metaphorically both as a deity and as irresponsible human activity.

I will begin with the former. Ancient Greeks frequently told stories about Hypnos, the god of sleep, and his role in the life and death of humans. In particular, Hypnos was usually thought of as a winged youth who stealthily put people to sleep by either touching their foreheads with a branch (e.g., Virgil, *Aen.* 5.854) or by pouring sleep-inducing liquid from

---

[14]Cf. Dennis R. MacDonald, "Luke's Eutychus and Homer's Elpenor: Acts 20:7-12 and *Odyssey* 10-12," *JHC* 1 (1994): 5-24. MacDonald argues that Luke's story about Eutychus is literarily dependent upon Homer's story about Elpenor. I, on the other hand, am arguing that the notions about sleep seen in Acts 20:7-12 are representative of a common thought pattern in the Fertile Crescent and the Mediterranean regions that likely predates the *Odyssey*.

a horn over them.[15] For instance in *Iliad* 14, which likely dates to the eighth century BCE,[16] the goddess, Hera, devises a scheme to distract Zeus temporarily so that Poseidon can deliver a staggering blow to the Trojans (*Il.* 14.153-60). To accomplish her goal Hera travels to Lemnos and begs Hypnos saying, "Sleep, lord of all gods and all men. . . . Lull to sleep the gleaming eyes of Zeus beneath his brows for me" (14.231-37).[17] Subsequently, while carrying out Hera's request, Hypnos hides behind a tree, takes on the disguise of a bird (14.282-91), and works under the cover of a dense cloud. As a result, Hypnos is able to overcome Zeus temporarily with a deep sleep (14.357-60).

On another occasion in *Iliad* 16, once Sarpedon's soul (ψυχή) and life have left him, Hypnos ("Υπνος), the god of Sleep, and his twin brother Death (Θάνατος) carry Sarpedon's body to the underworld (16.451-54, 666-82). Likewise, in the *Theogony*, which was likely written in the eighth century BCE,[18] Hesiod claims that Hypnos's mother is Night (Νὺξ); he has no father; and his siblings are Doom, Fate, Death, Dreams, Blame, and Woe (*Theog.* 211-12, 758).[19] Thus, in the works of Homer and Hesiod, we see a common belief that Hypnos, the god of Sleep, has the power to put both humans and gods to sleep at will. He, along with his twin brother Death, transports the souls of those who have died to the underworld.

Yet, the Greeks also associated sleep with irresponsible human behavior. For instance, in Homer's *Odyssey*, Elpenor, the youngest of Odysseus's men whom Homer describes as not "over valiant in war nor

---

[15]George M. A. Hanfmann, "Hypnos," in *The Oxford Classical Dictionary*, 3rd rev. ed., ed. Simon Hornblower and Antony Spawforth (Oxford UK: Oxford University Press, 2003) 737.

[16]Richmond Lattimore, *The Iliad of Homer*, trans. and introduced by Richmond Lattimore (Chicago: University of Chicago Press, 1951) 28-29.

[17]Homer, *Iliad*, trans. A. T. Murray, 2nd ed., rev. William F. Wyatt; LCL (Cambridge MA: Harvard University Press, 1999). All citations of the *Iliad* are taken from this translation.

[18]Hugh G. Evelyn-White, *Hesiod, the Homeric Hymns and Homerica*, LCL (Cambridge MA: Harvard University Press, 1914) xxvi.

[19]All citations are taken from *Hesiod, the Homeric Hymns and Homerica*, trans. Hugh G. Evelyn-White. In the Evelyn-White's LCL edition the paragraphs are not numbered. Therefore, the reader can find these lines on pages 95 and 133-34 of this volume.

sound of understanding" (10.553-554), falls asleep on a rooftop while in a drunken stupor.[20] The next morning, however, Odysseus finally issues the long-overdue call to all of his men to board the ship and to leave behind Circe's island and their beds of sweet sleep (ὕπνος) (10.548-49). Unfortunately, however, when Elpenor springs up without realizing he is on a rooftop, he falls to the ground, breaks his neck, and dies (10.555-60). In essence, his irresponsible behavior combined with his sleep result in a tragic outcome.

Perhaps even more helpful, consider Plato's references to sleep in the *Apology*. Socrates acknowledges that his divine calling annoys his fellow Greeks because he has been called to rouse them from sleep (νυστάζω) (30e). As a result, he says to the jury, "But you . . . might . . . easily kill me; then you would pass the rest of your lives in slumber (καθεύδω), unless God, in his care for you, should send someone else to sting you" (31a).[21] Thus, in this passage Plato uses sleep as a metaphor to describe humans who are out of step with the gods. Their sleep represents a spiritual, moral, or philosophical haze. Hence, in Greek literature, sleep routinely functioned metaphorically. At times, sleep referred to a mysterious god; at other times it characterized those who were out of step with the gods.

C. Roman Literature. In *The Aeneid* Virgil most certainly uses the term "sleep" to refer to bodily rest[22] and as a metaphorical allusion to death (e.g., 6.1211), but he also prominently refers to sleep metaphorically as a distinguishing mark between humans and the gods, as Somnus, the god of sleep, and as an obstacle that must be overcome by pious humans.[23]

---

[20]Homer, *Odyssey*, trans. A. T. Murray, rev. George E. Dimock, LCL (Cambridge MA: Harvard University Press, 1999). All citations of the *Odyssey* are taken from this translation. Dimock places this author in the eighth century BCE (5).

[21]*Euthyphro, Apology, Crito, Phaedo, Phaedrus*, trans. Harold N. Fowler, vol. 1 of *Plato in Twelve Volumes*, LCL (Cambridge MA: Harvard University Press, 1967). All citations of the *Apology* are taken from this translation. Plato wrote this text in the early portion of the fourth century BCE (xiv-xv).

[22]E.g., 1.930; 2.13, 360-407; 3.205, 677; 4.724, 730, 772; 6.698; 7.572; 8.41-42. All citations and translations of *The Aeneid* are taken from Virgil, *The Aeneid*, trans. Robert Fitzgerald (New York: Vintage, 1990).

[23]See, e.g., "Somnus" in *Lempriere's Classical Dictionary of Proper Names Mentioned in Ancient Authors*, 3rd ed., ed. John Lempriere (London: Routledge, 1986) 591.

Moreover, at points Virgil actually weaves these last three ideas together. First, Virgil repeatedly portrays the gods as being active during the night hours, whereas humans are typically asleep.[24] Hence the nocturnal activity of the gods reinforces the notion that the gods and humans are very different. As a result, at numerous points in *The Aeneid* the gods must first wake Aeneas and his men from their sleep in order to guide them.

For instance, in *Aen.* 4.772-803 a god appears to Aeneas in the middle of the night to warn him that he must leave Carthage immediately because Dido's anger is building. The god says, "Son of the goddess, sleep away this crisis, can you still? Do you not see the dangers growing round you? . . . Will you not be gone in flight, while flight is still within your power?" (4.777-81, 785-86). As a result, "Aeneas broke from sleep and roused his crewman" (4.794-95) in the middle of the night. Hence, in this passage sleep represents Aeneas's choice. If pious Aeneas chooses to fulfill his destiny as the founder of Rome, he must break from sleep and take immediate action. Alternatively, if he chooses to sleep through the night, he will find himself acting contrary to the will of the gods.

This dichotomy between good and bad decisions, which is then portrayed metaphorically through either night time vigilance or sleep, is perhaps even more striking in Virgil's portrayal of Palinurus. Palinurus is the chief helmsman of the Trojan fleet. While all of Aeneas's cohorts are sleeping on the beach at Ceraunia (3.671-77), Palinurus turns out briskly even before the midpoint of the night. The watchful Palinurus then rouses the rest of the Trojans so that they can catch the favorable sailing winds (3.678-92). Hence, at this point in the story, it is Palinurus's mastery over sleep that profits the entire group of future Romans.

Two chapters later in *Aen.* 5, however, Virgil portrays Palinurus in antithetical terms. Sailing along around midnight while his entire crew is sleeping, Palinurus's duty requires him to be alert and vigilant during the night as he was before. Yet, Somnus, the god of sleep, glides down from the stars "in quest" of Palinurus (5.1097-99). "Upon the high poop deck the god sat down in Phorbas' guise, and said: 'Palinurus, the very sea itself moves the ship onward. There's a steady breeze. The hour for rest has come. Put down your head and steal a respite for your tired eyes. I'll man your tiller for a while'" (5.1100-1107).

---

[24]E.g., 1.930, 3.205-38; 4.772-803; 8.40-92.

At first, Palinurus resists. Yet, Somnus is both more determined and more powerful. Therefore, Virgil writes:

> Now see the god, his bough a-drip with Lethe's dew, and slumberous with Stygian power, giving it a shake over the pilot's temples, to unfix, although he fought it, both his swimming eyes. His unexpected drowse barely begun, Somnus leaned over him and flung him down in the clear water, breaking off with him a segment of the stern and steering oar. Headfirst he went down, calling in vain on friends. (5.1117-25)

Then, the deed done, "the god himself took flight into thin air, but still the fleet ran safely on" (5.1128-30).[25] Thankfully, pious Aeneas somehow senses that the ship is drifting off course. As a result, Aeneas, himself, takes over and sets the fleet on the correct course while mourning his friend (5.1134-41).

Conversely, Virgil portrays the duty-bound Aeneas in almost opposite terms to those of the conquered Palinurus. For instance, as Aeneas and a group of his men are sailing down the river at night, Aeneas remains vigilant and stays awake. Virgil describes the scene, "Now daylight left the sky, and the mild moon, in mid-heaven, rode her night-wandering car, but duty would not give Aeneas rest: He held the tiller still, still shifted sail" (10.297-300). At that point, one of the nymphs, whom Cybele sends to inform Aeneas that his men are under attack, speaks to Aeneas. She says, "Still awake, Aeneas, kin to gods?" (10.315-16). Now certainly, Aeneas is literally kin to the gods, but here, Aeneas's fulfillment of his duty even in the middle of the night, unlike Palinurus, makes the observation all the more salient. Duty bound and pious Aeneas refuses to give in to Sleep's

---

[25]It is also noteworthy that Aeneas meets up with Palinurus at a later time. While Aeneas journeys in the underworld, he sees Palinurus among the unburied souls of those who have died but remain unburied (6.456-59). Consequently, Aeneas asks: "Which god took you away from us and put you under, Palinurus?" (6.462-64). In response Palinurus provides an allusive answer and begs Aeneas to give his body a proper burial so that he might be freed from the realm of the unburied souls (6.472-94). See W. S. M. Nicoll, "The Sacrifice of Palinurus," *CQ* 38/2 (1988): 459. Nicoll comments that Palinurus "gives Aeneas an account of his own death which differs substantially from the one given by Virgil himself as narrator in *Aen.* 5."

sweet distraction. Instead, he stays the course through the dark of night, and his men are the beneficiaries of his duty-bound actions.

In short, the *Aeneid* provides us with a glimpse of how ancient Romans, living roughly at the same time as Luke, viewed sleep.[26] More precisely, in *The Aeneid* Virgil portrays sleep both as a god and as irresponsible human behavior. Somnus approaches humans by disguise during the night hours, tempts them with distraction in the form of sleep, and prevents them from fulfilling their duties as well as their destinies. Hence, at times in *The Aeneid*, sleep functions metaphorically both as a Tempter and as a temptation.

D. Jewish Literature. Likewise, at points in the Hebrew Bible, sleep functions metaphorically. Yet here, rather than a personification of sleep it is primarily associated with irresponsible human behavior. Obvious examples include Samson in Judges 16. Twice, Delilah waits until Samson falls asleep before she first weaves the locks of his hair and then eventually cuts his hair (16:14, 19).[27] Unfortunately, when Samson wakes from his sleep, he is unaware "that the LORD has left him" (16:20 NRSV). Most certainly, Samson is lax in many of areas in his life. Yet, Samson's sleep is both physically and metaphorically illustrative of his dormant relationship with the LORD.

Similarly, when Nahum taunts and rebukes the Assyrian rulers of Nineveh, he criticizes them by saying, "Your shepherds are asleep, O king of Assyria; your nobles slumber" (Nah 3:18a). When Nahum describes the rulers as being oblivious to what God is about to do, he describes them as sleeping shepherds who should be alert and watching their sheep. Additionally, Jonah provides us with another example of one whose sleep is also related to his distraction from the will of the LORD. Jonah is sleeping in the boat even as the LORD is sending a storm to alter his course (Jon 1:1-9).

In later Jewish writings we continue to see sleep employed as a literary metaphor. For instance in *The Sentences of the Syriac Menander* (3rd c. CE), sleep is negatively associated with the kind of human actions that lead to

---

[26]Ovid, a Roman author writing around the same time period, expresses similar ideas about Somnus in *The Metamorphoses* 11.585-632.

[27]I will point out some of the Greek terminology that appears in the Septuagint as a way of demonstrating the commonality of thought between the Hebrew Bible and Luke's writings.

death. The author wrote, "Hateful is the custom of lying down at an improper time" because "sleep carries (us) into Sheol" (II.67-68).[28] In psalm 16 of the *Psalms of Solomon* (1st c. BCE), sleep clearly functions as a metaphor for sinful human behavior. The author writes:

> When my soul slumbered, (I was far away) from the Lord, wretched for a time; I sank into sleep (ὑπνόω), far from God. For a moment my soul was poured out to death; (I was) near the gates of Hades with the sinner. Thus my soul was drawn away from the Lord God of Israel, unless the Lord had come to my aid with his everlasting mercy. He jabbed me as a horse is goaded to keep it awake; my savior and protector at all times. (vv. 1-4)

Likewise in the *Testament of Reuben* 3.1-9 (2nd c. BCE), sleep (ὕπνος) is wed with the seven spirits of deceit: promiscuity, insatiability, strife, flattery and trickery, arrogance, lying, and injustice. The author writes:

> With all these the spirit of sleep (ὕπνος) forms an alliance, which results in error and fantasy. And thus every young man is destroyed, darkening his mind from the truth, neither gaining understanding in the Law of God nor heeding the advice of his fathers–just this was my plight in my youth. (3.7-9)

Thus, in ancient Hebrew and Jewish texts sleep often referred to more than mere physical rest. Instead at times it functions as a negative metaphor for inattentiveness toward the LORD. Whereas it may have been natural for Samson, the Assyrian rulers, Jonah, and the authors of the *Psalms of Solomon* and the *Testament of Reuben* to rest physically, in these passages their physical sleep illustrates far more. It illustrates their spiritual dullness. Moreover, at least for the author of the *Testament of Reuben*, this spiritual dullness developed during his youth.

E. Early Christian Literature. Similar metaphorical uses of sleep imagery can be seen in early Christian writings as well. These texts further demonstrate that at least some early Christians were recipients of the stream of ideas about sleep in antiquity that I am chronicling. First, sleep commonly functions as a metaphor or euphemism for physical death in the

---

[28] All citations and translations in this section derive from *The Old Testament Pseudepigrapha*, 2 vols., ed. James H. Charlesworth (New York: Doubleday, 1983, 1985).

New Testament. For instance in 1 Thess 4:13-18, Paul repeatedly refers to believers who are dead (νεκρός) as those who have fallen asleep (κοιμάομαι). Similar references to death as sleep can be found in John 11:11-13, 1 Cor 15:51, and 1 Thess 5:10.

Alternatively, we also see metaphorical references to sleep in which sleep alludes to spiritual dullness or distraction. For instance in 1 Thess 5:1-8, while discussing the Parousia, Paul writes "But you, beloved, are not in darkness, for that day to surprise you like a thief; for you are all children of light and children of the day; we are not of the night or of darkness. So then let us not fall asleep (καθεύδω) as others do, but let us keep awake and be sober" (1 Thess 5:4-6 NRSV). Here, sleep indicates that a believer is ill-prepared for the return of Christ, whereas being awake indicates that a believer is vigilant and ready for the return of Christ.[29] In a similar context in Romans, Paul exhorts his readers to "wake from sleep (ὕπνος). For salvation is nearer to us now than when we became believers" (Rom 13:11).[30]

In addition, consider the *Acts of Paul*, which was likely composed before 200 CE.[31] It includes a couple of stories in which sleep (or the lack thereof) and the act of sitting in a window play pivotal roles. Moreover, both of these stories may well be in dialogue with Luke's narration of the events in Acts 20:7-12 involving Eutychus and Paul.

---

[29]Earl J. Richard, *First and Second Thessalonians*, SP 11 (Collegeville MN: Liturgical Press, 1995) 253-54. See also, F. F. Bruce, *1 & 2 Thessalonians*, WBC 45 (Waco TX: Word, 1982) 116. Bruce writes: "The call for vigilance is voiced in terms of keeping awake and having one's wits about one, rather than being overcome by drowsiness and intoxication; it is voiced also in military terms. Spiritual armor is a necessary defense against spiritual assaults."

[30]James D. G. Dunn, *Romans 9-16*, WBC 38B (Dallas: Word, 1988) 786. In regard to Paul's reference to sleep, Dunn writes, "Here obviously . . . the connotation is eschatological and moral."

[31]For a conversation about the uncertain formation and history of the *Acts of Paul*, see Wilhelm Schneemelcher, "Acts of Paul," in *Writings Relating to the Apostles; Apocalypses and Related Subjects*, vol. 2 of *New Testament Apocrypha*, rev. ed., ed. Wilhelm Schneemelcher, trans. R. McL. Wilson (Louisville: Westminster, 1992) 213-35, and Jan N. Bremmer, ed., *The Apocryphal Acts of Paul and Thecla*, Studies in the Apocryphal Acts of the Apostles 2 (Kampen, Netherlands: Kok-Pharos, 1996).

First, in the *Acts of Paul and Thecla*, the third division of the composite *Acts of Paul*, Thecla's actions show her to be the ideal convert who is capable of living the Christian life in a manner superior to that of most. When Paul arrives in Iconium, Onesiphorous welcomes Paul as his house guest and provides Paul with an opportunity to spread his message.

> And while Paul was thus speaking in the midst of an assembly in the house of Onesiphorous, a virgin (named) Thecla . . . who was betrothed to a man (named) Thamyris, sat at a near-by window and listened night and day to the word of the virgin life as it was spoken by Paul; and she did not turn away from the window, but pressed on in the faith rejoicing exceedingly. (*Acts of Paul* 3.7)[32]

Hence, the author constructs a similar setting to that of Eutychus in Acts 20:7-12. Thecla is listening to the evangelist, Paul, while sitting in a window. Yet, unlike Eutychus, who falls asleep in a similar setting, Thecla listens "night and day to the word of the virgin life."

In fact, because Thecla "did not move from the window," her mother sends for Thamyris, the man to whom Thecla is betrothed, in order to complain about Paul's influence upon Thecla (*Acts of Paul* 3.8). When he arrives, the mother says, "For indeed for three days and nights Thecla has not risen from the window either to eat or to drink, but gazing steadily as if on some joyful spectacle she so devotes herself to a strange man" (*Acts of Paul* 3.8). The mother goes on to explain, "And my daughter also, who sticks to the window like a spider, is (moved) by his words (and) gripped by a new desire and a fearful passion; for the maiden hangs upon the things he says, and is taken captive" (*Acts of Paul* 3.9). Finally, despite both the pleas and the extreme displeasures of Thamyris, her mother, and her mother's maidservants, the author praises Thecla by letting us know that, "while this was going on (all around her) Thecla did not turn away, but gave her whole attention to Paul's word" (*Acts of Paul* 3.10).

Thus, in the *Acts of Paul*, the author portrays Thecla's attentiveness in terms that are antithetical to Eutychus's sleep in Acts 20:7-12. Whereas Luke tells us that Eutychus is overcome by sleep and therefore is not attentive to Paul's preaching, the second century Christian author of the *Acts of Paul and Thecla* shows that Thecla overcomes sleep and distraction

---

[32]All citations from the *Acts of Paul* are taken from the translation by Schneemelcher in *New Testament Apocrypha* 2:237-65.

while focusing upon Paul's words. For at least three days and nights, she is not distracted by any of her physical needs. To Thecla, Paul's message is simply too important to sleep, eat, or drink. In the end, this story encourages young Christians to emulate the attentiveness of Thecla.

Second, the author of the *Acts of Paul* includes a story about Patroclus in the eleventh chapter of this text. Paul arrives in Rome, is greeted by Luke and Titus, and rents a barn, which he uses as a place for teaching fellow Christians. Paul's ministry and message then draw a crowd, many of whom are from the house of Caesar. In particular, Patroclus, Caesar's cup-bearer, arrives late, cannot enter the barn due to the crowd, and therefore chooses to sit "at a high window" and to listen to Paul teach the word of God (*Acts Paul* 11.1). Tragically, however, things take a turn for the worse at this point. Patroclus falls from the window and dies (*Acts Paul* 11.1). Hence, this story has a great deal in common with that of Eutychus in Acts 20:7-12.[33] Both Eutychus and Patroclus are sitting in a high window listening to Paul teach a crowd of believers, and both young men fall to their deaths.

Interestingly, even though temporally it is "late," the author never says Patroclus falls asleep. Instead, the author indicates that Patroclus falls from the window because "the wicked devil" is at work. Similar to many of the texts we have examined from antiquity, we cannot assume that the earliest readers of the *Acts of Paul* would have differentiated the work of "the wicked devil" from the action of falling asleep. As we have repeatedly seen,

---

[33]Gerd Lüdemann, *Early Christianity according to the Traditions in Acts: A Commentary*, trans. John Bowden (London: SCM, 1989) 224. Lüdemann refers to this story as "an imitation of the story of the disciple Eutychus." For more complete discussions see Françios Bovon, "La vie des apôtres: traditions bibliques et narrations apocryphes," in *Les Actes des apôtres: christianisme et monde païen*, ed. Bovon, Publication de la faculté de théolgie l'université de Genève 4 (Geneva: Labor et Fides, 1981) 150, and MacDonald, "Luke's Eutychus and Homer's Elpenor," 10-11. MacDonald claims that the similarities "between the stories derive from literary dependence." Alternatively see Willy Rordorf, "In welchem Verhältnis stehen die apokryphen Paulusakten zur kanonischen Apostelgeschichte und zu den Pastoralbriefen?" in *Text and Testimony: Essays on New Testament and Apocryphal Literature in Honor of A. F. J. Klijn*, ed. Tjitze Baarda and A. F. J. Klijn (Kampen, Netherlands: Kok, 1988) 232-37. Rordorf argues that the similarities result from a common oral tradition rather than literary dependence.

sleep in antiquity was often metaphorically associated with a personified force that has the power to overcome humans.

The author writes, "But since the wicked devil was envious of the love of the brethren, Patroclus fell from the window and died, and the news was quickly brought to Nero" (*Acts of Paul* 11.1). At that point, Paul responds quickly.

> But Paul, perceiving it in the spirit, said: "Brethren, the evil one has gained an opportunity to tempt you. Go out, and you will find a youth fallen from a height and already on the point of death. Lift him up, and bring him here to me!" So they went out and brought him. And when the crowd saw (him), they were troubled. Paul said to them: "Now, brethren, let your faith be manifest. Come, all of you, let us mourn to our Lord Jesus Christ, that this youth may live and we remain unmolested." But as they all lamented the youth drew breath again, and setting him upon a beast they sent him back alive with the others who were of Caesar's house. (*Acts of Paul* 11.1)

Hence, just as we saw in Acts 20:7-12, the young man who falls out of the window is raised to life.

For our purposes, the *Acts of Paul* provides us with two distinct pictures of young people who are listening to the teachings of Paul while sitting in a window. Thecla functions as the ideal disciple when she denies her natural desires for sleep and a spouse. In fact, she remains vigilant in the window listening to Paul for three days and nights. Alternatively, Patroclus is conquered by the devil while sitting in a window listening to Paul preach. As a result, Paul goes on to warn the other believers against temptation and molestation from this evil force. Hence, the author of the *Acts of Paul* portrays sleep metaphorically in at least two ways: both as human negligence and as an external, wicked force. Yet, even then, in the Patroclus narrative, the author actually merges the two concepts. Paul's final exhortation to the believers about avoiding temptation and molestation actually links the work of the devil with human temptation.

III. Sleep in Luke-Acts

Sleep is not only treated metaphorically in ancient Sumerian, Greek, Roman, Jewish, and early Christian texts in general,[34] but Luke himself

---

[34]For an additional discussion about the use of sleep imagery in antiquity see

employs sleep imagery metaphorically, though he typically limits his metaphorical use of sleep to spiritual dullness or distraction. Luke's treatment of sleep is not surprising since Luke and his readers were participants in the broader cultural milieu of Mediterranean antiquity. For instance, at the transfiguration (Luke 9:28-36), Peter, James, and John almost miss Jesus' glory because they are weighed down by sleep (9:32). Notably, Luke alone includes this detail about the disciples' sleep at the transfiguration.[35] Similarly, in the garden of Gethsemane (Luke 22:39-46), Jesus prays with great vigilance even as the disciples fall asleep. Jesus is therefore provoked and asks, "Why are you sleeping? Get up and pray that you may not come into the time of trial (πειρασμός)."[36]

Furthermore, in Luke's writings we often hear Jesus and Paul contrast spiritual lethargy with vigilant faithfulness. For example, in Luke 12:35-37, Jesus says, "Be dressed for action and have your lamps lit, be like those who are waiting for their master to return. . . . Blessed are those slaves whom the master finds alert when he comes." Similarly, in Luke 21:34-36 Jesus says, "Be on guard so that your hearts are not weighed down" (21:34), and "Be alert at all times, praying that you may have the strength to escape all these things" (21:36). Here, Jesus metaphorically employs the idea of his followers being ready and alert in the middle of the night. In essence, he wants his disciples to be alert rather than asleep to God's work in the world.[37]

Finally, consider Paul's sermon to the Ephesian elders in Acts 20, which begins only five verses after the Eutychus narrative. Here, Paul addresses the Ephesian elders for the last time. He says, "Keep watch over

---

Horst Balz, ὕπνος, ἀφυπνόω, ἐνύπνιον, ἐνυπνιάζομαι, ἔξυπνος, ἐξυπνίζω, *TDNT* 8:545-50.

[35]Joseph A. Fitzmyer, *The Gospel according to Luke*, 2 vols., AB 28, 28A (New York: Doubleday, 1981, 1985) 1:800.

[36]Fitzmyer, *Gospel according to Luke* 2:1438. I concur with Fitzmyer when he argues that, unlike Mark, Luke provides a rationale and an excuse for the sleep of the disciples; Luke attributes their sleep to grief (22:39). Yet, despite the rationale, the disciples are still distracted from the purposes of God at a crucial juncture. As a result, Fitzmyer writes, "one cannot help but detect even in this account the lack of comprehension on their part" (2:1440).

[37]Charles H. Talbert, *Reading Luke: A Literary and Theological Commentary*, rev. ed., Reading the New Testament (Macon GA: Smyth & Helwys, 2002) 231-32.

yourselves and over the flock" (20:28), and "Be alert, remembering that for three years I did not cease night or day to warn everyone with tears" (20:31). In part, Paul exhorts them to vigilance because he believes heretical "wolves" will come and seek to persuade the flock (20:29-30). In this sermon, Paul lifts himself up as a positive example of what the elders should do. Paul, like a good shepherd, was vigilant both night and day to guard against spiritual pitfalls. Now Paul wants the elders to do the same. Importantly, the most vivid example of Paul's alertness and watchcare over his fellow Christians came earlier in chapter 20 when Paul cared for, protected, and restored the youthful Eutychus who had fallen asleep.

IV. Reading Acts 20:7-12 Metaphorically

I began by claiming that Acts 20:7-12 is structured in a chiastic fashion, which places the stress of the passage upon Eutychus's sleep. As a result, I have consulted a variety of ancient texts while paying attention to the role of sleep. My survey has shown that it would have been quite natural for Luke to employ metaphorical references to sleep, and it would have been quite natural for his first audience to interpret the text metaphorically. Yet, as I mentioned earlier, even if the evidence emboldens us to interpret Eutychus's sleep in Act 20:7-12 metaphorically, we still have to ask how the metaphor functions. Luke's audience would have been quite familiar with at least four different metaphorical understandings of sleep—sleep as death, as a marker of human mortality, as a nonhuman external force, and as spiritual or moral distraction.

First, it is certainly possible that some early readers interpreted Eutychus's sleep as nothing more than biological rest; this is, of course, the prevailing viewpoint of most Acts scholars today.[38] Yet, given that metaphorical references to sleep were commonplace in ancient texts and given that Luke himself draws attention to the disciples' sleep at crucial junctures, one at least has to ask whether Luke's first audience would have interpreted Eutychus's sleep as something more than mere biological rest. Second, metaphorical understandings of sleep as death or as a mark of mortality simply do not fit the context of Acts 20.

---

[38]E.g., C. K. Barrett, *A Critical and Exegetical Commentary on the Acts of the Apostles*, 2 vols., ICC (Edinburgh: T.&T. Clark, 1998) 2:950. Barrett claims that up to this point "attempts to find allegorical intention in the story are unconvincing."

Hence, we are left with two options: Would Luke's earliest readers have seen Eutychus as an innocent victim who was conquered by a non-human external force (e.g., Hypnos or the devil), or would they have seen Eutychus as a negligent sinner whose sleep illustrates his spiritual dullness? Even though it may be possible to argue that sleep in Acts 20:7-12 represents an adversarial deity (e.g., Hypnos or the devil) who defeats a helpless Eutychus,[39] it is difficult to interpret Luke's grammar in this fashion. For instance, on the first occasion when Luke tells us that Eutychus is being overcome (καταφέρω) by sleep (ὕπνος) in verse 9b, sleep is joined by an adjective creating a reference to a type of sleep: a deep (βαθύς) sleep. Here, it is less likely that Eutychus's sleep in Acts 20:7-12 could be interpreted metaphorically as the result of an assault from an adversarial deity.

As a result, it is far more likely that Luke's audience would have envisaged Eutychus's sleep in Acts 20:7-12 as a metaphorical indicator of Eutychus's own spiritual distraction or dullness.[40] In fact, we see antithetical images in this pericope. Paul and the majority of the congregation at Troas are attentive to God even during the dark of night, but Eutychus represents the young believer who is not. Paul looks more like Jesus in Gethsemane while Eutychus looks more like the disciples who succumb to temptation. Eutychus begins by straddling the boundary between the realm of dark and the realm of light.[41] Eventually, however, he falls asleep to God and the congregation. He falls away from the community that breaks bread on the Sabbath in an upper room while waiting for the dawn to arrive, and

---

[39]If the Patroclus narrative in the *Acts of Paul* 11.1 is literarily dependent upon Acts 20:7-12 and if it is expanding upon Acts 20:7-12, then one would place that type of interpretation in this category—i.e., the devil conquered Eutychus with sleep. Thus, one might argue that the author of the *Acts of Paul* was an early Christian who interpreted Acts 20:7-12 in this manner. Yet, even then, it must be noted that the author of the *Acts of Paul* constructed a narrative that was quite distinct from Acts 20:7-12 as he or she set forth this idea.

[40]F. Scott Spencer, *Journeying through Acts: A Literary-Cultural Reading* (Peabody MA: Hendrickson, 2004) 191. Also see Robert C. Tannehill, *The Acts of the Apostles*, vol. 2 of *The Narrative Unity of Luke-Acts: A Literary Interpretation* (Minneapolis: Fortress, 1990) 250; and Balz, *TDNT* 8:554. Balz writes: "The idea of man's sinful stupor in relation to salvation might account for the reference to sleep along with the raising again."

[41]Trémel, "À propos d'Actes 20,7-12," 359-69.

he dies. Conversely, the ministry of Paul as well as that of the early church consists of more than mere instruction and worship. Instead, it also includes the ministry of reconciliation for "fallen" believers.

Consequently, if we interpret Eutychus's sleep as a metaphorical reference to spiritual or moral distraction, then Eutychus functions as a negative example for early believers. His fall was his own fault. His sleep illustrates his sinfulness. As a result, Eutychus's story also functions as a stern warning to Luke's readers. Vulnerable believers should be aware of the severe consequences that come with spiritual or ecclesiological distraction.

Conclusion

Despite Bede's interpretation of Eutychus's sleep in the eighth century CE, Bernard Trémel became perhaps the first modern scholar to suggest that Acts 20:7-12 should be interpreted metaphorically in his 1980 article entitled, "À propos d'Actes 20,7-12: Puissance du Thaumaturge ou du témoin?" Subsequently, even though Trémel's thesis has gained a sympathetic hearing among a handful of scholars over the last twenty-five years,[42] it certainly has not garnered the support of the majority of those who write commentaries on the book of Acts. My research on the literary depictions of sleep in antiquity, however, reinforces and advances a metaphorical interpretation of Acts 20:7-12 in at least two ways. First, we have seen that the structure of Acts 20:7-12 emphasizes Eutychus's sleep. Structurally, Luke draws his readers' attention to Eutychus's sleep by referring to it twice in the center of this chiastic passage and by guiding his readers to reflect upon Eutychus at the end of the passage even after Paul has departed from Troas. Second, after recognizing the prominent role of Eutychus's sleep in Acts 20:7-12, I have been able to situate the discussion about a metaphorical reading of Acts 20:7-12 within the broader context of ancient Near Eastern and Mediterranean thought as it relates to sleep. Through this study we can readily see that ancient authors routinely employed metaphorical references to sleep. As a result, we can now conclude that a metaphorical interpretation of Acts 20:7-12 is not merely wishful hermeneutics or medieval invention.

---

[42]E.g., Gerhard Schneider, *Die Apostelgeschichte*, HTKNT 5/2 (Freiburg: Herder, 1982) 284-85; Rudolf Pesch, *Die Apostelgeschichte*, EKKNT 5 (Düsseldorf: Benziger/Neukirchener, 1995) 2:191; Tannehill, *Acts of the Apostles*, 249-50; and Beverly Roberts Gaventa, *The Acts of the Apostles*, ANTC (Nashville: Abingdon, 2003) 279-80.

Rather, a metaphorical and even negative interpretation of Eutychus and his sleep in Acts 20:7-12, as Bede espoused, is both a historically appropriate and exegetically fruitful avenue of interpretation. Many of Luke's first readers likely interpreted the story of Eutychus in this manner.

Prophets, Priests, and Godfearing Readers: The Priestly and Prophetic Traditions in Luke-Acts

Thomas E. Phillips

Trends within scholarship, as within fashion, change with dizzying speed. The themes that dominate the runways of Biblical scholarship in any given year are often relegated to the scholarly equivalent of the local thrift store just a few years later. For better or worse, the ideas that captivate scholarly audiences one season often fade into obscurity the next. In the publish-or-perish world of Biblical scholarship, where the goal is to continuously say something very new about the same very ancient texts, clinging to any trend long enough to consider its true value can be a *faux pas* on the order of wearing tube socks with sandals. Biblical scholars, like the editors behind *Vogue* and *Vanity Fair*, often move on to some newer fashion before the utility, beauty and intrinsic value of their earlier productions have been fully appreciated and exploited. Sometimes, even amid the marketing blitz for the newest fashions, some interesting ensembles can be generated from earlier, now disregarded, trends.

In this brief paper, I want to pick up three once prominent, but now less fashionable, concerns within Lukan scholarship and to mold these themes into a new ensemble that may once again bring these neglected themes back into the spotlight. In the coin of the scholarly realm, my thesis is that Luke-Acts presumes a distinction between the priestly and prophetic traditions within Judaism and that Luke-Acts places Christian believers within the prophetic tradition, while Judaism is placed within the priestly tradition. I will further argue that the Lukan writings portray the priestly tradition as divinely "muted" and supplanted by the prophetic tradition with which it has always competed. I will ultimately suggest that this textual strategy would be ideally suited to the purpose of drawing godfearing Gentiles away from Judaism and toward the church.

This reading of Luke-Acts is particularly persuasive when one draws upon earlier scholarship regarding Luke's portrayal of Jews and Judaism,[1]

---

[1]For a bibliography on this topic through 1998, see my "Subtlety as a Literary Technique in Luke's Characterization of Jews and Judaism," in *Literary Studies in Luke-Acts*, ed. Richard P. Thompson and Thomas E. Phillips (Macon GA: Mercer

regarding the Lukan tendency to portray key Christian leaders as prophetic figures,[2] and regarding the prominence of godfearers in the implied

University Press, 1998) 313-26. Among the most important subsequent contributors to the discussion are M. Bachmann, "Die Stephanusepisode (Apg 6,1-8,3): Ihre Bedeutung für die Lukanische Sicht des Jerusalemischen Tempels und des Judentums," in *The Unity of Luke-Acts*, ed. J. Verheyden (Leuven: Leuven University Press, 1999) 545-62; Robert L. Brawley, "Ethical Borderlines between Rejection and Hope: Interpreting the Jews in Luke-Acts," *CTM* 6 (2000): 415-23; G. P. Carras, "Observant Jews in the Story of Luke and Acts: Paul, Jesus and Other Jews," in *The Unity of Luke-Acts*, 693-708; Jay Eldon Epp, "Anti-Judaic Tendencies in the D-Text of Acts: Forty Years of Conversation," in *The Book of Acts as Church History*, ed. Tobias Nicklas and Michael Tilly, BZNW 120 (Berlin: Walter de Gruyter, 2003) 111-46; Joachim Jeska, *Die Geschichte Israels in der Sicht des Lukas*, FRLANT 195 (Göttingen: Vandenhoeck & Ruprecht, 2001); Paul Metzger, "Zeitspiegel: Neutestamentliche Handschriften als Zeugnisse der Kirchengeschichte: Die Frage nach einer Hoffnung für Israel bei Lukas," in *The Book of Acts as Church History*, 241-62; David P. Moessner and David L. Tiede, "Conclusion: 'And Some Were Persuaded . . . ' " in *Jesus and the Heritage of Israel*, ed. David P. Moessner (Philadelphia: Trinity Press International, 1999) 358-68; Martin Rese, "The Jews in Luke-Acts: Some Second Thoughts," in *The Unity of Luke-Acts*, 185-202; Michael Tilly, "Juden, Christen und Heiden im Actatext de Peschitto: Beobachtungen zu einer Syrischen Übersetzung der Apostelgeschichte," in *The Book of Acts as Church History*, 321-43; and Joseph B. Tyson, *Luke, Judaism, and the Scholars: Critical Approaches to Luke-Acts* (Columbia: University of South Carolina Press, 1999).

[2]The most important and frequently cited advocate for the importance of this theme within Luke-Acts is Luke Timothy Johnson, *The Literary Function of Possessions in Luke-Acts*, SBLDS 39 (Missoula MT: Scholars Press, 1977). More recently see Luke Timothy Johnson, *The Gospel of Luke*, SP 3 (Collegeville MN: Michael Glazier, 1991); Johnson, *Acts of the Apostles*, SP 5 (Collegeville MN: Michael Glazier, 1992); Brigid Curtin Frein, "The Literary Significance of the Jesus-as-Prophet Motif in the Gospel of Luke and the Acts of the Apostles" (Ph.D. diss.; St. Louis University, 1989); R. J. Irudhayasamy, *A Prophet in the Making: A Christological Study on Lk 4.16-30 in the Background of the Isaianic Mixed Citation and the Elijah and Elisha References* (Frankfurt: Lang, 2002); Mark McVann, "Rituals of Status Transformation in Luke-Acts: The Case of the Prophet," in *The Social World of Luke-Acts*, ed. Jerome Neyrey (Peabody MA: Hendrickson, 1991) 333-60; David L. Tiede, *Prophecy and History in Luke-Acts* (Philadelphia: Fortress, 1980); Paul S. Minear, *To Heal and to Reveal: The*

readership of Luke-Acts.[3] Admittedly, these three scholarly discussions are less prominent in Lukan studies today than they were in the previous decade, but in this essay I wish to revive interest in these earlier trends and to supplement them with a few new accessories. My wish is not merely to offer a retro perspective on Luke-Acts or to return a stock of threadbare ideas back to fashion. Rather my desire is to weave this patchwork of earlier discussions together using a new line of inquiry and thereby to establish a fresh reading of Luke-Acts that draws together these previously loosely related discussions. The thread that I will use to pull these discussions taut is Luke's treatment of the priestly and prophetic traditions in the Septuagint and first century Judaism. Before returning to these themes, however, I will offer a brief survey of the priestly and prophetic traditions in Luke and Acts.

Prophetic Vocation according to Luke (New York: Crossroads, 1976); and Thomas L. Brodie, *The Crucial Bridge: The Elijah-Elisha Narrative as an Interpretive Synthesis of Genesis-Kings and a Literary Model for the Gospels* (Minneapolis: Liturgical Press, 2000).

[3]This interpretation of Luke's readership was popularized by John Nolland's three-volume commentary on the gospel. See John Nolland, *Luke*, 3 vols., WBC (Dallas: Word, 1989) particularly 1:xxxii-xxxiii. For the other significant contributors to this discussion, see Martinus de Boer, "God-Fearers in Luke-Acts," in *Luke's Literary Achievement*, ed. Christopher M. Tuckett (Sheffield UK: Sheffield Academic Press, 1995) 50-71; Sarah Henrich, "Godfearing in Acts 10: The Changing Rules of Hospitality in Early Christianity" (Ph.D. diss.; Yale University, 1994); Jacob Jervell, "The Church of Jews and Godfearers," in *Luke-Acts and the Jewish People: Eight Critical Perspectives*, ed. Joseph B. Tyson (Minneapolis: Augsburg, 1988) 11-20; A. Thomas Kraabel, "The Disappearance of the 'God-Fearers,' " *Numen* 28 (1981): 113-26; Kirsopp Lake, "Proselytes and God-Fearers," in *The Beginnings of Christianity*, 5 vols., ed. Henry J. Cadbury et al., (Repr.: Grand Rapids MI: Baker, 1965) 5:74-95; Judith M. Lieu, "The Race of God-Fearers," *JTS* 46/2 (1995): 483-501; Wolfgang Stegemann, *Zwishen Synagogue und Obrigkeit: Zur historischen Situation der Lukanischen Christen* (Göttingen: Vandenhoeck & Ruprecht, 1991); Joseph B. Tyson, "Jews and Judaism in Luke-Acts: Reading as a Godfearer," *NTS* 41 (1995): 19-38; *Images of Judaism in Luke-Acts* (Columbia: University of South Carolina Press, 1992); Robert C. Tannehill, " 'Cornelius' and 'Tabitha' Encounter Luke's Jesus," *Int* 48/4 (1994): 347-56; and Roman Garrison, *The Significance of Theophilus as Luke's Reader* (Lewiston NY: Edwin Mellen Press, 2004).

I. Priests and Prophets in Luke's Birth Narratives

Priests make their first appearance in Luke's gospel in the first sentence after the gospel's preface. There the reader encounters Zechariah, who is identified as a "priest," "belonging to the priestly order" (1:5). He is married to Elizabeth, who is herself of Aaronite lineage (1:6). This priestly couple is "barren" (1:7). Their barrenness is, as has been widely recognized, a literary device to emphasize both their son's miraculous birth and the parallels between John and Jesus.[4] However, I want to suggest that their barrenness is also a metaphor for the barrenness of the priestly tradition. This indictment against priestly barrenness explains why the story, which has already twice identified Zachariah as a priest, continues by adding yet another double affirmation of Zechariah's priestly status. He is in the sanctuary serving "as a priest . . . according to the custom of the priesthood" when an angel appears to him (1:8-9).[5] Normally, an angelic visit would elicit a spirit of diligent obedience,[6] but in this case, Zechariah, whose priestly identity has been established by the narrative in four redundant comments, doubts the angel's words and is rendered "mute" because he "did not believe" (1:19-20).

This first scene within Luke's Gospel reveals a basic theme within Luke-Acts—the priestly tradition is "barren," therefore, God has rendered it "mute." In Luke-Acts, a resuscitated prophetic tradition speaks for God. The Lukan birth narratives accomplish this diminishing of the priestly tradition and privileging of the prophetic tradition by echoing and intensifying similar themes in the LXX, particularly the account of Samuel's birth. The physical and emotional settings of both birth announcements are the same: Both pregnancies were announced in the temple in the presence of priests (1 Sam 1:9-18; Luke 1:8-14). Both Hannah, the mother of Samuel, and Elizabeth, the mother of John, were distressed by their inability to conceive children, but both were able to conceive after receiving divine favor (1 Sam 1:5, 15; Luke 1:5, 25). The theme of divine calling and unique training is

---

[4]E.g., Nolland, *Luke* 1:20-23, 27.

[5]On the specific "customs" to which Luke refers, see Joel B. Green, *The Gospel of Luke*, NICNT (Grand Rapids MI: Eerdmans, 1997) 68-69.

[6]Although the reception of the visits was vastly different, Zechariah's angelic visit is modeled after the angelic visits to the prophet Daniel. See Raymond E. Brown, *The Birth of the Messiah*, 2nd ed. (New York: Doubleday 1993) 270-71.

the same for each child: Both babies were set apart for service before birth (1 Sam 1:11; Luke 1:15b-17) and both children were to abstain from wine and strong drink all of their lives (1 Sam 1:11; Luke 1:15). Even the narrator's reports of each child's healthy growth and development are parallel (1 Sam 1:26; Luke 1:80). Observation of such parallels is common among scholars,[7] and few scholars would doubt Joseph Fitzmyer's judgment that the Lukan correlation between Samuel and John "is hinting at his [John's] prophetic role."[8] Just as Hannah gave birth to the prophet Samuel in a day when the word of the Lord was rare (1 Sam 3:1), so also Elizabeth gave birth to a prophet—in the spirit and power of the prophet Elijah (Luke 1:17), in a day when the word of Lord was rare.[9]

As is also commonly noted, the Hannah/Samuel parallels are continued in the subsequent narrative of Jesus' birth. As Raymond Brown noted, many of the themes and linguistic structures of the famed *Magnificat* (Luke 1:46-55) have their "antecedent" in Hannah's prayer of thanksgiving (1 Sam 2:1-10).[10] In addition to sharing many of the same literary structures and soteriological themes common to LXX poetry, this song is particularly interesting for its prophetic emphasis upon God's blessing on the neglected poor.[11] Even though the parallels between the Hannah/Samuel story and the Elizabeth/John and Mary/Jesus stories are widely recognized among scholars, another perhaps equally significant observation is commonly overlooked—the accounts in both 1 Samuel and Luke contain stinging rebukes of the priestly tradition.

---

[7]E.g., Nolland, *Luke* 1:30; I. Howard Marshall, *Commentary on Luke*, NIGTC (Grand Rapids MI: Eerdmans, 1978) 57, and Darrell L. Bock, *Luke*, 2 vols., BECNT 3 (Grand Rapids MI: Baker, 1994) 1:84-85.

[8]Joseph A. Fitzmyer, *The Gospel according to Luke*, 2 vols., AB 28, 28A (Garden City NY: Doubleday, 1981, 1985) 1:326.

[9]By the first century, "Jewish authorities had promulgated the idea that prophecy had ceased." See Alan F. Segal, *Paul the Convert and the Apostasy of Saul the Pharisee* (New Haven CT: Yale University Press, 1990) 8-10.

[10]Brown, *Birth of the Messiah*, 357. James A. Sanders insists, with only slight hyperbole, that "Mary's Magnificat is but a bare reworking of the song of Hannah." Sanders, "Isaiah in Luke," in *Luke and Scripture*, ed. Craig A. Evans and James A. Sanders (Minneapolis: Fortress, 1993) 17.

[11]For a thorough analysis, see Brown, *Birth of the Messiah*, 356-65, 378-89.

Craig Evans's recent discussion typifies this scholarly oversight. After noting the parallels between Luke's infancy narratives and 1 Samuel's infancy narrative, Evans concluded that "the pro-Jewish stance of the [Lukan] infancy narratives is obvious."[12] In his rejection of Jack Sanders's much-debated assertions of Luke's anti-Jewish bias,[13] Evans asked:

> Luke's point [in the birth narratives], according to Sanders, is to show that in rejecting Jesus, Judaism has deviated from the path of *biblical faith and piety*. No doubt there is an element of truth in this. Luke certainly does wish to show that Christianity has its origins in *the best of Jewish piety*. But if that was his main point, why does the evangelist over and over again say that *Israel's fondest hopes* have been realized when in fact they have not?[14]

The answer to Evans's question is, I believe, that Luke-Acts does not presume a unified "biblical faith and piety." Luke-Acts presumes that "the best of Jewish piety" and "Israel's fondest hopes" belonged to the prophets and that this *prophetic piety* and this *prophetic hope* are realized in Christianity. However, Luke-Acts also presumes that the priestly tradition did deviate from the path of faithfulness. In other words, Evans is half-right. The *pro-prophetic* stance of the infancy narratives is obvious. However, he is also half-wrong. The *anti-priestly* stance of the infancy narratives is equally obvious. Both 1 Samuel and Luke offer significant rebukes of the priestly tradition, particularly when the priestly tradition is compared to the prophetic tradition. As Hannah's son, the prophet Samuel, was growing "both in stature and in favor with the Lord and with the people" (1 Sam 2:26), Eli, the priest, was hearing that his two sons were guilty of a "greedy eye" and of exploiting God's people. They were both to die. Not only that, but they and their children were also to be "cut off" from God's people (1 Sam. 2:27-36). The contrast between the divine favor enjoyed by Samuel and the divine judgment meted out against Eli's sons fulfills Hannah's prophetic announcement that God

> will guard the feet of his faithful ones,
> but the wicked shall be *cut off* in darkness. (1 Sam 2:9)

---

[12]Craig A. Evans, "Prophecy and Polemic: Jews in Luke's Scriptural Apologetic," in *Luke and Scripture*, 174.

[13]See Jack T. Sanders, *The Jews in Luke-Acts* (Philadelphia: Fortress, 1987).

[14]Evans, "Prophecy and Polemic," 175; emphasis added.

In Samuel's birth narrative, the prophetic tradition is narrated as faithful and enjoying divine favor, while the priestly tradition is characterized as wicked and cut off from divine favor. In the narrative of John's birth, this same pattern emerges. The priestly tradition of Zechariah is depicted as "barren" and unbelieving. Therefore, God renders it "mute." This divinely imposed priestly silence is broken only when Zechariah takes on the role of a prophet and prophesies (Luke 1:67). Zechariah's prophecy announces that salvation will arrive from "the prophet of the Most High" (Luke 1:76). In both 1 Samuel and Luke, unfaithful and unbelieving priests are eclipsed by divinely sanctioned prophets.

II. Priestly Hostility to the Prophetic Voice

In the subsequent rapid survey of Luke-Acts, I hope to demonstrate that Luke-Acts consistently associates the priestly tradition with hostility to the prophetic voice of God—as a (Jewish) institution which opposes God's messengers.

In the previously mentioned work, Craig Evans acknowledged the mixed treatment of Jews and Judaism in Luke-Acts, but argued that the negative images of Jews and Judaism in Luke-Acts stem from the ongoing debate between Christians and Jews over interpretation of the LXX. Christians were making claims about Jesus and the validity of his message on the basis of their interpretation of the LXX. According to Evans, the negative aspects of Luke's treatment of Judaism should be read in the context of this interpretive debate. Luke-Acts is not anti-Jewish *per se*, but it is highly critical of anyone who challenges Christian claims regarding the LXX—and because the LXX was Jewish Scripture, Jewish leaders often challenged Christian claims about the LXX. According to Evans, Luke-Acts therefore presumes that "the opponents of Christian claims are 'the Jews.'"[15] Understanding Luke's characterization of Jews against the backdrop of these interpretive struggles over the LXX has considerable merit. However, by painting that backdrop in terms of a Jewish/Christian dichotomy, Evans has missed a significant and necessary nuance. In Luke-Acts, it is not "the Jews" who oppose Christian claims. Rather it is a specific group of Jews, the priests, who oppose Christian claims.

---

[15]Evans, "Prophecy and Polemic," 211.

Of all the Jewish groups mentioned in Luke-Acts, only the priests are consistently portrayed as opponents of Christian claims. Contrary to Evans's claim, "the Jews" rarely appear in Luke's Gospel as one unified group of people—and when they do appear in the gospel, they neither utter any words nor perform any actions (i.e., 7:3; 23:3, 37, 38). Admittedly, "the Jews" are a more unified group in Acts, but their response to the Christian message is mixed in Acts. Sometimes they seek to kill or otherwise oppose Christian messengers (e.g., 9:23; 13:50; 14:2-5; 20:3, 19). Yet at other points, the Jews are persuaded by the Christian message (e.g., 13:43; 17:4, 12; 18:24). Equally inconsistently in Acts, the Jews frequently bring accusations against Paul (e.g., 22:30; 24:9, 19; 25:7, 11, 15; 26:2, 7), but Paul defends himself by twice insisting "I am a Jew" (21:39; 22:3).

Even when the focus is narrowed to specific Jewish groups—either sects or functionaries, these groups also tend to receive similarly mixed reviews in Luke-Acts. The sect of the *Pharisees* is frequently involved in controversies with Jesus (e.g., Luke 5:21, 30; 6:2, 7; 14:3) and they commonly find themselves sternly rebuked by Jesus as those who neglect justice and love (Luke 11:42-43), as those who reject the baptism of John (Luke 7:30), and as those who love money (Luke 16:14).[16] Yet a nameless Pharisee warns Jesus of Herod's plot to kill Jesus (Luke 13:31); the Pharisee, Gamaliel, intervenes in behalf of the imprisoned Peter and the apostles (Acts 5:34);[17] and the Pharisees on the council even strongly defend Paul (διαμάξομαι, Acts 23:9). Perhaps most importantly, Paul himself asserts, "I am a Pharisee" (Acts 23:6). Although the Pharisees are prominent in Luke and Acts, the sect of the *Sadducees* makes only one innocuous appearance in the gospel where they ask a question about the resurrection (20:27). In Acts, they reappear as consistently antagonistic to both the apostles (4:1; 5:17) and the Pharisees (23:6-8).

---

[16]It is significant to note that even the harshest criticisms of Jews in Luke-Acts are no harsher than the intra-Jewish criticisms offered by the Hebrew prophets. See Marilyn Salmon, "Insider or Outsider? Luke's Relationship with Judaism," in *Luke-Acts and the Jewish People: Eight Critical Perspectives*, ed. Joseph B. Tyson (Minneapolis: Augsburg, 1988) 76-82.

[17]Cf. John A. Darr, "Irenic or Ironic? Another Look at Gamaliel before the Sanhedrin (Acts 5:33-42)," in *Literary Studies in Luke-Acts*, ed. Richard P. Thompson and Thomas E. Phillips (Macon GA: Mercer University Press, 1998) 120-39.

Several Jewish groups are identified by their function in Luke-Acts. The characterization of most of these functionaries—scribes (γραμματεύς), lawyers (νομικός), teachers of the law (νομοδιδάσκαλος), and elders (πρεσβύτερος)—is mixed. The most common set of these functionaries is the scribes, but even this most common group does not have "a distinct and independent role" in Luke-Acts and functions almost as "an appendage of the Pharisees."[18] Like the Pharisees with whom they are closely identified, the Jewish *scribes* commonly engage in controversy with Jesus (e.g., Luke 5:21, 30; 6:7), receive his rebukes (e.g., Luke 20:46), and even plot to kill Jesus and his followers (e.g., Luke 9:22; 19:47; 20:19; 22:2; Acts 4:5; 6:12-13). Yet, even the scribes can express apparent satisfaction with Jesus' answers (Luke 20:39)[19] and can rally to Paul's defense (Acts 23:9). A closely corresponding group, *teachers of the law* (νομοδιδάσκαλος), appears only once in the gospel (5:17) where their distinctive title is quickly replaced by the more common "scribes" (5:21). They likewise appear only once in Acts where a teacher of the law is also identified as a Pharisee who defends the apostles' right to teach (Acts 5:34). Another close functional correspondence, *lawyers* (νομικός), makes a few appearances in Luke's Gospel (7:30; 10:25; 11:45-52; 14:3; and no appearances in Acts), but this title is also essentially synonymous with the more common title of scribe. Like the scribes and teachers of the law, the lawyers debate biblical interpretation with Jesus (Luke 10:25-37; 14:3), reject John's baptism (Luke 7:30) and are rebuked by Jesus (11:45-52).

The function of the people behind all three of these titles, scribes, teachers of the law, and lawyers, is essentially the same—to teach the people regarding biblical interpretation. As teachers and interpreters of Scripture, these scribes, lawyers, and teachers frequently come into conflict with Jesus over the meaning and use of Scripture. Throughout his ministry, Jesus challenged scribal authority and interpretation and offered his own teachings and interpretations of Scripture (Luke 4:31-32; 5:17; 6:6;11:1;

---

[18]Anthony J. Saldarini, *Pharisees, Scribes and Sadducees in Palestinian Society* (Collegeville MN: Michael Glazier, 1988) 181-82. For a succinct overview of the scribes, Pharisees, and Sadducees in Luke-Acts, see 177-87.

[19]The scribes' response ("Well said, teacher.") is generally taken as sincere agreement with Jesus at this point, e.g., Green, *Gospel of Luke*, 722-23 and Marshall, *Commentary on Luke*, 743. However, Johnson is skeptical (*Gospel of Luke*, 314).

13:10, 22; 19:47; 20:1, 21; 21:37; 23:5; Acts 1:1). Some people accepted Jesus' role as "teacher" and addressed him accordingly (Luke 7:40; 8:49; 9:38; 10:25; 11:45; 12:13; 18:18; 19:39; 20:21, 28, 39; 21:7). Sometimes Jesus even identified himself as a teacher (Luke 22:11; cf. 6:40). Jesus' followers emulated his example and also became teachers (Luke 3:12; Acts 2:42; 4:2; 5:21, 25, 28, 42; 13:1, 12; 18:11; 21:21, 28) as Jesus had expected they would (Luke 6:40). However, Jesus and his followers modified the teaching and interpretative function which they co-opted from the scribes, lawyers and teachers of the law. Jesus and his followers taught, but they did not teach the law. When confronted with "individuals" (not "brothers" or "believers," but unnamed people from among the Jews), who were teaching that they should teach people to obey "the customs of Moses" (Acts 15:1), the apostles and leaders of the early church soundly rejected the idea (Acts 15:2-29). For the believers in Acts, Moses was a prophet (Acts 3:22), not a teacher of the priestly practices!

In Luke-Acts, the Jewish *elders* are distinguished from the scribes, lawyers and teachers of the law, but, like the other Jewish functionaries in Luke-Acts, they are characterized in both positive and negative terms. Jewish elders were frequent opponents of Jesus and the early church (Luke 9:22; 20:1; 22:52, 66; Acts 4:5, 8, 23; 5:22; 6:12), but even they can act as intermediaries between Jesus and the recipients of his ministry (Luke 7:3). Eventually, the function (and even the title) of the "elders" was, like the function of the scribal teachers (of the law), adopted by the Christians who assumed leadership of the Christian community (Acts 11:30; 14:23; 15:2, 4, 6, 22, 23; 16:4; 20:17, 18).

The characterization of most Jewish sects and functionaries is therefore mixed—neither consistently negative nor positive. Of course, my observation in this essay of what Joe Tyson has called as an "ambiguous" portrayal of Jews and Judaism in Luke-Acts is not new.[20] And, likewise, attempts to account for that ambiguity are not new either. Jacob Jervell has argued that Luke-Acts tells the story of a divided people of God into believing and unbelieving Jews.[21] Mark Powell has suggested that Luke-Acts is hostile

---

[20]See Joseph B. Tyson, *Images of Judaism in Luke-Acts* (Columbia: University of South Carolina Press, 1992) and *Luke, Judaism, and the Scholars* (Columbia: University of South Carolina Press, 1999).

[21]Jacob Jervell, *Luke and the People of God* (Minneapolis: Augsburg, 1972).

toward the Jewish leadership, but not the Jewish people (λαός) *per se.*[22] Robert Tannehill explained the ambiguity in terms of Luke's confrontation with tragedy, an elect Jewish people who have rejected the Christ.[23] While this essay does not reject those earlier insights, it wishes to introduce an element which has been missing in the discussion to date. It is my contention that in Luke-Acts, the Jewish people are divided—and have been divided—along the lines of the prophetic and priestly traditions; the Jewish leadership is characterized negatively because it is allied to the prophet-rejecting priestly tradition; and the tragedy of the Jewish story is the rejection of the prophetic tradition and the embrace of the priestly tradition.

Throughout Luke-Acts, the priests—unlike other Jewish sects and functionaries—are never presented in positive terms. In a few places, Luke-Acts refers to the priesthood as an institution within Jewish history (Luke 6:4) or as an authority within Jewish life (Luke 3:2; 5:14; 17:14). But when Luke-Acts reveals clear value judgments on the role of the priests and the priesthood, those judgments are consistently negative. The priests provide examples of conduct to be avoided (e.g., Luke 10:31; Acts 19:14), and violating priestly taboos can be justified in Jesus' eyes (Luke 6:3-5). More importantly, the priests are stereotypically associated with opposition to Jesus and his followers. In Luke's Gospel, the priests are the primary agents behind Jesus' death. Jesus predicts that he "must suffer many things and be rejected by the elders, chief priests and teachers of the law, and [that] he must be killed" (Luke 9:22). In the gospel, the priests' actions consistently bear out the accuracy of Jesus' prediction as they repeatedly plot his demise (Luke 19:47; 20:19; 22:2, 4) and then ultimately take a leading role in his arrest (22:50-54) and trial (22:66; 23:4-20). When Luke eventually portrays the disciples looking back on the crucifixion in retrospect, they laid the blame for Jesus' death squarely on the shoulders of the priests. Cleopas and another unnamed disciple insisted that the "chief priests and leaders handed him [Jesus] over to be condemned to death and crucified him" (24:20). As

---

[22]Mark Allan Powell, "The Religious Leaders in Luke: A Literary-Critical Study," *JBL* 109/1 (1990): 93-110.

[23]Robert C. Tannehill, "Israel in Luke-Acts: A Tragic Story," *JBL* 104/1 (1985): 68-85.

historically dubious as the claim is,[24] in Luke's gospel, prediction, narrative, and retrospection all blame the priests for Jesus' death.

In Acts, the priests are equally culpable for the persecution of early Christianity. The priests preside over the first arrests and imprisonments of the apostles in Jerusalem (4:1-6, 23; 5:17-27) and the high priest is present at Stephen's death (7:1). The pre-Christian Saul (Paul) claims to have been authorized by the chief priest to violently persecute Christians (9:1, 14, 21; 22:5; 26:10-12). Eventually, the priests become Paul's primary accusers while he is in Roman custody (22:30; 23:2-5; 24:1; 25:2, 15) and they even devise an unsuccessful plot to kill Paul (23:14).

On the one occasion when Luke-Acts breaks with this uniformly negative evaluation of the Jewish priests, the reference occurs in a summary statement with very little accompanying narrative to provide interpretive context.[25] Luke records that many priests became obedient to the faith (Acts 6:7). Some interpreters have speculated that these priestly converts to Christianity came from the swollen ranks of the marginalized priests who populated Jerusalem.[26] Regardless of their status within Judaism, these priests are portrayed as converts to faith (thus the imperfect tense[27])—and Gerhard Krodel is probably correct to suggest that the mention of their conversion to Christian faith at this point in Luke-Acts probably signifies

---

[24]See John Dominic Crossan, *Who Killed Jesus?* (San Francisco: HarperSanFrancisco, 1995).

[25]The priests are consistently portrayed negatively in the narratives of both Luke and Acts. Because this uncharacteristically positive portrayal appears in a Lukan summary, it is probable that Luke's sources were more hostile toward the priests than was Luke—and that this one positive portrayal reflects a Lukan attempt to show that all true Jews, including the priests, accepted the Christian message.

[26]Jeremias's estimation of 8,000 priests in Jerusalem in the first century is widely accepted: e.g., Ernst Haenchen, *The Acts of the Apostles: A Commentary*, ed. and trans. Bernard Noble et al. (Oxford: Blackwell; Philadelphia: Westminster, 1971) 264, and James D. G. Dunn, *The Acts of the Apostles*, Narrative Commentaries (Valley Forge PA: Trinity Press International, 1996) 85. Fitzmyer discusses, and wisely rejects, the suggestion that these priests were the Essene priests who supposedly resided at Qumran. Joseph A. Fitzmyer, *The Acts of the Apostles*, AB 31 (New York: Doubleday, 1998) 351-52.

[27]On the inceptive force of the imperfect tense which connotes conversion, see C. K. Barrett, *The Acts of the Apostles*, 2 vols., ICC (Edinburgh: T.&T. Clark, 1994) 1:316-17.

their agreement with Stephen's impending criticisms of the temple (Acts 7:2-53, esp. vv. 47-50).[28] The conversion of these priests in Acts therefore intensifies Luke's rejection of the priestly tradition. Ironically, these priests escape Luke's criticism of the priestly tradition only by their conversion from that tradition![29]

The other Jewish functionaries are at their worst when they are in league with the priests. Each time that the *scribes* commit to violence against Jesus, they are teamed up with the chief priests (Luke 9:22; 19:47; 20:19; 22:2, 66; 23:10). Even when the scribes accost Stephen in Acts (6:12), it is the high priest who interrogates Stephen (7:1). The priests have a similar effect upon the Jewish *elders*. The elders commit to violence only in the company of the priests (Luke 9:22; 22:52, 66; Acts 6:12-7:1; 23:14; 24:1; 25:15). Although the *Pharisees* are portrayed negatively in much of Luke-Acts, they never actively plot violence in Luke-Acts. The Pharisees are sometimes in league with the scribes in testing or even opposing Jesus (e.g., Luke 5:21; 6:7; 11:53; 15:2), but in the absence of the priests, the Pharisees and scribes create no plans for violence. The *Sadducees* often oppose the Christian message in Luke-Acts, but they never collectively plot violence.[30] *In Luke-Acts, enticement to violence against the Christian message always involves priestly influence.* Other groups may join the priests in violence, but no Jewish group promotes violence apart from priestly participation.

Not surprisingly, therefore, in Luke-Acts, Christians can identify with the Pharisees (Paul insisted that he was a Pharisee, Acts 23:6), but they do not identify with the Sadducees from whose ranks Luke assumes the priests are drawn (Acts 5:17). Christians can assume most traditional Jewish titles and roles like elders (Acts 14:23; 15:2-6; 15:22-23; 16:4; 20:17; 21:18) and prophets (Luke 4:24; 7:26; 13:33; 20:6; 24:20; Acts 2:18; 3:22; 7:37; 11:27; 13:15; 15:32; 19:6; 21:9-10). Christ and his followers can even assume the lawyer-like and scribal duty of teaching and of interpreting the Scripture. In Luke-Acts, there are Christian Pharisees, Christian elders, Christian

---

[28]Gerhard A. Krodel, *Acts*, ACNT (Minneapolis: Augsburg, 1986) 134.

[29]The two appearances of *Levites* in Luke-Acts (Luke 10:32; Acts 4:36) similarly recount a negative role model and a convert to Christianity.

[30]Luke-Acts asserts that the priests were members of the sect of the Sadducees (Acts 5:17), but it clearly does not presume that all Sadducees were priests.

prophets and Christian teachers, but no Christian priests.[31] In fact, the only non-Jewish priest in Luke-Acts is not a Christian, but rather a pagan who cannot adjust to Christian thought (Acts 14:13-18). In Luke-Acts, pagans and Jews may have priests, but Christians do not. Christians can identify with various Jewish sects and offices, but Christians cannot identify with the priests in Luke-Acts. The priestly tradition is the unrelenting opponent of the Christian community in Luke-Acts.

III. Resuscitation of the Prophetic Voice

In the subsequent rapid survey of Luke-Acts, I hope to demonstrate that Luke-Acts consistently associates the prophetic tradition with salvation and the voice of God—as a (Christian) tradition which now faithfully conveys the word of God.

One of the most powerful arguments against reading Luke-Acts as consistently anti-Jewish is the extremely high regard that the text has for the Old Testament prophets. Luke-Acts repeatedly draws upon the writing prophets, particularly Isaiah, as unquestioned authorities (Luke 1:70; 3:4; 4:17; Acts 2:16; 3:18-24; 7:42, 48; 8:28-34; 10:43; 13:27, 40; 15:15; 26:27; 28:25). It also draws authoritative anecdotes from the non-writing prophets (Elisha, Luke 4:27; Samuel, Acts 3:24; 13:21; even David, Acts 2:29-30) and treats other unnamed prophets from the past as examples of virtue (Luke 10:24; 11:47; 13:28; Acts 3:25). In Luke-Acts, the prophets are placed on the same plain as Moses (Luke 16:16, 29, 31; 24:27, 44; Acts 13:15; 24:14; 26:22; 28:23). Or perhaps, more accurately, Moses, who describes himself as a prophet (Acts 3:22), is placed on the same plain as the prophets in Acts.

As has been widely observed, Luke-Acts transfers the authority of the prophets to early Christian leaders by developing the theme of a resuscitated prophetic tradition. In Luke's Gospel, Jesus insists: "the wisdom of God said, 'I will send them prophets and apostles'" (Luke 11:49). Although the source of this saying is obscure,[32] its promise of a divine renewal of

---

[31]The development of a priesthood within Christianity is a post-Lukan phenomenon. The Lukan criticism of the ancient Jewish priestly tradition cannot be appropriately transferred to the contemporary Christian priesthood.

[32]The phrase "wisdom of God" could refer to a now lost Jewish writing, to an oral tradition, to an insight originating from God's direction, or to Jesus' words. Whatever the exact identity of this wisdom, the gospel regards this wisdom as an

prophecy is central to Christian identity in Luke-Acts. As we have seen, the priestly tradition was rendered mute in the opening chapters of the gospel. However, the muting of the priestly tradition provided opportunity for the resuscitation of the prophetic tradition. The silence of the priest Zechariah was broken when he began to speak as a prophet, *prophesying* (Luke 1:67) that his son, John, would be "called a prophet" (Luke 1:76). The gospel's birth narratives established the status of both John and Jesus as prophets, a status that becomes a recurring point of debate among those who hear their message (7:16, 26, 39; 9:8, 19). Although some of the characters in Luke-Acts remain reluctant to accept the resuscitation of prophecy in the ministries of John and Jesus, the narrator of Luke-Acts shares none of this reluctance.

For Luke-Acts, the prophetic tradition was not only resuscitated by John and Jesus, but it was also carried forward by Jesus' followers, who also assumed the role of prophets. In Luke-Acts, these Christian prophets met with rejection and violence in a pattern consistent with the lives of the earlier prophets (Luke 6:23; 11:47-48; Acts 7:52). Accordingly, the prophet John was accused of having a demon (Luke 7:33) and the prophet Jesus was rejected in his hometown (Luke 4:24). Jesus eventually died in Jerusalem as had all the prophets of God (Luke 13:33-34; 23:13-39). Even after his resurrection, Jesus' followers continued to proclaim him as a prophet like the long gone Moses (Acts 3:22; 7:37). In Luke-Acts, Jesus' ministry fulfilled the promise of Joel that the Spirit of God would once again enable God's people to prophesy (Acts 2:16-18). After the resuscitation of prophecy in the ministries of John and Jesus, Christians routinely hear prophets and prophetic activity in their midst (Acts 11:27; 13:1; 19:6; 21:9-10)—even women got into the act of prophesying (Luke 2:36; Acts 21:9). However, among non-Christian Jews in Luke-Acts, there are only false prophets (Acts 13:6). The resuscitation of prophecy was a Christological and Christian phenomenon.[33] In Luke-Acts, false prophets have traditionally been more widely appreciated than true prophets among the Jews (Luke 6:26). In Luke-Acts, the Christians have prophets; the Jews have priests

---

unquestioned authority. On the interpretation of this expression, see Marshall, *Luke*, 502-503.

[33]The prophetess, Anna (Luke 2:36), is the only Jewish prophet in Luke-Acts. Although she is a prophet, her role as a prophet is specifically tied to her recognition of the soteriological significance of Jesus' birth (Luke 2:38).

(and false prophets). According to Luke-Acts, true prophets have always received contempt and violence from the unbelieving and disobedient elements within Judaism (Luke 6:23; 11:47-48; 13:34; Acts 7:52).

Perhaps the key episodes for understanding the roles of the priestly and prophetic traditions in Luke-Acts are the birth narratives and the Emmaus Road narrative. In the birth narratives, as we have seen, the priestly tradition was muted and Zechariah's voice was resuscitated as a prophetic voice (1:67). John and Jesus then perpetuated this resuscitated prophetic voice. At the other end of the gospel, as Cleopas walked along the Emmaus Road and reflected back on "the things about Jesus of Nazareth," he explained how Jesus

> was a prophet mighty in deed and word before God and all the people, and how our chief priests and leaders handed him over to be condemned to death and crucified him. (Luke 24:19)

In Luke-Acts, Jesus was a prophet and the priests killed the prophet. Jesus and those who associated with him resuscitated the spirit of prophecy and the priests rejected this resuscitated prophetic message. For Luke, the prophets have a history of being persecuted, but in the present, a deadly tension exists between the priestly tradition and the resuscitated prophetic tradition. Therefore, God has muted the priestly tradition and replaced it with a resuscitated prophetic tradition.

It is important to understand how remarkable this Christian claim to a resuscitated prophetic spirit was. As the Jewish scholar, Alan Segal, has noted:

> Claims of prophetic appointment were not commonplace in the first-century Judaism. The Jewish authorities had promulgated the idea that prophecy had ceased. A self-proclaimed prophet would therefore attract powerful enemies in the Jewish community.[34]

The prophet Jesus and his followers attracted powerful enemies and Luke-Acts identifies these enemies with the priests. Luke-Acts presumes that God had acted decisively in Jesus of Nazareth to mute the prevailing priestly voice and to resuscitate the long-suppressed prophetic voice.

---

[34]Segal, *Paul the Convert*, 9.

IV. Returning to Neglected Themes in Lukan Scholarship

If the preceding analysis is persuasive and Luke-Acts does conceive of the Christianity as the persecuted, but faithful, heir to a divinely resuscitated prophetic voice and of Judaism as the dominant, but unfaithful, heir to a divinely muted priestly voice, then the question arises: For what readership would such textual strategies be particularly effective?

At this point, I return to the opening paragraphs of this essay and suggest that the textual strategies explored in this paper would be particularly appealing to an audience of godfearers in the ancient world. For godfearers, Gentiles who were attracted to Judaism but who were reluctant to accept all the requirements of the Jewish law, Luke-Acts could be read as a godsend. In Luke-Acts, they could find all the themes that drew them to Judaism—monotheism, a rejection of idolatry, a just ethic, and an alternative to the Roman Empire—without any of the practices that repelled them from Judaism—circumcision, dietary and ritual laws, and Jewish exclusivism. Luke-Acts offered reflective godfearers an opportunity to locate everything they admired about Judaism within the prophetic (and Christian) tradition and to locate everything they disdained about Judaism within the priestly (and Jewish) tradition. Luke-Acts offered godfearers the opportunity to adopt a form of Judaism (Christianity) that perfectly suited their law-disdaining tendencies. In Christianity, they could have the prophetic tradition which had attracted them to Judaism without the priestly tradition that forced them to the periphery of Judaism.

The Christianity found in Luke-Acts was true to the words of the prophets—even the prophet Moses—without becoming mired in the teachings of the law. Christianity offered prophets and teachers galore, but no teachers of the law. Christianity expounded all the teachings that had attracted them to Judaism without any of the practices that made conversion to Judaism impractical. They could eat whatever was set before them (Luke 10:7) and set aside all demands for circumcision and ritual purity (Acts 15:23-29). Even a godfearing eunuch could read the prophets and convert to Christianity via baptism (Acts 8:26-40).

Conclusion

I have argued that Luke-Acts presents Christianity as a divinely resuscitated prophetic voice, which was opposed and persecuted by the disbelieving priests. Luke-Acts finds this priestly hostility to prophecy deeply rooted in

Israel's history. In Luke-Acts, this hostility is laid at the feet of the priests who are the unrelenting opponents of Jesus and his followers. This view of the Jewish priesthood, regardless of its historical accuracy, enabled Luke-Acts to present the Christian movement as the true heirs to the best of the Jewish tradition (the prophetic tradition), while associating non-Christrian Jews with the worst of Judaism (the priestly tradition). This consistent distinction between the priestly and prophetic elements within Judaism accounts for both the positive and negative images of Judaism within Luke-Acts. The priestly tradition is portrayed quite negatively (and violently), while the prophetic tradition is portrayed quite positively (and victimized). This mixed characterization of Judaism could be quite appealing to god-fearing Gentiles, who existed in a conflicted relationship with Judaism. By associating Jewish priests with the aspects of Judaism that the godfearers likely regarded as the least appealing aspects of Judaism, Luke-Acts may have offered godfearers a way to isolate their reservations about Judaism in a Jewish tradition that the Christians in Luke-Acts specifically rejected. By associating Christian prophets with the aspects of Judaism that godfearers likely regarded as the most appealing aspects of Judaism, Luke may have offered godfearers a way to adopt the most appealing aspects of Judaism in the competing claims of Christianity.

Contributors

ANDREW E. ARTERBURY is an assistant professor of Christian Scriptures at George W. Truett Theological Seminary, Baylor University, Waco, Texas. He is the author of *Entertaining Angels: Early Christian Hospitality in Its Mediterranean Setting* (Sheffield Phoenix Press, 2005).

FRANÇOIS BOVON is Frothingham Professor of the History of Religion, Harvard Divinity School. He was a professor at the University of Geneva, in its Divinity School, from 1967 to 1993. His four-volume critical commentary on Luke will soon be completed in German, French, Spanish, and Italian. (Volume 1, in English, appeared in the Hermeneia series in 2002.) His *The Last Days of Jesus* was published in 2006, followed by a Spanish translation in 2007.

ANDREW F. GREGORY is chaplain and fellow of University College, Oxford. He is the author of *The Reception of Luke and Acts in the Period before Irenaeus* (Mohr Siebeck, 2003) and editor (with Christopher Tuckett) of *The Reception of the New Testament in the Apostolic Fathers* (Oxford University Press, 2005) and *Trajectories through the New Testament and the Apostolic Fathers* (Oxford University Press, 2005).

RAIMO HAKOLA is docent of New Testament Studies and researcher at the University of Helsinki, Finland. He is the author of *Identity Matters: John, the Jews, and Jewishness* (Brill, 2005).

JUSTIN R. HOWELL is a Ph.D. candidate in New Testament and Early Christianity at the University of Chicago Divinity School, Chicago, Illinois.

JOHN B. F. MILLER is assistant professor of Religion at McMurry University, Abilene, Texas. He is the author of *Convinced That God Had Called Us: Dreams, Visions, and the Perception of God's Will in Luke-Acts* (Brill, 2007).

RICHARD I. PERVO is retired in St. Paul, Minnesota. He is the author of *Dating Acts: Between the Evangelists and the Apologists* (Polebridge, 2006) and, most recently, *Acts: A Commentary* in the Hermeneia series (Fortress, 2008).

THOMAS E. PHILLIPS is professor of New Testament and Early Christian Studies at Point Loma Nazarene University, San Diego, California. He is the author of *Acts in Diverse Frames of Reference* (Mercer University Press, 2009), *Paul, His Letters and Acts* (Hendrickson, 2009), and editor of *Acts and Ethics* (Sheffield Phoenix, 2005).

JAMES N. RHODES is visiting assistant professor in Religious Studies at Saint Michael's College, Colchester, Vermont. He is the author of *The Epistle of Barnabas and the Deuteronomic Tradition: Polemics, Paraenesis, and the Legacy of the Golden-Calf Incident* (Mohr Siebeck, 2004).

DAVID E. SMITH is associate professor of Religion and Philosophy at Taylor University, Upland, Indiana. He is the author of *The Canonical Function of Acts: A Comparative Analysis* (Liturgical Press, 2002).

JULIEN C. H. SMITH is a Ph.D. candidate in New Testament at Baylor University, Waco, Texas.

JOSEPH B. TYSON is professor emeritus of Religious Studies at Southern Methodist University, Dallas, Texas. His most recent book is *Marcion and Luke-Acts: A Defining Struggle* (University of South Carolina Press, 2006).

Bibliography

Abrams, Dominic, J. M. Marques, N. Brown, and M. Henson. "Pro-Norm and Anti-Norm Deviance within and between Groups." *Journal of Personality and Social Psychology* 78 (2000): 906-912.

Adler, Nikolaus. *Das erste christliche Pfingstfest: Sinn und Bedeutung des Pfingst-berichtes Apg 2,1–13*. NTAbh 18/1. Münster i. W.: Aschendorff, 1938.

Aejmelaeus, Lars. *Die Rezeption der Paulusbriefe in der Miletrede*. Helsinki: Suomalienen Tiedeakatemia, 1987.

Alexander, Loveday C. A. "Acts and Ancient Intellectual Biography." In *The Book of Acts in Its Ancient Literary Setting*, 31-63. Edited by Bruce W. Winter and Andrew D. Clarke. BAFCS 1. Grand Rapids MI: Eerdmans, 1993.

_____. *Acts in Its Ancient Literary Context: A Classicist Looks at the Acts of the Apostles*. LNTS 8. London: T.&T. Clark, 2005.

Amphoux, Christian-Bernard. "Les premières editions des Luc, I: Le texte de Luc 5." *ETL* 67 (1991): 312-27.

_____. "Les premières editions des Luc, II: Le histoire du texts au II siècle." *ETL* 68 (1992): 38-48.

Aphthonius. "The Preliminary Exercises." In *Progymnasmata: Greek Textbooks of Prose Composition and Rhetoric*, 89-128. Translated by George Alexander Kennedy. Writings from the Greco-Roman World. Atlanta: Society of Biblical Literature, 2003.

Aune, David E. *The New Testament in Its Literary Environment*. Cambridge UK: James Clarke & Company, 1987.

Bachmann, M. "Die Stephanusepisode (Apg 6,1-8,3): Ihre Bedeutung für die Lukanische Sicht des Jerusalemischen Tempels und des Judentums." In *The Unity of Luke-Acts*, 545-62. Edited by J. Verheyden. BETL 142. Leuven: University Press, 1999.

Balch, David L. "The Areopagus Speech: An Appeal to the Stoic Historian Posidonius against Later Stoics and the Epicureans." In *Greeks, Romans and Christians*, 52-79. Edited by David L. Balch, Everett Ferguson, and Wayne A. Meeks. Minneapolis: Fortress, 1990.

Balz, Horst. ὕπνος, ἀφυπνόω, ἐνύπνιον, ἐνυπνιάζομαι, ἔξυπνος ἐξυπνίζω. *Theological Dictionary of the New Testament* 8:545-50. Edited by Gerhard Kittel. Translated by Geoffrey Bromiley. Grand Rapids MI: Eerdmans, 1964.

Barnard, L. W. "Saint Stephen and Early Alexandrian Christianity." *NTS* 7 (1960–1961): 31-45.

Barrett, C. K. *The Acts of the Apostles*. Two volumes. ICC. Edinburgh: T.&T. Clark, 1994, 1998.

_____. "Quomodo Historia Conscribenda Sit." *NTS* 28 (1982): 303-20.

Bauckham, Richard. "The *Acts of Paul* as a Sequel of Acts." In *The Book of Acts in Its Ancient Literary Setting*, 105-52. BAFCS 1. Edited by Bruce W. Winter and Andrew D. Clarke. Grand Rapids MI: Eerdmans, 1993.

_____. "The *Acts of Paul*: Replacement of Acts or Sequel to Acts?" *Semeia* 80 (1997): 159-68.

Baur, Ferdinand Christian. *Paul, the Apostle of Jesus Christ, His Life and Work, His Epistles and His Doctrine: A Contribution to the Critical History of Primitive Christianity*. Two volumes. Edited by Eduard Zeller. Translated from the second edition by A. Menzies. London: Williams & Norgate, 1876.

Beissel, Stephan. *Entstehung der Perikopen des römischen Meßbuches: Zur Geschichte der Evangelienbücher in der ersten Hälfte des Mittelalters*. Reprint: Rome: Herder, 1967.

Benoit, André. *Saint Irénée: Introduction à L'Étude de sa Théologie*. Paris: Presses Universitaires de France, 1960.

Bethge, Hans-Gebhard. "Der Brief des Petrus an Philippus (NHC VIII, 2)." In *Nag Hammadi Deutsch* II, 663-76. Edited by Hans-Martin Schenke, Hans-Gebhard Bethge, and Ursula Kaiser. Koptisch-Gnostische Schriften 3. Berlin: Walter de Gruyter, 2003.

Bieder, Werner. *Die Apostelgeschichte in der Historie: Ein Beitrag zur Auslegungs-geschichte des Missionsbuches der Kirche*. Theologische Studien 61. Zurich: Theologischer Verlag Zürich, 1960.

Blaisdell, James. "The Authorship of the 'We' Sections of the Book of Acts." *HTR* 13 (1920): 136-58.

Bock, Darrell L. *Luke*. Two volumes. BECNT 3. Grand Rapids MI: Baker, 1994.

Boismard, Marie-Émile, and André Lamouille. *Le texte occidental des Actes des apôtres: Reconstitution et réhabilitation*. Synthèse 17. Two volumes. Paris: Recherches sur les civilisations, 1984.

Bonner, Stanley F. *Education in Ancient Rome: From the Elder Cato to the Younger Pliny*. Los Angeles: University of California Press, 1977.

Bonz, Marianne Palmer. "Luke's Revision of Paul's Reflections in Romans 9–11." In *Early Christian Voices in Texts, Traditions, and Symbols: Essays in Honor of François Bovon*, 143-51. Edited by Ann Graham Brock, David W. Pao, and David H. Warren. Boston: Brill, 2003.

Borgen, Peder. *Philo, John and Paul: New Perspectives on Judaism and Early Christianity*. BJS 131. Atlanta: Scholars Press, 1987.

Bori, Pier Cesare. *Chiesa primitiva. L'immagine della comunità delle origini: "Atti 2,42-47; 4,32-37." Nella storia della chiesa antica*. Testi e ricerche di scienze religiose 10. Brescia: Paideia, 1974.

Bovon, François, Bertrand Bouvier, and Frédéric Amsler. *Acta Philippi. Textus*. Corpus Christianorum Series Apocryphorum 11. Turnhout, Belgium: Brepols, 1999.

_____. "The Apostolic Memories in Ancient Christianity." In *Studies in Early Christianity*, 1-16. WUNT 161. Tübingen: Mohr Siebeck, 2003.

_____. *De Vocatione Gentium: Histoire de l'interprétation d'Act. 10, 1 – 11, 18 dans les six premieres siècles*. BGBE 8. Tübingen: Mohr Siebeck, 1967.

_____. "Eusebius of Caesarea's Ecclesiastical History and the History of Salvation." In *Studies in Early Christianity*, 271-83. Grand Rapids MI: Baker Academic, 2003.

_____. "L'Origine des récits concernant les apôtres." *Revue de théologie et de philosophie* 3/17 (1967): 345-50. Reprint in *L'Oeuvre de Luc: Études d'exégèse et de théologie*. LD 130. Paris: Cerf, 1987.

_____. "The Reception and Use of the Gospel of Luke in the Second Century." In *Reading Luke: Interpretation, Reflection, Formation*, 379-97. Edited by Craig Bartholomew, Joel B. Green, and Anthony C. Thiselton. Grand Rapids MI: Zondervan, 2005.

_____. "Tradition et redaction en Actes 10,1-11,18." *TZ* 36 (1970): 22-45.

_____. "La vie des apôtres: Traditions bibliques et narrations apocryphes." In *Les Actes des apôtres: christianisme et monde païen* 150. Edited by François Bovon. Publication de la faculté de théolgie l'université de Genève 4. Geneva: Labor et Fides, 1981.

Brawley, Robert L. "The God of Promises and the Jews in Luke-Acts." In *Literary Studies in Luke-Acts: Essays in Honor of Joseph B. Tyson*, 279-96. Edited by Richard P. Thompson and Thomas E. Phillips. Macon GA: Mercer University Press, 1998.

_____. "Ethical Borderlines between Rejection and Hope: Interpreting the Jews in Luke-Acts." *CurTM* 6 (2000): 415-23.

_____. *Luke-Acts and the Jews: Conflict, Apology, and Conciliation*. SBLMS 33. Atlanta: Scholars Press, 1987.

_____. "Social Identity and the Aim of Acomplished Life in Acts 2." In *Acts and Ethics*, 16-33. Edited by Thomas E. Phillips. Sheffield UK: Sheffield Phoenix Press, 2005.

Brehm, H. Alan. "Vindicating the Rejected One: Stephen's Speech as a Critique of the Jewish Leaders." In *Early Christian Interpretation of the Scriptures of Israel: Investigations and Proposals*, 266-99. Edited by Craig A. Evans and James A. Sanders. JSNTSup 148. Sheffield UK: Sheffield Academic Press, 1999.

Bremmer, Jan N., editor. *The Apocryphal Acts of Paul and Thecla*. Studies in the Apocryphal Acts of the Apostles 2. Kampen, Netherlands: Pharos, 1996.

Brodie, Thomas L. *The Crucial Bridge: The Elijah-Elisha Narrative as an Interpretive Synthesis of Genesis-Kings and a Literary Model for the Gospels*. Minneapolis: Liturgical Press, 2000.

Brown, Raymond E. *The Birth of the Messiah: A Commentary on the Infancy Narratives in the Gospels of Matthew and Luke*. Second edition. New York: Doubleday, 1993.

Brown, Rupert. "Social Identity Theory: Past Achievements, Current Problems and Future Challenges." *European Journal of Social Psychology* 30 (2000): 745-78.

Bruce, F. F. *Commentary on the Book of the Acts. The English Text with Introduction, Exposition, and Notes.* Second edition. NICNT. Grand Rapids MI: Eerdmans, 1977; 1st ed., 1954.

_____. *The Canon of Scripture.* Downers Grove IL: InterVarsity Press, 1988.

_____. *1 & 2 Thessalonians.* WBC 45. Waco TX: Word Books, 1982.

_____. "Stephen's Apologia." In *Scripture: Meaning and Method*, 37-50. Edited by Barry P. Thompson. Hull UK: Hull University Press, 1987.

Bureau, Bruno. *Lettre et sens mystique dans l'"Historia apostolica" d'Arator: Exégèse et épopée.* Études augustiniennes: Antiquité 153. Paris: Études augustiniennes, 1997.

Cabié, Robert. *La Pentecôte: L'évolution de la Cinquantaine pascale au cours des cinq premiers siècles.* Bibliothèque de liturgie. Paris: Desclée, 1965.

Cadbury, Henry J., F. J. Foakes-Jackson, and Kirsopp Lake. "The Greek and Jewish Traditions of Writing History." In *The Beginnings of Christianity* 2:7-29. Five volumes. Edited by F. J. Foakes-Jackson and Kirsopp Lake. London: Macmillan, 1920–1933.

_____. *The Making of Luke-Acts.* New York: Macmillan, 1927.

_____. *The Making of Luke-Acts.* Second edition. London: MacMillan, 1958. Reprint: Peabody MA: Hendrickson, 1999.

_____. "The Speeches in Acts." In *The Beginnings of Christianity* 5:402-27. Five volumes. Edited by F. J. Foakes-Jackson and Kirsopp Lake. London: Macmillan, 1920–1933.

_____. " 'We' and 'I' Passages in Luke/Acts." *NTS* 3 (1957): 128-32.

Calvin, John. *The Acts of the Apostles, 14-28.* Translated by John W. Fraser. London: Oliver & Boyd, 1966.

Cambe, Michel. *Kerygma Petri: Textus et commentarius.* CCSA 15. Turnhout, Belgium: Brepols, 2003.

Campbell, William S. "Who Are We in Acts?: The First-Person Plural Character in the Acts of the Apostles." Ph.D. dissertation, Princeton Theological Seminary, 2000.

Campenhausen, Hans von. "Die Apostelgeschichte finden wir vor Irenäus überhaupt nicht bezeugt." In *Die Entstehung der christlichen Bibel.* Tübingen: Mohr Siebeck, 1968.

_____. *The Formation of the Christian Bible.* Translated by J. A. Baker. London: A&C Black, 1972.

Cancik, Hubert. "The History of Culture, Religion, and Institutions in Ancient Historiography: Philological Observations concerning Luke's History." *JBL* 116 (1997): 681-703.

Cerfaux, Lucien. "Le chapitre XVe du Livre des Actes à la lumière de la littérature ancienne." In *Miscellanea Giovanni Mercati*, 107-26. Studi e Testi 121. Vatican City: Biblioteca Apostolica Vaticana, 1946.

_____. *Recueil: Études d'exégèse et d'histoire religieuse*. Three volumes. BETL 6, 7, 71. Gembloux: Duculot, then Leuven: Leuven University Press and Peeters, 1954–1985.

Charlesworth, James H., editor. *The Old Testament Pseudepigrapha*. Two volumes. New York: Doubleday, 1983, 1985.

Chatman, Seymour. *Coming to Terms: The Rhetoric of Narrative in Fiction and Film*. Ithaca NY: Cornell University Press, 1990.

Christe, Yves. "Apocalypse et 'Traditio legis'." *Römische Quartalschrift für christliche Altertumskunde und Kirchengeschichte* 71 (1976): 42-55.

Clark, Andrew. *Parallel Lives: The Relation of Paul to the Apostles in the Lucan Perspective*. Carlisle UK: Paternoster Press, 2001.

Clark, Donald Lemen. *Rhetoric in Greco-Roman Education*. New York: Columbia University Press, 1957.

Clarke, G. W. *The Octavius of Marcus Minucius Felix*. ACW 39. New York: Newman Press, 1974.

Coleman, Raymond Samuel, Jr. "Embedded Letters in Acts and in Jewish and Hellenistic Literature." Ph.D. dissertation, Southern Baptist Theological Seminary, 1994.

Conybeare, F. C. "The Commentary of Ephrem on Acts." In *The Beginnings of Christianity* 3:380-453. Five volumes. Edited by F. J. Foakes-Jackson and Kirsopp Lake. London: Macmillan, 1920-1933.

Conzelmann, Hans. *Acts of the Apostles: A Commentary on the Acts of the Apostles*. Hermeneia. Translated by James Limburg, A. Thomas Kraabel, and Donald H. Juel. Philadelphia: Fortress, 1987.

_____. "Luke's Place in the Development of Early Christianity." In *Studies in Luke-Acts*, 298-316. Edited by Leander E. Keck and J. Louis Martyn. Nashville: Abingdon, 1966. Reprint: Minneapolis: Fortress, 1980.

_____. "Die Schule des Paulus." In *Theologia Crucis-Signum Crucis: Festschrift E. Dinkle*, 85-96. Tübingen: J. C. B. Mohr, 1979.

Cosgrove, Charles. "The Divine DEI in Luke-Acts." *NovT* 26 (1984): 168-90.

Cribiore, Raffaella. *Gymnastics of the Mind: Greek Education in Hellenistic and Roman Egypt*. Princeton NJ and Oxford UK: Princeton University Press, 2001.

Crossan, John Dominic. *Who Killed Jesus?* San Francisco: HarperSanFrancisco, 1995.

d'Alexandrie, Athanase. *Les Trois Discours contre les Ariens*. Donner raison 15. Traduction et notes Adelin Rousseau, ouverture et guide de lecture René Lafontaine. Bruxelles: Lessius, 2004.

Darr, John A. "Irenic or Ironic? Another Look at Gamaliel before the Sanhedrin (Acts 5:33-42)." In *Literary Studies in Luke-Acts*, 120-39. Edited by Richard P. Thompson and Thomas E. Phillips. Macon GA: Mercer University Press, 1998.

_____. *On Character Building: The Reader and the Rhetoric of Characterization in Luke-Acts*. LCBI. Louisville: Westminster/John Knox, 1992.

Day, Michael. "The Function of Post-Pentecost Dream/Vision Reports in Acts." Ph.D. dissertation, Southern Baptist Theological Seminary, 1994.

Deissmann, Adolf. *Light from the Ancient East: The New Testament Illustrated by Recently Discovered Texts of the Graeco-Roman World.* (First edition: 1910.) New and completely revised edition. Translated by Lionel R. M. Strachan. London: Hodder & Stoughton; New York: Doran; New York: Harper and Brothers, 1927. Reprints: Grand Rapids MI: Baker, 1995; 1978; Peabody MA: Hendrickson, 1995.

Dibelius, Martin. *Studies in the Acts of the Apostles.* Edited by Heinrich Greeven. Translated by Mary Ling. New York: Charles Scribner's Sons, 1956. Reprint: Mifflintown PA: Sigler Press, 1999. (Original, 1951.)

_____. *The Acts of the Apostles: What Really Happened in the Earliest Days of the Church.* Amherst NY: Prometheus Books, 2005.

Droge, Arthur J. "Apologetics, NT." *The Anchor Bible Dictionary on CD-ROM.* Logos Library System Version 2.0c. 1995, 1996.

Dunn, James D. G. *The Acts of the Apostles.* Epworth Commentaries. Peterborough UK: Epworth, 1996.

_____. *Romans 9-16.* WBC 38B. Dallas: Word Books, 1988.

Dupont, Jacques. "Le salut des Gentils et la signification théologique du Livre des Actes." *NTS* 6 (1960): 132–55.

_____. *The Sources of Acts.* London: DLT, 1964.

Ehrlich, Ernst Ludwig. *Der Traum im Alten Testament.* BZAW 73. Berlin: Alfred Töpelmann, 1953.

Epp, Eldon J. "Anti-Judaic Tendencies in the D-Text of Acts: Forty Years of Conversation." In *The Book of Acts as Church History*, 111-46. Edited by Tobias Nicklas and Michael Tilly. BZNW 120. Berlin: Walter de Gruyter, 2003.

_____. *Theological Tendency of Codex Bezae Cantabrigiensis in Acts.* SNTSMS 3. Cambridge UK: Cambridge University Press, 1966.

Esler, Philip Francis. *Community and Gospel in Luke-Acts: The Social and Political Motivations of Lucan Theology.* SNTSMS 57. Cambridge UK: Cambridge University Press, 1987.

_____. *Conflict and Identity in Romans: The Social Setting of Paul's Letter.* Minneapolis: Fortress Press, 2003.

_____. *Galatians.* London and New York: Routledge, 1998.

Evans, Craig A., R. L. Webb, and R. A. Wiebe, editors. *Nag Hammadi Texts and the Bible: A Synopsis and Index*. NTTS XVIII. Leiden: Brill, 1993.

Evans, Craig A. "Prophecy and Polemic: Jews in Luke's Scriptural Apologetic." In *Luke and Scripture*, 171-211. Edited by Craig A. Evans and James A. Sanders. Minneapolis: Fortress, 1993.

Farahian, Edmond. "Paul's Vision at Troas (Acts 16:9-10)." In *Luke and Acts*. Edited by Gerald O'Collins and Gerald Marconi. Translated by Matthew O'Connell. New York: Paulist, 1993.

Ferguson, Everett. "Factors Leading to the Selection and Closure of the New Testament Canon: A Survey of Some Recent Studies." In *Canon Debate*, 295-320. Edited by Lee Martin McDonald and James A. Sanders. Peabody MA: Hendrickson, 2002.

Ferrarese, Gianfranco. *Il concilio di Gerusalemme in Ireneo di Lione. Ricerche sulla storia dell'esegesi di Atti 15,1-29. (e Galati 2,1-10) nell II secolo*. Testi e ricerche di scienze religiose 17. Brescia: Paideia, 1979.

Fitzmyer, Joseph A. *The Acts of the Apostles*. AB 31. New York: Doubleday, 1998.

_____. *The Gospel according to Luke*. Two volumes. AB 28, 28A. New York: Doubleday, 1981, 1985.

Foakes-Jackson, Frederick John. *The Acts of the Apostles*. Moffatt New Testament Commentary. London: Hodder and Stoughton; New York and London: Harper and Brothers, 1931.

Foakes-Jackson, F. J., Kirsopp Lake, and Henry J. Cadbury, editors. *The Beginnings of Christianity*. Five volumes. London: Macmillan, 1920–1933.

Foster, Benjamin R. *The Epic of Gilgamesh: A New Translation, Analogues, Criticism*. Norton Critical Edition. New York: W. W. Norton, 2001.

Frein, Brigid Curtin. "The Literary Significance of the Jesus-as-Prophet Motif in the Gospel of Luke and the Acts of the Apostles." Ph.D. dissertation, St. Louis University, 1989.

Gamble, Harry Y. *Books and Readers in the Early Church: A History of Early Christian Texts*. New Haven CT: Yale University Press, 1995.

_____. *The New Testament Canon: Its Making and Meaning*. Philadelphia: Fortress Press, 1985.

_____. "The New Testament Canon: Recent Research and the Status Quaestionis." In *The Canon Debate*, 296-94. Edited by Lee Martin McDonald and James A. Sanders. Peabody MA: Hendrickson, 2002.

Garrison, Roman. *The Significance of Theophilus as Luke's Reader*. Lewiston NY: Edwin Mellen Press, 2004.

Gaventa, Beverly R. *The Acts of the Apostles*. ANTC. Nashville: Abingdon Press, 2003.

_____. "Theology and Ecclesiology in the Miletus Speech: Reflections on Content and Context." *NTS* 50 (2004): 37-43.

Geckle, Richard Patrick. "The Rhetoric of Morality in Sallust's Speeches and Letters." Ph.D. dissertation, Columbia University, 1995.

George, Andrew R., editor. *The Babylonian Gilgamesh Epic: Introduction, Critical Edition, and Cuneiform Texts*. Two volumes. Oxford UK: Oxford University Press, 2003.

_____, editor. *The Epic of Gilgamesh: The Babylonian Epic Poem and Other Texts in Akkadian and Sumerian*. London: Penguin, 1999.

Gignac, Francis T. "Evidence for Deliberate Scribal Revision in Chrysostom's *Homilies on the Acts of the Apostles*." In *Nova et Vetera: Patristic Studies in Honor of Thomas Patrick Halton*, 209-25. Edited by John Petruccione. Washington DC: Catholic University of America Press, 1998.

_____. "The New Critical Edition of Chrysostom's *Homilies on Acts*: A Progress Report." In *Text und Textkritik: Eine Aufsatzsammlung*, 165-68. Edited by Jürgen Dummer. TU 133. Berlin: Akademie Verlag, 1987.

Gnuse, Robert Karl. *Dreams and Dream Reports in the Writings of Josephus: A Traditio-Historical Analysis*. AGJU 36. Leiden: Brill, 1996.

Godu, G. "Épîtres." In *Dictionnaire d'archéologie chrétienne et de liturgie*. Fifteen volumes. Edited by F. Cabrol. Paris: Letouzey et Ané, 1907–1953.

Gowler, David B. *Host, Guest, Enemy, and Friend: Portraits of the Pharisees in Luke and Acts*. Emory Studies in Early Christianity 2. New York: Peter Lang, 1991.

Grant, Robert M. *Greek Apologists of the Second Century*. Philadelphia: Westminster, 1988.

Green, Joel B. *The Gospel of Luke*. NICNT. Grand Rapids MI: Eerdmans, 1997.

Gregory, Andrew. "The Reception of Luke and Acts and the Unity of Luke-Acts." *JSNT* 29 (2007): 459-72.

_____. *The Reception of Luke and Acts in the Period before Irenaeus*. WUNT 169. Tübingen: Mohr Siebeck, 2003.

Gregory, Andrew and Christopher Tuckett. "What Constitutes the Use of the New Testament in the Apostolic Fathers? Reflections on the Methodological Issues." In *The Reception of the New Testament in the Apostolic Fathers*, 61-82. Edited by Andrew Gregory and Christopher Tuckett. Oxford UK: Oxford University Press, 2005.

Haacker, Klaus. "Dibelius und Cornelius: Ein Beispiel formgeschichtlicher Überlief-Erungskritik." *BZ* 24 (1980): 234-51.

Haenchen, Ernst. *The Acts of the Apostles: A Commentary*. Edited and translated by Bernard Noble, Gerald Shinn, Hugh Anderson, and R. McL. Wilson. Oxford UK: Basil Blackwell; Philadelphia: Westminster, 1971. (English version of the fourteenth edition of the following.)

_____. *Die Apostelgeschichte, neu übersetzt und erklärt*. Sixth edition. KKNT 3. Göttingen: Vandenhoeck und Ruprecht, 1968.

Hägg, Tomas. *Narrative Technique in Ancient Greek Romances: Studies of Chariton, Xenophon Ephesius, and Achilles Tatius.* Skrifter Utgivna av Svenska Institutet i Athen 2.8. Stockholm: Svenska Institutet i Athen, 1971.
_____. *The Novel in Antiquity.* Los Angeles: University of California Press, 1983.

Hakola, Raimo. "Social Identities and Group Phenomena in Second Temple Judaism." In *Explaining Christian Origins and Early Judaism: Contributions from Cognitive and Social Science.* Biblical Interpretation Series 89. Edited by Petri Luomanen, Ilkka Pyysiäinen, and Risto Uro. Leiden: Brill Academic Publishers, 2007.
_____. *Identity Matters: John, the Jews, and Jewishness.* NovTSup 118. Leiden: Brill, 2005.

Handy, David. "The Gentile Pentecost: A Literary Study of the Story of Peter and Cornelius (Acts 10:1–11:18)." Ph.D. dissertation, Union Theological Seminary (Richmond), 1998.

Hanfmann, George M. A. "Hypnos." In *The Oxford Classical Dictionary.* Third revised edition. Edited by Simon Hornblower and Antony Spawforth. Oxford UK: Oxford University Press, 2003.

Hansen, William. *Anthology of Ancient Greek Popular Literature.* Bloomington: Indiana University Press, 1998.

Hanson, John. "Dreams and Visions in the Graeco-Roman World and Early Christianity." *ANRW* 23/2 (1980): 1395-1427.
_____. "The Dream-Vision Report and Acts 10:1–11:18: A Form-Critical Study." Ph.D. dissertation, Harvard University, 1978.

Harnack, Adolf von. *The Acts of the Apostles.* Translated by J. R. Wilkinson. New York: G. P. Putnam's Sons, 1909.
_____. *The Date of Acts and of the Synoptic Gospels.* Translated by J. R. Wilkinson. New Testament Studies 4. New York: G. P. Putnam's Sons, 1911.
_____. *Marcion: Das Evangelium vom fremden Gott.* Second edition. Leipzig: J. C. Hinrichs'sche Buchhandlung, 1924.

Haslam, S. Alexander. *Psychology in Organizations: The Social Identity Approach.* London: Sage Publications, 2001.

Heath, Malcolm. "Invention." In *Handbook of Classical Rhetoric in the Hellenistic Period: 330 B.C.–A.D. 400*, 89-119. Edited by Stanley E. Porter. Leiden: E. J. Brill, 1997.
_____. *Unity in Greek Poetics.* Oxford: Clarendon Press, 1989.

Hemer, Colin J. *The Book of Acts in the Setting of Hellenistic History.* Edited by Conrad Gempf. Winona Lake IN: Eisenbrauns, 1990.

Hill, Craig C. *Hellenists and Hebrews: Reappraising Division within the Earliest Church.* Minneapolis: Fortress, 1992.

Hillier, Richard. *Arator on the Acts of the Apostles: A Baptismal Commentary.* Oxford UK: Clarendon, 1993.

Hills, Julian V. "The Acts of the Apostles and the *Acts of Paul.*" In SBLSP 1994, 24-54. Edited by Eugene Lovering. Atlanta: Scholars Press, 1994.

_____. "The *Acts of Paul* and the Legacy of the Lukan Acts." *Semeia* 80 (1997): 145-58.

_____. *Tradition and Composition in the Epistula Apostolorum.* HDR 24. Minneapolis: Fortress Press, 1994.

Hock, Ronald F. "The Educational Curriculum in Chariton's *Callirhoe.*" In *Ancient Fiction: The Matrix of Early Christian and Jewish Narrative*, 15-36. Edited by Jo-Ann A. Brant, Charles W. Hedrick, and Chris Shea. SBLSymS 32. Atlanta: Society of Biblical Literature, 2005.

_____. "The Rhetoric of Romance." In *Handbook of Classical Rhetoric in the Hellenistic Period: 330 B.C.–A.D. 400*, 445-65. Edited by Stanley E. Porter. Leiden: E. J. Brill, 1997.

Hoffman, R. Joseph. *Marcion: On the Restitution of Christianity: An Essay on the Development of Radical Paulinist Theology in the Second Century.* AAR Academy Series 46. Chico CA: Scholars Press, 1984.

Hogg, Michael A. and Dominic Abrams. *Social Identifications: A Social Psychology of Intergroup Relations and Group Processes.* New York: Routledge, 1988.

Irudhayasamy, R. J. *A Prophet in the Making: A Christological Study on Lk 4.16-30 in the Background of the Isaianic Mixed Citation and the Elijah and Elisha References.* Frankfurt: Lang, 2002.

Jervell, Jacob. *Die Apostelgeschichte.* Seventeenth edition. KKNT 3. Göttingen: Vandenhoeck & Ruprecht, 1998.

_____. "The Church of Jews and Godfearers." In *Luke-Acts and the Jewish People: Eight Critical Perspectives*, 11-20. Edited by Joseph B. Tyson. Minneapolis: Augsburg, 1988.

_____. "The Future of the Past: Luke's Vision of Salvation History and Its Bearing on His Writing of History." In *History, Literature, and Society in the Book of Acts*, 104-26. Edited by Ben Witherington III. Cambridge UK: Cambridge University Press, 1996.

_____. "Das gespaltene Israel und die Heidenvölker: Zur Motivierung der Heidenmission in der Apostelgeschichte." *ST* 19 (1965): 68-96.

_____. *Luke and the People of God: A New Look at Luke-Acts.* Minneapolis: Augsburg, 1972.

_____. "The Problem of Tradition in Acts." In *Luke and the People of God*, 19-39. Minneapolis: Augsburg, 1972.

_____. *The Theology of the Acts of the Apostles.* NTT. Cambridge UK: Cambridge University Press, 1996.

_____. *The Unknown Paul: Essays on Luke-Acts and Early Christian History.* Minneapolis: Augsburg Publishing House, 1984.

Jeska, Joachim. *Die Geschichte Israels in der Sicht des Lukas.* FRLANT 195. Göttingen: Vandenhoeck & Ruprecht, 2001.

Johnson, Luke Timothy. *The Acts of the Apostles.* SP 5. Collegeville MN: Michael Glazier, 1992.

_____. *The Gospel of Luke.* SP 3. Collegeville MN: Michael Glazier, 1991.

_____. *The Literary Function of Possessions in Luke-Acts.* SBLDS 39. Missoula: Scholars Press, 1977.

_____. "The New Testament's Anti-Jewish Slander and the Conventions of Ancient Polemic." *JBL* 108 (1989): 419–41.

_____. *Septuagintal Midrash in the Speeches of Acts.* The Père Marquette Lecture in Theology. Milwaukee: Marquette University Press, 2002.

Jokiranta, Jutta. "Social Identity Approach: Identity-Constructing Elements in the Psalms Pesher." In *Defining Identities: We, You, and the Other in the Dead Sea Scrolls. Proceedings of the Fifth Meeting of the IOQS in Gröningen.* Studies on the Texts of the Desert of Judah 70. Edited by Florentino G. Martínez and Maden Popovic. Leiden: Brill, 2008.

Jones, F. Stanley. *An Ancient Jewish Christian Source on the History of Christianity: Pseudo-Clementine Recognitions 1.21-71.* SBLTT 37. Atlanta: Scholars Press, 1995.

Judge, E. A. "A State Teacher Makes a Salary Bid." In *A Review of the Greek Inscriptions and Papyri Published in 1976,* 72-78. New Documents Illustrating Early Christianity 1. Edited by G. H. R. Horsley. North Ryde NSW: The Ancient History Documentary Research Centre, Macquarie University, 1981.

Kee, Howard Clark. *To Every Nation under Heaven: The Acts of the Apostles.* Harrisburg PA: Trinity Press International, 1997.

Kennedy, George A. *The Art of Rhetoric in the Roman World: 300 B.C.–A.D. 300.* Princeton NJ: Princeton University Press, 1972.

_____. *A New History of Classical Rhetoric.* Princeton NJ: Princeton University Press, 1994.

_____. *New Testament Interpretation through Rhetorical Criticism.* Chapel Hill: University of North Carolina Press, 1984.

_____. *Progymnasmata: Greek Textbooks of Prose Composition and Rhetoric.* Writings from the Greco-Roman World 10. Atlanta: Society of Biblical Literature, 2003.

Kessler, Herbert L. "Scenes from the Acts of the Apostles on Some Early Christian Ivories." *Gesta* 18 (1979): 109-19.

Kilgallen, John J. "The Function of Stephen's Speech (Acts 7,2–53)." *Bib* 70 (1989): 173-93.

_____. *The Stephen Speech: A Literary and Redactional Study of Acts 7,2-53*. AnBib 67. Rome: Pontifical Biblical Institute, 1976.

Kingsbury, Jack Dean. "The Pharisees in Luke-Acts." In *The Four Gospels: Festschrift Frans Neirynck* 2:1497-1512. Edited by F. van Segbroeck, Christopher M. Tuckett, G. van Belle, and J. Verheyden. BETL 100. Leuven: Leuven University Press, 1992.

Klauck, Hans-Josef. *Ancient Letters and the New Testament: A Guide to Context and Exegesis*. Translated by Daniel P. Bailey. Waco TX: Baylor University Press, 2006.

_____. *Magic and Paganism in Early Christianity: The World of the Acts of the Apostles*. Minneapolis: Fortress, 2003.

Klijn, A. F. J. "The Apocryphal Acts of the Apostles." *VC* 37 (1983): 193-99.

Klingenhardt, Matthias. "Markion vs. Lukas: Plädoyer für Wiederaufnahme eines alten Falles." *NTS* 52 (2006): 484-513.

Knox, John. *Marcion and the New Testament: An Essay in the Early History of the Canon*. Chicago: University of Chicago Press, 1942.

Koester, Craig R. *The Dwelling of God: The Tabernacle in the Old Testament, Intertestamental Jewish Literature, and the New Testament*. CBQMS 22. Washington DC: Catholic Biblical Association of America, 1989.

Koester, Helmut. *Ephesos: Metropolis of Asia*. HTS 41. Valley Forge PA: Trinity Press International, 1995.

_____. *Trajectories through Early Christianity*. Edited by James M. Robinson and Helmut Koester. Philadelphia: Fortress Press, 1971.

Koschorke, Klaus. "Eine gnostische Pfingspredigt: Zur Auseindandersetzung zwischen gnostischem und kirchlichem Christentum am Beispiel der 'Epistula Petri ad Philippum' (NHC VIII,2)." *ZTK* 74 (1977): 323-43.

Koskenniemi, Heikki. *Studien zur Idee und Phraseologie des griechischen Briefes bis 400 n. Chr*. Suomalaisen Tiedeakatemian Toimituksia/Annales Academiae Scientiarum Fennicae B, 102.2. Helsinki: Akateeminen Kirjakauppa, 1956.

Kraabel, A. Thomas. "The Disappearance of the 'God-Fearers.' " *Numen* 28 (1981): 113-26.

Krenkel, Max. *Josephus und Lukas: Der schriftstellerische Einfluß des jüdischen Geschichtschreibers auf der christlichen nachgewiesen*. Leipzig: H. Hässel, 1894.

Krodel, Gerhard A. *Acts*. ACNT. Minneapolis: Augsburg, 1986.

Kuntz, Kenneth. *The Self-Revelation of God*. Philadelphia: Westminster, 1967.

L'Hoir, Francesca Santoro. *The Rhetoric of Gender Terms: 'Man,' 'Woman,' and the Portrayal of Character in Latin Prose*. MBCBS 120. Leiden: E. J. Brill, 1992.

La Bonnardière, Anne-Marie. *Biblia Augustiniana*. Seven volumes. Antiquité 11, 18, 21, 26, 42, 49, 67. Paris: Études augustiniennes, 1960–1975.

Labriolle, Pierre de. *Histoire de la littérature latine chrétienne.* Third edition. Revue et augmentée par Gustave Bardy. Études anciennes. Paris: Belles Lettres, 1947.

Lagrange, Marie-Joseph. *Histoire ancienne du canon du Nouveau Testament.* Paris: Gabalda, 1933.

Lake, Kirsopp. "Proselytes and God-Fearers." In *The Beginnings of Christianity* 5:74-95. Five volumes. Edited by Henry J. Cadbury. Reprint: Grand Rapids MI: Baker, 1965.

Laplace, Marie Marcelle Jeanine. "Le Roman de Chariton et la Tradition de l'Éloquence et de la Rhétorique: Constitution d'un Discourse Panégyrique." *RMP* 140 (1997): 38-71.

Lara, Carlos Hernandez. "Rhetorical Aspects of Chariton of Aphrodisias." *Giornale Italiano di Filologia* 42 (1990): 267-74.

Lattimore, Richmond. *The Iliad of Homer.* Translated and introduced by Richmond Lattimore. Chicago: University of Chicago Press, 1951.

Lempriere, John, editor. *Lempriere's Classical Dictionary of Proper Names Mentioned in Ancient Authors.* Third edition. London: Routledge, 1986.

Levine, Amy-Jill. *The Misunderstood Jew: The Church and the Scandal of the Jewish Jesus.* San Francisco: HarperSanFrancisco, 2006.

Lietzmann, Hans. *Petrus und Paulus in Rom.* Second edition. Arbeiten zur Kirchengeschichte 1. Berlin-Leipzig: de Gruyter, 1927.

Lieu, Judith M. "The Race of God-Fearers." *JTS* 46.2 (1995): 483-501.

Lindemann, Andreas. *Paulus im Ältesten Christentum.* BHT 58. Tübingen: J. C. B. Mohr, 1979.

Löning, Karl. "Paulinismus in der Apostelgeschichte." *Paulus in den Neutestamentlichen Spätschriften: Zur Paulusrezeption im Neuen Testament.* Edited by Karl Kertelge. QD 89. Freiburg: Herder, 1981.

Lüdemann, Gerd. *Early Christianity according to the Traditions in Acts: A Commentary.* Translated by John Bowden. London: SCM, 1989.

Luttikhuizen, Gerard P. "The Letter of Peter to Philip and the New Testament." In *Nag Hammadi and Gnosis.* Edited by R. McL. Wilson. Leiden: Brill, 1979.

Lyons, William John. "The Words of Gamaliel (Acts 5.38-39) and the Irony of Indeterminacy." *JSNT* 68 (1997): 23-49.

MacDonald, Dennis R. "Luke's Eutychus and Homer's Elpenor: Acts 20:7-12 and *Odyssey* 10-12." *JHC* 1 (1994): 5-24.

McDonald, Lee Martin, and James A. Sanders, editors. *The Canon Debate.* Peabody MA: Hendrickson, 2002.

McGushin, P. C, *Sallustius Crispus, Bellum Catilinae: A Commentary.* MBCBS 45. Leiden: E. J. Brill, 1977.

McKinlay, A. P., editor. *Aratoris subdiaconi de Actibus apostolorum.* CSEL 72. Vienna: Hoelder-Pichler-Tempski, 1951.

McVann, Mark. "Rituals of Status Transformation in Luke-Acts: The Case of the Prophet." In *The Social World of Luke-Acts*, 333-60. Edited by Jerome Neyrey. Peabody MA: Hendrickson, 1991.

Malherbe, Abraham J. *The Cynic Epistles: A Study Edition*. SBLSBS 12. Missoula MT: Scholars Press, 1977.

_____. *Paul and the Popular Philosophers*. Minneapolis: Fortress, 1989.

Malina, Bruce J. and Richard L. Rohrbaugh. *Social-Science Commentary on the Gospel of John*. Minneapolis: Fortress Press, 1998.

Man, Ronald E. "The Value of Chiasm for New Testament Interpretation." *BSac* 141 (1984): 147-51.

Marguerat, Daniel. "The 'Acts of Paul' and the Canonical Acts: A Phenomenon of Rereading." Translated by Ken McKinney. *Semeia* 80 (1997): 169-83.

_____. *The First Christian Historian: Writing the 'Acts of the Apostles.'* SNTSMS 121. Cambridge UK: Cambridge University Press, 2002.

_____. "L'Image de Paul dans les Actes des Apôtres." In *Les Actes des Apôtres: Histoire, récit, théologie*, 121-54. Edited by Michel Berder. Association catholique française pour l'étude de la Bible. Paris: Les editions du Cerf, 2005.

Marques, José M. "The 'Black-Sheep Effect:' Outgroup Homogeneity in Social Comparison Settings." In *Social Identity Theory: Constructive and Critical Advances*, 131-151. Edited by Dominic Abrams and Michael A. Hogg. London: Harvester Wheatsheaf, 1990.

Marques, José M., Dominic Abrams, D. Páez and C. Martinez-Taboada. "The Role of Categorization and In-Group Norms in Judgments of Groups and Their Members." *Journal of Personality and Social Psychology* 75 (1998): 976-88.

Marques, José M., Dominic Abrams, D. Páez, and Michael A. Hogg. "Social Categorization, Social Identification, and Rejection of Deviant Groups Members." In *Blackwell Handbook of Social Psychology: Group Processes*, 400-24. Edited by Michael A. Hogg and R. Scott Tindale. Oxford UK: Blackwell, 2001.

Marques, José M., V. Y. Yzerbryt and J.-P. Leyens. "The 'Black-Sheep Effect': Extremity of Judgments towards Ingroup Members as a Function of Group Identification." *European Journal of Social Psychology* 18 (1988): 1-16.

Marques, José M., and V. Y. Yzerbryt. "The Black-Sheep Effect: Judgmental Extremity towards Ingroup Members in Inter- and Intra-Group Situations." *European Journal of Social Psychology* 18 (1988): 287-92.

Marques, José M., E. M. Robalo, and S. A. Rocha. "Ingroup Bias and the 'Black Sheep' Effect: Assessing the Impact of Social Identification and Perceived Variability on Group Judgments." *European Journal of Social Psychology* 22 (1992): 331-52.

Marrou, H. I. *A History of Education in Antiquity.* Translated by George Lamb. New York: Sheed and Ward, 1956.

Marshall, I. Howard. *Commentary on Luke.* NIGTC. Grand Rapids MI: Eerdmans, 1978.

Mason, Steve. "Chief Priests, Sadducees, Pharisees, and Sanhedrin in Acts." In *The Book of Acts in Its Palestinian Setting*, 115-77. Edited by Richard Bauckham. BAFCS 4. Grand Rapids MI: Eerdmans, 1995.

_____. *Josephus and the New Testament.* Peabody MA: Hendrickson, 1992.

Meade, David G. *Pseudonymity and Canon.* Grand Rapids MI: Eerdmans, 1987.

Meiser, Martin. "Texttraditionen des Aposteldekrets—Textkritik und Rezeptionsgeschichte." In *Apostelgeschichte als Kirchengeschichte: Text, Texttradition und antike Auslegeen*, 373-98. Edited by Tobias Nicklas and Michael Tilly. BETL 120. Berlin: de Gruyter, 2003.

Merenlahti, Petri. *Poetics for the Gospels? Rethinking Narrative Criticism.* Studies of the New Testament and Its World. London: T.&T. Clark, 2002.

Merenlahti, Petri and Raimo Hakola. "Reconceiving Narrative Criticism." In *Characterization in the Gospels*, 13-48. Edited by David Rhoads and Kari Syreeni. JSNTSup 184. Sheffield: Sheffield Academic Press, 1999.

Merk, A. "Der neuentdeckte Kommentar des hl. Ephraim zur Apostelgeschichte." *ZTK* 48 (1924): 52-53.

Metzger, Paul. "Zeitspeigel: Neutestamentliche Handschriften als Zeugnisse der Kirchengeschichte: Die Frage nach einer Hoffnung für Israel bei Lukas." In *The Book of Acts as Church History*, 241-62. Edited by Tobias Nicklas and Michael Tilly. BETL 120. Berlin: de Gruyter, 2003.

Meyer, Marvin. *The Letter of Peter to Philip.* SBLDS 53. Chico CA: Scholars Press, 1981.

_____. "NHC VII, 2: The Letter of Peter to Philip, Introduction." In *Nag Hammadi Codex VIII*, 229. Edited by John H. Sieber. NHS 31. Leiden: Brill, 1991.

Miesner, Donald R. "Chiasm and the Composition and Message of Paul's Missionary Sermons." S.T.D. thesis, Lutheran School of Theology at Chicago, 1974.

Migne, J.-P., ed. *Patrologia graeca.* 167 volumes. Paris, 1857–1886.

Miller, John B. F. *Convinced That God Had Called Us: Dreams, Visions, and the Perception of God's Will in Luke-Acts.* BINS 85. Leiden: Brill, 2006.

Minear, Paul S. *To Heal and to Reveal: The Prophetic Vocation according to Luke.* New York: Crossroads, 1976.

Mitchell, Margaret M. *Paul and the Rhetoric of Reconciliation: An Exegetical Investigation of the Language and Composition of 1 Corinthians.* Louisville: Westminster/John Knox, 1991.

_____. "Rhetorical and New Literary Criticism." In *The Oxford Handbook of Biblical Studies*, 615-33. Edited by J. W. Rogerson and Judith M. Lieu. New York: Oxford University Press, 2006.

Mittelstädt, Andreas. *Lukas als Historiker: Zur Datierung des Lukanischen Doppelwerkes*. Texte und Arbeiten zum neuestestamentlichen Zeitalter 43. Tübingen: Francke, 2006.

Moessner, David P. " 'The Christ Must Suffer': New Light on the Jesus—Peter, Stephen, Paul Parallels in Luke-Acts." *NovT* 28 (1986): 220-56.

Moessner, David P. and David L. Tiede. "Conclusion: 'And Some Were Persuaded. . . . ' " In *Jesus and the Heritage of Israel*, 358-68. Edited by David P. Moessner. Philadelphia: Trinity Press International, 1999.

Morgan, Teresa. *Literate Education in the Hellenistic and Roman Worlds*. Cambridge Classical Studies. Cambridge UK: Cambridge University Press, 1998.

Mount, Christopher. *Pauline Christianity: Luke-Acts and the Legacy of Paul*. NovTSup 104. Leiden: E. J. Brill, 2002.

Müller-Abels, Susanne. "Der Umgang mit 'schwierigen' Texten der Apostelgeschichte in der Alten Kirche." In *Apostelgeschichte als Kirchengeschichte. Text: Texttraditionen und antike Auslegungen*, 347-72. Edited by Tobias Nicklas and Michael Tilly. BETL 120. Berlin: de Gruyter, 2003.

Murphy, R. P. R. "Jewish Christianity." In *A Dictionary of Biblical Interpretation*. Edited by R. J. Coggins and J. L. Houlden. Philadelphia: Trinity Press International, 1990.

Nanos, Mark D. *The Irony of Galatians: Paul's Letter in First-Century Context*. Minneapolis: Fortress Press, 2002.

Nelson, Robert S. "Rabbula Gospels." In *The Oxford Dictionary of Byzantium* 3:1769. Three volumes. Oxford UK: Oxford University Press, 1991.

Neudorfer, Heinz-Werner. *Der Stephanuskreis in der Forschungsgeschichte seit F. C. Baur*. Monographien und Studienbücher 309. Giessen: Brunnen, 1983.

Neusner, Jacob. "Vow-Taking, the Nazirites, and the Law: Does James' Advice to Paul Accord with Halakhah?" In *James the Just and Christian Origins*, 59-82. Edited by Bruce Chilton and Craig Evans. Leiden: Brill, 1999.

Newman, Barclay M., and Eugene A. Nida. *A Translator's Handbook on The Acts of the Apostles*. Helps for Translators 12. London: United Bible Societies, 1972.

Neyrey, Jerome H. "Acts 17, Epicureans and Theodicy: A Study in Stereotypes." *Greeks, Romans, and Christians: Essays in Honor of Abraham J. Malherbe*, 118-34. Edited by David L. Balch, Everett Ferguson, and Wayne A. Meeks. Minneapolis: Fortress Press, 1990.

Nicoll, W. S. M. "The Sacrifice of Palinurus." *CQ* 38/2 (1988): 459-72.

Nock, Arthur D. "The Apocryphal Gospels." *JTS* n.s. 11 (1960): 63-70.

Oakes, Penelope J., S. Alexander Haslam, and John C. Turner. *Stereotyping and Social Reality*. Oxford: Blackwell, 1994.

O'Neill, J. C. *The Theology of Acts in Its Historical Setting*. London: SPCK, 1961.
_____. *The Theology of Acts in Its Historical Setting*. Second revised edition. London: SPCK, 1970.

Orbán, A. P., editor. *Aratoris subdiaconi: Historia apostolica*. CCSL 130, 130A. Turnhout, Belgium: Brepols, 2006.

Pagels, Elaine. "Visions, Appearances and Apostolic Authority: Gnostic and Orthodox Tradition." In *Gnosis*, 415-30. Edited by Barbara Aland. Göttingen: Vandenhoeck & Ruprecht, 1978.

Palmer, Darryl W. "Acts and the Ancient Historical Monograph." In *The Book of Acts in Its Ancient Literary Setting*, 1-29. Edited by Bruce W. Winter and Andrew D. Clarke. BAFCS 1. Grand Rapids MI: Eerdmans, 1993.

Parsons, Mikeal C. "Luke and the *Progymnasmata*: A Preliminary Investigation into the Preliminary Exercises." In *Contextualizing Acts: Lukan Narrative and Greco-Roman Discourse*, 43-64. Edited by Todd C. Penner and Caroline Vander Stichele. SBLSymS. Atlanta: Society of Biblical Literature, 2003.
_____. " 'Nothing Defiled AND Unclean': The Conjunction's Function in Acts 10:14." *PRS* 27 (2000): 263–74.

Parsons, Mikeal C., and Richard I. Pervo. *Rethinking the Unity of Luke and Acts*. Minneapolis: Fortress Press, 1993.

Pecere, Oronzo. *La letteratura di consumo nel mondo greco-latino*. Edited by Oronzo Pecere and A. Stramaglia. Cassino: Università degli studi di Cassino, 1996.

Penner, Todd C. *In Praise of Christian Origins: Stephen and the Hellenists in Lukan Apologetic Historiography*. Emory Studies in Early Christianity 10. New York: T.&T. Clark, 2004.

Perkins, Pheme. *Gnosticism and the New Testament*. Minneapolis: Fortress, 1993.
_____. *The Gnostic Dialogue: The Early Church and the Crisis of Gnosticism*. New York: Paulist Press, 1980.

Pernot, Laurent. *Rhetoric in Antiquity*. Translated by W. E. Higgins. Washington DC: Catholic University of America Press, 2005.

Pervo, Richard I. *Dating Acts: Between the Evangelists and the Apologists*. Santa Rosa CA: Polebridge Press, 2006.
_____. "Direct Speech in Acts and the Question of Genre." *JSNT* 28 (2006): 285-307.
_____. "A Hard Act to Follow: The *Acts of Paul* and the Canonical Acts." *JHC* 2/2 (1995): 3-32.
_____. "Israel's Heritage and Claims upon the Genre(s) of Luke and Acts: The Problems of a History." In *Jesus and the Heritage of Israel: Luke's Narrative*

Claim upon Israel's Legacy, 127-43. Edited by David P. Moessner. Harrisburg PA: Trinity Press International, 1999.

_____. "Meet Right—and Our Bounden Duty." *Forum* n.s. 4/1 (2001): 45-62.

_____. *Profit with Delight: The Literary Genre of the Acts of the Apostles.* Philadelphia: Fortress Press, 1987.

Pesch, Rudolf. *Die Apostelgeschichte.* Two volumes. EKKNT 5. Neukirchen-Vluyn: Neukirchener Verlag, 1986, 1995.

Petzer, J. H. "Tertullian's Text of Acts." *SecCent* 8/4 (1991): 201-15.

Phillips, Thomas E. "The Genre of Acts: Moving Toward a Consensus?" *CBR* 4 (2006): 365-96.

_____. "Narrative Characterizations of Peter and Paul in Early Christianity." *ARC: Journal of the Faculty of Religious Studies at McGill University* 30 (2002): 139-57.

_____. "Paul as Role Model in Acts 16 and Beyond." In *Acts and Ethics*, 49-63. Edited by Thomas E. Phillips. Sheffield UK: Sheffield Phoenix, 2005.

_____. "Subtlety as a Literary Technique in Luke's Characterization of Jews and Judaism." In *Literary Studies in Luke-Acts*, 313-26. Edited by Richard P. Thompson and Thomas E. Phillips. Macon GA: Mercer University Press, 1998.

Pichler, Josef. "Das theologische Anliegen der Paulusrezeption im lukanischen Werk." In *The Unity of Luke-Acts*, 731-44. Edited by J. Verheyden. BETL 142. Leuven: Leuven University Press, 1999.

Pietri, Charles. "Concordia apostolorum et renovatio urbis." *Mélanges d'archéologie et d'histoire* 73 (1961): 275-322.

Porter, Stanley E. *The Paul of Acts: Essays in Literary Criticism, Rhetoric and Theology.* WUNT 115. Tübingen: Mohr Siebeck, 1999.

Poupon, Gérard. "Fiche signalétique: Les Actes de Pierre." In *Les Actes apocryphes des apôtres. Christianisme et monde païen*, 299-301. Publications de la Faculté de théologie de l'Université de Genève 4. Geneva: Labor et Fides, 1981.

Powell, Mark Allan. "The Religious Leaders in Luke: A Literary-Critical Study." *JBL* 109/1 (1990): 93-110.

Praeder, Susan Marie. "The Problem of First-Person Narration in Acts." *NovT* 29 (1987): 193-218.

Räisänen, Heikki. *Jesus, Paul and Torah: Collected Essays*, 149-202. JSNTSup 43. Sheffield: JSOT Press, 1992.

Ramsey, J. T. *Sallust's Bellum Catilinae: Edited with Introduction and Commentary.* Edited by Gilbert W. Lawall. APATS 9. Chico CA: Scholars Press, 1984.

Rapske, Brian. *The Book of Acts and Paul in Roman Custody.* BAFCS 3. Grand Rapids MI: Eerdmans, 1994.

Reardon, B. P. "Chariton." In *The Novel in the Ancient World*, 309-35. Edited by Gareth Schmeling. MBCBS 159. Leiden: E. J. Brill, 1996.

Rebenich, Stefan. "Historical Prose." In *Handbook of Classical Rhetoric in the Hellenistic Period: 330 B.C.–A.D. 400*, 265-337. Edited by Stanley E. Porter. Translated by R. McL. Wilson. Leiden: E. J. Brill, 1997.

Reimer, Ivoni Richter. *Women in the Acts of the Apostles: A Feminist Liberation Perspective*. Translated by Linda M. Maloney. Minneapolis: Fortress, 1995.

Rese, Martin. "The Jews and Luke-Acts: Some Second Thoughts." In *The Unity of Luke-Acts*, 185-202. Edited by Joseph Verheyden. BETL 142. Leuven: Leuven University Press, 1999.

Richard, Earl. *Acts 6:1–8:4: The Author's Method of Composition*. SBLDS 41. Missoula MT: Scholars Press, 1978.

_____. *First and Second Thessalonians*. SP 11. Collegeville MN: Liturgical, 1995.

Richter, Wolfgang. "Traum und Traumdeutung im AT: Ihre Form und Verwendung." *BZ* 7 (1963): 202-20.

Robbins, Vernon K. "The Social Location of the Implied Author of Luke-Acts." *The Social World of Luke-Acts: Models for Interpretation*, 305-32. Edited by Jerome H. Neyrey. Peabody MA: Hendrickson, 1991.

_____. "Writing as a Rhetorical Act in Plutarch and the Gospels." In *Persuasive Artistry: Studies in New Testament Rhetoric in Honor of George A. Kennedy*, 142-68. Edited by Duane F. Watson. JSNTSup 50. Sheffield: JSOT Press, 1991.

Roberts, Alexander, James Donaldson et al., editors. *Ante-Nicene Fathers. Translations of the Writings of the Fathers Down to A.D. 325*. American edition, revised and chronologically arranged with brief prefaces and occasional notes by Arthur Cleveland Coxe (1885–1896). Facsimile reprint: Peabody MA: Hendrickson, 1994, 2007. Online: the online Library of Liberty (Indianapolis: Liberty Fund Inc., ©2008). New York: Christian Literature Publishing Co., 2008.

Robinson, J. A. T. *Redating the New Testament*. Philadelphia: Westminster, 1976.

Roloff, Jürgen. "Die Paulus-Darstellung des Lukas: Ihre geschichtlichen Voraussetzungen und ihr theologisches Ziel." *EvT* 39 (1979): 510-31.

Rordorf, Willy. "In welchem Verhältnis stehen die apokryphen Paulusakten zur kanonischen Apostelgeschichte und zu den Pastoralbriefen?" In *Text and Testimony: Essays on New Testament and Apocryphal Literature in Honor of A. F. J. Klijn*, 232-37. Edited by T. Baarda and A. F. J. Klijn. Kampen, Netherlands: Kok, 1988.

_____. "Paul's Conversion in the Canonical Acts and in the *Acts of Paul*." Translated by Peter Dunn. *Semeia* 80 (1997): 137-44.

Rosenmeyer, Patricia A. *Ancient Epistolary Fictions: The Letter in Greek Literature*. Cambridge UK: Cambridge University Press, 2001.

Rothschild, Clare K. *Luke-Acts and the Rhetoric of History: An Investigation of Early Christian Historiography*. WUNT 2. Reihe 175. Tübingen: Mohr Siebeck, 2004.

Rowe, C. Kavin. "History, Hermeneutics and the Unity of Luke-Acts." *JSNT* 28 (2005): 131-57.

_____. "Literary Unity and Reception History: Reading Luke-Acts as Luke and Acts." *JSNT* 29 (2007): 449-57.

Saldarini, Anthony J. *Pharisees, Scribes and Sadducees in Palestinian Society*. Collegeville MN: Michael Glazier, 1988.

Salmon, Marilyn. "Insider or Outsider? Luke's Relationship with Judaism." In *Luke-Acts and the Jewish People: Eight Critical Perspectives*, 76-82. Edited by Joseph B. Tyson. Minneapolis: Augsburg, 1988.

Sanders, Jack T. "Can Anything Bad Come Out of Nazareth, or Did Luke Think That History Moved in a Line or in a Circle?" In *Literary Studies in Luke-Acts*, 297-312. Edited by Richard P. Thompson and Thomas E. Phillips. Macon GA: Mercer University Press, 1998.

_____. *The Jews in Luke-Acts*. Philadelphia: Fortress, 1987.

_____. "The Pharisees in Luke-Acts." In *The Living Text: Essays in Honor of Ernest W. Saunders*, 141-88. Edited by D. E. Groh and Robert Jewett. Lanham MD: University Press of America, 1985.

_____. "The Prophetic Use of the Scriptures in Luke-Acts. In *Early Jewish and Christian Exegesis*, 191-97. Edited by Craig A. Evans and William F. Stinespring. Atlanta: Scholars Press, 1987.

Sanders, James A. *Canon and Community: A Guide to Canonical Criticism*. Philadelphia: Fortress Press, 1984.

_____. "Isaiah in Luke." In *Luke and Scripture*, 13-25. Edited by Craig A. Evans and James A. Sanders. Minneapolis: Fortress, 1993.

Schaff, Philip, editor. *Nicene and Post-Nicene Fathers*. First series (1886–1890). Facsimile reprint: Peabody MA: Hendrickson, 2004.

Schaff, Philip, and Henry Wace, editors. *Nicene and Post-Nicene Fathers*. Second Series (1886–1890). Facsimile reprint: Peabody MA: Hendrickson, 2004.

Schenke, Hans-Martin. "Das Weiterwirken des Paulus und die Pflege seines Erbes durch die Paulus-Schule." *NTS* 21 (1974-75): 505-18.

Schmeling, Gareth L. *Chariton*. TWAS 295. New York: Twayne, 1974.

Schmidt, Daryl D. "The Greek New Testament as a Codex." In *The Canon Debate*, 469-84. Edited by Lee Martin McDonald and James A. Sanders. Peabody MA: Hendrickson, 2002.

Schneckenberger, Matthias. *Über den Zweck der Apostelgeschichte*. Bern: Fischer, 1841.

Schneemelcher, Wilhelm, editor. *New Testament Apocrypha*. Two volumes. Revised edition translated by R. McL. Wilson. Cambridge UK: J. Clark; Louisville: Westminster/John Knox, 1991–1992.

_____, editor. *Bibliographia Patristica*. Thirty-five volumes. Berlin: de Gruyter, 1956–1990.

Schneider, André and Luigi Cirillo. "Roman pseudo-clémentin, Reconnaissances." In *Écrits apocryphes chrétiens*, 2:1602-1605. Edited by Pierre Geoltrain and Jean-Daniel Kaestli. La Pléiade 516. Paris: Gallimard, 2005.

Schneider, Gerhard. *Die Apostelgeschichte*. HKNT 5.2. Freiburg: Herder, 1982.

Schrader, Richard J., Joseph L. Roberts III, and John F. Makowski. *Arator's on the Acts of the Apostles*. Atlanta: Scholars Press, 1987.

Schulz, S. "Gottes Vorsehung bei Lukas." *ZNW* 54 (1963): 104-16.

Segal, Alan F. *Paul the Convert and the Apostasy of Saul the Pharisee*. New Haven CT: Yale University Press, 1990.

Shepherd, William. *The Narrative Function of the Holy Spirit as a Character in Luke-Acts*. SBLDS 147. Atlanta: Scholars Press, 1994.

Sieben, Hermann Josef. *Kirchenväterhomilien zum Neuen Testament: Ein Repertorium der Textausgaben und Übersetzungen. Mit einem Anhang der Kirchenväter-kommentare*. Instrumenta Patristica 11. The Hague: Martinus Nijhoff International, 1991.

Simon, Marcel. "Saint Stephen and the Jerusalem Temple." *JEH* 2 (1951): 127-42.

Skarsaune, Oskar. *The Proof from Prophecy*. NovTSup 56. Leiden: Brill, 1987.

Smith, David E. *The Canonical Function of Acts: A Comparative Analysis*. Collegeville MN: Liturgical Press, 2002.

Smothers, Edgar R. "Le texte des Homélies de saint Jean Chrysostome sur les Actes des apôtres." *RECHSR* 27 (1937): 513-48.

Soards, Marion L. *The Speeches in Acts: Their Content, Context, and Concerns*. Louisville: Westminster/John Knox Press, 1994.

Speiser, E. A. "The Epic of Gilgamesh." In *Ancient Near Eastern Texts: Relating to the Old Testament*, 72-99. Third edition with Supplement. Edited by James B. Pritchard. Princeton NJ: Princeton University Press, 1969.

Spencer, F. Scott. *Acts*. Readings: A New Biblical Commentary. Sheffield UK: Sheffield Academic Press, 1997.

_____. *Journeying through Acts: A Literary-Cultural Reading*. Peabody MA: Hendrickson, 2004.

_____. "Wise Up, Young Man: The Moral Vision of Saul and Other νεανίσκοι in Acts." In *Acts and Ethics*, 34-48. Edited by Thomas E. Phillips. Sheffield UK: Sheffield Phoenix, 2005.

Spengel, Leonard, editor. *Rhetores Graeci*. Three volumes. Leipzig: Teubner, 1853–1856.

Squires, John T. *The Plan of God in Luke-Acts.* SNTSMS 76. Cambridge UK: Cambridge University Press, 1993.

Stegemann, Wolfgang. *Zwishen Synagogue und Obrigkeit: Zur historischen Situtation der Lukanischen Christen.* Göttingen: Vandenhoeck & Ruprecht, 1991.

Stenberg, Meir. *The Poetics of Biblical Narrative: Ideological Literature and the Drama of Reading.* Bloomington: Indiana University Press, 1985.

Sterling, Gregory E. *Historiography and Self-Definition: Josephos, Luke-Acts and Apologetic Historiography.* NovTSup 64. Leiden: E. J. Brill, 1992.

Stirewalt, M. Luther, Jr. *Studies in Ancient Greek Epistolography.* SBLRBS 27. Atlanta: Scholars Press, 1993.

Stoops, Robert F. "Riot and Assembly: The Social Context of Acts 19:23-41." *JBL* 108 (1989): 73-91.

Stuhlfauth, Georg. *Die apokryphen Petrusgeschichten in der altchristlichen Kunst.* Berlin: de Gruyter, 1925.

Sylva, Dennis D. "The Meaning and Function of Acts 7:46–50." *JBL* 106 (1987): 261–75.

Syreeni, Kari. "Peter as Character and Symbol in the Gospel of Matthew." In *Characterization in the Gospels*, 106-152. Edited by David Rhoads and Kari Syreeni. JSNTSup 184. Sheffield UK: Sheffield Academic Press, 1999.

_____. "Wonderlands: A Beginner's Guide to Three Worlds." *Svensk exegetisk årsok* 64 (1999): 33-46.

Tajfel, Henri W. and John Turner. "An Integrative Theory of Intergroup Conflict." In *The Social Psychology of Intergroup Relations*, 33-47. Edited by W. G. Austin and S. Worchel. Monterey: Brooks/Cole, 1979.

_____. *Human Groups and Social Categories: Studies in Social Psychology.* Cambridge UK: Cambridge University Press, 1981.

Tajra, Henri W. *The Trial of St. Paul: A Juridical Exegesis of the Second Half of the Acts of the Apostles.* WUNT 2. Reihe 35. Tübingen: Mohr Siebeck, 1989.

Talbert, Charles H. *Literary Patterns, Theological Themes, and the Genre of Luke-Acts.* SBLMS 20. Missoula: Scholars Press, 1974.

_____. *Luke and the Gnostics.* New York: Abingdon, 1966.

_____. *Reading Acts: A Literary and Theological Commentary on the Acts of the Apostles.* New York: Crossroad, 1997.

_____. *Reading Luke: A Literary and Theological Commentary.* Revised edition. Reading the New Testament. Macon GA: Smyth & Helwys, 2002.

_____. *Reading Luke-Acts in Its Mediterranean Milieu.* NovTSup 107. Leiden: E. J. Brill, 2003.

_____. *Romans.* Smyth & Helwys Bible Commentary. Macon GA: Smyth & Helwys, 2002.

Tannehill, Robert C. *The Acts of the Apostles*. Volume 2 of *The Narrative Unity of Luke-Acts: A Literary Interpretation*. Minneapolis: Fortress, 1990.

_____. "'Cornelius' and 'Tabitha' Encounter Luke's Jesus." *Int* 48/4 (1994): 347-56.

_____. "Israel in Luke-Acts: A Tragic Story." *JBL* 104/1 (1985): 68-85.

_____. "Should We Love Simon the Pharisee? Hermeneutical Reflections on the Pharisees in Luke." *CTM* 21 (1994): 424-33.

Taylor, Nicholas. "Luke-Acts and the Temple." In *The Unity of Luke-Acts*, 709-21. Edited by Joseph Verheyden. BETL 142. Leuven: Peeters, 1999.

Théon, Aelius. *Progymnasmata*. Translated by Michel Patillon with Giancarlo Bolognesi. Collection des universités de France. Paris: Belles Lettres, 1997.

Thraede, K. "Arator: Nachtrag zum RAC." *JAC* 4 (1961): 187–96.

Tiede, David L. *Prophecy and History in Luke-Acts*. Philadelphia: Fortress, 1980.

Tigay, Jeffrey H. *The Evolution of the Gilgamesh Epic*. Philadelphia: University of Pennsylvania Press, 1982.

Tilly, Michael. "Juden, Christen und Heiden im Actatext de Peschitto: Beobachtungen zu einer Syrischen Übersetzung der Apostelgeschichte." In *The Book of Acts as Church History*, 321-43. Edited by Tobias Nicklas and Michael Tilly. BETL 120. Berlin: de Gruyter, 2003.

Tomson, Peter J. "Gamaliel's Counsel and the Apologetic Strategy of Luke-Acts." In *The Unity of Luke-Acts*, 585-604. Edited by J. Verheyden. BETL 142. Leuven: University Press, 1999.

Townsend, John T. "The Date of Luke-Acts." In *Luke-Acts: New Perspectives from the Society of Biblical Literature Seminar*, 47-62. Edited by Charles H. Talbert. New York: Crossroad, 1984.

Trapp, Michael., editor. *Greek and Latin Letters: An Anthology, with Translation*. Cambridge UK: Cambridge University Press, 2003.

Trebilco, Paul R. *The Early Christians in Ephesus from Paul to Ignatius*. WUNT 166. Tübingen: Mohr Siebeck, 2004.

Trémel, Bernard. "À propos d'Actes 20, 7-12: Puissance du Thaumaturge ou du témoin?" *RTP* 112 (1980): 361-62.

Trites, Allison A. "The Importance of Legal Scenes and Language in the Book of Acts." *NovT* 16 (1974): 278-84.

Tuckett, Christopher M. "How Early Is the 'Western' Text of Acts?" In *The Book of Acts as Church History. Apostelgeschichte als Kirchengeschichte: Text, Texttraditionen und antike Auslegungen*, 69-86. Edited by Tobias Nicklas. BETL 120. Berlin: de Gruyter, 2003.

Turner, John C. "Some Current Issues in Research on Social Identity and Self-Categorization Theories." In *Social Identity: Context, Commitment, Content*, 6-34. Edited by Naomi Ellemers, Russell Spears, and Bertjan Doosje. Oxford UK: Blackwell, 1999.

Tyson, Joseph B. "The Date of Acts: A Reconsideration." *Forum* n.s. 5 (2002): 33-51.

_____. *Images of Judaism in Luke-Acts*. Columbia: University of South Carolina Press, 1992.

_____. "Jews and Judaism in Luke-Acts: Reading as a Godfearer." *NTS* 41 (1995): 19-38.

_____. *Luke, Judaism, and the Scholars: Critical Approaches to Luke-Acts*. Columbia: University of South Carolina Press, 1999.

_____. *Marcion and Luke-Acts: A Defining Struggle*. Columbia: University of South Carolina Press, 2006.

_____, editor. *Luke-Acts and the Jewish People: Eight Critical Perspectives*. Minneapolis: Augsburg, 1988.

Vielhauer, Philip. *Geschichte der urchristlichen Literatur*. Berlin: de Gruyter, 1975.

_____. "On the 'Paulinism' of Acts." In *Studies in Luke-Acts: Essays Presented in Honor of Paul Schubert*, 33-50. Translated by William C. Robinson, Jr. and Victor P. Furnish. Edited by Leander E. Keck and J. Louis Martyn. Nashville: Abingdon Press, 1966. Reprint: Minneapolis: Fortress, 1980.

_____. "Zum 'Paulinismus' der Apostelgeschichte." *EvT* 10 (1950-51): 1-15.

Walker, William O. "Acts and the Pauline Corpus Revisited: Peter's Speech at the Jerusalem Conference." In *Literary Studies in Luke-Acts: Essays in Honor of Joseph B. Tyson*, 77-86. Edited by Richard P. Thompson and Thomas E. Phillips. Macon GA: Mercer University Press, 1998.

Watson, Francis. " 'In Whom are Hid All the Treasures of Wisdom and Knowledge': Colossians and the Autonomy of the Gospel." Paper presented at the annual meeting of the Society for New Testament Studies. Halle, Germany, 5 August 2005.

_____. *Paul and the Hermeneutics of Faith*. London: New York: T.&T. Clark, 2004.

Wellhausen, Julius. *Kritische Analyse der Apostelgeschichte*. Abhandlungen der königlichen Gesellschaft der Wissenschaften zu Göttingen: Philologisch-historische Klasse 15.2. Berlin: Weidmanns, 1914.

Welliver, Kenneth Bruce. "Pentecost and the Early Church: Patristic Interpretation of Acts 2." Ph.D. dissertation, Yale, 1961.

Wikenhauser, Alfred. "Religionsgeschichtliche Parallelen zu Apg 16, 9." *BZ* 23 (1935–1936): 180-86.

Wiles, James W. *A Scripture Index to the Works of St. Augustine in English Translation*. Lanham MD: University Press of America, 1995.

Wiles, Maurice. *The Divine Apostle: The Interpretation of St Paul's Epistles in the Early Church*. Cambridge UK: Cambridge University Press, 1967.

Wilkins, Ann Thomas. *Villain or Hero: Sallust's Portrayal of Catiline*. AUS. New York: Peter Lang, 1994.

Williams, Kathryn F. "Manlius' *Mandata*: Sallust *Bellum Catilinae* 33." *CP* 95 (2000): 160-71.

Wilson, Stephen G. "Lucan Eschatology." *NTS* 14 (1970-71): 330-47.

Winter, Bruce W. "Official Proceedings and the Forensic Speeches in Acts 24-26." In *The Book of Acts in Its Ancient Literary Setting*, 305-36. Edited by Bruce W. Winter and Andrew D. Clarke. BAFCS 1. Grand Rapids MI: Eerdmans, 1993.

Witherington, Ben. *The Acts of the Apostles: A Sociorhetorical Commentary*. Grand Rapids: Eerdmans, 1998.

Woodman, Anthony John. *Rhetoric in Classical Historiography: Four Studies*. Portland OR: Areopagitica Press; London and Sydney: Crown Helm; London and New York: Routledge, 1988.

Wuellner, Wilhelm. "Arrangement." In *Handbook of Classical Rhetoric in the Hellenistic Period: 330 B.C.–A.D. 400*, 51-87. Edited by Stanley E. Porter. Leiden: E. J. Brill, 1997.

Wylie, A. L. B. "John Chrysostom and His Homilies on the Acts of the Apostles: Reclaiming Ancestral Models for the Christian People." Ph.D. dissertation, Princeton Theological Seminary, 1992.

_____. "John Chrysostom's Homilies on Acts." In *Biblical Hermeneutics in Historical Perspective: Studies in Honor of Karlfried Froelich on His Sixtieth Birthday*, 59-72. Edited by Mark S. Burrow and Paul Rorem. Grand Rapids MI: Eerdmans, 1991.

Zeev, Miriam Pucci Ben. "The Uprisings in the Jewish Diaspora, 116–17." In *The Cambridge History of Judaism* 4:93-104. Edited by Steven T. Katz. Cambridge UK: Cambridge University Press, 2006.

Index of Modern Authors

Index of Biblical References

Index of Other Ancient Writings

2